90 Broad Street
Bloomfield, NJ 07003
973-566-6200

Atomic Blonde

Atomic Blonde

The Films of Mamie Van Doren

BARRY LOWE

— *Foreword by* MAMIE VAN DOREN —

McFarland & Company, Inc., Publishers
Jefferson, North Carolina, and London

LIBRARY OF CONGRESS CATALOGUING-IN-PUBLICATION DATA

Lowe, Barry.
Atomic blonde : the films of Mamie Van Doren /
Barry Lowe ; foreword by Mamie Van Doren.
p.   cm.

Includes bibliographical references and index.

ISBN 978-0-7864-3138-0 ∞
illustrated case binding : 50# alkaline paper

1. Van Doren, Mamie.   I. Title.
PN2287.V33L69   2008   791.4302'8092 — dc22   2007047448

British Library cataloguing data are available

©2008 Barry Lowe. All rights reserved

*No part of this book may be reproduced or transmitted in any form
or by any means, electronic or mechanical, including photocopying
or recording, or by any information storage and retrieval system,
without permission in writing from the publisher.*

On the cover: Mamie Van Doren in a publicity shot for the 1953 film *Forbidden*.
Front cover by TG Design.

Manufactured in the United States of America

*McFarland & Company, Inc., Publishers
Box 611, Jefferson, North Carolina 28640
www.mcfarlandpub.com*

For Walter Figallo, with love

Acknowledgments

Books like this one are a collaborative effort just as much as movies are. So I need to thank, in no particular order (this is not billing after all), Barry Schultz for introducing me all those years ago to the movies of Mamie Van Doren. To the actors, directors and others who took the time to answer my questions by phone, email and letter even when they could not help out: the gracious Rhonda Fleming, Peter Bogdanovich, June Wilkinson, the original Gill Man Ben Chapman, Bill Gray, George Dzundza, Jan Merlin, Robert Carradine, Tom Smothers, Hugh Hefner, Ronald Godfrey, John Kenrick, G. William Oakley, Gino Colbert, Alan Traynor, and Elinor Donahue, who went beyond the call of duty with her reminiscences. Day-to-day support and encouragement from Terry O'Brien, Carol Langley, Graham Fuller, Mary Richards-Rocos, John Rocos, Frank Garfield, David Butler, Darrin Redgate, Margaret McNiven and Robert Henry kept me plugging away when all seemed hopeless. And especially to my partner, Walter Figallo, without whose love and support this book would never have reached fruition.

And to the incomparable Mamie Van Doren, a woman of resilience, humor and eternal sex appeal.

Table of Contents

Acknowledgments vi
Foreword by Mamie Van Doren 1
Preface 3
Introduction 5

BIOGRAPHY 11
THE FILMS 57

AS JOAN OLANDER

Footlight Varieties (1951)	57
His Kind of Woman (1951)	58
Two Tickets to Broadway (1951)	59

AS MAMIE VAN DOREN

All American (1953)	62
Forbidden (1953)	66
Hawaiian Nights (1954)	68
Yankee Pasha (1954)	69
Francis Joins the WACS (1954)	74
Ain't Misbehavin' (1955)	78
The Second Greatest Sex (1955)	82
Running Wild (1955)	90
Star in the Dust (1956)	95
Untamed Youth (1957)	100
The Girl in Black Stockings (1957)	106
Jet Pilot (1957)	110
Teacher's Pet (1958)	112
High School Confidential! (1958)	116
Born Reckless (1958)	125
The Big Operator (1959)	130
Guns, Girls and Gangsters (1959)	135
The Beat Generation (1959)	140
Le Bellissime Gambe di Sabrina (*The Beautiful Legs of Sabrina*) (1959)	146
Girls Town (1959)	148
Vice Raid (1960)	155
College Confidential (1960)	157
Sex Kittens Go to College (1960)	163
The Private Lives of Adam and Eve (1960)	167
Una Americana en Buenos Aires (*The Blonde from Buenos Aires*) (1961)	171
The Candidate (1964)	172
3 Nuts in Search of a Bolt (1964)	174
Freddy und das Lied der Prärie (*The Sheriff Was a Lady*) (1964)	179
Las Vegas Hillbillys (1966)	181
The Navy vs. the Night Monsters (1966)	183
You've Got to Be Smart (1967)	188

Voyage to the Planet of Prehistoric Women (1968)   190

I Fratelli di Arizona (*The Arizona Kid*) (1971)   192

That Girl from Boston (1975 — never completed)   194

Free Ride (1986)   194

Glory Years (1987)   196

The Vegas Connection (1999)   197

Slackers (2002)   197

TELEVISION APPEARANCES 203

RECORDINGS 211

Bibliography 215

Index 219

Foreword by Mamie Van Doren

Who is Mamie Van Doren? That's a fair question. I've written quite a few words that I thought answered that question pretty well. Barry Lowe, however, has come up with more answers to that question. I can't wait to read it myself and find out what they are.

The more difficult question is: Why is Mamie Van Doren? What caused Mamie to POOF! materialize into existence in 1953 and launch a career that has lasted far, far longer than the careers of most of her contemporaries?

When is Mamie Van Doren? That's more complicated yet, since it involves time. How old is she *really*? This is a question much debated and researched. It is always a preoccupation of interviewers, writers, and show business pundits.

What is Mamie Van Doren? Is she an actress, model, movie star, glamour goddess, or sex symbol? I have been called those things and many more. Many less flattering.

How is Mamie Van Doren? What were the steps? What were the decisions she made to make a movie star–style career into a lifelong passion for, well, *life*? What is life, after all, except a story about the journey?

I've written a couple of forewords over the years, mostly for books about Marilyn. It's really an odd feeling to write one for a book about me. It is eerie, kind of like writing your own obit, then reading it in the papers.

Being Mamie Van Doren, much like in *Being John Malkovich*, exists very much in the head of the one being. The existential fact of being me is an ongoing adventure in the moment. That Barry Lowe has tapped a bit into that cramped little portal behind a filing cabinet somewhere, leading to The Being of Mamie, is an admirable piece of work. That he conveys it so skillfully is Barry's art and the good fortune of you, the reader.

There used to be a blonde would-be actress who went around Hollywood claiming to be me. I kept hearing about how I had attended this party, or had been seen on the town at this restaurant or that club. Often I heard how drunk or promiscuous I had been; as long as my alter ego hadn't done something to get me sued or jailed, I thought it was sort of amusing. It always made me wonder, though, about people who slip into a well-known person's identity and pretend to be them. Like Elvis impersonators, donning the white jumpsuit and cape and mumbling, "Thank you very much, ladies and gentlemen," becoming more than they usually are, infused by the power of the King, and rock and roll, and the adulation that he always triggered from his fans. I can't imagine that the Mamie impersonator got much more than a good table from the maitre d' or a drink from the guy at the end of the bar, but, hey, whatever makes you happy.

In a way, I'm a Mamie Van Doren impersonator too. Over the years I've become so much

Mamie in May, 2006, at the Sportsman's Lodge in Studio City to pay tribute to Johnny Grant, a recipient of a Broadcasting Pioneer Award (photograph by Thomas Dixon).

a part of the fans, Hollywood, movies, and, lately, cyberspace, that I find myself resonating between the me I see while putting on my makeup, and the me I read about in letters, magazine articles, and emails. Somewhere in the middle of all that is Mamie Van Doren.

I can't wait to read about the me that Barry Lowe has found. And so, let's push aside the filing cabinet, pry open the trap door, and duck into the tunnel.

May 29, 2006

Preface

Someone once said, "Sex symbols are born, not made," and I agree with that. I think it's something you are gifted with — it's a magic that comes from within. When you walk into a room, you know that you'll light it up and when I do, I think, I've done what I was supposed to do. I've done my job.
— Mamie Van Doren
to *MAO Mag*, Spring 2006

Indeed, Mamie Van Doren does light up a room — the cinema — every time she appears on screen. That she has never been given her due as an actress is apparent from entries (or lack thereof) in film histories. They are either superficial, as demonstrated by Leonard Maltin's assessment of her career: "Platinum blonde bombshell often referred to as the poor man's Lana Turner ... is best remembered for a series of showy roles in cheap 1950s melodramas that emphasized her physical endowments rather than her somewhat meager dramatic abilities" (*Leonard Maltin's Movie Encyclopedia*, 897–98); or just plain wrong (and downright nasty):

> As another Monroe spin-off Van Doren starred in around twenty exploitation flicks during the Fifties, all of them purely designed to give audiences a long, lurid look at as much of her body as the Production Code would permit. Of all the Bombshells she was the only one who really looked dirty. Glamour and insensibility were her trademarks, along with a huge pair of knockers that seemed endlessly to be tumbling out of her clothes [George Robert Kimball, *The Movie* #55, 1091–1092].

This book is an attempt to counteract the prevailing attitudes about Mamie Van Doren's film career and to put paid to salacious nonsense like the above. It's an attempt to place Mamie in the context of her era, to examine her good, bad and indifferent film output, and to show she was as much an auteur as any other actor in Hollywood.

Critics, film historians and even fans seem to project their own fantasies and/or moral biases on Mamie and, in so doing, feel no compunctions about using the most demeaning and sexist of terms to describe her attributes. Some believe she has probably brought this on herself with her progression of lurid "tell-all" biographies. But this is to confuse the actress with the woman.

Mamie was very much a product of post–World War II America. She was very much a part of the atomic age. She was its number one blonde. She resonated with popular youth culture of the era in a way that the more middle-brow Marilyn Monroe and Jayne Mansfield did not although, in all fairness, it's doubtful that they were inclined to pursue this demographic. Mamie's career may have been (mis)guided by the whims and fancies of middle-aged and middle-class men but they were astute enough, nonetheless, to recognize the talents that made Mamie so appealing to a subculture for whom she was not only a star but an icon of the underestimated B movies of the period.

3

This book, an attempt to place Mamie at the center of youth-oriented movies of the 1950s, is split into two major sections: Mamie's biography, then a film-by-film analysis of her films including cast and crew lists, plot synopsis, song lists and who sang them (when the movie contained songs), notes on each film including comments from Mamie and her co-stars wherever possible, memorable quotes, and reviews of the period as well as more recent reviews to show how opinions have changed, or hardened, about her work.

Because there is so much second-hand paraphrasing when it comes to Mamie's films, as so few of them are available, I have gone back to the originals (not always easy to find), sometimes bootleg copies of poor quality. To date very few of her films have been issued on DVD. A few of the films I have not been able to find and some, *The Candidate* for example, even Mamie has never seen. For these films, I have relied on publicity, plot synopses and interviews. For the others I have taken cast and credit lists from the actual film as well as augmenting them from sources such as the Internet Movie Database where they could be verified. A list of Mamie's television work and her recordings rounds out this volume.

Like any such work, mistakes will inevitably creep in and I gratefully seek any corrections of fact. However, opinions, like sex appeal, are very much in the eye of the beholder.

Glamour publicity photograph of Mamie, taken circa 1960.

I have credited magazines from which I gleaned reviews and, where possible, attributed dates but some libraries have clippings which are minus this important information or page numbers. Rather than leave such vintage material from the book, I have included it date-free. Source notes appear at the bottom of pages. I have referred to Mamie as Joan Olander, her birth name, in the biographical chapter up until her name was changed by Universal Studios. I have also standardized different spellings in the credits of films. For example, makeup is spelled variously as make up, make-up and makeup on film credits and, rather than change spellings each time I have resorted to the simple expedient of using "makeup."

This book is a historical and critical homage to one of the great blonde bombshells of the screen. If her career never reached the heights of a Davis, a Crawford or a Garbo, Mamie is nonetheless as distinctive and iconic in her way as these other screen goddesses. To some of us, more so.

Introduction

In Quentin Tarantino's iconic 1994 *Pulp Fiction*, there's a scene in which hit man–minder Vincent (John Travolta) takes Mia (Uma Thurman), his boss's wife, to Jackrabbit Slim's, a retro 1950s restaurant and "the next best thing to a time machine" in which the diners sit in cars of the era to be served by waiters and waitresses dressed and made up to resemble stars of the period. Vincent orders a Douglas Sirk steak and Mia a five dollar shake, Martin and Lewis. Tarantino himself describes the restaurant as having "posters from 1950s AIP movies all over the wall ('ROCK ALL NIGHT,' 'HIGH SCHOOL CONFIDENTIAL,' 'ATTACK OF THE CRAB MONSTER' [sic] and 'MACHINE GUN KELLY.'"*

Vincent patrols the premises and in the background we catch a glimpse of a platinum blonde in tight pants, bullet bra, and cowgirl hat.

Later, Mia comes back from snorting coke in the ladies room.

MIA: Mmm, don't you just love it when you come back from the bathroom and find your food waiting for you?

VINCENT: We're lucky we got anything at all. I don't think Buddy Holly's much of a waiter. Maybe we should have sat in Marilyn Monroe's section.

MIA: Which one? There's two Monroes.

VINCENT: No, there's not. (*Pointing at Marilyn in the white dress serving a table*) That's Marilyn Monroe ... (*Then, pointing at a Blonde Waitress in a tight sweater and Capri pants, taking an order from a bunch of film geeks*) ... and that's Mamie Van Doren. I don't see Jayne Mansfield; she must have the night off or something.†

In this one scene, Tarantino elevates Mamie Van Doren, a cult figure, to iconic status—and simultaneously damns her to eternal comparisons to the other two great blonde bombshells of the era.

It has been the curse of Mamie's career that she has been compared to Monroe (in particular) and Mansfield (in passing) and has been found wanting. This comparison diminishes the particular oeuvre of all three actresses, for each found her niche and blossomed within its fairly narrow parameters. Marilyn was the vulnerable, kittenish Barbie doll; Jayne was a pneumatic parody of womanhood; and Mamie was the sexual aggressor struggling against the streak of Puritanism that ran, and stills runs, through American movies and society. In fact, Mamie was the most modern of the three in her portrayals, especially of teenagers and young women, her characters more attuned to contemporaneous youth culture.

The U.S. quite rightly takes great pride in its cultural inventions: jazz, and the American musical, for example. After World War II, the newest, and least wanted, of inventions was the teenager, the mainly affluent child of a mainly middle-class and upper–working-class society.

---

*Pulp Fiction, 52. Only Rock All Night *(1957) and* Machine-Gun Kelly *(1958) were AIP movies although* High School Confidential! *(1958) and* Attack of the Crab Monsters *(1957) certainly fit the bill as an example of retro 1950s cinema.*

†Pulp Fiction, 59–60.

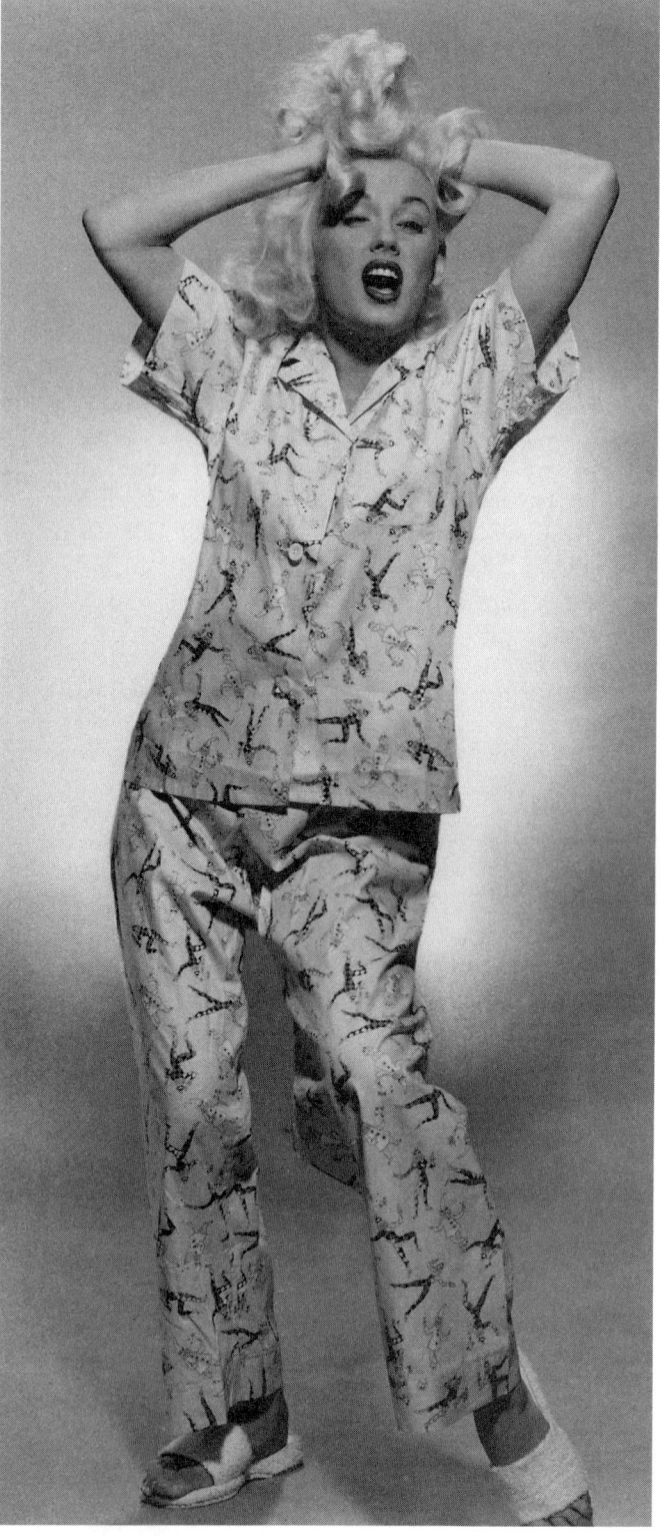

Mamie in 1958 posed to look like her rival, Marilyn Monroe.

Up to that time the human hierarchy tended to be divided into children and adults. The emerging teenage class had leisure time and ready money but little of interest on which to spend it. That would have to wait for business to discover the new substrata's economic clout.

It was a period of fear as well as prosperity, the anxiety whipped up by the media, the House Un-American Activities Committee, and the advent of the nuclear era which threatened to bring American life as we knew it to an end. In its crudest form, Hollywood supported the political and economic status quo with sloganeering films such as *I Married a Communist* (1949) and *I Was a Communist for the FBI* (1951), while others cloaked their propaganda in the more esoteric world of space and alien invaders and allowed viewers to draw ideological comparisons if they wished to: *Red Planet Mars* (1952), *Invasion of the Body Snatchers* (1956). These films fed into American paranoia and made palpable the attack on the American values of democracy and private enterprise by the alien forces of communism.

When youth culture did arrive, it would seem like yet another alien invasion. English-speaking western societies have never had a tradition of readily engaging new ideas or traditions—they usually attack first and ask questions later—until big business discovers there's a buck to be made and then the new culture is assimilated (swallowed) and blanded down until it's palatable to the conservative society at large. Those adherents who refuse to assimilate are ostracized.

Nowhere was this more apparent than in the full frontal attack of rock 'n' roll. It burst on the scene like the atomic bomb and blew away the stuffy image of a servile, suited Andy Hardy who really did believe that Father Knows Best. That there is no immediately identifiable female Andy Hardy is testimony to Hollywood sexism. Rock 'n' roll became the soundtrack of modern youth culture. Now father was likely to be condemning that devil music, just as it was being condemned in the nation's newspapers and pulpits as a sign of degeneracy in youth, another "ism" to be swatted down in the name of The American Dream.

In attempting to keep the lid on an increasingly youthful population which cared little about the austerity of the war years, arbiters of taste and values were breeding rebellion. The inevitable result was that youth culture met rock 'n' roll and exploded into juvenile delinquency. In western cultures it's not books, plays, films or even television that ferment cultural revolution — it's music. For rock, the pivotal moment was the release of *Blackboard Jungle* (1955) which featured Bill Haley and the Comets singing "Rock Around the Clock" on the soundtrack. It was a Road to Damascus moment.

Mamie was uniquely positioned to embrace the new music. Marilyn had already surrendered to non-threatening middle-brow Hollywood-Broadway music. Jayne was happy to headline *The Girl Can't Help It* (1957) but the rock music was on the soundtrack. Mamie mainlined rock 'n' roll by performing it. She had a less developed image than her sister blondes and was floundering at Universal in a series of bimbo roles or blonde and bosomed wallpaper in supporting leads. In *Running Wild* (1955) Mamie met juvenile delinquency and rock 'n' roll in a movie she had, at first, been reluctant to make. That movie set the mold. But it was *Untamed Youth* (1957), with Mamie as a basically good kid sent to a prison farm after being arrested for skinny dipping, which refined it. Incarceration brings out the hip-swiveling (based on Elvis Presley's gyrations), rock-singing Mamie. Her impact was immediate and she was feted, as well as decried, as "the girl built like a platinum powerhouse."

In *Teacher's Pet* (1958) Mamie's role was small but telling and she cemented her reputation as the screen's premier female rock 'n' roller with the song "The Girl Who Invented Rock and Roll," even though she wasn't, and neither was the song. The song was, in many respects, meant to be a symbol of vulgarity and immaturity (i.e., teen). But set against the more austere Doris Day character, Mamie looked like more fun.

So why is Mamie so overlooked by serious film critics and historians today? One reason is the lack of access to most of her films. A handful are available on video or DVD or shown widely on television. Some turn up at retrospectives of, especially, the thrillers and film noir. The lack of firsthand familiarity with Mamie's movies has led to a certain second-handedness in writing about her, a certain facile thumbnail biography and talent appraisal.

Snobbery also plays a part in the relegation of Mamie and her films to the slagheap of exploitation. "Exploitation" is a dirty word in critical, but not cult, circles. And movies aimed at a teen market are rarely taken as anything but popular fodder. No matter how well made or how good the production values of movies made on minuscule budgets, they are dismissed as hack work for directors and other screen artisans on their way up or down. Jack Arnold's helming of *High School Confidential!* (1958) is dismissed as slumming.

But the combination of producer-director Albert Zugsmith and actress Mamie Van Doren produced some of the best B movies between 1957 and 1960; in fact — why not say it? — some of the best movies of the decade. Equally as impressive were the roles she undertook for other independent producers of the period.

Later, Mamie's image was compromised and tarnished by "nudie" appearances in pics such as *3 Nuts in Search of a Bolt* (1964) in which she disrobes to take a beer bath. But then, if it was good enough for the French and the Italians, why wasn't it good enough for a red-blooded American girl? Why? Europeans were bred to be sex goddesses; American women were bred to

Mamie and dance partner, Lou Southern, meet rock 'n' roll head on in *Running Wild* (Universal, 1955).

be wives and mothers. It was expected of those exotic Europeans such as Brigitte Bardot and Sophia Loren. And the movies usually had subtitles giving them a sense of sophistication they often did not deserve. Sleaze is a precept only if it's in English, it seems.

Realizing she had nothing to lose, Mamie began peddling the sex angle. In her photo shoots and in her revelations in four autobiographical tomes since the mid–1960s, she has set out to live up to her reputation, deserved or otherwise. As a result, too many historians equate her freewheeling sexual life with her ability as an actress. There's more than a whiff of the "slut" about Mamie in some of the critical appraisals of her oeuvre.

Mamie may have started out as the dumb blonde (*Yankee Pasha* and *The Second Greatest Sex*) or the loyal wife in waiting (*Star in the Dust*) but she was never passive like Monroe and Mansfield. Mamie went after her man. If marriage was the ultimate prize in the early films, later it became sexual gratification. She played men at their own game and, most times, won. There is a refreshing lack of talk of love in Mamie's best films. This may have been threatening

Introduction

to the male critics of the time who preferred their sex symbols matronly (Monroe), or pneumatic parodies (Mansfield), where Mamie was a temptress. And a temptress who knew what she wanted and went after it. She didn't always get it (in *High School Confidential!* after attempting unsuccessfully to seduce Russ Tamblyn, her "nephew," she goes back to her husband), but that was of little breast-beating consequence and she quickly moved on to the next conquest.

Perhaps it's not a feminist manifesto but her portrayals were more flesh and blood and sexual longing than many of her contemporaries. While characters portrayed by Doris Day, Debbie Reynolds, Annette Funicello and even Ann-Margret held out for commitment culminating in a wedding ring, Mamie's never seemed to give it a thought (or else were already married and looking to stray).

Only the strongest of men could stand up to Mamie's sexual onslaught. Marilyn, for example, rarely, if ever, was paired with a strong leading man. She was seen opposite milquetoasts such as Tom Ewell, Tommy Noonan, and Joseph Cotten, as if to confirm to the male audience that even the wimpiest of them could win her. Mamie went for virility, the rugged toughs whose faces looked lived in (Jan Merlin, Steve Cochran), or older guys with money (Reginald Gardiner, John Holland). Occasionally, if there was no one else around, she would opt for pretty boys such as Russ Tamblyn or Keith Andes.

Mamie was vulgar, common, brassy. You could never imagine her going the route that Piper Laurie's character took in twisting her personality out of shape to (mistakenly) please the wealthy Rory Calhoun in *Ain't Misbehavin'*. There is a directness to Mamie's characters which cries out: accept me as I am or fuck off. She was the good bad girl. She rarely took a drink or smoked — sex was her recreational drug of choice. And if some men found her threatening, it was perhaps because they felt they were not up to Mamie's brazen come-on.

As Molly Haskell says of the 1950s in *From Reverence to Rape*: "[T]he stars who

Quintessential Mamie. The look that launched a thousand wet dreams in the late 1950s.

stood out from it in papier-mâché relief—Jerry Lewis and Elvis Presley, Marilyn Monroe and Doris Day—had an unreal quality, images at once bland and tortured. They were all *about* sex, but *without* sex. The fabulous fifties were a box of Cracker Jacks without a prize; or with the prize distorted into a forty-inch bust, a forty-year-old virgin" (235).

What she's too polite to say is movies in the 1950s were all about giving the heterosexual male an erection without the money shot. American movies, and most of the female characters who peopled them, were a tease. What men wanted was a pliant, busty Stepford Wife.

Juxtaposed against the mammary brigade (and let's face it, Doris Day was a blonde bombshell herself) and the elfin gamins of Audrey Hepburn, et al. (perhaps the beginning of the anorexic look), Mamie was all sexual being. And to a country already under siege (mentally at least if not in reality) by atomic weapons, communism, juvenile delinquency, and rock 'n' roll, Mamie was the last straw. And in today's sexually regressive climate, with the resurgence of moral fundamentalism, Mamie and her screen characters are subversive oases, untamed by age: Think of her septuagenarian tit flashing in the teen flick *Slackers,* which brought forth howls of derision.

Mamie is a survivor. Granted, her heyday as a sex siren has passed, although a naked photo in the October 2006 issue of *Playboy* belies that. But since *Pulp Fiction* her profile has increased. Not that she wasn't always around—just not as visible. She got involved with the fight against AIDS and discrimination against those suffering from the disease in the 1980s and 1990s. And she has a provocative website (making her the first sex kitten in cyberspace), a star on the Hollywood Walk of Fame, has been an honored guest at numerous film festivals, and was one of the guests of honor (with Carroll Baker) at the Palm Springs Blonde Bombshells art show in January 2006.

Interviews with her, and articles about her, are on the increase and a recent personal highlight was posing for a full-page spread for the March 2006 Hollywood issue of *Vanity Fair* under the creative directorship of fashion titan, Tom Ford. As if that's not enough to keep her busy, Mamie also has her own net blog on which, among other things, she continues to rail against George W. Bush and his administration over U.S. involvement in Iraq.

The world and the movies could well do with a few more like Mamie Van Doren.

Biography

EARLY YEARS

The future Mamie Van Doren was born Joan Lucille Olander in the small town of Rowena, South Dakota, on February 6, 1933, to Warner and Lucille Olander; her parents met at the town's Swedish Lutheran church. The passion that resulted led to a rushed wedding, Mamie making her debut a mere six months later.

Warner knew all there was to know about farming including that he didn't want to make it his living. Although his natural inclination was for mechanical tinkering, he took what jobs he could find during the Depression. When Joan was born he was eking out a living in a local rock quarry, making 35 cents a load. Life for the Olanders improved when he found employment as a mechanic in Sioux City, ninety miles away, and went to live there with Lucille. Little Joan was left behind with her maternal grandparents, the Bennetts, on their 160-acre farm in Rowena. There, at least, she was assured of a stable environment as well as a warm bed and three square meals a day.

It was an austere existence as the farm had no electricity, no gas and no running water. Joan would walk the mile and a half to the two-room schoolhouse in all kinds of weather—wind, snow or rain. But there was always entertainment via the radio and often live music as her grandfather played violin in a trio that entertained at parties. He also encouraged little Joan to sing and dance.

Frequently ill, she had three operations before the age of seven, on one occasion when she was four almost dying of a prolonged hemorrhage that followed surgery. Even at a young age, Joan was aware that appearances accounted for a lot; her major post-appendectomy concern was that the scar would show. She had a "cystoid bump" removed from her face because her schoolmates made fun of it. From that surgery she does have a scar. "It is not a bad scar," Mamie admits. "Even many people who know me well are not aware it exists. But, to me, of course, it stands out like a lighted match in a coal bin."*

After two years she moved to Sioux City to be with her parents, both of whom were now working. Because her mother was kept busy by her job in a local store, one of the three city movie houses became her babysitter when Joan wasn't at school.

> When I look back on my early days in Rowena and Sioux City, it seems to me I must have been born into show business. I was always dancing and singing (sometimes like a little show-off, I guess) but I really liked to appear in front of people. This I first did at parties, and later in declamatory contests. I was also a musician, believe it or not, a cellist. And I loved to have an audience. I think I developed much of this liking for the stage from my mother's ambitions for me. She always

---

*Mamie Van Doren, *My Naughty, Naughty Life!*, 7.

wanted me to become a motion picture star. And that, I guess, was all right with daddy, inasmuch as I had been born a girl and as such could not become a great baseball player.[†]

It has become a cliché but Joan found in the movies the perfect antidote to the dark days of the Depression: the promise of fairy tale romance, living happily ever after with the man she loved. It was in the darkness of those peddler palaces of movie fantasy that Joan set her heart on becoming a Hollywood star. She was to learn the celluloid world had little relationship to the real world.

With the country preparing for war and defense plants springing up along the West Coast, her father received a military deferment because he was considered to be in a strategic industry and got a job in San Diego before moving on to his intended destination of Los Angeles. The idea of Los Angeles and its adjunct, Hollywood, appealed to the star-struck young Joan and, eventually, in May, 1942, a letter arrived containing enough money to transport her and her mother to the film mecca.

It was on the long, crowded train

The young Joan Olander as a brunette at 13, and as a blonde at 20 as she lays siege to Hollywood.

*Van Doren, My Naughty, Naughty Life!, 10–11.

journey that Joan had a brush with the harsh realities of randy men. The train was full of soldiers in various states of undress accompanied by girls who were there, as Mamie puts it, "for love or profit." The liquor was flowing and some of the soldiers were having sex with their women friends across the seats. A young handsome soldier called her "doll" and flirted with her, which went some way toward helping her survive the terrible conditions on the train: "Our day-coaches were crowded, noisy and smelly—from the odor of liquor, smoke, and the sweat of human beings crowded together. I was flustered by the eagerness of the men, the crushing and the pawing. My God, I thought, it looked exciting but so violent. This was all new to me. My mother had for some time protected me against the more sordid side of sex but here it was in the open. I felt a fear but a forming need and passion."*

Not long after she arrived in Los Angeles, Joan met her first bona fide star. A gala party was being held at the famed nightclub, the Mocambo,† and her parents took her along to ogle from the sidewalk as the celebrities paraded up the red carpet. Joan plucked up the courage to approach Mae West for an autograph and was rewarded with the message: *Best of luck to Joanie, a very pretty girl.*

"I stood in the walkway looking after her until my mother pulled me back behind the barrier. The doors of the Mocambo opened and closed repeatedly that night, swallowing up celebrities and stars. More than anything in the world I wanted to be behind those doors. I, too, wanted to be the toast of Hollywood, adored, envied, catered to."‡

The family's first apartment was at 2420 Raymond Avenue; they later moved to a more spacious house at 1421 South Harvard Boulevard. Joan had difficulty adapting to the big city after her life in a small town, especially since the new schooling was so radically different. But Los Angeles had its compensations. Sometimes she and her mother would go to see a vaudeville show at the Orpheum. And, at the grand old age of 11, Joan could head downtown on a Saturday morning unaccompanied to do some window shopping and, when finances permitted, take in a movie matinee.

However, one afternoon on her way home, she got more of a show than she wanted: a man in a car exposed himself, traumatizing her. "For weeks—and occasionally even years later—that man returned to me in my sleep, leaving me a neurotic young girl and even upsetting me as a young woman. For several months after that experience I found myself hating boys, and looking upon men as animals. But I'm glad that hatred never lasted."**

Nevertheless she did not hate her first kiss. "No phase of lovemaking stands out more vividly than my first kiss from a half-frightened 13-year-old boy! In a way, I suppose, it marked the day I quit being wholly a girl and became, ever so slightly, something of a woman. I can trace back my own sex life to my first kiss—and after that wham! Zowie! Whoops! I remember it as if it were yesterday. It was in a hallway during a party. I was 12. My young lover was frightened after he had stolen the kiss and I was angry. I liked it so much I wanted more. Much more."††

She got much more from the crush she had on "Benny,"‡‡ a boy about two years her senior who drove a Cadillac to school. They became inseparable and even talked of marriage though Joan was only 14, until the FBI put an end to their relationship. "Benny" gave her hard-to-get

---

*Van Doren, My Wild Love Experiences, 16.
†Famed Latin American–themed West Hollywood nightclub (8588 Sunset Boulevard) which opened on January 3, 1941, with glass cages of live birds along the walls. From the beginning it attracted the movie colony's A-list with its big band dance music and nightclub performers which included Frank Sinatra and Ella Fitzgerald. The club closed to 1959 and the site is now a car park.
‡Van Doren, Playing the Field, 23.
**Van Doren, My Naughty, Naughty Life!, 34.
††Van Doren, I Swing, 89.
‡‡"Benny" is the pseudonym Mamie gives him in Playing the Field.

Mamie early in her career in a cheesecake pose.

ration coupons which Joan distributed indiscriminately to friends and neighbors. She never saw him again although he continued to send birthday and Christmas cards for the next ten years.

Joan found herself a job as an usherette, wearing a uniform with a pillbox hat and carrying a flashlight, at the Pantages Theater* on Hollywood Boulevard. In her spare time she hung out at the nearby Schwab's Drugstore[†] even though she knew the story of Lana Turner's being plucked from anonymity there was a myth. But to encourage anyone who might want to discover her, she had dyed her hair platinum.

---

*The Pantages Theater at 6233 Hollywood Boulevard was built in 1930 at a cost of $1.25 million to accommodate the newly invented talking pictures. It hosted a number of glamorous movie premieres before it was bought from the Fox cinema chain by Howard Hughes in 1949. During the 1950s it was home to the annual Academy Awards; the Emmy Awards were held there until 1977, moving when the grand old theater became a home for live theater, especially touring productions of Broadway musicals.

[†]Schwab's Drugstore at 8024 Sunset Boulevard was demolished in 1988 to make way for a large shopping complex. Its owner Leon Schwab, with an eye for publicity, promoted the false claim that Lana Turner was discovered there, sitting on a stool at the soda fountain. It was, though, a popular hangout for actors and writers looking for work and the Lana Turner myth is still potent, even today.

Against all odds, discovered she was— by Nils Thor Granlund* who hosted a show broadcast live from the Florentine Gardens nightclub on the new medium of television. She was offered her first role as decoration: a pretty face in the background, given the sobriquet Little Joanie the Flower Girl. Her decorative services also entailed modeling clothes and jewelry from local businesses and extolling their virtues on the program. Because television in that period was broadcast in black and white, "They coated all the girls appearing on the show with thick white Pancake makeup and brown lipstick. We looked like creatures in a horror movie," Mamie remembers.[†]

In a precursor of the modern talk show, Granlund would interview a movie star, tell jokes, and talk with the audience. Joan worked for the live weekly show on and off for over a year but in lieu of cash payment the girls received a pair of stockings and the hopeless dream of becoming stars. Disillusionment set in quickly even though she was in show business (of a sort).

MISS PALM SPRINGS

While Joan was vacationing with her mother at the Montecito Motel in Palm Springs, the manager suggested that Joan take part in the Miss Palm Springs competition which the motel was sponsoring. With her mother's permission, the 15-year-old entered. And won. Other beauty crowns quickly followed, including the title of Miss Eight Ball from the Los Angeles Press Club (photos of Mamie would now feature heavily in both Los Angeles and Palm Springs). Not surprisingly, she received a phone call from RKO Studios and was contracted for a bit role in their variety omnibus film, *Footlight Varieties* (1951). She had one brief scene and no dialogue.

Joan got to meet the secretive head of RKO, Howard Hughes, after he saw her either at the Mocambo Club or at the Miss Palm Springs Pageant (sources differ); he had her invited to lunch at which he asked her if she were a virgin. A flabbergasted Joan retorted: "That's something you'll never know, Howard." He did, however, get to know Joan on a more intimate level over the months that followed but "not of a penetrative kind,"[‡] she has reported. After a series of personal questions during which he ascertained, to his obvious satisfaction, that she was not dating any boy in particular, he told her he might have a role for her in a film, *Jet Pilot*, that RKO was shooting near Las Vegas. Hughes invited her to spend the weekend with him but Joan was already committed to an engagement as the reigning Miss Palm Springs for the city's Chamber of Commerce. He engaged a limousine to drive Joan and her mother, but once in Palm Springs he demanded she forego her booked engagement and spend time with him. When she refused, she discovered the limousine was no longer available to drive her back to Los Angeles.

Joan was nevertheless told to report to Las Vegas for a bit role in *Jet Pilot*. She spent two days on the film during which time she never saw its star, John Wayne, not surprising since she was cast as a member of the Soviet air force. And the film itself would not surface until 1957 after Howard Hughes had endlessly tinkered with it. More small non-speaking roles followed in the Jane Russell–Robert Mitchum film noir *His Kind of Woman* and the Janet Leigh–Ann Miller–Tony Martin musical, *Two Tickets to Broadway* (both 1951). Realizing she needed acting lessons, Joan enrolled with Berlin-born Natasha Lytess (1913–1964) who had been a student of famed theatre and film director, Max Reinhardt, and who had appeared in a small number

---

*Swedish-born Nils Thor Granlund (1882–1957), or NTG as he liked to be called, was an entertainment legend. He is considered the first radio DJ and pioneered the use of paid advertising on the medium. He also packaged variety shows and owned a number of nightclubs. During Prohibition he and singer Harry Richman opened the up-market speakeasy, Club Richman. As an innovator it was only natural he would get involved with movies and appeared on screen, as himself, in Mr. Broadway (1933), The Girl from Paradise (1934), Rhythm Parade (1942), Take It Big (1944), and Goin' to Town (1944). After movies the natural next step was to television.

†Van Doren, *Playing the Field*, 27–28.

‡Phone interview with the author, May 23, 2006.

of U.S. films, including *Comrade X* (1940) and *Once Upon a Honeymoon* (1942). She was also Marilyn Monroe's acting coach from 1948 to 1955. The lessons were short-lived because "I felt I wasn't learning anything — Natasha couldn't or wouldn't stop talking long enough to teach."*

With a lifetime of bit parts seemingly ahead of her at RKO and rejection from MGM where she screen tested in a scene from *Mildred Pierce* and from 20th Century–Fox where she did a scene from a Susan Hayward film, and feeling smothered at home, Joan took the opportunity to marry successful sportswear manufacturer, Jack Newman, ten years her senior; she'd met him at Friday night boxing matches she attended with her father. Jack was wealthy and experienced. Mamie was poor and oversexed, although still a virgin. Aged 17, she eloped to Santa Barbara and lied about her age to the judge who married them. Although the sex was athletic and lived up to her expectations, by the time the married couple returned to Los Angeles from their honeymoon, Joan realized she may have been too hasty.

They had little in common apart from their love of sex. Joan discovered that Jack suffered from erratic mood swings probably caused by an old war wound. His jealous rages culminated in an argument during which he tried to throw Mamie from the second-story balcony of their apartment. She moved back in with her parents and began legal proceedings to get out of her short marriage.

Taken to Las Vegas to get over the break-up, Joan succeeded in picking up a job as a showgirl at the El Rancho Hotel and Casino. During her summer there she became friends with Danielle Corey, who had also worked at RKO, and who made a lesbian pass at her. It was to be the first of many such passes from women such as Coco Chanel and Marlene Dietrich. Joan rejected the pass. One she did not reject was from mobster Charlie Fischetti, a cousin and henchman of Al Capone, although at first she did not know who he was. Even when she did, the relationship continued. Charlie showered Joan with gifts and cash and their relationship continued, on and off, until Charlie's death in 1951.

Back in Los Angeles after her stint as a showgirl, she considered herself now too mature to go back to school and auditioned to become a model for the famed Alberto Vargas.† Joan's mother accompanied her to the modeling assignment because Joan was under 18 but she and the artist were left alone for the session. "He explained what he wanted from me — the wild, saucy expression of a real sexy girl, blended with a suggestion of wholesomeness of the all–American girl type."‡ The painting was completed in one sitting for which Joan was paid $200. When the picture appeared in the July 1951 edition of *Esquire*, her modeling profile skyrocketed. She quickly chafed at the early nights and the lack of a social life required of models. In an attempt to break free she auditioned at the Beverly Hills Hotel for a New York revival of the Morton Gould–Betty Comden and Adolph Green Broadway musical *Billion Dollar Baby* and was cast in the chorus. Her mother again signed the necessary papers giving her permission and Joan headed to the Big Apple for the first time. The show was at Monte Prosser's Café Theater, which he had set up after relinquishing the Mocambo Club in Los Angeles. Joan was a showgirl and "wore a scanty (for its day) butterfly costume with a pair of green wings."**

---

*Van Doren, Playing the Field, 37.

†Peruvian-born Alberto Vargas (real name: Joaquin Alberto Vargas y Chavez) (1896–1982) was famed for his cheesecake paintings, especially during his 16 years illustrating for Playboy in the 1960s and 1970s. His major influence was La Vie Parisienne artist Raphael Kirchner, whose rendering of the female form he admired and adapted. Vargas settled in the U.S. to escape World War I and continued painting as well as retouching photographs. He worked with Florenz Ziegfeld in the 1920s, perfecting his depiction of the idealized female body. Throughout the Depression he was a step away from poverty until he was contracted to Esquire for whom he created the Vargas Girl. At the age of 64, when he was hired by Hugh Hefner to paint nudes for Playboy, his reputation and his financial security were assured. It was the air-brushed ethereal quality of his nudes that made Vargas justly famous.

‡Van Doren, My Naughty, Naughty Life!, 60.

**Van Doren, Playing the Field, 47.

Biography 17

Mamie in 2006 as a modern-day Vargas Girl (photograph by Alan Mercer).

The theater, situated at 49th and Broadway, was close to Jack Dempsey's restaurant so it was only natural she would meet the famed boxer.* More surprising was that she began a sex-

---

*Jack Dempsey (William Harrison Dempsey, 1895–1983) originally boxed as Kid Blackie before adopting the name Jack Dempsey around 1914 and going on to claim the World Heavyweight Champion title July 14, 1919, retaining it until September 23, 1926. He lost a rematch with new champion Gene Tunney the following year and retired, opening the restaurant in New York.

ual liaison with Dempsey, a man, her mother kept reminding her, older than her own father. But she was too young to be restricted sexually and began secretly seeing margarine heir Micky Jelke, and was also preparing a visit to Charlie Fischetti in Chicago when he died suddenly of a heart attack. Eddie Fisher,* then an up-and-coming crooner on the brink of super success, also succumbed to Joan's charms. According to Fisher,

> Joan Olander was a gorgeous eighteen-year-old chorus girl. She had a perfect figure. Better than perfect. I was told she had been married and divorced at fifteen, and had been dating former heavyweight champion Jack Dempsey since she was sixteen.... We made a very cute couple. She fell in love with me and told Dempsey, but what was he going to do about it? He was married. Every time we went out she insisted we go to places where we could be seen; she was desperate for attention. I thought the whole thing was ridiculous, and I knew she was using me, but ... Joan was gorgeous. She was the last woman I slept with before I was inducted.[†]

Two years later when he returned from Korea, Joan was the first person he called, telling her to book a room at the Beverly Hills Hotel. While he found the sex still as good as ever and Joan, now renamed Mamie Van Doren, as gorgeous as ever, he wanted a little more intellectual stimulation. According to Eddie their relationship fell apart permanently one night at the Mocambo Club when he refused to be photographed with her, opting instead to be photographed with Edward G. Robinson. Mamie walked out.

After the dispiritingly unsuccessful season of *Billion Dollar Baby*, Joan was near penniless, out of work, and frightened for the future. "I could sing a little, dance a little, but not enough to get any attention. I'd go to parties and other places and start to meet people and pay close attention to what they were and what they could do for me. I know that is callous, but that's how I made it. Slowly I began to realize what I needed. That was most important — to know my goal. I needed a man who would like me and at the same time be a kind of a genius who would teach me to sing and teach me how to present a night club act. I had to get lucky."[‡]

That man turned out to be acclaimed songwriter Jimmy McHugh (1894–1969), composer of a number of hit songs including "I Can't Give You Anything But Love," "Don't Blame Me," and "I'm in the Mood for Love" with lyricist Dorothy Fields. Joan met him in Los Angeles and he signed her to a personal management contract arranging for her to attend acting classes with Ben Bard. A former movie heavy, Bard's acting school had an attached theater famed for its productions of classic and contemporary plays. Bard's students over the years included such screen stalwarts as Alan Ladd, Jack Carson, Shirley Temple, Gower Champion, Angie Dickinson, Cliff Robertson and Gig Young. At the theatre with Joan were director Aaron Spelling, years before going on to a successful career in television production, and his then girlfriend, actress Carolyn Jones (who would later enjoy success in the movies and as Morticia on *The Addams Family*).

Joan appeared in Bard theater productions of *Once in a Lifetime* by Kaufman and Hart, *At War with the Army* by James B. Allardice and then played Dixie in Clifford Odets' *The Big Knife*. She screen tested for Paramount performing *The Big Knife*'s climactic scene after being coached by Spelling and Jones but she was not offered a contract. She believes she was rejected because of the intervention of gossip columnist Louella Parsons,** then Jimmy McHugh's lady friend,

---

*Eddie Fisher (1918–) rose to fame on Eddie Cantor's radio program (after years of amateur contests), Arthur Godfrey's radio show and later with the bands of Charlie Ventura and Buddy Morrow. He was signed to a recording contract with RCA Victor on the strength of his nationwide popularity on Cantor's program but in 1951, just as his career was gaining momentum he was drafted into the U.S. Army. His time in the service enhanced his standing with the public and upon discharge he went on to greater fame.
[†]Eddie Fisher with David Fisher, Been There, Done That, 61.
[‡]Van Doren, I Swing, 107–08.
**Louella Parsons (real name: Louella Rose Oettinger) (1881–1972) was a small-town journalist until the breakup of her marriage, after which she moved to Hollywood and began writing scripts. She is credited with writing the first movie gossip column, for the Chicago Record-Herald in 1914, but lost her job when William Randolph Hearst bought

Mamie in her brief segment miming "You Belong to Me" in *Forbidden* (Universal, 1953).

the paper. She wrote for various news outlets until 1925 when she moved to Los Angeles fearing she was dying of tuberculosis. She went to work for Hearst on the Los Angeles Examiner *and was eventually syndicated in over 600 newspapers and magazines worldwide. Her power increased when she added radio broadcasts to her talents. She was a ruthless arbiter on all things moral and cinematic and could destroy (or revive) careers at the stroke of a pen. Her power was diluted marginally when Hedda Hopper began writing in opposition in 1937. Parsons' power waned in the late 1950s and she retired in 1965.*

who erroneously believed that Joan and Jimmy were having an affair. To make matters worse, Parsons also threatened Ben Bard with adverse publicity if he did not dismiss Joan from his acting school. Joan planned the only revenge on Parsons available to her: "I convinced myself that no matter how unlikely it seemed, somehow, someday, I was going to be a star."*

McHugh managed to get a despondent Joan into acting classes at the prestigious Bliss Hayden Theater and she was offered the ingénue role of Marie in their production of William Inge's *Come Back, Little Sheba*. "We played to an enthusiastic first night audience and the crowd obviously liked me. The next day Jimmy got a call from Phil Benjamin, a casting director from Universal who had been in the audience. Benjamin thought I would be right for the role of a nightclub singer in a Universal picture called *Forbidden* starring Tony Curtis and Joanne Dru. Things began happening fast. I drove to Universal the next day and met Benjamin, veteran producer Ted Richmond, and the director Rudy Maté."† These men liked what they saw. They gave her a song and accompanying movements to learn over the weekend and told her to be prepared to shoot the scene on the Monday.

> At the studio the wardrobe people sewed me into the long white satin gown while makeup people glued on fake fingernails. I was in a fog, concentrating on my song while everyone orbited me pinning, sewing, dabbing, retouching. Finally I was led onto the elegant nightclub set, and when Tony Curtis, Joanne Dru, and the other actors were in place, Rudy Maté shouted, "Action!" It was over in one take but Ted Richmond came over and told me what a great job I'd done. "Everyone thinks you're just dynamite, Joan. We've been talking about a contract for you here at the studio." He gestured to a group of men disappearing through the back door of the sound stage. As luck would have it, the top executives—including Milton Rachmil, head of Universal's parent company, Decca Records—had flown out the day before from New York to meet with the local studio execs.‡

Jimmy McHugh negotiated a seven-year Universal contract with two-year options and a starting salary of $260 a week. The studio also agreed to pay for her singing lessons and her wardrobe. Looking back on her early career, Mamie wrote in 1997: "A star emerging from one studio had a galvanizing effect on the others. Marilyn Monroe's light winked on at 20th Century–Fox, and the other studios, seeing her popularity expressed in box office receipts, immediately began to develop their own 'answers.' Each studio began searching for its own dumb blonde. As luck would have it, Universal International decided I was theirs. I became Universal's answer to Marilyn Monroe, though I (and they) had no idea what the real question was."**

Enter Mamie Van Doren

Universal's contract came with a price: a name change. Mamie, after Dwight D. Eisenhower's wife and the country's First Lady, and the Van Doren came about as the studio hierarchy thought she looked more Dutch than Swedish. In an interview with modamag.com, Mamie revealed her new double-barreled last name "came from a young actor, his name was Robert Van Doren. He came to me and said, 'Mamie, you've got my last name.' ... They had changed his name to John Smith. He was tall, blonde and good looking." While the studio could have had the striking blond contract player in mind when they chose Mamie's name, John Smith (1931–95), who appeared in a number of westerns and TV shows, had the birth name of Robert Van Orden, admittedly an anagram of Van Doren.

Mamie found the new moniker to her liking. "It had a certain quality about it, a ring to

---

*Van Doren, Playing the Field, 59.
†*mamievandoren.com*
‡Ibid.
**Van Doren, *Click: Becoming Feminists*, 9.

Biography 21

it. Nor did I mind discarding the name Joan Olander. It just didn't sound like a movie star's name. But Mamie Van Doren — now, that was something else."* She began attending classes at the Universal talent school along with Dennis Weaver, David Janssen, Jack Kelly, Julia Adams, Barbara Rush, Kathleen Hughes, Piper Laurie, Tony Curtis, Rock Hudson, Clint Eastwood and Anita Ekberg.

"They spent millions of dollars on training the young people who came in to be stars. They had people from UCLA giving classes in diction, which I took, and they had facilities for horseback riding on the back lot. Then you'd take fencing and you'd have classes in drama and improvisation. Everything. You can't believe what we did. They spent a lot of money and we had the best training there. I was lucky to get that studio because they had it and I needed it."†

In the summer of 1953, director Jesse Hibbs tested her for a role in the Tony Curtis starrer, *All American,* and let it be known she was expected to play with his crotch while she read lines. She got the part and was fourth-billed after Curtis, Lori Nelson and Richard Long. "The studio publicity department had more or less groomed me for the part because they decided I was the sexy type. They photographed me in bathing suits, sweaters and Sheath gowns. They mentioned my walk, in fact, they mentioned anything about me that made their point, until I

Mamie on the beach for her first series of Universal cheesecake photographs in 1953.

*Van Doren, Playing the Field, *62–63.*
†Van Doren, Click: Becoming Feminists, *9.*

found myself concentrating on what makes a girl sexy. I decided it was not a wiggle, or wearing clothes that fitted like wallpaper, it was more than that; it was something in a girl's eyes ... even beyond that, it has to be something deep in a girl, a great desire to please, to be admired. So I decided it took brains as well as curves to be sexy."*

It was an auspicious beginning to her career at Universal as the film was released a few months before the earlier lensed *Forbidden*. Then she was rushed into *Yankee Pasha* as Lilith the harem girl given as a slave to Jeff Chandler. Mamie was billed below Chandler and his screen love interest Rhonda Fleming. The schizophrenic storyline begins as a western before becoming a pirate movie and then an Arabian Nights–style action-adventure. It was Universal's first CinemaScope movie and they pulled out all the stops to make it a box office success.

> I had a really cute part — it wasn't a small role, Lilith was one of the main characters. Jeff Chandler was super to work with, and the guy who played the king, Lee J. Cobb, he came on to me — he used to call me at night and ask me to go out with him. Of course, I thought he was ancient. A lot of these guys would try to get me, and I said to myself, "How can they expect me to go out with them? They're just too old!" I mean, I really liked him as a friend, but to get involved with him emotionally — well, I was too immature. I always looked at actors like that as father figures. But they had other ideas.†

Getting a reputation as Universal's answer to Marilyn Monroe wasn't hurting her career and being squired to film premieres by some of the country's best-looking men guaranteed she would have her photo appear in newspapers worldwide. Nicky Hilton, recently divorced from Elizabeth Taylor, was Mamie's escort to the premiere of *The Glenn Miller Story* (1954) and, against the wishes of Nicky's father Conrad, head of the Hilton hotel chain, they began dating seriously. But while Nicky was "generously endowed" as a lover, Mamie found "there was a sadness about having sex with him" caused by his huge appetite for alcohol which impaired his performance. She began secretly dating a dance teacher at the studio, Dwayne Ratliff, who had appeared in *The I Don't Care Girl* (1953), a Fox film starring Mitzi Gaynor as Eva Tanguay.

Mamie was next cast in a Francis the Talking Mule series entry, *Francis Joins the WACS* (1954), one of the inevitable chores that many Universal contractees had to undertake. Although the actors hated playing second fiddle to the mule, they found it preferable to playing second fiddle in Universal's other cash cow, the Ma and Pa Kettle franchise. Then she was sent to test for the lead in what Universal hoped would be its answer to MGM musicals, *The Third Girl from the Right*. Mamie was in far from fine form: She had been with Ratliff when he collapsed and was rushed to a hospital. He was subsequently diagnosed with polio and Mamie underwent a painful spinal tap to test for the disease and was still debilitated when she turned up for her screen test. As a result she was cast not in the lead role of the singer-dancer who weds the Nob Hill millionaire but as one of her roommates. "The leading role went to Piper Laurie," Mamie writes in *Playing the Field*. "It was a mystifying choice in some ways. Piper was (and still is) a fine dramatic actress, but she is not primarily a song-and-dance performer."

Although happy to be steadily employed, she began to seriously question the dumb-blonde roles in which she was being typecast at Universal. She seemed to be going backwards. "Unfortunately, Universal was clueless when it came to developing female talent. They could build Rock Hudson or Tony Curtis into major stars, but they were baffled as to how to cultivate their actresses. It is difficult to name a woman of similar stature to Rock and Tony who emerged from that era at Universal."‡

Mamie's relationship with Nicky Hilton was going backwards and it finally ended during the filming of *Ain't Misbehavin'* (as *The Third Girl from the Right* had been renamed). But a

---
*Picturegoer Annual 1956.
†*Movie Club*, 15–16.
‡*Van Doren*, Click: Becoming Feminists, 10.

Mamie with Nicky Hilton at a Hollywood premiere in 1953.

chance phone call from pal Bob Francis,* a Columbia contractee she'd met at acting classes, led to a dinner date with bandleader Ray Anthony, in town to test for a role in the Fred Astaire vehicle *Daddy Long Legs* for 20th Century–Fox; a romance ensued. Mamie and the famed bandleader shared a similar sense of humor, a Midwest background and a love of music. Ray was born Raymond Antonioni in Bentleyville, Pennsylvania, in 1922 and raised in Cleveland, Ohio. He became a trumpeter with the Glenn Miller band between 1941 and 1942 and was with Jimmy Dorsey's band for six months before spending four years in the U.S. Navy heading his own orchestra in the Pacific. Upon his discharge he formed a civilian orchestra under his own name.

Pointing out the morals clause in her contract, the studio warned her off seeing Ray because he was a married man, albeit separated from his wife. But, by now, both Mamie and Ray were deeply in love and, after Ray's quickie divorce in Mexico, they flew out for a holiday in Hawaii. "Ray was that combination that every woman looks for: aggressive but gentle, ardent but cool, devastatingly skilled, and handsomely equipped."†

Before the getaway Mamie had to take care of business that had been nagging at her. Jimmy McHugh's Svengali-like grip on her career had been noticeably lessened of late. True, illness

---

*Robert Francis (1930–1955) was one of Columbia's most promising young actors when he was killed piloting a light plane. He made just four films: They Rode West, The Caine Mutiny, The Bamboo Prison *(all 1954) and* The Long Gray Line *(1955).*
†*Van Doren,* Playing the Field, *107.*

had slowed him down, but a number of loan-outs to other studios for quality films had fallen through thanks to Louella Parsons' interference, Mamie believes. Her roles at Universal were getting smaller and depressingly similar. Encouraged by Ray Anthony she went to celebrity lawyer Jerry Geisler* who had helped her mother a few years before when a drunk ran a red light and hit the car in which she was traveling, injuring her severely. Mamie turned to him to extricate her from her contract with McHugh. It was an easy matter. Mamie, under legal age when she signed, did not get her parents' signatures on the contract; plus Jimmy McHugh was not registered as an artists' manager in California. Mamie was free to seek representation elsewhere.

But on returning to Los Angeles from Hawaii she was confronted with one of the nastiest scandals of all. The studio had received advance warning of a story that *Confidential* magazine was about to run: that Mamie and her mother had been prostitutes. The accusation was false but its mere publication would have been enough to end her Hollywood career. Mamie headed straight to Jerry Geisler, who rang the publisher and threatened a lawsuit so huge it would close down his magazine if he didn't have iron-clad proof of the accusation. The story never appeared.

Mamie with ducks in a typical cheesecake pose of the 1950s.

*In Hollywood's Golden Age, the criminal defense attorney everyone used was Jerry Geisler. The precursor to celebrity lawyers like Robert Shapiro and Johnny Cochran, Geisler had successfully defended Charlie Chaplin and Errol Flynn on rape charges, and represented Marilyn Monroe in her divorce from Joe DiMaggio. He was expensive but no one in Los Angeles could match Geisler's skill before a jury.

Mamie found out the source of the scurrilous rumors was none other than her old nemesis, Louella Parsons.

Back at Universal, Mamie segued from dumb blonde chorus girl in contemporary San Francisco in *Ain't Misbehavin'* to dumb blonde in the American West in *The Second Greatest Sex* (1955). The studio pulled out all stops for its CinemaScope musical starring George Nader, Jeanne Crain, Bert Lahr and Keith Andes. But during filming Mamie suffered morning sickness, not realizing its significance even though her period was weeks late. When she began bleeding while on the set, she went immediately to her family physician who informed her she'd had a miscarriage. A baby out of wedlock was more than enough to get an actress fired from a studio and Mamie dictated that Ray would have to use condoms in future.

In March, 1955, a movie that led ultimately to a change in Mamie's career opened in New York. It was MGM's *Blackboard Jungle* starring Glenn Ford. But for the choice of "Rock Around the Clock" by Bill Haley and the Comets on the soundtrack, it may have been merely another in a long line of teen-bashing movies that were popular in the period, particularly with the rise of Marlon Brando in Columbia's *The Wild One* (1954) and James Dean in Warner Bros.' *Rebel without a Cause* (1955). However, that auspicious choice launched the era of rock 'n' roll. The studios began to turn out movies aimed at a well-heeled juvenile market which was alienated by bland adult cinema fare. Nik Cohn best summed up the general scramble to get on the bandwagon: "Churchmen offered spiritual comfort, psychologists explained, magistrates got tough, parents panicked, businessmen became rich and rock exploded into a central issue."[*]

Universal, fearing the trend would not last but also fearful of being left behind, rushed to join the stampede with *Running Wild* (1955). It was another juvenile delinquent movie, this time juvenile car thieves, based on a superior detective thriller by Ben Benson. Keenan Wynn played the adult head of the car-stripping operation, supported by a Who's Who of the Universal charm school: William Campbell, Kathleen Case, Jan Merlin and John Saxon. Feeling it was a step backwards (it was filmed in black and white and it would be her first "bad girl" role), Mamie told the studio she would rather go on suspension. But Universal prevailed. In the process of doing a wild jitterbug to "Razzle Dazzle" by Bill Haley and the Comets on a jukebox, Mamie discovered the joys of rock 'n' roll and, in so doing, invented a niche for herself and a place in cinema history.

During the filming of *Running Wild*, Mamie was approached about appearing on Broadway in the lead role in a new play by George Axelrod titled *Will Success Spoil Rock Hunter?*,[†] a satire on Hollywood and the cult of Marilyn Monroe. Mamie's role was to be that of Rita Marlowe, the Monroe caricature. Jule Styne, who was producing the show, came to Los Angeles to audition Mamie and liked her reading of the part. He invited her to travel to New York to meet writer-director Axelrod but, in one of those moments she regrets in hindsight, she turned him down. Her complex reasoning was colored by a career that was continually in Marilyn Monroe's shadow, and that it was a spoof on dumb blondes which meant it was a spoof on her as well. And, most importantly, it meant time away from Ray Anthony with whom she was deeply in love. The role went to the little-known Jayne Mansfield whose career to that point had been in bit roles in a small number of films. The Broadway production catapulted her to stardom and a return to Hollywood in films the likes of which Mamie could only dream about.

On completing *Running Wild*, Mamie found she was pregnant again. Her resolve to make

---

[*]Nik Cohn, Awopbopaloobop AlopBamBoom: Pop from the Beginning *(London: Paladin, 1973), 19.*
[†]*Opened at the Belasco Theater, New York, on October 13, 1955, and played 444 performances. The cast was Orson Bean, Jayne Mansfield, Martin Gabel, Walter Matthau, Tina Louise, Harry Clark, Carol Grace and Michael Tolan. The Frank Tashlin–directed film version (1957) starred Mansfield with Tony Randall, Joan Blondell, Betsy Drake and John Williams. For the screen, Tashlin cut out a major role to expand the role of Rock Hunter for Tony Randall.*

Ray wear a rubber had proven short-lived but, when she told him, he was reluctant to commit to a marriage that mere months before he himself had proposed. He told Mamie he had changed his mind and headed out on the road with the band. The only thing that kept her going through the heartache was work. Producer Albert Zugsmith, who began his film career with low-budget science fiction quickies before joining Universal for the Joan Crawford–Jeff Chandler thriller *Female on the Beach* (1955), wanted Mamie for his upcoming Western *Star in the Dust* (1956). "*Star in the Dust* was Universal's answer to *High Noon*. That was one of U.I.'s problems—they had an 'answer' to everything rather than doing something original."*

Fighting morning sickness and a constricting corset, Mamie struggled through five weeks of the grueling shoot wondering if the studio would invoke the morals clause in her contract. However, a repentant Ray Anthony rang and confessed he could not live without her, something he'd realized after six lonely weeks on the road. She flew to Toledo where the band was playing and they were wed on August 29, 1955. But almost from the beginning of their married life, Ray showed a jealous streak that would eventually drive the couple apart. On March 18, 1956, Mamie gave birth to 6 lb. 1 oz. Perry Ray Anthony at St. John's Hospital in Santa Monica after twelve hours in labor. Newspapers carried the report of Perry's "premature" birth. While still in hospital she received a visit from an executive from Universal who informed her that her new status as a married woman and a mother did not fit the image the studio had carved out for her, and that they would not be renewing her contract when it expired in 1957. Worse, they would not be using her in any more films before then although she was free to work for other studios. They did allow her to continue dance and voice lessons at Universal.

The cheesecake gave way to glamour in this 1953 publicity shot.

THE FREELANCE YEARS

In later years Mamie would rail against the studio system and male-dominated Hollywood of the era. "The movie scene in

*Van Doren, Playing the Field, 124.

the 1950s was to feminism what a cleaver is to meat. The studio system had been in charge of what audiences saw on the screen for thirty years. Precious few films of the period contain strong feminine characters because the studios—in concert with the half-assed piety and thinly veiled hypocrisy of the censorship boys from the Johnson and Hays offices—created images of women dreamed up by men. There were very few women then in executive positions at the studio. There were no women as studio heads. If you were an actress called upon to portray one of those images, you were required to live your life in accordance with the restrictions of that image—or else. There was no tolerance of illegitimate children, extramarital affairs, or nude layouts in men's magazines."*

Salvation came in the form of a script from her new agent, Maurie Gutterman. It was the bleakly cynical film noir *The Girl in Black Stockings* (1957) in which she was typecast as a young blonde gold-digger opposite Lex Barker, Anne Bancroft, Marie Windsor, Ron Randell and John Dehner. It was shot on location in Kanab, Utah, which meant a two-week separation from Ray and Perry. Back in their small apartment on Shirley Place in Beverly Hills, the marriage became even more poisonous when Ray was cast in *The Girl Can't Help It* (1956), a vehicle for Jayne Mansfield. To further aggravate the Mansfield connection, Mamie was offered the Los Angeles production of *Will Success Spoil Rock Hunter?* She turned it down.

By this time the comparisons with Marilyn and Jayne were becoming a burden. "I never could see the necessity of being compared to anyone—just because I'm blonde, and I can wiggle, wriggle and jiggle, when the occasion calls for it. I'm not trying to duplicate anyone. I would much rather be a mediocre original, than an outstanding carbon copy."[†]

Married life began to improve when Ray was signed to host an ABC-TV variety show, *The Ray Anthony Show*, in 1956. The extra money meant they could move into more spacious surroundings: a three-story, six-bedroom Spanish-style stucco house with swimming pool and tennis court on La Presa Drive in Hollywood. And, in keeping with their new accommodation, they employed a cook, a gardener, a maid and a nurse for Perry. But a larger house did not make it any more palatable to be playing at being Mrs. Ray Anthony even when she appeared on his show as a singer. A contract for a two-picture deal with Howard W. Koch, director on *Black Stockings*, got her out of the house.

As Mamie embraced rock 'n' roll to revitalize her career, big band leader and trumpeter Ray was finding his style of music heading the way of the dodo. Ray confided to *Picturegoer*, "It was quite a surprise to me to find that Mamie could sing. I knew she was a good little actress and I thought one musician in the family was enough.... One thing I'm thankful for. Mamie's taste is changing. She used to sing awful numbers, but now she's going over to ballads. And to sexy numbers, of course ... which she does darned well, I'd say."[‡] But their diverse music tastes was leading to conflict no matter what Ray said in print.

Untamed Youth (1957), one of Mamie's favorite starring films, is also one of her quintessential movies of the 1950s: a lurid melodrama created to fertilize teen paranoia. If there was a market for adult entertainment that was delusional about teens then, obviously, the reverse was equally true. It was another rung on the ladder of Mamie's cult superstardom. Released through Warner Bros., the plot featured Mamie and Lori Nelson as sisters who are incarcerated as slave labor in a correctional facility, picking cotton for the crime of skinny dipping. Mamie got to sing four of the songs including a calypso number in anticipation of a new "fad." Rocker Eddie Cochran was on hand to lend his talents to a bottom-drawer song and top-drawer performance of one of the film's better numbers penned by Les Baxter. During filming on location in

---

*Van Doren, Click: Becoming Feminists, 7–8.
[†]*Liberty, May, 1958, 34.*
[‡]*Ray Anthony, Picturegoer, October 12, 1957.*

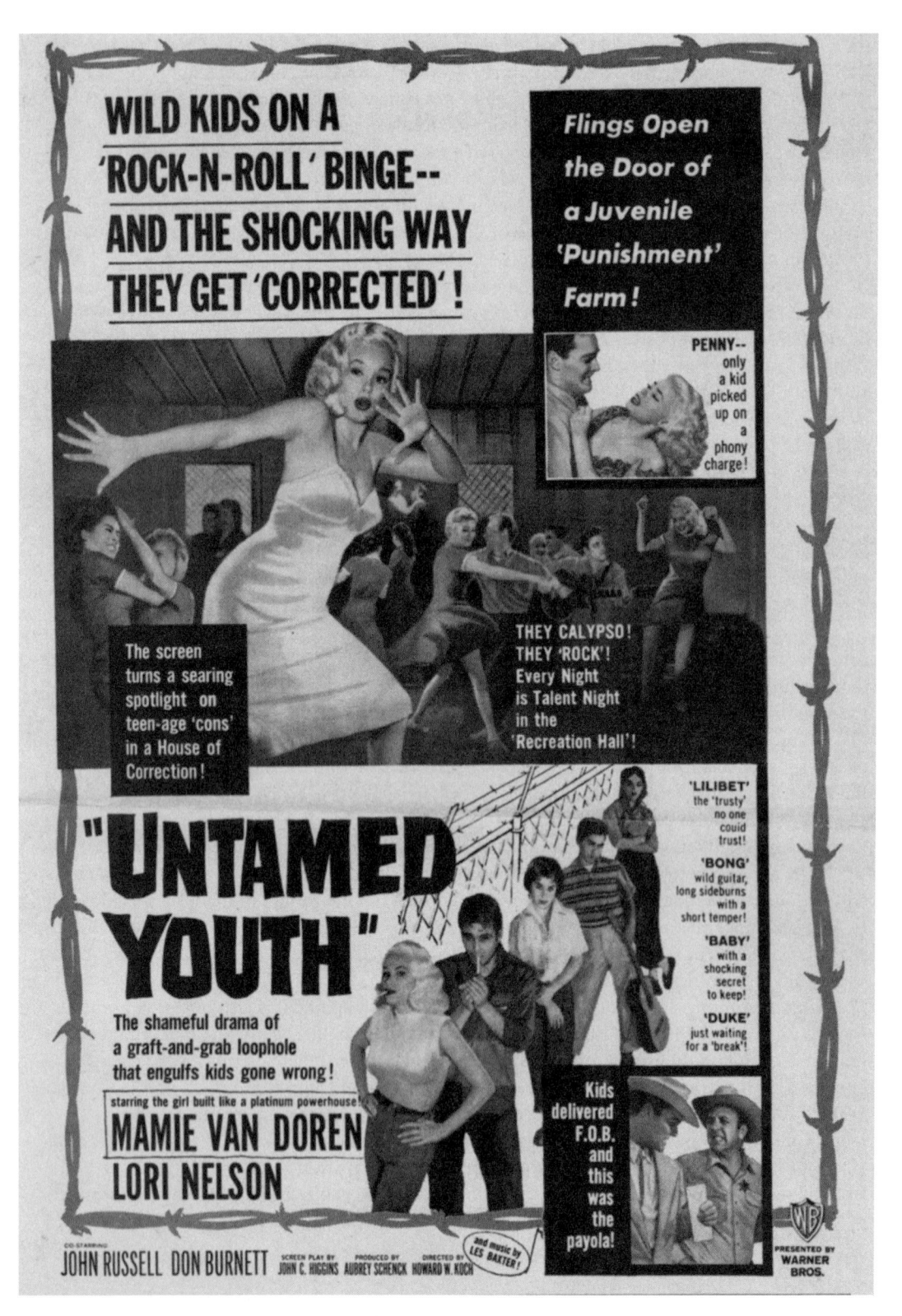

Press advertisement for *Untamed Youth* (Warner Bros., 1957).

Bakersfield, California, Mamie's dress supposedly got caught in a cotton-picking machine and her thigh was lacerated. The press duly reported the "accident" with revealing photos of Mamie's bandaged thigh.

Between acting and promotional chores (she was appointed official hostess at the Tournament of Champions golf classic played in Las Vegas in April), Mamie spent as much time as possible at home in 1957 bonding with son Perry and attempting to shore up her marriage. Then Gutterman negotiated a contract for her to star in Lou Walters' Latin Quarter Revue at the Riviera Hotel. The salary was too good to turn down: ten thousand dollars a week for four weeks to perform a 30-minute night club act opening October 2, 1957, with choreography by Jack Baker and gowns by Norman Norrell. While Ray continued his television show in Los Angeles, Perry and his nurse remained with Mamie in Las Vegas. One night during the run of her show, Elvis Presley came to admire Mamie and although their relationship never became physical both of them wanted it to. The money from the Vegas gig enabled Mamie to buy her own home on Rising Glen Road in the Hollywood Hills overlooking the Sunset Strip but, with a good dose of street smarts, she put the house in her parents' names.

In 1958 she was in the Warner Bros. commissary for lunch with producer Howard W. Koch (for whom she was shooting the rodeo musical *Born Reckless*) when Clark Gable saw her and requested her for the film he was about to make with Doris Day, *Teacher's Pet* (1958). In the movie, set in the world of academia and big city newspapers, she would be a nightclub singer, the third side of the love triangle, opposite Doris's new-fangled journalism teacher and Gable's old-fashioned city newspaper exponent. Mamie bonded with Gable but found the movie's female star aloof. For many years she blamed Doris's supposed jealousy for the excision one of her scenes from the movie. (She has since reappraised the situation.) The two-week shoot was one of the high points of her career. It was also the movie in which she sang the song that has become her unofficial anthem, "The Girl Who Invented Rock and Roll." Even if she didn't invent it, she certainly nudged it along.

Albert Zugsmith

Because the mainstream studios had been so slow to react positively to the new teen subculture (they mostly saw it as a threat), a new breed of independent producers moved in to fill the gap and grab market share. Without the huge studio overheads and the long lead-in times for a major film, they could exploit the new fads quickly, cheaply and, more importantly, effectively. But, as film historian Jack Stevenson points out, "the scenarios of their films would remain remarkably unchanged: naïve (and in the case of gals, good looking & well endowed) school kids playing with the matches of sex, drugs and now hotrods, and getting — you guessed it — burned, but not until audiences saw how much fun it was to sin. The concept of compensating moral values, firmly ingrained in the American mentality at large, still applied."[*]

Albert Zugsmith, who had produced Mamie's earlier *Star in the Dust*, was now freelancing after his separation from Universal and was one of the independent producers who spotted a cultural opening and moved in to fill it with a series of exploitation pictures. His aim was simple: "The box office success of a picture in today's market is in direct ratio to the talk it arouses. It is not enough for the picture to just entertain; the audiences must derive from it a reaction that will cause talk for weeks after."[†]

Zugsmith had begun as a newspaperman and his projects as producer and director reflect

---

[*]*Jack Stevenson*, Addicted: The Myth and Menace of Drugs in Film, *40–41.*
[†]"*From* Rock Around the Clock *to* The Trip: The Truth About Teen Movies." Rolling Stone.

Lori Nelson and Mamie on the set of *Untamed Youth* (Warner Bros., 1957). Although here they appear in bathing suits in the movie the two women are arrested for skinny dipping.

this in their immediacy: the choice of topical subjects (i.e., exploitation) and the punchy, pared-back style in which they were shot. After he sold his media interests in the East he headed to California and persuaded RKO to allow him to shoot three low-budget films at $100,000 each. He formed American Pictures Corporation and applied the same efficiency methods he had at his newspapers, radio and television stations. Cashing in on the Cold War concern over atomic bombs, his project *3000 A.D.* was renamed *Captive Women* (1952) by RKO. He followed up with the even more paranoid, and wildly successful, *Invasion USA* (1952) about a communist invasion of the U.S. and the nuking of Manhattan. He credits Ralph Black, the film's production manager, and Al Green, the director, with teaching him the motion picture trade on that film. Green even allowed him to co-direct the film. He added to the burgeoning field of giant sea creatures movies with *Port Sinister* (1953), which was notable for its cast of giant crabs; he also helmed a film version of the Phil Silvers stage success *Top Banana* (1954). After a dream run of six films, the other members of American Pictures wanted to dissolve their partnership to cash in on a tax break.

He had joined Universal under the stewardship of Ed Muhl, vice-president in charge of production, and while there had been responsible for *Written on the Wind* (1956) and *The Incredible Shrinking Man* (1957) and gave Orson Welles a stab at directing again with *Touch of Evil* (1958). But when Universal put Alfred Daff in charge of the studio's output, Zugsmith knew there would be more interference. Although he was offered a seven-year producer's contract he was, by this time, itching to take on director's chores. But Zugsmith's credo, and one of the main reasons for his success, was his skill as a wordsmith and a script doctor. "The writing is the main thing, and no matter how adept you are in the production end, the physical production, or anything else, first came the word, you know," he told Todd McCarthy and Charles Flynn.*

In his perceptive article "Albert Zugsmith's Opium Dreams" in *Bright Lights*, C. Jerry Kutner sums up Hollywood's reigning view (then and now) of the producer-director: "Hollywood preferred to view Zugsmith as an exploitation filmmaker, one who was all too willing to capitalize on unwholesome subject matter — miscegenation, drug abuse, disturbed sexuality — in a word, the FORBIDDEN. In those days the arbiters of taste rarely considered that sleaze could coexist on the same plane as visual fluency and high artistic expression. Indeed, what can one say about a producer who voluntarily made no less than seven films with Mamie Van Doren? Only, as Dietrich says at the end of *Touch of Evil*, that he was 'some kind of man.'"

Between 1958 and 1960 Mamie would be the mainstay of Albert Zugsmith's repertory company which included Jackie Coogan, Ray Anthony, Norman "Woo Woo" Grabowski, Charles Chaplin Jr., Ziva Rodann, Cathy Crosby, Mickey Rooney, Vampira, and Mel Tormé. Only Mamie would appear in seven. They ran the gamut of contemporary issues such as drug running in high schools in *High School Confidential!* (1958), union corruption and stand over tactics in *The Big Operator* (1959), beatniks and serial rape in *The Beat Generation* (1959), juvenile gangs, drag racing and female delinquency in *Girls Town* (1959), and teen sexuality in *College Confidential* (1960). Then there were the juvenile sex farces *Sex Kittens Go to College* (1960) and *The Private Lives of Adam and Eve* (1960). It was fun while it lasted.

Mamie's film work with Zugsmith led to the press announcement in September, 1960, that Mamie was to star in a Broadway musical, *Sin, Sin, Sin*, to be produced by Zugsmith in 1961. The projected plotline "tells about a congressional committee which investigates a confession-type magazine and is in turn investigated itself." The project never eventuated but has a few similarities to a later "lost" Mamie movie, *The Candidate* (1964).

Mamie also worked for other independent producers which she admits "marked a period

---

*Todd McCarthy and Charles Flynn, eds., Kings of the Bs, 414–15.

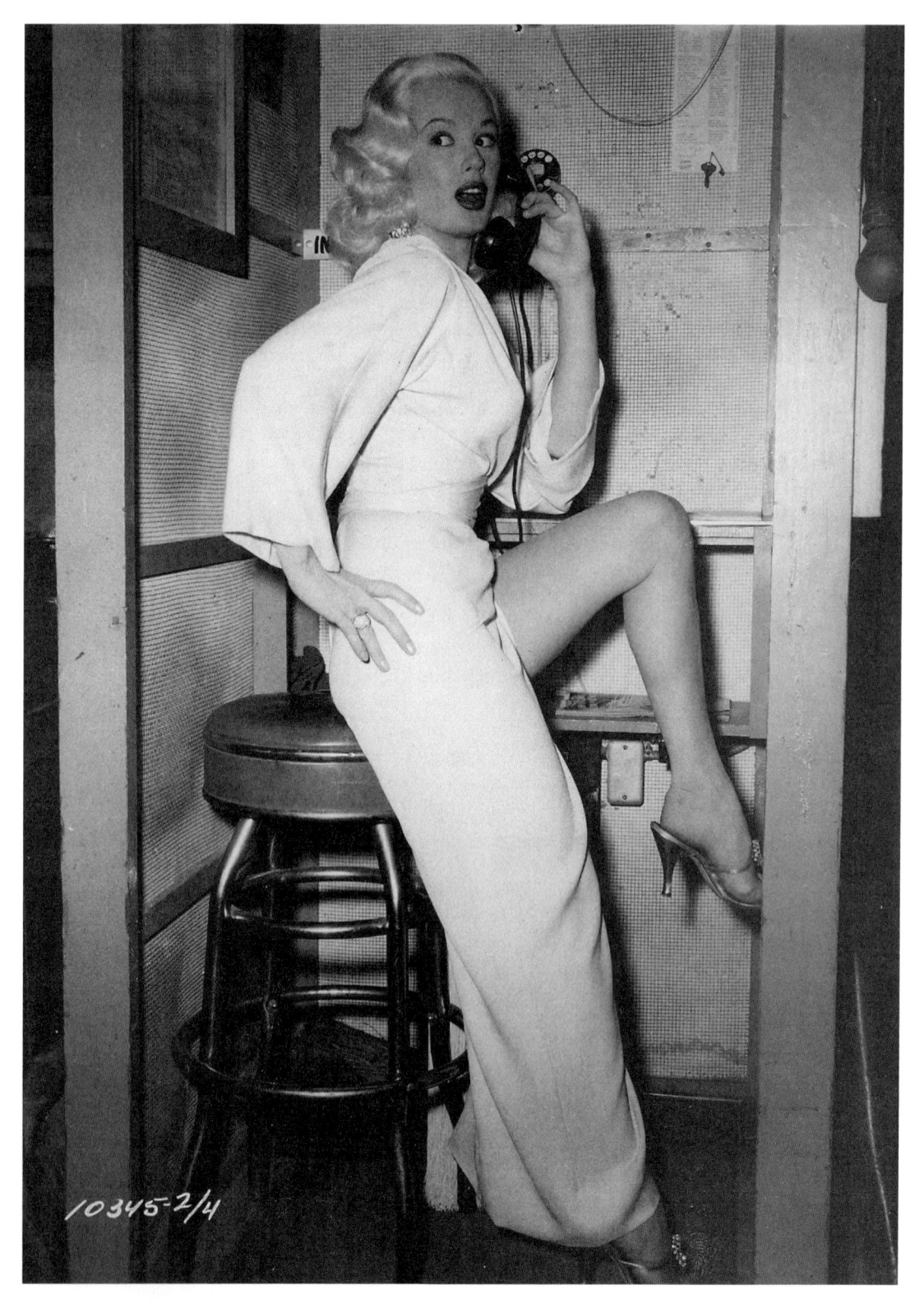

Mamie shows a bit of leg in a publicity shot for *Teacher's Pet* (Paramount, 1958).

when I began making movies strictly for the money."* She realized her marriage was on the rocks and she needed to squirrel away savings in the event of a break-up.

Edward Small offered Mamie a deal for two low-budget black and white crime thrillers to be released through United Artists. The first was a taut film noir, *Guns, Girls and Gangsters* (1959), about an armored car hold-up; Mamie played the not-quite-rotten wife of jailbird Lee Van Cleef. Edward L. Cahn did the directorial chores as he did for the second film, *Vice Raid* (1960). The pictures were shot in less than four months and Mamie walked away with close to one hundred thousand dollars, good money in those days. And her opinion of the films' quality has mellowed over the years.

In 1958, Mamie was called up for a television pilot. "I was offered a role in a proposed TV series, titled *The Body, the Face and the Brain*. For a fleeting instant, I thought how wonderful it would be to play a triple role. But I don't have to tell you which part they figured fitted me. It called for a Jayne Mansfield type."†

Tension in the marriage escalated after *The Ray Anthony Show* was cancelled in 1957. During yet another argument, Mamie was so provoked, she hit Ray with a red patent-leather Pappagallo pump, the spiked-heel connecting with the top of his head. Ray's subsequent ultimatum that Mamie forego her next movie in Italy and cut back spending on clothes meant the marriage

Mamie singing in the shower in the scene cut from **Girls Town** (MGM, 1959) when the Catholic Church objected.

*Liberty, May, 1958, 34.
†Telephone interview with the author, May 23, 2006.

was over. Mamie headed to Italy, her first trip to Europe, for an all-expenses-paid eight weeks away from Ray and a salary of over sixty thousand dollars.

Mamie told the press: "We regret very much that we haven't been able to make a go of it because of our son, Perry, too, whom we both adore. It has been difficult for us because our careers have kept us separated so much of the time."* Mamie hinted at a reunion but said if it did not occur there would be an amicable divorce. The fact that Mamie referred to Ray as "Mr. Anthony" whenever she mentioned him meant there was little surprise when she filed for divorce on September 9, 1958.

Meanwhile, Nino Crissman, actor-turned-director of *Le Bellissime gambe di Sabrina* [*The Beautiful Legs of Sabrina*] (1959), was none too pleased with the news of the impending divorce of his leading lady; he feared a backlash in Catholic Italy. But the Italians mobbed her and an affair with co-star Antonio Cifariello helped her forget her separation from Ray. A sidelight of her European sojourn was a trip to a film festival in Taormina, Sicily to pick up an acting award for Marilyn Monroe for her performance opposite Laurence Olivier in *The Prince and the Showgirl* (1957). Marilyn had been unable to attend.

Back in the U.S., Mamie filed for legal separation from Ray, asking that he take care of Perry's college education. The divorce would not become final until 1960. Judge Edward Brand awarded her a dollar a month as token alimony and three hundred dollars a months for the support of Perry. Ray also agreed to maintain a $25,000 insurance policy for his son. "Any actress with a career such as mine in mind is better off without a husband. A woman simply can't make a complete success of both job and husband! One has to come first — with me it's got to be career."†

She traveled to South America for *Una Americana en Buenos Aires* [*The Blonde from Buenos Aires*] (1961), lured in part by the financial incentive of owning all English-speaking rights.

As well as finally cutting the ties with Ray, Mamie cut ties with her old agents and signed up with Lutz and Loeb, run by Bill Loeb, who suggested that as movie offers were drying up she consider a nightclub act. Jack Brooks‡ was hired to write comedy material and customize lyrics to a popular song to suit Mamie's image, Jack Baker put her male dancers through their choreographic paces and the musical arrangements were by Johnny Mandel.** As a spot to try the act out, the Chi-Chi Club in Palm Springs was chosen and booked. With Mandel conducting the band, Mamie played five nights and on the strength of the positive reviews she landed a gig at the Latin Quarter in New York. But to further refine the show, Bill Loeb first booked it into the Lotus Club, an intimate supper club in Washington, D.C.

The four-week New York season was also a success and led to bookings across the country as well as in Mexico and Argentina. She also took her cabaret act to Australia, opening at Sydney Chevron Silver Spade, the city's premier night spot, on January 28, 1963. The critic for *The Sun* wrote that Mamie "is a talented entertainer with an original and well-presented act." The anonymous critic went on: "Every bit as pretty as her picture, she is not the statuesque, brassy blonde many of those pictures suggest. Beneath that piled up hairdo is a small, dainty person with a quiet but engaging personality. In a variety of numbers she exploits with the utmost skill the flexibility of a pleasant but otherwise limited voice." The highlight of the act was said to be Mamie's rendition of "A Good Man Is Hard to Find," a novelty number in which

---

Uncredited newspaper article reproduced in Mamie Van Doren Fan Club Journal, *Volume 6, Number 1.*
†*Sun-Herald (Sydney), October 23, 1961.*
‡*Liverpool, England-born Jack Brooks (1912–71) migrated to the U.S. in 1916 and wrote songs for Bing Crosby, Phil Harris and Fred Allen. A prolific lyricist and sometime composer, he is perhaps best known for "Ole Buttermilk Sky" (with Hoagy Carmichael) plus "That's Amore" and "Inamorata" (Harry Warren). Brooks worked with composers David Raksin, Leigh Harline, Norman Berens, Edgar Fairchild, Walter Scharf, Saul Chaplin and Frank Skinner.*
**Johnny Mandel (1925–) is a film composer best remembered for "Suicide Is Painless" from the 1970 film M.A.S.H (and later used as the theme for the television series of the same name) and "The Shadow of Your Smile" (Paul Francis Webster).*

Lobby card for *The Beat Generation* (MGM, 1959).

she introduced several men she admired, all impersonated by her male dance partner (Alexander Plaatschaert) wearing face masks.*

Just before her trip to Australia, Mamie was reported to have pulled out of a planned co-starring role with Jayne Mansfield in *Promises! Promises!* because she discovered that Jayne would receive two-and-a-half percent more of the film's profits. Her part was taken by Marie McDonald.†

Cheering news was the all-expenses-paid offer of the Lucille Ball role in a dinner theater version of the Broadway musical *Wildcat*‡ at the Meadowbrook Theater in New Jersey. Mamie was accommodated at the Salisbury Hotel in New York and a limo drove her to and from the engagement for which she was receiving five thousand dollars a week. "Oh God, it was such a

---

*The Sun *(Sydney), January 29, 1963.*
†*Marie McDonald (1923–1965, real name: Cora Marie Frye) was the daughter of a former Ziegfeld girl. She became a model at age 15 and went on to win minor titles in beauty competitions such as Miss Yonkers and the Queen of Coney Island before being crowned Miss New York in 1939. That same year she appeared on Broadway in* George White's Scandals of 1939 *and sang with Tommy Dorsey and His Orchestra on Dorsey's radio show. Her beauty and physical attractions gained her the tag "The Body" when she tackled Hollywood but her career stalled and she spent time touring in bus-and-truck productions of Broadway successes. She was involved in a number of scandals throughout her life and died of a self-administered overdose in 1965.*
‡*Wildcat, a vehicle for the then-popular television star Lucille Ball, opened at the Alvin Theater on Broadway on December 16, 1960 and closed June 3, 1961 after 171 performances and two previews. Music was by Cy Coleman, lyrics by Carolyn Leigh and book by N. Richard Nash. Directed and choreographed by Michael Kidd, it also starred Keith Andes, Swen Swenson, and Paula Stewart, with a young Valerie Harper in the dancing chorus.*

Going nowhere fast: publicity shot of Mamie about to paddle her canoe in 1960. Note the chess set on board and the rope that is tying the canoe to the pier.

hard show. My character was a tomboy, and she beat the drum and sang. It was hard but at least it was over in two hours and I could go home and sleep and gas-up for the next performance. I didn't have to worry about dancers, temperamental conductors and hair and all. I got my check at the end of the week and deposited it, and that was it."*

MAMIE, MARILYN AND MANSFIELD

It was during Mamie's run in *Wildcat* that Marilyn Monroe died of a drug overdose in California. It was a wake-up call and a time for reflection for Mamie whose career was closely aligned to both Marilyn and Jayne Mansfield. "The similarities between us were frightening. I tried to keep in mind that what had happened to Marilyn need not happen to me. Nonetheless, with Marilyn's death, the entire world recognized that an era was over. The days of the sex goddesses and blonde bombshells had officially been laid to rest."†

After Marilyn's death, Mamie received overtures from the John F. Kennedy camp to become her sexual replacement but she wasn't tempted. She thought the approach was distasteful and remembered what Truman Capote had said about the Kennedys: that he'd seen an awful lot of cocks in his time and that if you put all the Kennedys together it wouldn't make one good one.

Back in Los Angeles after the run of *Wildcat*, Mamie was invited to meet famed baseball star, Bo Belinsky.‡ The attraction was instant and their escapades began appearing in newspapers across the world. It was short-lived, however, as Bo headed off to play winter baseball in South America, and Mamie began dating dog-food millionaire Clement Hirsch.

"I never tried to hide the fact that I was interested in somebody sexually. I didn't sleep with everybody I ever met. I dated a lot of guys who I didn't go to bed with. But when I wanted to do something with somebody, I just went ahead and did it. I was very much my own woman when it came to sexual matters, and I know it ended up hurting my career because there were no women in control in those days, and I didn't seem to be fucking the right men. Behind the scenes my reputation was bouncing back and hurting me. I knew early on I would never get the Legion of Decency from the Catholic Church.... I liked sportsmen. I liked athletes and guys who kept in shape. I loved boxers and baseball players, guys who could really move, but there were a lot of Hollywood people who fit that description."**

Mamie resurrected her cabaret act to keep busy but downsized the operation in order to turn a more handsome profit. Don Morand gave her a new hairstyle for her return engagement at the Chi-Chi Club where she opened in February, 1963, just after her 30th birthday. Bo Belinsky was in the opening night audience which also included Frank Sinatra and his cronies. The relationship with Bo was reignited, the romance often conducted via long distance phone as Mamie continued to tour her nightclub act and Bo was under curfew because it was baseball season.

In November, 1963, she was a special guest at a convention of strippers at the Bel-Air Hotel in Los Angeles to announce the formation of the Exotique Dancers' League and to announce the League's first awards for the 10 Best Undressed Women in America.†† Mamie reportedly

---

*Femme Fatales, *February, 1997, 22.*
†*Van Doren*, Playing the Field, *175.*
‡*Famed left-handed pitcher Robert "Bo" Belinsky (1936–2001) threw the first no-hitter for the Los Angeles Angels. Famed as much for his life off the mound as on, he was linked romantically with a bevy of female stars such as Connie Stevens, Ann-Margret and Tina Louise. As his life became more dissipated and his career plummeted, he fought and overcame alcoholism and found solace in Christianity. He died of a heart attack after years of battling bladder cancer.*
**Femme Fatales, *September-October, 2001, 25.*
††*They were (in order) Lili St. Cyr, Jennie Lee, Rita Atlanta, Tempest Storm, Sally Rand, Ann Corio, Tinker Bell, Naja Karamaru, Virginia Bell and Tura Satana.*

Lobby card for one of Mamie's great films, *Guns, Girls and Gangsters* (Imperial Pictures, 1959).

threw herself enthusiastically into an exotic dance and was unanimously elected an honorary member of the League.

Following an appearance on *The Tonight Show with Johnny Carson* came more nightclub work, which meant a heart-wrenching separation from Perry. Then Tommy Noonan offered her a role in his sex farce *3 Nuts in Search of a Bolt* (1964), in which he would co-star as himself. It would be her first movie in three years and had the added advantage that it was to be filmed in Los Angeles so she could spend time at home with Perry. And she would receive a percentage of the picture. Noonan also persuaded Mamie to pose naked for *Playboy*. In keeping with Jayne Mansfield's "reveal all" appearance in the earlier Noonan sexcapade *Promises! Promises!** (1963), a nude beer bath scene was added to *3 Nuts* to lure cinema patrons. As Mamie was on a percentage, she agreed and the box office boomed.

Mamie's nude bath spread was featured over six pages in the June, 1964 *Playboy*. "I thought, 'Well, here is my body and I don't know what it's going to look like ten years, thirty years from now if I'm still around. I'm going to take pictures and be able to look at them when I get older and see how I stack up to the ones then.' As a matter of fact, I have nude pictures on my staircase that I had taken in the '60s and I look at them and say, 'Hmmm. Not bad.' I can stack up

---

**Promises! Promises!* is credited as the first movie in which a mainstream actress fully bared her breasts. Jayne Mansfield's two nude scenes appear fairly early in the film, which concerns two married couples on a cruise together during which, in a night of drunken lovemaking, the two women become pregnant but remain confused as to which man is the father.

to them very easily."* Mamie had already appeared in *Playboy* in February, 1964, in a series of less-revealing photos taken before and during her nightclub act, four poses shot exclusively for the magazine.

In early 1964 Bill Loeb secured a role for Mamie in a German-Yugoslav co-production, *Freddy und das Lied der Prärie* [*The Wild, Wild West*†], starring popular singer Freddy Quinn, then being touted as the German-speaking answer to Elvis Presley. It would be her first trip back to Europe since *The Beautiful Legs of Sabrina* in 1959. Filming took place in Berlin and Dubrovnik in Yugoslavia (now Croatia). After completion, Mamie and Don Morand, whom she had brought along as secretary-hairstylist, headed for Paris to recover from the grueling shoot and to find a dress for Mamie to feature in her advertising gig for the men's aftershave, Aqua Velva.

She found a dress she wanted at a fashion show at Coco Chanel's salon but because she needed it in a matter of weeks, the salon said they could not oblige until Coco, herself intervened; Mamie was sold the dress the model had worn. It was upstairs from the salon, in Coco Chanel's inner sanctum, that Chanel attempted to seduce Mamie. "I never explored the other side. I had plenty of opportunities. I could have done it with Coco Chanel or Marlene Dietrich. I would now like a shot but back then I was so young. Now I know it isn't wrong."‡

Mamie purred her way through "There's something about an Aqua Velva man" on screen and in print for about a year, which helped replenish the coffers. She then became a party animal and was squired around town by singer Johnny Rivers, whose career had taken off as a result of his gigs at Whisky A Go Go** and who had recently had a hit record with Chuck Berry's "Maybelline." On one auspicious occasion at the discothèque, Mamie and Johnny found themselves at a booth with Jayne Mansfield and Beatles, John Lennon and George Harrison; when a photographer snapped a picture, George retaliated by throwing a drink at the intruder. It hit Mamie in the face instead.

It was also at the famed discothèque that she met Steve McQueen and, after initial resistance because he was married, Mamie succumbed. She also had her first acid with him at a party at the home of famed hairdresser Jay Sebring (a Tudor mansion which had once belonged to Jean Harlow and Paul Bern). The relationship was purely physical but eventually fizzled out because of McQueen's repeated use of drugs, acid and amyl nitrite, and because he never intended divorcing his wife. Mamie consoled herself with a four-week appearance at the Thunderbird Hotel in Las Vegas in October, 1964, and a return engagement at the Latin Quarter in New York.

Bo Belinsky was proving to be a marathon man not only in bed but also in his staying power as a prospective partner. When Bo proposed marriage, on April Fool's Day, 1965, Mamie accepted without hesitation. According to Bo, Mamie released the details to the press and kept pressuring him to name a day and buy a ring to make it official. "So, right away, I feel the pressures of being engaged. I went to my attorney and I says, 'My heavens, I'm engaged to be married.' I don't

---

*Femme Fatales, *February 1997, 20.*
†*Released on video and DVD under the erroneous title,* The Sheriff Was a Lady.
‡*Phone interview with the author, May 23, 2006.*
**Whisky A Go Go, *famed nightclub at 8901 Sunset Boulevard in West Hollywood, opened January 11, 1964, as a discothèque although they had live music as well as a DJ playing records in a suspended cage, which led to the creation of the Go-Go dancer. It was at the forefront of a number of musical trends and also promoted the careers of then lesser known bands. It was also the center of police harassment in the mid–1960s not least because wowsers objected to the word "whisky" in its name. Johnny Rivers (1942, real name: John Ramistella), singer-songwriter, formed his first band, The Spades, while still in high school and later, via Alan Freed, got a number of recording contracts through the late 1950s. But his career did not take off until Ricky Nelson recorded one of his songs and he made a living as a songwriter and musician. In 1963 he took over as a fill-in act at Gazzari's nightclub after the night spot's jazz trio walked out. Word of mouth drew huge crowds to the venue and the next year Johnny was offered a one-year contract to sing at Whisky A Go Go.*

Press advertisement for *3 Nuts in Search of a Bolt* (Harlequin, 1964).

want to get out of it yet, yet I do. I'm confused. So the attorney says, 'It was April Fool's Day when you got engaged. You can make a statement to the press that it was just a big joke.' But I says, 'What about the goddam girl? It would make her look sick.' So there we are, engaged.

"Everybody was ripping me about the engagement. They're telling me, 'You're gonna distract yourself. She's no good for the game, Bo.' But every time I would introduce Mamie to them, their goddam tongues would hang out, from [Angels boss] Gene Autry on down. Everybody wanted to take a nip at her."*

When the engagement was announced, Bo was told by the Angels front office that his relationship was ruining his career, an opinion reinforced in print by some sports journalists. His heavy drinking combined with his heavy smoking made Mamie ill and the long phone calls ate into her sleeping time when she was touring in a summer stock production of *Silk Stockings*, the Cole Porter musical version of *Ninotchka*, with Earl Wrightson and Lee Grant,† directed by Arthur Storch. Mamie was Janice Dayton, the role played on Broadway by Gretchen Wyler and on screen by Janis Paige, and got to sing "Stereophonic Sound," "Satin and Silk" and "Josephine." While the production was playing Springfield, Massachusetts, Bo broke off the engagement, accusing Mamie of being unfaithful with her driver. But when Mamie confronted him later in Los Angeles, he admitted the Angels had given him the choice: break off

Although Mamie was continually going to Europe to appear in foreign-language films, it's doubtful these are her traveling clothes.

---

*Myron Cope, "A Dialogue Between Baseball's Bigmouths: Bo Belinsky, Dick Stuart," August, 1965.

†Lee Grant started out on Broadway, winning acclaim in Detective Story (1951), and went to Hollywood to reprise her role in the film version (1951) for which she received an Academy Award nomination. She fell afoul of McCarthy's House Un-American Activities Committee when she refused to testify against her husband, writer Arnold Manoff, and film work dried up until the 1960s. She went on to win an acting Oscar for her performance in Shampoo (1975). In later years she added directing to her list of accomplishments, winning an Oscar for Down and Out in America (1986).

the relationship with Mamie or be relegated to their minor-league team in Hawaii. The engagement was rekindled and Bo headed to Hawaii but Mamie called a halt to it a short time later when she discovered *he* had been cheating on *her*.

The following year brought what many consider two of her worst movies: The "vegetarian horror" *The Navy vs. the Night Monsters* and the first and last teaming of the two remaining blonde bombshells in *Las Vegas Hillbillys*. There *was* a disagreement over *Las Vegas Hillbillys* billing but none of the overt hostilities the press played up at the time. Mamie and Mansfield were cool to each other, brought on perhaps by the realization that they were the last of the blonde bombshell dinosaurs.

The work offers were drying up but Loeb managed to secure her a nightclub tour of Central and South America which lasted several months. She played Mexico City, Buenos Aires, Rio de Janeiro and Managua, among others. On her return to the U.S. she began dating football star Joe Namath.*

Perry, her son, was proving a problem at a private school so enrollment at Harding Military Academy was fortuitous (he knuckled down under the discipline and loved playing trumpet in the marching band). Another problem was her home. She moved out after finding it ransacked on her return from her nightclub tour of South America and one night when she watched fearfully as a man with a drawn gun on her patio tried to break in. She moved into the Shoreham Towers Hotel. Adding to her woes, she found she was pregnant although her relationship with Joe Namath had run its course.

Her choices were to raise the child as an unmarried mother, have an abortion, or marry quickly. The answer came in the form of 19-year-old Lee Meyers, whom she married secretly on May 6, 1966, in Boise, Idaho, one of the few U.S. states in which a man under 21 could marry without parental consent. Lee was heir to a $2 million inheritance that he would receive on his 21st birthday. He and Mamie spent their two-day honeymoon in Oregon after which Lee, a ball player, left to join his team, the

Mamie as the sultry seductress.

---

*Joe Namath (1943–) was a quarterback who played for the AFL's New York Jets and Los Angeles Rams in the 1960s and 1970s. Rookie of the Year in 1965, he went on to become an All-Star in 1965, 1967, 1968 and 1969. He retired with a record of 77 wins, 108 losses, and 3 ties. In his career he threw 173 touchdowns and 220 interceptions. Because of his love of New York nightlife, he was dubbed "Broadway Joe" by the press. He later went on to an unspectacular acting career in movies and on television.

Dallas–Fort Worth Spurs, on the road, and Mamie headed for New Jersey to star in *Gentlemen Prefer Blondes* at the Meadowbrook Theater. They kept their marriage a secret until June 22 when it made international news. Concerning the age difference, Mamie quipped: "Lee is mature enough to marry — he even shaves."*

But, realizing the marriage was a mistake, Mamie had an abortion, told Lee the reason was she didn't want to begin a marriage pregnant. Once news of their marriage got out, Lee was traded to the Chicago Cubs who capitalized on the exposure. Lee seemed to lose his enthusiasm for the game once married and was transferred four times in two years. He was more than happy to spend Mamie's money although he would soon inherit $2 million from his grandfather's estate. But he did convince her to move from Los Angeles to the more salubrious surroundings of Newport Beach, 50 miles south of the city. Another advantage was that Perry could move into the apartment and attend a local school.

While Mamie was repeating her performance in *Gentlemen Prefer Blondes* in the summer of 1967 at the Wedgwood Dinner Theater in Glen Cove, Long Island, she heard of Jayne Mansfield's tragic death in a car accident. It brought home her mortality like nothing else. She was the one remaining of the blonde bombshell triumvirate. The jobs were drying up and all she was being offered was a non-speaking role in added scenes in the dubbed English-Soviet science fiction film unleashed on a disinterested American public as *Voyage to the Planet of Prehistoric Women* (1967).

"I began to be jealous of Jayne and Marilyn in an odd way. Interviewers invariably asked me about them, it was as if *they* had won the beauty contest and *I* was the runner-up. They were dead and therefore frozen in time — the stuff of legends. I was a face still alive, trying to earn a living, making mistakes in front of everyone. Hollywood never appreciated my talent. I was just another blonde lucky to have a good body. They never looked past that. They never allowed me to be my own woman. So you know what? I said, 'Fuck you, Hollywood.' I just didn't care anymore."†

The marriage to Lee was on the rocks, however, and after she discovered his involvement with hashish, she filed for divorce.‡ "We had two wonderful years together, but he has been acting differently lately. We had a bad scene and he packed up and went home to his mother. I don't know why I cannot get a good solid man who will appreciate me."**

Mamie never told Lee the baby wasn't his. How does she feel about it today? "Are you expecting me to say remorse? Well, I won't. I did what I had to do. I couldn't have had the baby, it would have looked like a tiny Joe Namath."††

Mamie was forced to sue Tommy Noonan for her share of the profits of *3 Nuts in Search of a Bolt* but in August, 1968, Superior Court Judge Ben Koenig ruled that five percent of gross receipts after the producers received $150,000 amounted to zero. (Noonan and co-producer Ian McGlashan were able to convince the court they had received less than $130,000.)

VIETNAM

There was only one place to go to gain an appreciation for life: Vietnam, to entertain the troops. The effect of the tour on Mamie was total and even today when she recounts her expe-

---

*Sunday Telegraph *(Sydney), June 26, 1966.*
†*salon.com, July 19, 2000.*
‡*Lee Meyers was later arrested in Hawaii for attempting to smuggle hashish into the country but tried on a lesser charge and given probation. He died in a car crash at the age of 25.*
**Daily Mirror *(Sydney), September 10, 1968.*
††*Phone interview with the author, September 15, 2006.*

riences she chokes up with emotion and fights back tears. Because the fighting was at its fiercest when she arrived in the war zone in 1968, her shows were cancelled in that country but she did tour the Philippines where the enlisted men and officers went for the R&R. More importantly, it was where the injured were taken to military hospitals at the Clark and Subic Bay bases. Here, Mamie came face to face with the horrors of the Vietnam conflict, particularly in the burn units. Her visit to the hospital was like a "journey down through hell."*

During her Asian sojourn, Mamie played nightclubs and service clubs in Japan, Hong Kong, Taiwan and Thailand. On her return to the U.S. and realizing son Perry would be of draft age in a short six years, she prayed that the war be over soon. In 1971 she returned to the area for another series of concerts which began at the safer Rama Hilton Hotel in Bangkok. She later performed for troops at the Ubon Air base near the border with Laos.

Once in Vietnam, Mamie entertained troops in the field at small fire stations and outposts. "While most of the places I was to work were considered pacified, there were many that could never be fully declared safe. Often I made do with a truck bed or the back of a tank for a stage. My little five-piece Filipino band would be wailing away while I sang through the mike of our hastily connected sound system."† Later, of the time she spent entertaining in the south of Vietnam, Mamie wrote, "If it was a budding death wish that led me to Vietnam, the wish came to full flower at the fire stations down near the Mekong Delta."‡

She kept a diary, for the first time in her life, of the three months she spent there. Of May, 1971, she wrote:

> It is already dark as I put on my makeup in a makeshift dressing room. These Spartan quarters have been set up for me by a senior sergeant and a couple of grunts at this remote fire base. It is really a small trailer that feels like a sauna. It is humid and hot as only Vietnam's Mekong Delta can be, even though the sun has gone down an hour ago. As fast as I put on the makeup, it runs off my face in little brown rivulets of sweat.
>
> I hear helicopters in the distance, a sound as common in Vietnam as the honk of taxicab horns in Manhattan.
>
> My thoughts are back home. I have been here only a few weeks, but I am very, very homesick for my son,

Glamour shot of Mamie in her 1960s nightclub period.

*Van Doren, Playing the Field, 235.
†Ibid, 241.
‡Ibid, 243

Perry, and my mother and father. They did not want me to come here and risk my life. And they could not understand why I insisted. I had felt that I could come to Vietnam and end my life in a blaze of glory. Now I marveled at the stupidity of my suicide mission. What was I trying to prove?

Suddenly there is a deafening explosion. I am thrown from my chair. Makeup scatters across the room. Another explosion follows, not quite as close, drowning out my screams.

The sergeant dashes in the door and helps me up. "It's okay," he reassures me. "It's okay, really."

"Okay? What's going on? Is it an attack?"

The sergeant grins. "Hell, that's nothing compared to the real thing. This is just fireworks. Charlie's celebrating Ho Chi Minh's birthday."

"Couldn't they just send a card? I thought I was dead."*

During the latter stages of her tour, Mamie became so debilitated she had difficulty getting out of bed. Admitted to the Field A Hospital in Saigon (now Ho Chi Minh City), she was diagnosed with amoebic dysentery and told there could be damage to her liver. The hospital didn't have the equipment necessary to test her but they were reluctant to have her medically evacuated until she was well. Catch-22. Her health deteriorating, she threatened to contact President Richard Nixon, whose letter she carried thanking her for her support of the troops in Vietnam. It did the trick and a week later space was found on a Medevac flight to Hawaii. Her recovery continued apace and a scan cleared her of liver damage.

"Now I could put the war behind me. Except that like everyone else who came in contact with Vietnam, I could never leave it nor would it ever leave me. The memories were always waiting there, in the dark."†

Between her South East Asia tours, Mamie continued to perform on stage and in 1970 appeared in Toledo in the Frank Loesser Pulitzer Prize — winning musical *How to Succeed in Business Without Really Trying*. It was directed by Leslie B. Cutler with Bob Cummings as J.B. Biggley, the role played by Rudy Vallee on Broadway and in the film version. Mamie was (type)cast as the bubble-headed blonde Hedy, a role essayed on Broadway by Virginia Martin and in the film by Maureen Arthur. Among the other productions in which Mamie toured were *In One Bed — and Out the Other* (adapted by Ed Fielbert and Mawby Green from the French farce *Une Nuit Chez Vous*

Glamour shot of Mamie in the early 1960s.

*Vietnam Stories, mamievandoren.com
†Van Doren, Playing the Field, 248.

Madame by Jean de Letraz); *See How They Run* by Philip King; *Two and Two Make Sex* and *Scandalous Follies*.

After her second tour she opted for a complete change and headed to London to seek work, renting an apartment in Montague Square. But, in March, 1972, after a miserable six months of damp and despondency, she headed home and into the arms of Burt Reynolds. It lasted all of one night. It was over almost before it had begun and Burt made the mistake of calling out "Judy," the name of his former wife Judy Carne, at the moment of climax.

Back in California, Mamie became involved in politics with the campaign to help re-elect Nixon president. It was a natural as Mamie lived in a Republican hub, the conservative moneyed class of Newport Beach. She toured the country raising funds for Nixon's coffers and met with high-ranking administration officials including John Mitchell; her offer to strip at a fundraiser was firmly squelched. But she was invited to the White House for a dinner in honor of German Chancellor Willy Brandt and found herself seated next to Henry Kissinger, who later gave her a personal tour of the White House. His attempts to seduce Mamie were to no avail; his breath kept her at arm's length.

Her plunge into party politics also landed her another husband, Ross McClintock, executive vice-president of the Fluor Corporation. Mamie is forthright about her reasons for marrying him: "I did not love Ross. I looked at my marriage to him as one of convenience and companionship. He lived well and moved in a circle of important friends, [and] I thought that was what I wanted. My marriage to Ross was the only time I ever postponed having sex with my spouse-to-be until after we tied the knot. The experience lives in my memory as a terrific recommendation for premarital sex."*

They were married in Las Vegas in 1972; like her previous forays into wifehood, it was destined to fail. She was expected to conform to the rules of a corporate housewife which, given her background, was never going to work. It came to a head when McClintock became angry about a nude photo spread in a magazine Mamie had posed for before their engagement. His outburst and his demands about her future behavior ended the marriage. McClintock was granted an annulment.

Mamie and Thomas

In March, 1974, Mamie began a tour of *Will Success Spoil Rock Hunter?* in Florida with local actor Thomas Dixon playing the male lead. He was thirteen years Mamie's junior and married, but on the subsequent tour of the play they became lovers.

> The first time I was with Thomas that way [sexually] was in St. Petersburg, Florida. It was a very warm, balmy night and I was living in a place on the bay. I had a beautiful condominium that the theater had set me up in. It was a lovely place overlooking the water and it was decorated like a palace.
> After the show one night, he came over and we had a drink. Champagne, it was. I don't drink hard liquor. We relaxed. And it was a natural thing. I felt like I'd known him all my life. It wasn't ever hard to talk to him; it was never hard to do anything with him. So it was easy to make love.†

They lived together for five years at Newport Beach and, after Thomas's divorce was finalized, they married on June 26, 1979, to the disapproval of both sets of parents. As of this writing, they are still together. Mamie believes it's the things they have in common that bind them together: "We share a love of animals, of laughing, and of being together; a love of silences, and

---

*Van Doren, Playing the Field, *257*.
†Van Doren, The First Time, *37–38*.

of each other's privacy. We live at the beach, comforted by the sound of distant surf, warmed by a mutual respect, and fed on the promise of the next sunrise."*

They worked together over the years in theatre and nightclubs until Thomas gave up his acting career to concentrate on writing.

In 1980 Mamie toured in the national road company of *Whoopee!* with Imogene Coca and Ted Pritchard. It was not a happy experience for either side. Mamie was unhappy with unwanted sexual advances and the cast found her aloof and unfriendly. Mamie bailed out of the production at the Christmas break. To add to a bad year, she was nominated for a "Life Achievement Award: The Worst Actress of All Time" in Harry and Michael Medved's best-selling but far-from-subtle book, *The Golden Turkey Awards* (Perigee). She was in stellar company along with fellow nominees Candice Bergen, Vera Hruba Ralston and Raquel Welch. The book which brought notorious "bad" director, Edward D. Wood Jr. to world prominence, gave the "coveted" worst actress to Ms. Welch.

Strapless Mamie in one of the many glamour photographs for which she posed (and yet another in which her cleavage has been subtly altered by airbrushing).

Mamie's screen career had essentially dried up but she made television appearances on *Vega$* (1978) and *Fantasy Island* (1979). She was settled into married life and semi-retirement in 1984 when her new public relations manager, Alan Eichler, persuaded her to participate in a tribute to her film career at the Nuart Theater on Santa Monica Boulevard. Three of her movies were screened with some of her old co-workers in attendance: Aubrey Schenck, Al Zugsmith and Howard W. Koch turned up to pay their respects to their former leading lady and the night was a huge success.

In February 1985 Mamie appeared at Palomino with her hour-long cabaret act consisting of three segments: a rock 'n' roll tribute, an homage to the 1940s and a disco segment, all conducted by pianist Andy Howe. In the rock segment she told stories about her brushes with rock gods Bill Haley, Eddie Cochran and Elvis Presley. In the disco segment she sang her record "State of Turmoil" which had made it onto the dance charts the previous year. *Variety* opined: "Turned out in hot pink mini-skirt and loose-fitting white blouse, Van Doren's sincerity overcomes a voice which, while not disagreeable, is less than power-packed. Her '40s medley of such vintage ballads as 'As Time Goes By,' 'Time after Time,' 'The More I See You' and 'I'll Be Seeing

*Van Doren, Playing the Field, *272.*

You' works perhaps best with her pipes, since she doesn't have to force matters to get across here."*

Then it was back to running an antiques business in Newport Beach and making a big screen foray from time to time just for the money. The movie roles were lackluster. *Free Ride* (1986), merely one of a burgeoning number of gross-out teen comedies, cashed in on the perceived Mamie Van Doren image.

As the 1980s progressed and AIDS' insidious death rattle was heard across the world, particularly targeting the U.S. entertainment industry, Mamie raised funds and became a pin-up of the gay community. She had been asked to appear at an AIDS benefit at the Roxy in the early '80s when little was known about the disease. Invitations were sent out to people in the entertainment industry but there were few acceptances. Ten female stars showed up, including Mamie, Jean Simmons, Terry Moore and Sheree North. "The gay men didn't come. They were scared."†
She did concerts at Probe and Studio One and other gay clubs. She was Queen of the 1986 Gay Pride Parade but was accused of doing it merely for publicity. This was a strange accusation considering the opprobrium connected with the disease, particularly in its early years. The following year she was Grand Marshall of Gay Pride in West Hollywood.

On August 5, 1986, Mamie was one of the speakers at the annual Westwood Village Memorial Park memorial service for Marilyn Monroe; the event was organized by the Los Angeles–based organization, Marilyn Remembered. Soprano Therese Lee sang Elton John's Marilyn tribute "Candle in the Wind," and Mamie paid tribute: "She paved the way for all of us. To define glamour, one only needs to say 'Marilyn.' She had that unique ability to look straight up out of her soul and project what was there into the lens of a camera…. Our purpose here today is to reach across that chasm of years and honor a quiet, talented, difficult, lovely, chatty, simple, complex, witty, superlative friend. Darling Marilyn, we miss you."‡

In 1987 she hosted a series of teenage movies released on Rhino Home Video. Among the titles were *Naked Youth* (1960), *The Violent Years* (1956), and *Carnival Rock* (1957). More controversial was the publication of her autobiography, *Playing the Field*, written with Art Aveilhe, in which she spoke frankly about her sexual escapades and dished dirt on some of her conquests and even some political figures. It garnered wide publicity and created a renewal of interest in Mamie, who was a regular on the party circuit, especially at Hugh Hefner's Playboy mansion for Halloween, birthdays, etc. Hefner's parties are still a mainstay of Mamie's social calendar.

Mamie's Memoirs

Playing the Field was not the first time she had penned her memoirs. In fact, this was her fourth volume of autobiography. In 1964 *My Naughty, Naughty Life!* as told to Richard Bernstein and Robert J. Rhodes was issued by Century Publishing. A year later she wrote solo *I Swing*, a 128-page paperback from Novel Books which contained 35 pages of black and white photos of Mamie including three from the notorious beer bath scene in *3 Nuts in Search of a Bolt*. A success, the first print run sold out in 10 days and Mamie followed up that same year "by popular demand" with *My Wild Love Experiences*, again from Novel Books of Chicago. It contained 30 pages of photos, many (including the beer bath pics) repeated from the earlier book. The books' sexual frankness was merely a foretaste of what Mamie would reveal in her 1987 memoir.

---

*Variety, February 13, 1985.
†Email to the author, August 23, 2005.
‡Hollywood Studio Magazine, May 1987, 41.

"In my autobiography, *Playing the Field*, I was one of the first women to discuss the penis size of men I knew. Because of that, the book caused quite a stir.... Talk show hosts, especially men, were intimidated by a woman who frankly evaluated men the way men had evaluated women over the years—by inches."* In the same magazine article, Mamie continued, "I said that seven and a half inches was my preferred minimum acceptable size, with eight as ideal. What, you may ask, is the basis for such a specific measurement? It is a complicated equation, to be sure—part astrology, part East Indian Kama Sutra, and part old-fashioned carpenter's tape measure. And experience. It's the scientific method: experimentation. Go figure. It's the right size."†

Her specified dimensions caused controversy—so much that Mamie was back in print the following issue attempting to placate some readers. "Small guys, please don't come crying to me. It's not the end of the world. You've probably compensated beautifully for your little shortcoming by developing a great sense of humor or becoming a smooth lambada dancer or a skillful bridge player. Or maybe you've trained your tongue to do things not even imagined by the guys with the maxi-salamis."‡

Mamie in fashionable and revealing costume in the 1970s, around the time she was performing in nightclubs.

In November she was in Chicago for a special edition of *The Oprah Winfrey Show* about blonde bombshells and for screenings of *Girls Town* and *Untamed Youth* by the Chicago Psychotronic Film Society. One of the corselets Mamie wore in the 1950s went on display, along with the bra Tony Curtis wore in *Some Like It Hot* (1959), Phyllis Diller's training bra and other celebrity bras, at an exhibition celebrating the 40th anniversary of Frederick's of Hollywood at their Hollywood franchise.

Mamie's higher public profile led to her special guest appearance at the Bumbershoot Film Festival at the Seattle Center Arena in September, 1988, for a 35mm screening of *Untamed Youth* and a Q&A session afterwards. A year later she was in Paris to promote the French edition of her autobiography, retitled *Hollywood Flash-Back* in a translation by Simone Huinh. She was met at the airport by a crowd of fans before being whisked away to her suite at Pierre Cardin's

---

*Glamour Girls: Then and Now, *Number 14, 68.*
†Ibid, *71.*
‡Glamour Girls: Then and Now, *Number 15, 76.*

Early glamour shot of Mamie showing her legs which weren't good enough for the Italians (they were body-doubled in 1959's *The Beautiful Legs of Sabrina*).

hotel, Residence Maxim in the Avenue Gabriel, near the Champs Elysee. At her disposal for the frantic round of photo shoots, interviews (including a one-hour interview on the top-rated *The Freddy Show*) and press parties was a 1951 Rolls-Royce complete with liveried chauffeur.

At the age of sixty, Mamie went under the knife for cosmetic facial surgery. She made the decision as a result of the promotional tour for her autobiography. She had been little seen and photographed since her marriage to Thomas. "I noticed that when I called myself a sex kitten, people looked embarrassed. That's when I realized you can't talk about yourself as a sex symbol when you no longer *are* one. People didn't see me that way any more. They saw an aging woman who was kidding herself."* The surgery was performed by top Beverly Hills plastic surgeon, Dr. George Brennan. "It was just a simple lift. I had a little pouch under my chin and droopy laugh lines around my mouth and he fixed them. He didn't touch my eyes or lips."

Mamie scoffed at the reports of breast enhancement surgery at the same time. "They're all me. I didn't have surgery on my breasts. Big breasts run in the family. My mother had them too."†

Also in 1991 Mamie headed to Belgium to appear at the Bertje Awards, the country's version of the Emmys. While she found Brussels a lovely old city, "The weather was so cold and the sun almost never shone. While walking around sight seeing and looking in shop windows, I noticed the people in the shops laughing and pointing. I finally caught on that they were laughing because I was wearing sunglasses in the dreary, overcast weather. Too Hollywood for Brussels." However, Mamie's appearance on the show was a huge success: "I sang an eight-minute medley of rock 'n' roll songs starting with 'The Girl Who Invented Rock and Roll' and ending with 'What'd I Say.' The audience was knocked out and the show won its time slot."‡

She hosted AIDS Walk Orange County and later was Guest of Honor at Europride '93 held in Berlin on June 26; at the latter she sang her new songs, "Edge of Hollywood" and "Marilyn," which had been recorded by a German company. As well, Kitchen Sink Press released a set of trading cards of Mamie; the first thousand cards were lip-printed and personally signed by Mamie. The specially signed cards, which featured photos from her films and more revealing cheesecake shots, were "sprayed for permanence."

That same year the Mamie vs. Mansfield feud was reignited, this time in print. Shake Books released *Jayne Mansfield vs. Mamie Van Doren — Battle of the Blondes: A Pictorial History* which, as the company blurb trumpeted, "In over 220 photos ... traces the films, recordings, TV appearances, books, scandals, products, tabloids and much more, of both Jayne and Mamie. The book is packed with rare photos, stills, candids, pin-ups, magazine covers, and reviews of Mansfield and Van Doren. This is the first time such a complete record of these two sexy powerhouses has been published in one volume." However, respectability and Hollywood inclusiveness were achieved on February 1, 1994 when Mamie got her star on the Hollywood Boulevard Walk of Fame at 7057 Hollywood Boulevard; it had been initially embedded in the wrong spot and had to be dug up and moved.

Pride was tinged with sadness when her beloved mom died on August 27 the following year.

THE NEW MILLENNIUM

In 1999 she joined the computer age by setting up her own website. "I thought it would be interesting to do something, and be able to get across *me* rather than someone else's version of

---

*Bob Michaels & Kathleen Tracy, Confidential (undated).
†Phone interview with the author, May 23, 2006.
‡Mamie Van Doren Fan Club Journal, Volume 6, Number 1, 3.

me. I've had journalists do interviews with me, and I've been on television, but I really have never been able to talk about things I wanted to talk about. So now I can get on the site and get something that represents the way I really am.... I want to consider myself the first authentic sex kitten in cyberspace."* From the website Mamie began a thriving business selling autographs and nipple prints.

She was fulfilling her destiny as a sex goddess. "We, the sex goddesses, became a sort of castrati in the movies—a class of performers locked into our roles by our physical attributes. Who could imagine seeing Mamie Van Doren playing a nun? Who would want to? No, glamour girls were born to be glamour girls. When they could no longer be glamour girls, many found life unbearable. How many succumbed to overdoses? How many sought solace in drinking? How many lived their lives in Hollywood's ever-crowded fast lane until they met the inevitable head-on collision with death? If you didn't die trying to fulfill someone else's idea of womanhood, you died when their idea no longer made sense in your life."[†]

On April 22, 2000, Mamie was a guest of honor at a screening of *Guns, Girls and Gangsters* at the American Cinematheque; she was introduced by the then mayor of Hollywood, Johnny Grant, who had been an usher at the Pantages Theater when Mamie started work there. She sat on stage for a Q&A session after the movie. Two years later, on October 11, 2002, she was inducted into the Las Vegas Casino Legends Hall of Fame.

The new millennium became a busy period for Mamie as there was an upsurge in interest in her career. She featured prominently on a giant banner outside the Hollywood in Vegas exhibition (dedicated to Hollywood stars who entertained in Las Vegas) at the Movie Museum on Hollywood Boulevard. It opened May 18, 2005 and ran through most of the year. On June 3, she attended the annual Palm Springs Film Noir Festival for another screening of *Guns, Girls and Gangsters* at the Camelot Theater followed by a Q&A. As an added treat, the day of the screening was declared Mamie Van Doren Day by Mayor Ron Oden. That same month, she was in West Hollywood for the Gay Pride Parade on June 12.

> I was so thrilled to accept an invitation to ride in the Gay Pride Parade this year. Alan Eichler, my publicist and long-time friend, arranged the details, right down to ordering up some fabulous cloudy weather! I rode in a gorgeously restored 1952 Chevy Belaire convertible owned by Lee Hoffman. Those pipes sounded sooooo sweet! And the back seat reminded me of all those steamy nights of my misspent youth. It was truly one great time. I had all my posse with me: Alan Eichler, Alan's partner Ralph, Alan Mercer, David Wills, Skip E. Lowe, Starlet [her dog] for protection, and [husband] Thomas (glued as always to his camera!).[‡]

Later in the year she attended the MAO Magazine Launch Party to kick off New York's Fashion Week on September 7, and attended the 50th anniversary Thalians Ball** at the Century Plaza Hotel in Los Angeles. But the most prestigious of all that year was her photo shoot, on November 21, for the special Hollywood issue of *Vanity Fair* that hit the stands in 2006. "Fashion maven Tom Ford conceived the idea for this shoot after seeing a picture of Pam Anderson and me, taken at Tom Ford's and Richard Buckley's Oscar party this year. This layout will celebrate the fusion between Hollywood glamour divas of two generations—looking like sisters. Photographer Ali Mahdavi and his crew were flown in from Paris, and *Vanity Fair* staffers ferried out from New York for this very special meeting of blonde bombshells."[††]

Designer Tom Ford, the former head of Gucci and Yves St. Laurent fashion houses, picked

---

*Femme Fatales, *August 20, 1999, 39, 43.*
[†]*Van Doren,* Click: Becoming Feminists, *11.*
[‡]*mamievandoren.com*
**Thalians *is a charitable organization set up by Ruta Lee and Debbie Reynolds in 1955 to help those with psychiatric problems mainly via the Thalians Mental Health Center.*
[††]*mamievandoren.com*

Biography 53

Mamie in a costume test for an unknown film early in her career.

Mamie for the *Vanity Fair* layout: "I actually don't think of Mamie as one of the last Hollywood blonde bombshells, as she is so completely current. She is so totally of our time — in fact, she may be more of our time than she was in the 1960s."*

And on December 3, Mamie received the accolade of a star on the Palm Springs Walk of Stars, the keynote address being given by Kaye Ballard.† In 2006, the 20th anniversary of the formation of Mamie's fan club, filmmaker Kevin Leadingham followed her around shooting a documentary, and Mamie hosted the January 14 opening of "Blonde Bombshells: An Examination of the Species" at the M Modern Gallery, Palm Canyon Drive, Palm Springs. She was one of the featured blondes along with Marilyn, Lana Turner, Jean Harlow, Veronica Lake, Pamela Anderson and others. David Wills, curator of the show, revealed he was obsessed with Mamie in his years growing up in Australia. "Mamie was a little more blonde, a little more buxom, a little more of a bombshell and she was a bad girl."‡

In March she addressed a peace rally in Orange County, condemning George W. Bush's

George Barton (Marty Milner) and Dr. West (Mamie) commiserate, perhaps over how they got in a stinker like this one (*Sex Kittens go to College*, Allied Artists, 1960).

*Peter Larsen, The Orange County Register, April 19, 2006, 10.
†Kaye Ballard (1926–) [RN: Catherine Gloria Balotta] has appeared on Broadway, most notably in Carnival and The Golden Apple, and on television's The Mothers-in-Law. She has not had the big screen career she deserves but was effective in the film version of Terrence McNally's The Ritz (1976).
‡Desert Magazine, January, 2006, 56.

warmongering. On May 19, she was one of the guests, along with Angie Dickinson, Jeanne Brown, Fred Travolina, Jamie Farr, Tippi Hedren, Buzz Aldrin, Terry Moore, Hal Kanter, and Gary Owens, who paid tribute to Johnny Grant, honored with the Broadcasting Pioneer Award at the Sportsman's Lodge in Studio City. One month later, on June 17, she was a celebrity guest at the Friar's Club* Lifetime Achievement banquet honoring George Barris, "King of the Kustomizers":

> I first met George on the set of *Running Wild* when I got to drive one of his cars because I was the only one on the set at the time who could drive a stick shift. I was making a slew of teenage movies at the time and the girls were all crazy for the boys who drove hot rods. George provided picture cars for the films. George and his brother Sam almost single-handedly created the custom car hot rod culture in Southern California after the Second World War. It spread through the rest of the country, but no one could create a custom car like George. In fact, George is the man who made stars of cars: the Batmobile, the Munsterkoach, ZZ Top's roadster, and many more."[†]

And what of Mamie as she heads toward her 80s?

> Memory gratifies. Time is a grand vintner, bottling up memories in your cerebral cellars to be mellowed with time, later decanted to the next generation. I have been blessed with a rich life during which I have met presidents, kings, racing drivers, jocks, and just about every other imaginable sort of celebrity. I am often asked to recall those encounters— and in the spirit of expanding the bounds of good taste, I often do. Who would have dreamed that the Eisenhower years or even the swingin' '60s would become so interesting to a generation that never lived through them? And who would have dreamed that I would get so much pleasure out of telling them about it?
>
> Personally, the greatest thing about getting older is being here to enjoy it.[‡]

---

*The Friars Club of Beverly Hills, a private club for show business stalwarts, was founded in 1947 by Milton Berle at the Savoy Hotel in Hollywood, moved to Beverly Hills in 1961 and became the home of celebrity roasts in which friends of a celebrity would devise every comic turn imaginable, clean and risqué, to embarrass the honoree. It has no connection with the Friars Club of New York which was founded in 1904.

[†]Van Doren, quoted from www.mamievandoren.com. George Barris (c. 1925–) built model airplanes and cars during his childhood before he and his older brother, Sam, turned their attention to the real thing as teenagers, learning their skills in local body shops and modifying cars for street use and drag racing. One of his first creations was used in High School Confidential! His expertise turned into a livelihood when he began customizing cars for Hollywood stars as well as creating idiosyncratic vehicles for shows such as The Beverly Hillbillies.

[‡]The Older the Fiddle, the Better the Tune, 152–53.

The Films

AS JOAN OLANDER

Footlight Varieties • RKO Radio Pictures, 1951

CREDITS: *Directors:* D.W. Griffith (*Confidence* sequence), Benjamin Stoloff (*Radio City Revels* sequence), Hal Yates (new footage); *Producer:* George Bilson; *Script:* D.W. Griffith (*Confidence* sequence), Felix Adler & Hal Yates (*He Forgot to Remember* sequence); *Music:* Sammy Timberg, Roy Webb; *Musical Director* (new material): C. Bakaleinikoff; *Musical Director* (*Radio City Revels*): Victor Baravalle; *Choreographer* (*Radio City Revels*): Hermes Pan; *Photography:* G.W. Bitzer & Arthur Marion (*Confidence* sequence), Jack MacKenzie & J. Roy Hunt (*Radio City Revels* sequence), J. Roy Hunt & Frank Redman (new footage); *Editors:* James [J.R.] Whittredge, Edward W. Williams; B&W; 60 minutes.

SONGS: "The Show Must Go On" (Gordon Jenkins; Tom Adair); "Good Night, Ladies" *The Sportsman Quartet*; "La Paloma" (Sebastian Yradier) *Frankie Carle Orchestra*; "Fantasie Impromptu" *Jerry Murad and His Harmonicats*; "The Galloping Comedians" (Kabelevsky) *Jerry Murad and His Harmonicats*; "I Get the Neck of the Chicken"; "Hungarian Rhapsody" (Franz Liszt) *Liberace*; "Love Rhumba"; "Dixieland Time" *Buster West & Melissa Mason*.

CAST: Jack Paar (*Himself*); Frankie Carle (*Himself— segment "Carle Comes Calling"*); The Sportsman Quartet [Bill Days, Martin Sperzel, Gurney Bell, Bob Stevens] (*Themselves*); Red Buttons (*Himself*); Liberace (*Himself*); Inesita (*Gypsy Dancer*); Grace Ramanos; Joan Olander [Mamie Van Doren] (*Blonde in Theater*); He Forgot to Remember Segment: Leon Errol (*Leon*); Dorothy Granger (*Vivian Errol*); Jerry Murad and The Harmonicats (*Themselves*); Byron Foulger (*Dr. Twitchell*); Elaine Riley; Harry Harvey (*Leon's Fishing Buddy*); Patti Brill; Emory Parnell (*Older Cop*); Eddie Kane (*Headwaiter*); Radio City Revels Segment: Buster West, Melissa Mason (*Dancers*)

NOTES: Mamie's very first appearance on the silver screen is in the very last scene of *Footlight Varieties*, a collection of old variety and short subject footage augmented with new material from Hal Yates, including Liberace playing Franz Liszt's "Hungarian Rhapsody."

Variety reported, "RKO has a diverting entry in this musical review.... There's a lineup of 12 acts to make it a vaudeville show on film that will be acceptable for all lower-case bookings." (April 4, 1951)

But not everyone liked these compilation movies, pioneered by producer George Bilson in 1948 with *Variety Time*, also with Jack Paar as MC interlinking clips from RKO movies and full short subjects and taking part in new material. The second, *Make Mine Laughs* (1949), with Gil Lamb as MC, resulted in Ray Bolger and Jack Haley suing RKO for the unauthorized use of their names and performances. They both won cash settlements and the film was subsequently withdrawn from circulation in time for this, the third and final entry in the series.

Mamie recalls: "My scene was the final one of the movie, as the camera panned across an empty theater to find a boy and girl still necking in front of a blank screen. I played the girl; the boy was a good-looking young actor named Jack Paar. Paar was very sweet, a little shy. Even then he was wearing a toupee."*

His Kind of Woman · RKO Radio Pictures, 1951

The hottest combination that ever hit the screen!

CREDITS: *Presenter:* Howard Hughes; *Director:* John Farrow; *Executive Producer:* Robert Sparks; *Screenplay:* Frank Fenton and Jack Leonard, based on the story "Star Sapphire" by Gerald Drayson Adams; *Music:* Leigh Harline; *Musical Director:* C. Bakaleinikoff; *Photography:* Harry J. Wild; *Editors:* Eda Warren, Frederic Knudtson; *Production Design:* J. McMillan Johnson; *Art Director:* Albert S. D'Agostino; *Set Decorators:* Darrell Silvera, Ross Dowd; *Miss Russell's Gowns:* Howard Greer; *Hair:* Larry Germain; *Makeup:* Mel Berns; *Sound:* John E. Tribby, Clem Portman; B&W; 120 minutes.

SONGS: "Five Little Miles from San Berdoo" (Sam Coslow) *Jane Russell*; "You'll Know" (Jimmy McHugh, Harold Adamson) *Jane Russell*

CAST: Robert Mitchum (*Dan Milner*); Jane Russell (*Lenore Brent/Liz Brady*); Vincent Price (*Mark Cardigan*); Tim Holt (*Bill Lusk*); Charles McGraw (*Thompson*); Marjorie Reynolds (*Helen Cardigan*); Raymond Burr (*Nick Ferraro*); Leslye [Leslie] Banning (*Jennie Stone*); Jim Backus (*Myron Winton*); Philip Van Zandt (*Jose Morro*); John Mylong (*Martin Krafft*); Carleton G. Young (*Gerald Hobson*); *Uncredited*: Dorothy Abbott (*Card Player*); Tol Avery (*Fat Hoodlum*); Richard Bergren (*Milton Stone*); Danny Borzage (*Lodge Bartender*); Mary Brewer, Gwen Caldwell, Oliver Cross, Jim Davies, Barbara Freking, Stuart Holmes, Don House, Geraldine Jordan, Joy Windsor (*Lodge Guests*); Joan Olander [Mamie Van Doren] (*Lodge Guest at Bar*); Peter Brocco, Mike Lally (*Thompson's Henchman*); James Burke (*Barkeeper in Nogales*); Anthony Caruso (*Tony*); Robert Cornthwaite (*Hernandez*); Daniel De Laurentis (*Mexican Boy in Nogales*); King Donovan (*Reporter*); Marietta Elliott (*Redhead*); Paul Fierro (*Charles*); Joel Fluellen (*Sam*); Paul Frees (*Corley*); Gerry Ganzer (*Countess*); Ralph Gomez (*Mexican Foreman*); Joseph Granby (*Arnold*); Henry Guttman (*Man*); Stacy Harris (*Harry*); Len Hendry (*Customer*); Jerry James, Edwin Rand (*Policemen*); William Justine (*Gyppo*); Alberto Morin (*Lt. Rodriguez*); Bill Nelson (*Ship's Captain*); Bob Rose (*Corley's Servant*); John Sheehan (*Guitarist*); Mickey Simpson (*Hoodlum*); Ken Terrell (*Gunman*); Dale Van Sickel, Bud Wolfe (*Seamen*); Ernö Verebes (*Esteban*); Dan White (*Tex Kearns*); Sally Yarnell (*Pianist*); Maria Sen Young (*Swaying Waitress*).

DVD: As part of the *Film Noir Classic Collection Volume 3*. Also includes: *On Dangerous Ground, Border Incident, The Racket, Forbidden Passage, A Gun in His Hand, Women in Hiding* and *You, the People*.

NOTES: Although *His Kind of Woman* did not sit in the RKO vaults for anywhere near the time it took to release *Jet Pilot*, it still languished for over a year before a name change, from *Smiler with a Gun*, and a re-edit from Jerry Wald and Norman Krasna, the two men shepherding the studio's shelved films to release. The title change was indicative of the confusion over what sort of film it was. The initial title promised a crime melodrama, the second a love story. It had Louella Parsons' seal of approval ("The hottest combination that ever hit the screen") and an ad campaign that included a three-story high by 45-foot-wide billboard on Wilshire and Fairfax in Los Angeles painted by Marc Zamparelli[†] of Jane Russell, and her pert cleavage, draped over the recumbent Robert Mitchum. The box office kachinged, adding to RKO's coffers, although critics found the mixing of genres perplexing. *Newsweek* thought "it never is quite clear what the makers had

---

*Mamie Van Doren, Playing the Field, 30–31.
†Charles Higham, in his biography Howard Hughes: The Secret Life, tells the story of Hughes employing Zamparelli to paint his portrait — in two days. The artist said he could do it in three and worked 72 hours straight through. Presented with the finished work, the RKO boss gave it his okay, except that a 32nd of an inch needed to be taken off one ear and several other minuscule changes needed to be made. Zamparelli did as he was requested.

uppermost in mind: suspense, comedy or action."

The convoluted plot had gambler Dan Milner awaiting instructions at a resort in Mexico, the unknowing victim of a plot by exiled gangster honcho, Nick Ferraro. While he's waiting, Dan becomes involved with singer Lenore Brent and her lover, ham actor Mark Cardigan, before he learns he is to undergo experimental surgery, and then death, so Ferraro can enter the United States using his identity. After Dan is kidnapped and taken aboard a yacht, Lenore and Cardigan ride to his rescue. Cardigan gets the glory and Dan gets the girl.

In these more genre-savvy times, *His Kind of Women* comes across as an entertaining potboiler crime melodrama-film noir that mixes the different genre elements with glee. Vincent Price, as the petulant film star who is having a rather lethargic affair with Jane Russell's singer, walked away with the film and the reviews. This is understandable given that Price's screen time was enhanced when Howard Hughes "fell in love" with the character of Mark Cardigan. "We finished the film and I went to Rome for another picture," Vincent Price recalled in an interview.* "But he called us back for some new scenes. We all crowded in the boat and sailed off to save Mitchum from a fate worse than death."

Price garnered praise all round, *The Los Angeles Times* (September 1, 1951) saying, "Vincent Price is cast as a 'ham' screen actor spouting Shakespeare and strutting so preposterously that after a while, perversely, you begin to recognize some truth in the character." The film's two leads, however, fared less well. "Mr. Mitchum blinks sleepily into space and Miss Russell, strategically sheathed in some opulent gowns, merely and understandably arches her upper lip as though she were smelling something awful" was Howard Thompson's opinion in *The New York Times*; he called it "one of the worst Hollywood pictures in years."

Mamie spent three months on location for this film. Apart from earning enough money to buy a sports car, she managed a few moments of speechless screen time as she and another blonde are escorted to the resort bar by an older gentleman.

Two Tickets to Broadway • RKO Radio Pictures, 1951

Get set for a Racy Romp up and down the Big Street!

CREDITS: *Presenter*: Howard Hughes; *Director:* James V. Kern; *Producers:* Norman Krasna, Jerry Wald; *Script:* Sid Silvers and Hal Kantor, based on a story by Sammy Cahn; *Music:* Walter Scharf; *Musical Supervisor:* C. Bakaleinikoff; *Musical Numbers Created & Directed by* Busby Berkeley; *Vocal Arranger:* Eliot Daniel; *Photography:* Edward Cronjager, Harry J. Wild; *Editor:* Harry Marker; *Art Directors:* Albert S. D'Agostino, Carroll Clark; *Set Decorators:* Darrell Silvera, Harley Miller; *Gowns:* Michael Woulfe; *Hairstyles:* Larry Germain; *Makeup:* Mel Berns; *Sound:* Earl A. Wolcott, Clem Portman; Technicolor; 106 minutes.

SONGS: "Pelican Falls" incorporating "Auld Lang Syne" and "Yankee Doodle Dandy" with new lyrics: Chorus, Janet Leigh; "There's No Tomorrow" ["O Solo Mio"] (Al Hoffman, Leo Corday, Leon Carr) Tony Martin; "Manhattan" (Richard Rodgers; Lorenz Hart) Tony Martin, Janet Leigh, Chorus; "Baby You'll Never Be Sorry" (Jule Styne, Leo Robin) Eddie Bracken, Gloria DeHaven; chorus reprised by Tony Martin; "The Closer You Are" (Jule Styne, Leo Robin) Tony Martin, Janet Leigh; reprised Tony Martin; Joe Smith, Charles Dale; "The Worry Bird" (Jule Styne, Leo Robin) Gloria DeHaven, Janet Leigh, Ann Miller, Barbara Lawrence; "Let's Make Comparisons" (Bob Crosby; Sammy Cahn) Bob Crosby; "Prologue from 'Pagliacci'" (Leoncavallo) Tony Martin; "Big Chief Hole-in-the-Ground" (Jule Styne, Leo Robin) Tony Martin, Janet Leigh, Ann Miller, Gloria DeHaven, Barbara Lawrence; "Are You Just a Beautiful Dream" (Jule Styne, Leo Robin) Tony Martin

CAST: Tony Martin (*Dan Carter*); Janet Leigh (*Nancy Peterson*); Gloria DeHaven (*Han-*

---

*Gazette-Journal, Reno, Nevada, November 25, 1979.

Giant banner of Mamie outside the Hollywood Entertainment Museum on Hollywood Boulevard in September 2005, advertising the Hollywood in Vegas exhibition (photograph by the author).

nah Holbrook); Eddie Bracken (*Lew Conway*); Ann Miller (*Joyce Campbell*); Barbara Lawrence (*S.F. Rogers*); Joe Smith (*Harry*) and Charles Dale (*Leo*); Taylor Holmes (*Willard Glendon*); Buddy Baer (*Sailor*); Bob Crosby (*Himself*); The Charlivels (*Themselves*); *Uncredited*: Frieda Stoll (*Wardrobe Woman*); Fred L. Gillett (*Bus Driver*); Norval Mitchell (*Mr. Peterson*); Helen Spring (*Mrs. Peterson*); John Gallaudet (*McGiven*); Isabel Randolph (*Housekeeper*); Donald MacBride (*Bus Terminal Guard*); John Sheehan (*Desk Clerk*); Don Blackman (*Porter*); Vera Miles (*Chorus Girl*); Joi Lansing (*Redhead*); Joan Shawlee, Mara Corday, Joan Evans, June McCall, Joan Olander [Mamie Van Doren], Noreen Mortensen, Joel Robinson, Georgia Clancy, Elizabeth Burgess, Barbara Thatcher, Carol Brewster (*Showgirls*); George Nader (*TV Studio Mic Check Guy*); Linda Williams (*Brunette*); Angela Stevens (*Blonde*); Libby Taylor (*Maid*); Herman Cantor, Jimmy Dundee (*Doormen*); Millicent Deming (*Receptionist*); Jerry Hausner (*Agent*); Jack Gargan (*Dispatcher*); Jane Easton, Shirley Tegge, Martha O'Brian, Lucy Knoch, Rosalee Calvert, Joan Barton, Shirley Whitney, Marilyn Johnson, Gwen Caldwell, Barbara Freking, Mona Knox, Rosemary Knighton, Marie Thomas (*Girls*); Jean Corbett, Helen Hayden, Claudette Thornton, Hazel Shaw, Barbara Logan, Charlotte Alpert, Victoria Lynn, Jeane Dyer, Pat Hall, Maura Donatt (*Chorus Girls*); Billy Curtis (*Midget*); Mike Lally, Bennett Green (*Men with Tux*); Larry Barton (*Waiter*); Gene Banks (*Usher*); Vincent Graeff (*Cheerleader*); Maxine Willis, Joann [Joan] Arnold (*Secretaries*); Ann Melton, Ann Kramer (*Women in Evening Gowns*); Marg Pemberton (*Hotel Guest*); Ann Kimball (*Western Union Girl*); Lillian West (*Old Woman*); Sid Tomack (*Bus Driver*); Tony Felice, Marty Rhiel, Duris De Jong, Gene Marshall (*Ad-lib Men*); Marie Allison (*Ad-lib Woman*); Miles Shepard, Bob Thom (*Cops*); Ralph Hodges, Michael Pierce (*Hot Rod Passengers*); Suzanne Amers (*Beautiful Girl*); Kathy Case; Anne O'Neal; Lester Dorr; Charlete Hardy; Carry Owen; Shirley Buchanan; Mildred Carroll; Carmelita Eskew; Joanne Frank; Mary Ellen Gleason; Joan Jordan; Lola Kendrick; Shirley Kimball; Evelyn Lovequist; Kathleen O'Malley; June Paul; Marylin Symons; Beverly Thomas; Joan Whitney; Barbara Worthington; Eileen Coghlan.

NOTES: Mamie recalled *Two Tickets to Broadway* as "as garden-variety rags-to-riches story with every pretty unknown in Hollywood playing a bit role. If there had been a beauty contest on that set, I would have come in last."*

She is easy to spot in one scene: She enters the Palace Deli and sits at a table with friends in a scene involving Smith and Dale as the Deli proprietors and Tony Martin being taken for a ride by a man who is posing as the producer of Bob Crosby's TV show. It's an amiable musical which concerns the rather clichéd travails of small town (Pelican Bend) girl (Janet Leigh) traveling to New York to become a star. On the way she is befriended by a trio of showgirls (Ann Miller, Barbara Lawrence and Gloria DeHaven) and a male singer on the make (Tony Martin). Despite the best efforts of their incompetent manager (Eddie Bracken) they land a spot on Bob Crosby's television variety show just as Ms. Leigh boards a bus to head home in defeat.

A.H. Weiler in *The New York Times* wrote, "The producers have filled the screen with enough pulchritude to excite even the most hardened misanthrope. The tunes in *Two Tickets to Broadway* may not generate much whistling, but the girls will."

The musical numbers (helmed by veteran Busby Berkeley) and specialty acts were the reason for the film, the slim plotline, more aptly titled *Two Tickets to Television*, the excuse.

Mamie was close to turning 17 and her career at RKO was over. "I could see that there was no future for me at RKO outside of playing bit parts."†

---

*Mamie Van Doren, Playing the Field, 36.
†Ibid., 39.

AS MAMIE VAN DOREN

All American • Universal-International, 1953 (British Title: *The Winning Way*)

CREDITS: *Director:* Jesse Hibbs, All American, U.S.C. '27; *Producer:* Aaron Rosenberg, All American, U.S.C. '33; *Associate Producer:* William D. Powell; *Screenplay:* D.D. Beauchamp; *Adaptation by* Robert Yale Libott, *Based on a story by* Leonard Freeman; *Music:* Henry Mancini; *Musical Direction:* Joseph Gershenson; *Photography:* Maury Gertsman; *Film Editor:* Edward Curtiss; *Art Direction:* Bernard Herzbrun, Eric Orbom; *Set Decorations:* Russell A. Gausman, Julia Heron; *Sound:* Leslie I. Carey, Corson Jowett; *Gowns:* Rosemary Odell; *Hair Stylist:* Joan St. Oegger; *Makeup:* Bud Westmore; *Assistant Director:* Fred Frank; B&W; 83 minutes.

SONG: "Have a Beer" (Arnold Hughes; Frederick Herbert) *Male Students*

CAST: Tony Curtis (*Nick Bonelli*); Lori Nelson (*Sharon Wallace*); Richard Long (*Howard Carter*); Mamie Van Doren (*Susie Ward*); Gregg Palmer (*Hunt Cameron*); Paul Cavanagh (*Professor Banning*); Barney Phillips (*Clipper Colton*); Jimmy Hunt (*Whizzer*); Stuart Whitman (*Zip Parker*); Douglas Kennedy (*Tate Hardy*); Donald Randolph (*David Carter*); Herman Hickman, All American, Tenn. '52 (*Jumbo*); Frank Gifford, All American, U.S.C. '51 (*Stan Pomeroy*); Tom Harmon, All American, Mich. '39–40 (*Himself*); Jim Sears, All American, U.S.C., '52 (*Dartmore Quarterback*); Elmer Willhoite, All American, U.S.C. '52 (*Kenton*); Donn Moomaw, All American, UCLA '52 (*Jones*); *Uncredited*: Paul Smith (*Smith*); Morgan Jones (*Casey*); John Harmon (*Bartender*); Harris Brown (*Butler*); Bill Baldwin Sr. (*Announcer*); George Bozanic (*McManus*); Malcolm Cassell (*Louie*); Douglas Deems (*Usher*); Fortune Gordien (*Gronski*); Myrna Hansen (*Girl at Party*); Jim Hardy (*Dutch Wilson*); Bill Radovich (*Joe*); Al Carmichael; Earl Audet.

PLOT: After Nick Bonelli wins the game for Mid-State to become an All American, he is told by the coach that his parents were killed in a bus crash on the way to the game. He feels he is responsible for their deaths because they wanted him to better himself by accepting a scholarship in architecture at Ivy League Sheridan University in Chicago. Because of the coach's callous behavior (keeping the information from him purely to win the game), Nick travels to the college to plead for the scholarship. But right from the start he runs up against the college hierarchy as a result of his unconventional haircut, his lack of social status and his steadfast refusal to use the one social leveler at his disposal: his football prowess. He particularly falls foul of fellow student Howard Carter, whose family is a great benefactor to the university.

Nick attracts the attention of Sharon Wallace, secretary to Prof. Carl Banning. He is constantly in trouble for breaking the university rules, such as visiting an off-limits bar, The Pewter Mug, where he meets waitress Susie Ward. Howard turns up to warn Susie away from one of his more impressionable buddies and a fight ensues between Nick and Howard. After Susie and Nick leave, Howard is arrested and spends the night in jail for disturbing the peace. When Nick is confronted with the accusation that he was involved in the fight, he denies it and Howard is threatened with expulsion.

The college football team is on a losing streak but no amount of cajoling will entice Nick to help them out. At a high-class party Nick turns up with a dejected Susie to show they are as good as the rest of the college elite. Susie comes on to Howard using the same lines she uses on everyone. Eventually Nick's resistance is worn down by Sharon Wallace, who tells him it's to his own advantage to play football to win friends at the university, not because she cares whether the team wins or not.

With Nick on the team they go on to win game after game. When Nick is asked to move into the team's sorority house, Howard storms out in protest, also losing his spot on the team. Howard's dad returns unexpectedly from a European trip and Nick goes to find Howard at The Pewter Mug so he can salvage his father's respect. Howard has passed out; when Nick attempts to wake him up, a struggle ensues and

Nick (Tony Curtis) knows trouble when he sees it: Susie the waitress (Mamie) dances with sophomore Nick in the off-limits bar The Pewter Mug, in *All American* (Universal, 1953).

Susie, mistaking his intentions, smashes a bottle over his head. Nick is arrested and expelled from the university.

On the big day, the first time the university has a chance of winning the finals, Nick is listening to the game on the radio at The Pewter

Mug. Susie, realizing her mistake, begs the dean of men to allow Nick back into college and he runs onto the field in the third quarter in time to help win the game, Howard's friendship and the girl. Plus, the audience is expected to assume, a lucrative career in architecture.

NOTES: Mamie is fourth billed in *All American*,* a rather ordinarily plotted but otherwise interesting football melodrama, the first released with her new moniker since signing with Universal. Although the football scenes were enough to help the movie into profit in the U.S., elsewhere the game's rules were as arcane as, say, cricket to Americans. The film was shorn of 13 minutes of gridiron footage in the U.K.; it still flopped and never went into wide release. The banal "will he/won't he play the game and help the struggling college team to victory?" plot was so hackneyed by the '50s that *Monthly Film Bulletin* wrote "it has attempted little and achieved even less." A cast and crew littered with All Americans, a term obscure to the world outside North America, didn't help.

If the plot is shallow, then so is the character of Nick Bonelli, played by Tony Curtis, a character so dumb you marvel that he even knows what architecture is. For example, when he visits the Carter house he is told by the manservant that Mr. Carter will see him in the library.

NICK: I thought he wanted to meet me here.
MANSERVANT: The library is part of the house.

The most interesting aspect of the film is Mamie's character, the first in a long line of working class–lower middle class, good/bad girls that Mamie became so adept at playing. In fact, Mamie's character has a background not dissimilar to the actress' own — except this farm girl has come to the big college town with her sights set on attracting herself a rich husband. To that end she has taken a job in a dive to support herself and meet men.

We first meet her when Nick enters The Pewter Mug and persuades her to dance with him.

NICK: What are you doing in a dump like this?
SUSIE: Looking for a future
NICK: A future?
SUSIE: Why not? Most of you Sheridan boys come from wealthy families.
NICK: Well, if you picked me you picked the wrong guy.
SUSIE: What are you afraid of?
NICK: You.
SUSIE: Why?
NICK: I know trouble when I see it.
 (*Susie cuddles up to him*)
SUSIE: How could I cause you any trouble?
NICK: By doing just what you're doing now.

Susie is a girl with a reputation. But Mamie wasn't even old enough to serve beer.

Later, when she crashes the Carters' party and is introduced to Professor Banning, he says he's heard of her on several occasions in the past year.

SUSIE: You have?
BANNING: Yes, indeed. I believe you're now rated in second place to the original school charter of things to see on the campus.
SUSIE: Why second place?
BANNING: I'm beginning to wonder about that myself.

Tony Curtis's Nick and Mamie's Susie are one-of-a-kind underneath. But whereas Nick is sullen and uncooperative in the one area that will almost certainly gain him entrance to the ranks of the country's future high rollers, portrayed chillingly with ice-cool superiority by Richard Long, Mamie's Susie is eager to please. A little too eager although there is a naïve calculation behind her façade as witness her come-on line that she uses without variation on all the eligible men she meets. But the film is Nick's story, not Susie's. Nick has something that will enable his social superiors to turn a blind eye to his upstart desire to become an architect (on a scholarship): his talent at football. Susie has only her looks and sex appeal to hitch a ride up the social ladder. Her American Dream is predicated on sex and even the hollow ending to the movie, when she is hoisted on

---

*The title is variously given as The All American *or* All-American *but on the screen it is two words, no hyphen and no definite article.*

Susie (Mamie), Prof. Banning (Paul Cavanagh), Sharon Wallace (Lori Nelson) and David Carter (Donald Randolph) cheer on the home team in the climactic football game in *All American* (Universal, 1953).

the shoulders of the very college bachelors she is so eagerly pursuing, she doesn't realize there is a worm in the apple. Rich boys screw girls like Susie but marry girls of their own social standing. A few movies later, Mamie played second fiddle in a similar Hollywood fairy tale in which poor chorus girl Piper Laurie will marry rich Rory Calhoun and, after the *de rigueur* ups and downs and misunderstanding, they look like they will settle into domestic bliss and live happily ever after. A typical Hollywood fairy tale.

Ironically, as Mamie was hoisted above the actors in the last scene of *All American*, "One guy slipped his hand up my crotch. I was so mad. I'll never forget that I was so embarrassed because I was so young. Now I'd say, 'Oh, really? Shoot that one more time, honey, one more time.' Times change."

For half the film, the development of Susie's character and her desperate search for security through marriage to wealth is a telling example of the plight of unskilled women in western societies. With her only skill in waitressing, Susie faces a bleak future. But she is alluring and uses that allure to good effect. That she is using it on the wrong people is her tragedy. Even though for purposes of plot Susie has to betray Nick so that he is expelled from college (bad girl), she eventually realizes she must put things right and becomes the heroine of the hour.

Mamie's initial screen performance is mesmerizing. She hits the screen with force and makes Susie's obsessive tunnel vision and her desperation perfectly understandable. If the permutations of the script later let her down, it is nonetheless an auspicious dramatic debut. It also sets up recurring themes and patterns in Mamie's non-period films: Her characters are usually on the lowest socio-economic rung of society, working class, and cars become a feature of mobility, not only physical but social.

Curtis and Mamie make a superb team and it's to be regretted they were never paired up again although Mamie does make an unbilled cameo in the Tony Curtis starrer *Forbid-*

den. The chemistry between them is palpable. Two bruised creatures who, in a more supportive world, would have fallen in love with each other but are blinded by their struggle to lift themselves out of the mire of mediocrity (Nick through his relationship with the blandly beguiling Sharon Wallace, played by Lori Nelson, and Susie through marriage). In real life it would be a few more years before Mamie and Tony got together and, as she relates with her trademark candor on her website, he made her "clitty tingle."

There are homoerotic overtones in the relationship of Richard Long and Tony Curtis, Long circling and slagging off at the piece of rough trade that is Nick, criticizing his hair and his behavior until he falls under Nick's androgynous good looks and the two consummate their friendship on the playing field. Nick arouses stronger emotions in Richard Long than any woman who appears in his life.

Mamie had one regret. "I had a song but they cut it. I was singing around the juke box just before Tony Curtis comes into the bar where I'm working. It was Jimmy McHugh's 'I Can't Give You Anything but Love.' I was disappointed because I wanted to be known as a singer."*

REVIEWS: "Rah-rah football feature ... is an entertaining offering ... [W]hile no great classic of the gridiron in the handling of the subject or in the acting, it is plenty of fun for general audiences ... [An] entertaining mixture of formula film pigskin hokum ... Lori Nelson ... plays [her] part appealingly. A different kind of appeal was meant in the casting of Mamie Van Doren, blonde charmer who lures the players to an off-limits beer joint and gets them in trouble. She's up to the role's demands." *Variety*, July 22, 1953

"An old-fashioned drama with a football background." Clive Hirschhorn, *The Universal Story*, 210

"Mamie Van Doren does what Mamie Van Doren usually does. While the football sequences are exciting, the film is a bit hard to take at times, especially when the 20-plus college freshman Nick is advised by his professors to grin and bear it when he's hazed by the much-younger upper classmen." Hal Erickson, *All Movie Guide*

"Definitely a way below average grid-iron epic. The script has nothing new to offer that we haven't seen in countless films of this type before, the direction is the soul of mediocrity, the acting is steadfastly routine and production values are minimal." *Film Index*, #10

Forbidden • Universal-International, 1953

He's the kind of man who's out of bounds for any kind of woman!

CREDITS: *Director:* Rudolph Maté; *Producer:* Ted Richmond; *Script:* Gil Doud, William Sackheim, based on a story by William Sackheim; *Music:* Frank Skinner; *Photography:* William H. Daniels; *Editor:* Edward Curtiss; *Art Directors:* Bernard Herzbrun, Richard H. Riedel; *Set Decorators:* Russell A. Gausman, Ruby R. Levitt; *Costumes:* Bill Thomas; *Sound:* Leslie I. Carey, Joe Lapis; B&W; 85 minutes.

SONG: "You Belong to Me" (Pee Wee King,† Redd Stewart, Chilton Price) *Mamie Van Doren*‡

CAST: Tony Curtis (*Eddie Darrow*); Joanne Dru (*Christine Lawrence*); Lyle Bettger (*Justin Keet*); Marvin Miller (*Cliff Chalmer*); Victor Sen Yung (*Allan Chung*); Alan Dexter (*Barney Pendleton*); David Sharpe (*Henchman Leon*); Peter Mamakos (*Sam*); Howard Chuman (*Hon-Fai*); Weaver Levy (*Tang*); Harold Fong (*Wong*); Mae [*Mai*] Tai Sing (*Soo Lee*);

---

*Phone interview with the author, May 23, 2006.

†*Pee Wee King (Julius Frank Anthony Kuczynski) (1914–2000) was a bandleader and a composer who famously penned "The Tennessee Waltz" with his band's male vocalist Redd Stewart (1923–2003); their recording reached number 3 on* Billboard*'s country music chart in 1948. Patti Page had an even bigger mainstream hit with the song in 1950, selling over six million copies by 1967. It was declared the state song of Tennessee in 1965. King was elevated to the Country Music Hall of Fame in 1973.*

‡*Mamie's singing voice was dubbed by Virginia Rees who also dubbed for Lana Turner in* Ziegfeld Girl *(1941), Marlene Dietrich in* The Lady Is Willing *(1942), Angela Lansbury in* The Harvey Girls *(1946), Evelyn Keyes in* The Jolson Story *(1946), Lucille Ball in* Easy to Wed *(1946) and Vera Ralston in* Timberjack *(1955).*

Uncredited: Mamie Van Doren (*Nightclub Singer*); Barry Bernard (*Black*); Spencer Chan (*Chin*); Aen-Ling Chow, Leemoi Chu (*Girl Dealers*); Al Ferguson (*Harbormaster*); Jimmy Gray (*Guard*); Harry Lauter (*Holly*); Alphonse Martell (*Guest*); Reginald Sheffield (*Englishman*); Ray Engel.

PLOT: Eddie Darrow is in Macao to lure Christine Lawrence back to Philadelphia for crime boss Barney Pendleton, who hopes to get his hands on a sworn affidavit she has left in a safety deposit box as "insurance" (to be opened in the event of her sudden demise). Eddie has been sent because of his past association with her. On his way to the Lisbon Club, one of Christine's hangouts, Eddie saves the life of the club's owner, Justin Keet. Keet, who is engaged to Christine, hires Eddie to run the club. Although bitter at the way Christine dumped him to marry another man, Eddie finds he is still in love with her and is surprised to find she reciprocates. She reveals she only married a mobster to save Eddie's life. They realize they are both in danger, as Pendleton has taken out insurance for Eddie's return, in the form of backup mobster Cliff Chalmer.

Eddie concocts an elaborate ruse to escape the Portuguese colony but is caught. He attempts to convince Chalmer the escape plan is merely a ruse to lure an unsuspecting Christine back to the U.S. Christine overhears the plan and thinks Eddie has betrayed her. In retaliation she marries Keet but realizes too late that he is as big a racketeer as her first husband. With the help of the Lisbon Club pianist, who is really an undercover cop, she flees on a boat with Eddie to Kowloon with Keet and his heavies in hot pursuit. After an elaborate cat-and-mouse game aboard a cargo ship, Keet and his henchmen are blown apart in an explosion. Christine is also assumed dead when her ID is found on board the gutted vessel. This leads to the opening of the safety deposit box and the charging of Barney Pendleton. But both Christine and Eddie have survived and intend to sail back to the U.S. to start a new life together.

NOTES: *Forbidden* is an okay crime melodrama in which Mamie appears around the 33-minute mark as the chanteuse in the Lisbon Club singing, or rather miming, "You Belong to Me," the melody heard every time the lovers (Curtis and Dru) have a "moment." Mamie, at this stage still Joan Olander although unbilled, is mere background dressing as the former lovers sit miserably at a table regretting their lost relationship under the watchful eye of Dru's intended, Lyle Bettger, the nightclub's crooked owner. Mamie's "Lena Horne* moment," posed against a nightclub pillar, lasts a mere twenty seconds.

Stark black-and-white photography by William H. Daniels and polished direction by Polish-born Rudolph Maté cannot disguise the fact that the movie location got no further East than the back lot at Universal and the harbor at San Diego. The use of the very limited street set landscape is masterly, painting everything around the club as dark and dismal and a place of intrigue and assassination. The pace, however, is so labored that the audience is always one step ahead of the unnecessarily convoluted plot.

Mamie's role was essentially her screen test for Universal. "I was in the right place at the right time. My career had stagnated at RKO and I was doing *Come Back, Little Sheba*† in Beverly Hills when a talent scout from Universal saw me they had to have a singer in a movie they were shooting at that moment with Tony Curtis. They knew I could sing. Phil Benjamin, who was head of casting then, took me over to

---

*MGM never quite knew what to do with African-American Lena Horne, and so her screen career mainly consisted of musical numbers interpolated into nightclub sequences with her leaning against pillars or other set pieces. This allowed Southern exhibitors to excise the segments.

†Play by William Inge (1913–73). Inge was a major theatre writer of the 1950s with successes such as Bus Stop *and* Picnic. Come Back, Little Sheba, *his first Broadway play, opened at the Booth Theater on February 15, 1950, and ran for 190 performances. Lead actors Shirley Booth and Sidney Blackmer both won Tony awards under the direction of Daniel Mann but only Booth and Mann went west to Hollywood to repeat their success. Burt Lancaster played the Blackmer role on film.*

the stage to meet the producer* and director.† I did and they said 'Be ready Monday,' this was on a Friday, to shoot this song called 'You Belong to Me.' So I had the weekend to learn 'You Belong to Me.' Someone else had previously recorded it and I had to mouth it to the song and so all weekend I was learning the movements to it. I was so nervous it was termed as a screen test for me because all the executives from New York were there and they watched me do it live."‡

They liked what they saw and Mamie, as she would become under their tutelage, was signed to a seven-year contract. She was rushed into one of the lead roles opposite Tony Curtis in *All American*, which was released two months before *Forbidden*.

Rudolph Maté was a noted cinematographer in Europe before heading to Hollywood in 1935. He took up the directing reins in 1947 but never with the same kind of success. He directed a number of cult favorites, the best of which are the film noir classic *D.O.A.* (1950) and the sci-fi; *When Worlds Collide* (1951).

REVIEWS: "A regulation set of melodramatics concerned with hoodlum enterprise in Macao is offered in this shoot-'em-up, derrin'-do actioner." *Variety*, November 25, 1953

"It was nice to see Tony Curtis out of eastern garb and in Mufti ... but that was all that could be said in its favor. For the rest it was a relentlessly drab little caper..." Clive Hirschhorn, *The Universal Story*

"Many Far Eastern cities, with Shanghai and Hong Kong at the head of the list, have been the locale for more than a few movies, and they have almost always been steeped with intrigue, crime, assorted mayhem and obscure vices. *Forbidden* ... follows in the tradition.... As is usually the case with 'B' products of this caliber, *Forbidden* is an exercise in violent connivance just chock full of phony sets, and stock expressions on the faces of actors who find themselves in the caper. The production was directed by Rudolph Maté, who obviously was stumped by the scenario furnished by William Sackheim and Gil Doud. Their literary effort is the real villain of the piece." *The New York Times*, January 30, 1954

Hawaiian Nights • Universal-International, 1956

CREDITS: *Producer-Director:* Will Cowan; *Script:* Joe Twerp; *Editor:* Frank Gross; Black & White; 17 minutes.

SONGS: "Minoi Minoi Ay"; "Lovely Hula Girl" (Randy Oness, Jack Pitman); "Hawaiian Spear Chant"; "Kumu in the Muumuu"; "Ama Ama"; "Nohea"; "Hoku Okalania"

CAST: Pinky Lee; Mamie Van Doren; Lisa Gaye; Alfred Apaka; Tani Marsh and Her Dancers; Ben Chapman; Danny Stewart and His Islanders; Steve Steventon.

NOTES: Mamie and Lisa Gaye put in an appearance along with finalists from the 1953 Miss World competition, some of whom would pop up as harem girls in *Yankee Pasha*, in this Universal-International 17-minute short. Its slim storyline is woven around comedian Pinky Lee (1907–93), an acclaimed children's television show host in the early 1950s. His trademarks were a plaid suit and baggy checkered trousers, a lisp and a silly theme song. *The Pinky Lee Show* ran until 1955 and is considered the precursor of *Pee wee's Playhouse*.

"I was the female lead opposite Pinky Lee but I didn't have any songs to sing in that one. I can't remember the plot, it was so long ago. But they were trying out some of the Miss Universe finalists and putting them under contract. I don't think many of them went on to anything else much after *Yankee Pasha*."**

Universal was using some of its exotic talent with a view to reactivating "tropical-style" movies like those made by Maria Montez and Jon Hall in the previous decade. To that end

---

**Ted Richmond (1912–) also produced another Mamie vehicle,* Francis Joins the WACS *(1954).*
†*Rudolph Maté (1898–1964) was a Polish-born cinematographer who worked with Alexander Korda, Karl Freund, Carl Theodor Dreyer and Erich Pommer in Europe, before he went to Hollywood in 1935 as a cinematographer. He turned to directing in 1947.*
‡*Interview on the DVD of* 3 Nuts in Search of a Bolt.
***Phone interview with the author, May 23, 2006.*

they signed up Honolulu-born baritone Alfred Apaka,* known as "The Golden Voice of Hawaii," and Tani Marsh† and her dancing partner, Ben Chapman,‡ as well as her dance troupe.

Chapman recalled, "Tani and I were performing at the Islander Room in the Roosevelt Hotel on Hollywood Boulevard when she came in one night and said there were people coming from Universal Studios to look at us. They were doing a musical short for the Miss Universe girls. After the show they told us to come down to the studio the next day because they liked what they saw. They told me they were going to bring back tropical movies for me.

"Jon Hall, who made all those movies with Maria Montez, was my cousin and I'd already appeared as a dancer in one musical at MGM, *Pagan Love Song*, as Rita Moreno's boy friend. I joined the Marines and fought in Korea before I came back to California and resumed my dancing career. That's when the Universal scouts saw me and Tani.

"They signed me to a year contract but their South Sea Island movies never did take off and when my time was up they let me go. Before they did, though, I was lucky enough to be hanging around the studio when they cast me as the Gill Man in *Creature from the Black Lagoon*.

"Tani and I remained good friends. She had made a few movies before *Hawaiian Nights* and made a couple more after but neither of us made it big in films."**

Yankee Pasha • Universal-International, 1954

Forbidden Morocco ... ruled by a Yankee adventurer! Every thrilling moment of the great best seller!

CREDITS: *Director:* Joseph Pevney; *Producer:* Howard Christie; *Screenplay:* Joseph Hoffman, based on the novel by Edison Marshall; *Musical Direction:* Joseph Gershenson; *Music:* Hans J. Salter; *Photography:* Carl Guthrie; *Technicolor Color Advisor:* William Fritzche; *Film Editor:* Virgil Vogel; *Art Direction:* Bernard Herzbrun, Eric Orbom; *Set Decorations:* Russell A. Gausman; *Costumes:* Rosemary Odell; *Hair Stylist:* Joan St. Oegger; *Makeup:* Bud Westmore; *Assistant Director:* Joseph E. Kenny; CinemaScope; Technicolor; 84 minutes.

CAST: Jeff Chandler (*Jason Starbuck*); Rhonda Fleming (*Roxana*); Mamie Van Doren (*Lilith*); Lee J. Cobb (*Sultan*); Bart Roberts [Rex Reason] (*Omar Id-Din*); Hal March (*Hassan Serdar*); Tudor Owen (*Elias Derby*); Arthur Space (*Richard O'Brien*); Benny Rubin (*Zimil*); Phil Van Zandt (*Baidu Sa'id*); Harry Lauter (*Dick Bailey*); John Day (*First Mate Miller*); The Miss Universe Beauties: Christiane Martel (Miss Universe), Myrna Hansen (Miss United States), Kinuko Ito (Miss Japan), Emita Arosemena (Miss Panama), Synove Gulbrandsen (Miss Norway), Alicia Ibanez (Miss Uruguay), Ingrid Mills (Miss South Africa), Maxine Morgan (Miss Australia) (*Harem Girls*); *Uncredited*: Forbes Murray (*Roxana's Father*); Dan White (*Fur Trader*); John Barrie; Robert Bice; Harry Clexx; Louise Colombet; Mara Corday; Joan Danton; Bert Davidson; Marla English; Warren Farlow; Wayne A. Farlow; Lisa Gaye; Jean Hartelle; Jimmy Hawkins; Bob Hopkins;

---

*Alfred Aholo Apaka (1919–60) was a singer and recording artist who got his professional break when hired by orchestra leader Don McDiarmid Sr. A huge star on the Hawaiian hotel club circuit, he also tried his hand with Ray Kinney at New York's Hotel Lexington. Back in Hawaii he was "discovered" by Bob Hope who took him to Hollywood to appear on his TV show. He also made several appearances on *The Ed Sullivan Show* (1957). *Hawaiian Nights* was his one foray into movies.

†*Tani Marsh appeared as a dancer in *Song of the Islands*, *The Mad Doctor of Market Street* (both 1942), and *Sailor Beware* (1952). Her cinema career was over after *From Hell It Came* (1957) and *Blue Hawaii* (1961).

‡*Ben Chapman was born in California in 1925 and brought up in Tahiti by his Tahitian parents before he moved back to California in 1940. His 6'5" height made him the ideal candidate to play Universal's famed Gill Man in the iconic *Creature from the Black Lagoon* (1954); he is the on-land Gill Man to Ricou Browning's underwater Gill Man. Ben still does movie conventions and attends screenings with his *Creature* co-star and "love interest" Julie Adams (then billed as Julia Adams). He finished his feature film career with *Ma and Pa Kettle in Waikiki* (1955) and *Jungle Moon Men* (1955).

**Phone interview with the author, June 3, 2006.

Slave girl Lilith (Mamie) shows off a Rosemary Odell–designed harem costume in *Yankee Pasha* (Universal, 1954).

Donald Kerr; Henri Letondal; Alfred Linder; Mari Lynn; Matt Moore; Barry Norton; Carl O'Bryan; Eddie Parker; John Phillips; Ray Quinn; Lorin Raker; Allan Ray; Harry Tyler; Michael Vallon; Mel Welles.

PLOT: Fur trapper Jason Starbuck rides into 1800 Salem, Massachusetts looking for a new life and new adventure, and falls in love with the already promised Roxana. She is committed to marrying the town bully to please her father. Starbuck returns to the wilderness and Roxana, who has broken her engagement, sails for Marseilles with her father to escape the malicious gossip. Starbuck hears of Roxana's change of heart and goes after her only to discover she has been abducted and taken as a slave to Morocco.

Through the U.S. consul there, Starbuck is introduced as a marksman who can instruct the sultan's troops in the art of rapid arms firing and reloading in 15 seconds on a horse. Warlord Omar Id-Din is antagonistic to Starbuck as he has designs on usurping the sultan's throne. But Starbuck's skill wins the day and he moves into quarters in the palace and ingratiates himself further with the sultan by adopting Muslim customs and dress, although not the religion itself. He is assigned slave girl Lilith to be his companion.

News of Starbuck's advancement reaches Roxana, who is being held in Omar's harem. Learning of her whereabouts, Starbuck engineers a duel between himself and Omar, the prize being the other's slave girl. Starbuck wins but spares Omar's life. Roxana meets Lilith and a catfight for supremacy ensues. However, in the heat of battle, Roxana reveals the truth of her relationship with Starbuck and Lilith runs off to warn Omar of the treachery. Starbuck, who has organized passage on an American ship, sees Omar's men taking Roxana away.

Lilith begs Starbuck to forgive her and vows to undo the harm even if it means losing Starbuck (a pretty safe bet considering she's never had him in the first place). She goes to Omar's and trades places with Roxana. But in rescuing her, Starbuck's horse is shot out from under him and he's taken prisoner. There is only one punishment: death; the sultan reluctantly must apply the law equally to all. Starbuck is to be thrown from the castle wall onto sharp protruding hooks, a task which Omar has offered to handle personally.

Starbuck and other western prisoners free themselves from Omar's dungeon as Roxana arrives with Hassan, the sultan's troop commander, and some of his men. In the melee, Starbuck and Omar fight it out on the castle battlements and, to no one's surprise, Omar falls and is impaled on the deadly spikes.

Starbuck and Roxana are chased to the harbor, where they board the American ship. Hassan persuades the sultan that Starbuck should be pardoned for ridding him of the conspirator, Omar. The sultan is placated and allows the ship to leave the harbor unharmed — but as punishment Hassan is gifted with the talkative slave girl, Lilith.

NOTES: Mamie was third billed, below the title, after screen testing for the role against Mari Blanchard and Lisa Gaye, Debra Paget's sister. This big budget (for Universal) western-cum-swashbuckler, the studio's first in CinemaScope, starred one of its most bankable actors, Jeff Chandler. Chandler was joined by the beautiful Rhonda Fleming and Mamie plus a bevy of Miss Universe finalists, including Miss Universe herself, Christiane Martel. The beauty contestants, many of whom spoke little English, were used as harem background while Mamie and Rhonda slugged it out, literally, for the affections of strapping fur trapper-adventurer Chandler.

Mamie had reason to remember the catfight. "Movie fights are elaborately choreographed so that no one will get hurt. [Joseph] Pevney,* the director, blocked out the fight for us, and the stunt coordinator carefully rehearsed

---

Joseph Pevney (1911–), was an underrated Universal director who helmed a number of solid films including Meet Danny Wilson *(1952),* Flesh and Fury *(1952),* Six Bridges to Cross *(1955),* Away All Boats *(1956), and* Tammy and the Bachelor *(1957). He later turned to television, working on major series such as* Wagon Train, Bonanza, Marcus Welby M.D., The Alfred Hitchcock Hour, Star Trek, Fantasy Island *and* Trapper John M.D.

our movements. During the fight, Rhonda was to hit me, sending me sprawling across the bed. When the cameras rolled and the fight started, everything worked as it was supposed to— until the end. Rhonda's punch was supposed to miss me by a comfortable margin. The camera angle would make it look like her fist had landed squarely on my jaw. When the moment came, though, she landed a solid right cross."*

Based on the best-selling novel by Edison Marshall,[†] *Yankee Pasha* was Mamie's second major role on screen and her first in period costume. Studio designer Rosemary Odell[‡] did her proud in a series of harem pants, mainly in shades of yellow and rose, which highlighted Mamie's coloring and beauty. Mamie did balk at the hypocrisy of the screen's moral code which decreed women's navels be covered. "Of course men had no trouble baring their chest and navel in movies, like Jeff Chandler did in *Yankee Pasha*. My harem costume, though, had pants that covered my belly button in case it got some man excited so much he'd go out and violate the nearest woman."**

She was exhausted by the grueling six-days-a-week schedule over eight weeks on the Universal back lot and found that not only was she plagued with fatigue but that more disastrously she was losing weight — and she was losing her trademark figure. She took her problem to the costume department, who padded her bra — the first and last time she would ever do so on screen.

The film's subliminal message, that commonest of Hollywood themes, "there's no place like home," reinforced by the incipient anti–Muslim racism and the use of Arab stereotypes, was lost in the confusion of genres: what begins as a western becomes a pirate movie before moving into Arabian Nights territory. The portrayal of the Moroccan characters (the majority are Christian-hating fascists who lord it over women and use them as chattels for exchange or else as sex slaves) are as distasteful today as early screen depictions of African-Americans or Native Americans.

Considering the villainy of Omar Id-Din (Bart Roberts), it's ludicrous that Rhonda Fleming's Roxana is permitted to reject his advances; perhaps stereotyping Omar as a rapist or woman murderer was one stereotype too far even for Hollywood. Rex Reason, then billed as Bart Roberts, who played Omar, remembers Mamie as "a vivacious young starlet, with a good personality" and "perfect for the role."[††]

When Starbuck asks if Roxana is still alive in Morocco, he is told: "If so, it would be kinder to accept her as dead than to think she is a slave in Islam." And the U.S. Consul tells him when he arrives in Morocco: "The sultan considers all non-believers his subjects and his slaves. There are no free Christians in Morocco."

Although Rhonda Fleming had the lion's share of the scenes and the love interest, Mamie is superb in her comic characterization. Ms. Fleming has fond memories of her: "In working with Mamie (and Jeff Chandler) in *Yankee Pasha* (not one of our best, I'm afraid, but we had fun), she played a slave girl to the king and I was abducted from a ship and brought to the palace against my will. She was quite a little fighter on the jealousy fight scenes and we had a lot of tumbling and hair pulling. She played the role very well in spite of it not being a very complimentary role for her, but I enjoyed working with her. She was very pretty and a hard worker — knew her lines and was always on time — lots of energy!"[‡‡]

Mamie's headstrong harem sex slave, who is more than happy to have been assigned to Chandler's strapping Starbuck, has a fatal flaw: she doesn't know when to be quiet.

---

*Phone interview with the author, May 26, 2006.
[†]Other films based on novels by Edison Marshall (1894–1967) include Shadows of the North (1929), Son of Fury (1942), and The Vikings (1958).
[‡]A year later, Rosemary Odell (1924–92) designed the costumes for another Mamie vehicle, Ain't Misbehavin'.
**Phone interview with the author, March 25, 2006.
[††]Letter to the author.
[‡‡]Email to the author, September 30, 2005.

Lilith (Mamie) attempts unsuccessfully to have her master, Jason Starbuck (Jeff Chandler), make love to her in *Yankee Pasha* (Universal, 1954).

(*On being presented to Starbuck and having given him the once-over*)

LILITH: I'll obey your every word. I am by nature timid and silent and will not worry you with much idle talk as would other women. I will look after all your wants so all your wishes will be gratified before the words have even been spoken. All my days I will make offerings to our sovereign for having presented me to a master such as you. I feared you'd be so old that I'd have to aid you to your couch, or so ugly that I could not bear to look at you. Ah, truly a happy kismet has answered my prayers.

And later, after Starbuck has cursed her for her constant prattle:

LILITH: Truly an evil genie has cursed me so that my master regards me as a witch. And yet I can prove I have not the witch's mark. (*Reveals her naked back to Starbuck*) Look well, master; do you see the witch's mark?

STARBUCK: I see only a back that would tempt the devil.

LILITH: My master is too kind to his slave.

Even Roxana is keen to point out her fault.

(*Lilith laughs when Roxana is first introduced to Starbuck's harem*)

LILITH: So this is the moon of beauty for whom my master fought a great duel. You are but fit for cleaning his stable and hauling his wood.

* * *

(*Lilith starts ordering Roxana around*)

LILITH: I was here first. I am the mistress of this household. Do not forget that.

ROXANA: You may think so. If it pleases you.

LILITH: It is so and it will be so! And I will see to it that I remain in his favor since I've been well versed in the art of pleasing a man in a variety of ways. I can dance. I can sing. I can...

ROXANA: Evidently the one art you are best versed in is cackling.

If *Yankee Pasha* was no more than adequate Saturday-afternoon adventure hokum, it did give Mamie a chance to shine as a screen beauty and as a consummate comedy actress, and garnered her some of the best reviews she was ever to receive. But although *Yankee Pasha* looked spectacular with its widescreen Technicolor, outstanding costume design, and atmospheric music from an uncredited Henry Mancini, its ludicrous 1001 Nights plot did not prove a hit with the moviegoing public. It grossed a meager $1.25 million in the U.S.

REVIEWS: "Most of the fun results from surprising Mamie Van Doren, a real cutie in harem garb, who portrays a very loquacious slave girl given to Chandler by the Sultan. The American wants no part of her and her efforts to win his attentions, which include incessant chattering, gets several laughs." John L. Scott, *The Los Angeles Times*

"It's not much of a show, being shy of story merit and reasonably credible action and performances ... Edison Marshall's swashbuckling novel had a lot more punch in print than it does on the screen ... Mamie Van Doren, U's Monroe-ish blonde curve-pitcher, stirs up some chuckles as a talkative harem slave." *Variety*, March 17, 1954

"A long and obviously fabricated tale fanciful enough to turn Scheherazade green with envy." A. H. Weiler, *New York Times*

"Big surprise is Mamie Van Doren, who is excellent as a loquacious slave girl whose incessant chatter makes ownership of her a punishment. She also looks gorgeous in the flimsy, eye-popping costumes of Rosemary Odell." *The Hollywood Reporter*

"The action yarn takes on quite a lively air as Jeff [Chandler] meets every challenge to 'big man' his way among pirates and villains ... Worthy support is offered by Lee J. Cobb as the Sultan, Bart Roberts as a villain, Mamie Van Doren as a gabby slave girl, Phil Van Zandt as a slave dealer." Sara Hamilton, *Los Angeles Examiner*

"Studio-bound hokum..." *Halliwell's Film & Video Guide 2000*

"The gimmick of this production-line escapist fare was having dashing (silent but strong) hero Jeff Chandler surrounded not only by shapely Rhonda Fleming and Mamie Van Doren, but by a harem filled with finalists from the Miss Universe contest. The trappings may have been exotic, but the caliber of everything else in the picture was standard fare." James Robert Parish, *Pirates and Seafaring Swashbucklers on the Hollywood Screen*

"An adaptation of Edison Marshall's sex-in-the-sand novel which scenarist Joseph Hoffman cut and re-stitched in order to conform to the studio's highly profitable series of desert adventures.... Dotted around the harem was a bevy of Miss Universe finalists ... but they all paled into insignificance compared with Miss Fleming, in whom Technicolor brought out the very best. Sex of a more flagrant sort was represented by Mamie Van Doren as a loquacious slave girl." Clive Hirschhorn, *The Universal Story*

Francis Joins the WACS • Universal-International, 1954

"What trick is there in talking? Any fool can do it."—Francis the Talking Mule

CREDITS: *Director:* Arthur Lubin; *Producer:* Ted Richmond; *Script:* Devery Freeman and James B. Allardice, *Story by* Herbert Baker, *Additional Dialogue:* Dorothy Reid [Davenport]; *based on the characters created by* David Stern; *Music Supervisor:* Joseph Gershenson; *Photography:* Irving Glassberg; *Editors:* Ted J. Kent, Russell Schoengarth; *Art Direction:* Alexander Golitzen, Robert Clatworthy; *Set Decorators:* Russell A. Gausman, Oliver Emert; *Makeup:* Bud Westmore; *Hair:* Joan St. Oegger; *Special Photography:* David S. Horsley; *Assistant Director:* John Sherwood; *Sound:* Leslie I. Carey, Glenn E. Anderson; *Technical Advisor:* Lane Carlson, Major, W.A.C.; B&W; 95 minutes.

SONGS: "Women's Army Corps Song" (Jane Douglass, Camilla Mays Frank) *Women's Choir (Over opening and end credits)*; "Francis Joins the WACS" (Britt Wood, George Beatty; Frederick Herbert) *Chill Wills*; "She'll Be Comin' Round the Mountain" (Traditional, based on the Negro spiritual "When the Char-

Mamie and her best friend, Francis the Talking Mule, pose for a publicity shot for *Francis Joins the WACS* (Universal, 1954).

iot Comes," composer-lyricist unknown) *Mamie Van Doren, Donald O'Connor*

CAST: Donald O'Connor (*Peter Stirling*); Julia [Julie] Adams (*Capt. Jane Parker*); Chill Wills (*Gen. Kaye/voice of Francis*); Mamie Van Doren (*Corporal Bunky Hilstrom*); Lynn Bari (*Maj. Louise Simpson*); Zasu Pitts (*Lt. Valerie Humpert*); Francis, the Talking Mule; Joan Shawlee (*Sgt. Kipp*); Allison Hayes (*Lt. Dickson*); Mara Corday (*Kate*); Karen Kadler (*Marge*); Elsie Holmes (*Bessie*); Olan Soule (*Capt. Creavy*); Anthony Radecki (*Aide*); *Uncredited*: William Phipps, Richard Deems (*Jeep Drivers*); Charles Lane (*Reporter*); Patti McKay (*Lt. Burke*); Joel Allen; Dan Barton; Bobette Bentley; Henry Blair; Lyle Bond; Robert Bray; Rye Butler; John Close; James Coffey; Kathleen Dennis; Frances Farwell; Anthony Garcen; Phil Garris; Richard Grant; Robert Haines; Michael Hall; Ed Haskett; Bonnie Henjum; James Hyland; Mitchell Kowall; Paul Kruger; Harold Lockwood; Herbert Lytton; Muriel Mansell; Danna McGraw; Tyler McVey; Carl O'Bryan; Voltaire Perkins; John Phillips; Jeanne Shores; Barbara Smith; Jeanne Tatum; Rusty Wescoatt; Stuart Wilson; Sam Woody; Lynn Wright.

VIDEO: MCA Universal Home Video

PLOT: Army Reserve Officer Peter Stirling works in a bank but a glitch in the Pentagon's "classification machine" calls him up for duty in the WACs (the Women's Army Corps). At Fort Chase they are expecting female camouflage expert, Bunny Stirling, not Peter Stirling, and he manages to rile up Captain Parker, his commanding officer, with his sexist attitude about women in the military. In revenge, she assigns him WAC officer duties until his transfer comes through.

Through a series of misunderstandings on his first night at the base, Stirling is thought to be a pervert and is paraded before Major Simpson, who has read his record and is gobsmacked by his 27 incarcerations in neuro-psychiatric detention. She tells him not to pull any of that "mule hanky panky." Naturally, his old friend Francis, the Talking Mule, also arrives at the base, as does his psychiatric nurse from his days in Burma, Lieutenant Valerie Humpert.

Stirling is assigned to the demoralized Second Platoon but the top brass thinks he has been sent to spy on the WACs because of a forthcoming exercise against General Kaye's male troops. Through a series of tough assignments, Stirling comes to admire the women's skills as soldiers and is won over though his motives are still questioned. Stirling is locked up (on the eve of the great WACs White Army vs. General Kaye's Blue Army exercise) for saying that Francis stole a strategic map and memorized it. He is busted out the next morning by Captain Parker abetted by Lt. Humpert.

With Francis imitating the general's voice and Stirling in the field, the women win the day with just minutes to spare. General Kaye loses his voice just before he is to deliver a speech to a live TV audience and the well-hidden Francis does the honors, praising the WACs. General Kaye blows his top and wants the mule court-martialed. The film ends happily with General Kaye himself incarcerated in the psychiatric ward, finger painting while Stirling and Francis watch him from outside a window.

NOTES: Mamie is fourth-billed in the fifth of seven Francis movies* based on the popular satire of army incompetence, *Francis the Talking Mule* (1949) by David Stern.[†] The initial outing in the series, *Francis* (1950), was a runaway success for Universal, earning $3 million in the domestic market on a budget of around $150,000. So, in the tradition of "when

---

*The six movies are Francis *(1950)*, Francis Goes to the Races *(1951)*, Francis Goes to West Point *(1952)*, Francis Covers the Big Town *(1953)*, Francis Joins the WACS *(1954)*, Francis in the Navy *(1955)* and Francis in the Haunted House *(1956)*. Francis also made an appearance, albeit animated, in the 1954 UPA Gerald McBoing Boing short How Now Boing Boing *with a voice by Marvin Miller (who more famously supplied the voice of Robby the Robot in 1956's* Forbidden Planet*).*

[†]*David Stern (1909–2003) adapted his novel for the first of the Francis movies and co-wrote the second,* Francis Goes to the Races, *with Oscar Brodney from a story by Robert Arthur. He went on to write additional dialogue for* Rhubarb *(1951) and the screenplay for* Swamp Women *(1955). Stern also co-wrote, with Frank Thomas, a syndicated comic strip,* Francis, the Famous Talking Mule, *which was illustrated by Cliff Rogerson through 1952 53.*

you're onto a good thing milk it to death," the saga of the smart-talking, superior-brained mule, Francis, and his intellectually lightweight sidekick, Lt. Peter Stirling, continued. The Francis series, along with the Ma and Pa Kettle franchise,* kept Universal's coffers filled and kept the Universal stock company of actors in steady employment even though most shuddered at the thought of appearing in them.†

As Mamie remembers: "The *Francis* movies were something that contract players at Universal were expected to do, but were regarded by all of us as a pain. I counted myself as lucky to have had to appear in only one of them. But, faced with the prospect of Francis the Talking Mule or Ma and Pa Kettle, I would choose that oat-burning leading man every time. Of course, Francis was *really* a female because the censors would not allow a mule's cock on screen, effectively upstaging *everyone*."‡

Donald O'Connor, whose hapless Peter Stirling was one of the joys of the series, tired of playing second fiddle to a Talking Mule as his career outside Universal was full-steaming ahead with top drawer vehicles such as *Singin' in the Rain* (1952) and *Call Me Madam* (1953). When his contract with Universal expired he gladly handed the mule's reins over to Mickey Rooney, who played reporter David Prescott. According to O'Connor, after six movies the mule still received more fan mail than he did. However, O'Connor wasn't free of his four-footed friend even then. In 1980, by which time his film career was in decline, he announced plans to bring the mule in from pasture for *Francis Goes to Washington*. It never eventuated.

Mamie remembers O'Connor with fondness: "I enjoyed kissing Donald O'Connor, he was sweet. We remained friends and kept in touch."**

Director Arthur Lubin,†† who helmed all but the final in the *Francis* series, was a much underrated jobbing director with whom Mamie got on well. "Arthur Lubin liked me and was very creative in dreaming up extra little scenes for me to do. And, yes, he made sure there were plenty of handsome young men everywhere."‡‡

After *Francis* was retired, Lubin, still not finished with the concept, jumped species and medium and created television's popular talking horse *Mister Ed*. There were 143 episodes (1961–66) on CBS with Alan Young as the harassed dumb friend of the superior quadruped.

As an attack on male chauvinism, *Francis Joins the WACS* was two steps forward and one step back. While it purported to show the ingenuity and skill of women military personnel, it also took great pains to show WACS as

---

Ma (Marjorie Main) and Pa (Percy Kilbride) Kettle began life as supporting characters in The Egg and I *(1947) from Betty MacDonald's popular novel. Their spin-off franchise began with* Ma and Pa Kettle *(1949) and followed with annual installments:* Ma and Pa Kettle Go to Town *(1950),* Ma and Pa Kettle Back on the Farm *(1951),* Ma and Pa Kettle at the Fair *(1952),* Ma and Pa Kettle on Vacation *(1953), and* Ma and Pa Kettle at Waikiki *(1955). After Kilbride left the series,* The Kettles in the Ozarks *(1956) featured Arthur Hunnicutt as Pa's brother, Sedgewick Kettle, and* The Kettles on Old MacDonald's Farm *(1957) co-starred as Parker Fennelly as Pa. Old MacDonald's Farm was not only the last of the Kettles series but also Marjorie Main's final big screen outing.*

†*The Universal charm school trainees who appeared in the* Francis *series included Patricia Medina, Tony Curtis, Mikel Conrad in* Francis *(1950); Piper Laurie in* Francis Goes to the Races *(1951); Lori Nelson and Gregg Palmer in* Francis Goes to West Point *(1952); Yvette Duguay in* Francis Covers the Big Town *(1953); Mamie, Mara Corday and Julie [then Julia] Adams in* Francis Joins the WACS *(1954); and Martha Hyer, David Janssen, Clint Eastwood in* Francis in the Navy *(1955). By the final, and weakest, entry,* Francis in the Haunted House *(1956), Donald O'Connor as Peter Stirling and Chill Wills as the voice of Francis had deserted to be replaced by Mickey Rooney and Paul Frees, respectively.*

‡*Email to the author, November 8, 2002.*

**Ibid.

††*Arthur Lubin (1898–1995) brought out the best in Abbott & Costello in* Buck Privates *(1941),* Ride 'em Cowboy *(1942),* Keep 'em Flying *(1941),* Hold That Ghost *(1941), and* In the Navy *(1941), as well as helming the Nelson Eddy* Phantom of the Opera *(1943),* The Spider Woman Strikes Back *(1946),* New Orleans *(1947), and* Rhubarb *(1951).*

‡‡*Email to the author, November 8, 2002.*

sexily clad and as attractively proportioned as possible. But even though the film's "message" is that WACs are the equal of men and should be taken seriously as a fighting force, there is a wry "nudge nudge wink wink" that the women need a man (no matter how incompetent) or, better yet, a mule to get them across the line. Of course, subversively, the same duo also defeated the cream of the men's army. But this is reading too much into what is essentially light entertainment.

Mamie has little to do as Universal contract player Julie (then Julia) Adams is given the major share of screen time. One of the film's highlight's in Mamie, dressed in a flour sack, sistered to Donald O'Connor as a pair of yokels who warble their way through "She'll Be Comin' Round the Mountain" as the opposition Blue Army advances. Not surprisingly, even a flour sack looks good on Mamie.

REVIEWS: "Donald O'Connor and his loquacious friend, Francis the Talking Mule, are back for another laugh session ... The box office outlook is good, since the same type of amusing screwball comedy that has characterized the series is put forth slickly in this one ... O'Connor, Wills, the Misses Adams, Bari, Mamie Van Doren and ZaSu Pitts ... plus the other casters all deliver slickly to point the Ted Richmond production for a favorable reaction from the ticket buyers." *Variety,* July 7, 1954

"Francis ... stands head and withers above mere man, which includes the film's director, Arthur Lubin ... Francis, to be frank, is far more intelligent than the humans in the film. He outthinks, outplots and generally runs their show, from planning military operations to playing matchmaker. All the while he is sneering contemptuously. That animal is, to be truthful, a veritable Machiavelli with hocks..." *New York Times,* July 31, 1954

"As usual, the script ... gave the quadruped all the best lines ... [E]nsuring a steady ripple of laughter throughout was director Arthur Lubin." Clive Hirschhorn, *The Universal Story*

Mamie salutes Universal for teaming her with their cash mule, Francis, in a publicity shot for *Francis Joins the WACS* (Universal, 1954).

Ain't Misbehavin' • Universal-International, 1955

It's got that M-M-M-MAMBO! ... and that M-M-MAMIE!

CREDITS: *Director:* Edward Buzzell; *Producer:* Samuel Marx; *Screenplay:* Edward Buzzell, Philip Rapp and Devery Freeman, *Based on the story* "Third Girl from the Right" *by* Robert Carson; *Musical Supervision:* Joseph Gershenson; *Music (uncredited):* Frank Skinner, Henry Mancini; *Vocal Arrangements:* Johnnie Scott;

Choreography: Kenny Williams and Lee Scott; *Photography:* Wilfrid M. Cline; *Technicolor Color Consultant:* William Fritzsche; *Film Editor:* Paul Weatherwax; *Art Direction:* Alexander Golitzen, Alfred Sweeney; *Set Decorations:* Russell A. Gausman, Ruby R. Levitt; *Gowns:* Rosemary Odell; *Makeup:* Bud Westmore; *Hair Stylist:* Joan St. Oegger; *Sound:* Leslie I. Carey, John A. Bolger, Jr.; *Assistant Director:* Frank Shaw; Technicolor; 82 minutes.

SONGS: "The Dixie Mambo" (Sonny Burke; Charles Henderson) *Piper Laurie, Dani Crayne, Mamie Van Doren, chorus;* "A Little Love Can Go a Long, Long Way" (Sammy Fain, Paul Francis Webster) *Piper Laurie; reprised on piano at Nob Hill Party;* "I Love That Rickey Tickey Tickey" (Johnnie Scott; Sammy Cahn) *Piper Laurie, Dani Crayne, Mamie Van Doren, chorus;* "Ain't Misbehavin'"* (Thomas Waller, Harry Brooks, Andy Razaf) *Piper Laurie*

CAST: Rory Calhoun (*Kenneth Post III*); Piper Laurie (*Sarah Hatfield*); Jack Carson (*Harold North*); Mamie Van Doren (*Jackie*); Reginald Gardiner (*Piermont Rogers*); Barbara Britton (*Pat*); Dani Crayne (*Millie*); Carl Post (*Andre Banet*); Roger Etienne (*Corbini*); Harris Brown (*Randall*); Isabel Randolph (*Mrs. Moffit*); George Givot (*Native Boatman*); Peter Mamakos (*Andy*); *Uncredited:* Wilbur Mack, Voltaire Perkins, Peggy Leon (*Board Members*); Franz Roehn (*Mr. Zukerman*); Alexander Campbell (*Mr. Moffitt*); Jameson Shade (*Pop*); Nan Leslie (*Photographer*); Russell Gaige (*Henry Lamont*); Donald Kerr (*Fan at Ball Game*); Jerry Riggio (*Luigi*); William Forrest (*Mr. Dellaby*); Mary Bayless (*Mrs. Dellaby*); Sara Taft (*Mrs. Beaton*); Madge Blake (*Mrs. Grier*); Carlyle Mitchell (*Mr. Hall*); Jack Mower (*Husband*); Paul Thierry (*Maitre d'*); Frank Chase, William Murphy (*Sailors*); Joseph Mell (*Vendor at Ball Game*); Helen Spring (*Lady Next to Sarah*); Jane Buchanan (*Mrs. Carlson*); Lela Bliss (*Mrs. Hanover-Burke*); Lillian Culver (*Mrs. Hall*); Jack Daly (*Gardener*); Don Dillaway (*Mr. Warden*); Jean Fenwick (*Wife*); Bess Flowers (*Mrs. Grier's Friend*); Margaret Irving (*Mrs. Grumbacher*); Beth Marion (*Woman with Feather*); Madelon Mitchell (*Mrs. Warden*); Veronica Pataky (*Mrs. James*); Isabel Randolph (*Matron*); Gloria Ann Simpson (*Mrs. Hudson*); Elizabeth Slifer (*Mrs. Keys*); Dick Ryan (*Mr. Hicks*); Barry Norton, Sam Harris, Gail Bonney (*Dancers*); Lisa Gaye (*Chorus Girl*); Leslie Turner; Harte Wayne; Mack Williams; Jeane Wood; Jack Baston; Ella Ethridge; Lynn Malcolm; Norman Stevans.

PLOT: Post Enterprises has a finger in just about every money-making business in San Francisco, and head man Kenneth Post III has settled down to a life of corporate conformity after years of having a ringside table at every nightclub in America. But every now and then the raffish itch gets the better of him. He sees Sarah Hatfield and her two chorus girl roommates entertaining at the Rowdy Club via a new invention which anticipates Digital Television, and sets out to employ her for the company's new advertising campaign. There are suspicions on both sides initially, especially from Ken's cynical minder, Harold North, who believes Sarah only wants to get her hands on Ken's millions. But they fall in love and marry. Sarah falls victim to snobbishness and attempts a Pygmalion transformation from brassy showgirl to Nob Hill philanthropist with the help of the dissipated Piermont Rogers. Sarah's continual humiliation at the hands of Ken's intended fiancée, Pat, spurs her on to acquire the trappings of sophistication while simultaneously estranging the affections of her husband who married her for her down-to-earth quality.

The marriage's irrevocable breakdown leads to separation and a trip to Reno to get a divorce. Sarah, realizing she still loves Ken, flees to the Rowdy Club knowing Ken will pursue her and a happy reunion is a definite prospect.

NOTES: Mamie is fourth-billed above the title in this clichéd rich-boy (Calhoun)-meets-

---

*One of the 20th century's iconic songs, "Ain't Misbehavin'" was written by (Thomas) Fats Waller (1904–43) and Andy Razaf (1895–1973) and was used for the title of the Broadway jukebox musical based on the music of Waller which catapulted Nell Carter to stardom and a Tony Award.

Title lobby card for *Ain't Misbehavin'* (Universal, 1955) in which Mamie took a back seat to Piper Laurie.

marries-loses-chorus-girl (Laurie) story. She plays one of two chorines (the other is played by Dani Crayne*) with whom said chorus girl shares an apartment. It's a thankless supporting role and Mamie (as well as Dani) disappears from view early in the film but not before she's had a chance to sing, dance and play wisecracking gold digger, Jackie.

The throwaway plot is handled professionally by Piper Laurie and Rory Calhoun. Ms. Laurie is too much the lady to be really convincing as the brassy showgirl, a role that would have fitted Mamie much better. But Mamie gets the lion's share of the comic lines: When Sarah returns from her date with the mysterious Ken, she's asked "So, how was fat and 50?"

SARAH: Slender and 30 and very good-looking and you know how I was, I was so cute I couldn't stand myself.

JACKIE: Didn't he even kiss you goodnight?

SARAH: Of course he kissed me. He was a perfect gentleman.

JACKIE: Oh. A gentleman who's rich is as perfect as he can get.

But Mamie is merely chorus not only to the musical numbers but also to the general plot. Scripted from a story by Robert Carson, it is not on a par with his best work, the story and screenplay for the 1937 classic *A Star Is*

Dani Crayne (1934–) was signed up by Universal when she was "discovered" giving mambo lessons at a Hollywood dance school; Ain't Misbehavin' became her debut film. Gossip columnists linked her romantically with a fellow Universal-International contractee, the then closeted gay actor George Nader. Crayne married a series of high-profile industry members: Buddy Greco, David Janssen, and Hal Needham. Her last screen appearance was as Helen of Troy in The Story of Mankind *(1957). Her movie career lasted a meager two years.*

Jackie (Mamie) and Millie (Dani Crayne) pump their roommate Sarah (Piper Laurie) for gossip after her first date with Kenneth Post III (Rory Calhoun) in *Ain't Misbehavin'* (1955).

Born. Edward Buzzell co-wrote the screenplay with Devery Freeman and Philip Rapp and directed with the same sure hand with which he guided the earlier musicals *Honolulu* (1939), *Ship Ahoy* (1942) and *Neptune's Daughter* (1949). TV-standard choreography was by the head of Universal's dance department Kenny Williams and Lee Scott. That Mamie's character is not only a golddigger but a bubblehead is revealed when she wanders off at the Nob Hill party with disreputable Piermont Rogers, who promises her a job as model; she comes back fuming after he tried to take her measurements but didn't even have a tape. Good joke but inconsistent characterization. This is the sort of role that Mamie could do with her eyes closed but which was stereotyping her.

REVIEWS: "Up and coming hopefuls in the film arts have to cut their milk teeth somewhere, and *Ain't Misbehavin'* is the type of zwieback on which they chew.... The story line ... flits frantically about the place and never goes anywhere.... It's a forced, joyless thing that director Edward Buzzell has wrought. All surface and no distinction. The music is tired and the dances are flaccid repetitions of hundreds of other movie dances." *New York Times*, July 2, 1955

"Pleasant musical fluff..." *Leonard Maltin's Movie & Video Guide*

"Lively American version of *Pygmalion*, with musical numbers and some bright lines." *Halliwell's Film & Video Guide*

"A musical that rested on the oh-so-familiar cliché beloved of musicals in which a rich young man falls in love with a chorus girl..." Clive Hirschhorn, *The Universal Story*

"Frothy musical with likeable cast ... Many sprightly tunes lift average story line from the mediocre ... [P]roduction numbers [feature] a lot of hip-swinging from Laurie, Van Doren and Dani Crayne..." *Motion Picture Guide*

"A lightweight bit of musical comedy fluff that should prove mildly diverting escapism, and is peopled with such likeable cast toppers as Rory Calhoun, Piper Laurie, Jack Carson and Mamie Van Doren, who helps keep it going on a reasonably pleasant course ...Songs and terps are handled acceptably by Miss Laurie and the others, but sight appeal is the stronger asset." *Variety*

"A story with music, rather than a musical, but this time it is the story that sparkles, the music that seems irrelevant. That such a tired plot has yielded so much humor is due to some entertaining dialogue, delivered with considerable zest by piquant Piper Laurie. Jack Carson is endearingly himself, and Reginald Gardiner contributes an expertly timed study in cynical decay." *Film Index #7*

The Second Greatest Sex • Universal-International, 1955

The saga of those hilarious Kansas brawls set to singin' ... dancin' ... and mad, mad music! The boys were after the girls! The girls were after the boys! And both of them were after the same darn thing!

CREDITS: *Director:* George Marshall; *Producer:* Albert J. Cohen; *Written by:* Charles Hoffman; *Musical Supervision:* Joseph Gershenson; *Choreography:* Lee Scott and (uncredited) Jack Harmon, Lucille Lamaar; *Photography:* Wilfrid M. Cline; *Technicolor Color Consultant:* William Fritzsche; *Film Editor:* Frank Gross; *Art Direction:* Alexander Golitzen, Robert Clatworthy; *Set Decorations:* Russell A. Gausman, John P. Austin; *Costumes:* Jay A. Morley, Jr.; *Hair Stylist:* Joan St. Oegger; *Makeup:* Bud Westmore; *Sound:* Leslie I. Carey, Glenn E. Anderson; *Special Photography:* Clifford Stine; *Assistant Director:* William Holland; CinemaScope; Technicolor; 87 minutes.

SONGS: "What Good Is a Woman without a Man" (Pony Sherrell, Phil Moody) *Jeanne Crain,* Edna Skinner, Kitty Kallen, Mamie Van Doren, Mary Marlo, Women Townsfolk*; "Travelin' Man" (Pony Sherrell, Phil Moody) *Paul Gilbert, danced by Tommy Rall, Ward Ellis*; "My Love Is Yours" (Pony Sherrell, Phil Moody) *George Nader*†; "There's Gonna Be a Wedding" (Phil Moody; Pony Sherrell) *Bert Lahr, Mary Marlo, Sharon Bell, Edna Skinner, Jimmy Boyd*; "Down Yonder" (Gilbert) Danced by *The Midwesterners*; "What Good Is a Woman without a Man/Travelin' Man" (Pony Sherrell, Phil Moody) *Edna Skinner, Paul Gilbert*; "How Lonely Can I Get?" (Joan Whitney, Alex Kramer) *Kitty Kallen, danced by Tommy Rall*; "Send Us a Miracle" (Pony Sherrell, Phil Moody) *Keith Andes, Chorus*; "Lysistrata" (Pony Sherrell, Phil Moody) *Jeanne Crain, Edna Skinner, Mamie Van Doren, Kitty Kallen, Kathleen Case*; "The Second Greatest Sex" (Jay Livingston, Ray Evans) *Bert Lahr, Men Townsfolk*; "The Second Greatest Sex" (Jay Livingston, Ray Evans) Sung over the End Credits, *Singers Uncredited*

Jeanne Crain (*Liza McClure*); George Nader (*Matt Davis*); Kitty Kallen (*Katy Connors*); Bert Lahr (*Job McClure*); Paul Gilbert (*Roscoe Dobbs*); Keith Andes (*Rev. Maxwell*); Mamie Van Doren (*Birdie Snyder*); Tommy Rall (*Alf Connors*); Kathleen Case (*Tilda Bean*); Jimmy Boyd (*Newt McClure*); Edna Skinner (*Cassie Slater*); Cousin Emmy [Cynthia May Carver] (*Cousin Emmy*); Ward Ellis (*Zachary Bean*); Mary Marlo (*Sarah McClure*); Sheb Wooley (*Jones City Leader*); George Wallace (*Simon Clegghorn*); Harry Harvey ("*Doc*" *Grimshaw*); Sharon Bell (*Sally McClure*); The Midwesterners (*Square Dancers*).

PLOT: The town of Osawkie, Kansas, 1880, is a veritable man-free zone because the

---

**Jeanne Crain's singing voice was dubbed by Doreen Tryden, who also supplied the (uncredited) singing voice for Jo Ann Page in* Kismet *(1944), Donna Reed in* The Picture of Dorian Gray *(1945), Yvonne De Carlo in* Frontier Gal *(1945), and Angela Lansbury in* The Hoodlum Saint *(1946).*

†*Some sources credit George Nader's singing voice to Bill Lee (1916–80), who also supplied the (uncredited) singing voice for Tom Drake in* Words and Music *(1948), Matt Mattox in* Seven Brides for Seven Brothers *(1954), and Christopher Plummer in* The Sound of Music *(1965) as well as supplying the singing on a number of animated features including* Alice in Wonderland *(1951),* One Hundred and One Dalmatians *(1961), and* Hey There, It's Yogi Bear *(1964).*

Jackie (Mamie) flirts with old drunk Piermont Rogers (Reginald Gardiner), who promises her a modeling job in *Ain't Misbehavin'* (Universal, 1955).

husbands, sons, and boyfriends are all off attempting to wrest control of a small metal safe containing the county records, ballots and voting lists, as well as land grants from Washington, which mandate that the town possessing them is the lawful county seat. The towns of Osawkie, Mandaroon and Jones City are all vying for the rights to be the county seat and have been feuding for years. Osawkie is triumphant and it looks as if the County War is at

Beautiful Belgian poster for *Greve d'Amour,* also known as *The Second Greatest Sex* (Universal, 1955).

an end and Liza sets the date for her wedding to Matt Davis, something she has been reluctant to do because his passions have been elsewhere: with the safe. But on their wedding night the safe is stolen before Matt can consummate the marriage and he and the menfolk of the town head off to retrieve it, leaving the women frustrated and angry.

Liza has had enough and introduces the eligible women to the concept espoused in *Lysistrata*, the ancient Greek play by Aristophanes, in which the female population withheld conjugal couplings from their soldier spouses until peace was declared. To this end the women barricade themselves in an abandoned fort outside town. The men return despondent over the loss of the safe, which sank to the bottom of the river and the women are about to return home. But Matt then reveals the County War is not over as they can retrieve the safe when the level of the river falls. The men are thrown out of the fort and told their conjugal "rights" will be restored when they put in writing that they won't fight over the safe any more.

At the river, another melee ensues and the safe rolls down the bank into quicksand. Realizing the war is over, the men head back to the fort with a flag of truce. The women from all three warring factions won't open the gate until the men put it in writing that the conflict is over. The men of Mandaroon and Jones City threaten violence until Liza tells them that they certainly can drag the women away but that there's no power on Earth can make a woman love a man. Liza tells them of her idea of the three towns sharing the county seat. The men reluctantly agree.

Amongst the general rejoicing and flurry of new weddings, Matt and Liza go back to their cabin and rush inside. The camera remains primly outside as we hear the scramble for the bedroom and the consummation of the marriage.

NOTES: Mamie is seventh billed, below the title, as Birdie Snyder in this neglected B musical. Universal lavished Technicolor and CinemaScope, as well as a slew of popular singers, comedians and stalwarts of the Universal back lot, on Charles Hoffman's amusing but somewhat clichéd script, an updated and westernized version of Aristophanes' classic Greek play, *Lysistrata*.[*] It was one of their most expensive productions to that date.

Directed by veteran George Marshall,[†] Mamie is, once again, in dumb blonde mode, although she has a number of good lines as she woos reluctant town preacher Keith Andes.

(*Birdie examining the shipment of satin that has arrived for Liza's wedding dress*)

BIRDIE: Oh, if I had a white satin wedding dress, I'd never take it off.

(*Looking at Rev. Maxwell*)

Well, hardly ever. When are you going to set the day, Liza?

LIZA: There's ... there's plenty of time, Birdie.

BIRDIE: (*Opening a box she has received*)
I hope it's soon so I can wear my high button shoes with the French heels.

(*Holding them up*)

They came all the way from Paris.

(*Coquettishly*)

If you'll pardon the expression, Reverend Maxwell.

But this being the Wild West she is cosseted and corseted from neck to ankle in "period" costumes flatteringly and eye-poppingly designed by Jay A. Morley Jr., who would again dress her to good effect in another western, *Star in the Dust*, a year later.

When the man of her dreams is about to head out with the posse after the elusive safe:

BIRDIE: Be careful, Reverend Maxwell

REV. MAXWELL: The good Lord will watch over us, Miss Snyder, but I do appreciate your interest.

BIRDIE: *You do?!?* I'll remember that always. Even if I live to be 30.

---

[*]*The final play in Aristophanes' War and Peace trilogy, first produced in 411 B.C., tells the story of Lysistrata, leader of the women of Athens, who persuades them and the women of the other states of Hellas to withhold sexual favors from their men (it says nothing about lesbians) until they end their 21 years of war.*

[†]*George Marshall (1891–1975) began his career in the silent era and ended his prolific, artistic career on television. In between he helmed such classics as* Destry Rides Again *(1939) and* The Blue Dahlia *(1946), as well as another underrated 1950s musical,* Red Garters *(1954).*

And Birdie has something in common with most of the characters Mamie played: an overwhelming desire for love or, at the very least, a man.

(*Liza is rousing the women of the town to put Aristophanes' play into practice by going to the old Indian Fort outside town*)
LIZA: And we'll barricade ourselves in and the men out until they come to their senses.
BIRDIE: I don't want the Reverend Maxwell to come to his senses. I want him to come to *me*.

While Mamie does play a dumb blonde she manages to invest her non sequiturs with a warmth that imbues Birdie with charm and vulnerability.

(*The women are holed up in the fort when the men arrive with a flag of truce*)
LIZA: What did I tell you? And with a flag of truce.
(*Looking through a telescope, Cassie sees the flag of truce is a pair of bloomers*)
CASSIE: Hey, it's an unmentionable.
(*Birdie grabs the telescope and has a look*)
BIRDIE: I wondered what had happened to them.
KATY: It's working, Liza, it's working.
LIZA: Of course it's working. If it worked for the women of Greece, why wouldn't it work for the women of Kansas?
BIRDIE: For a while I was losing my faith in history.

Against a stellar array of actors Mamie is memorable, not only for her exquisite looks enhanced by the coloring of her costumes, particularly the startling initial yellow dress, but the delivery of her lines. Although she has no solo number, she does get to join the chorus of man-deprived townswomen, including the dubbed Jeanne Crain, Kitty Kallen, Cousin

Pitching horseshoes: Publicity photograph of Edna Skinner, Kitty Kallen, Mamie, and Kathleen Case for *The Second Greatest Sex* (Universal, 1955).

Mamie shows off her legs and her costume for the musical western *The Second Greatest Sex* (Universal, 1955).

Emmy, and Edna Skinner, on two songs: the plaintive "What Good Is a Woman without a Man" and "Lysistrata."

Every conceivable cliché has been thrown into the western pot: the bespectacled spinster schoolteacher with the dowdy clothes to match the dowdy life, the priapic traveling salesman, the sexually naïve boy on the verge of puberty, the smart-mouthed younger sister, the stoic ma and pa double, and the butch, strutting Calamity Jane wannabe. Scripter Charles Hoffman unabashedly milks the stereotypical characters and manages to come up with a rollicking sex farce set in the Wild West — albeit a milksop sort of Wild West. There's not a gun to be seen anywhere, battles are played out with fists, and in this pre–*Brokeback Mountain* era, all the men are red-blooded heterosexuals. Ironic, then, that the male lead is played by gay George Nader,* and that none of the love-deprived women turn to their sisters for Sapphic fulfillment.

There's a rich vein of misogyny running through the film. For example, when the safe goes missing again and the men are barred from sex with the women, they do the only "masculine" thing they can, they get drunk. And as they wallow in self-pity, Pa McClure serenades them in song about men being "the second greatest sex." Tellingly, Reverend Maxwell doesn't join in the chorus. The next morning Newt arrives with the news that the river level has dropped and the safe can be recovered. Half the men don't care any more until Matt incants the misogynist's creed: "Well, I'll tell you this. If we give in to them now, the war won't be the only thing that's finished around here. We'll be finished as far as any claim to self-respecting manhood is concerned and every time they snap their fingers we're going to have to jump and like it." The others, naturally, fall in line.

The Second Greatest Sex was Universal's bandwagon-jumping answer to MGM's musical western, *Seven Brides for Seven Brothers* (1954), itself based on a classical tale of the rape of the Sabine women, Warner Bros' *Calamity Jane* (1953), and Paramount's *Red Garters* (1954). The title song, supplied Jay Livingston and Ray Evans,[†] was not among their best work although Kitty Kallen[‡] released it as a 45. The main body of songs was from Pony Sherrell and Phil Moody. Keith Andes's "Send Us a Miracle" is stirring and 'Travelin' Man" memorable for Paul Gilbert's energetic rendition. Kitty Kallen's beautiful solo "How Lonely Can I Get?" was an interpolation from Joan Whitney and Alex Kramer.

What the four western musicals of the period shared was a strong-willed female central character. What *The Second Greatest Sex* excelled in was the dancing. The lively sequences, choreographed by Lee Scott, who had already worked with Mamie on *Ain't Misbehavin'* (1955) and would later do the honors on *Las Vegas Hillbillys* (1966), were high points of the film. Scott was blessed to have two spectacular dancers in Tommy Rall, who brought his energetic style over from *Seven Brides* and had appeared to good effect alongside Bob Fosse in *Kiss Me, Kate* (1953), and Ward Ellis, who would go on to create high-energy routines for television variety shows as well as supply the choreography for Mamie in *3 Nuts in Search of a Bolt*.

George Nader (1921–2002) was a Universal beefcake star who toiled in the shadow of his more highly promoted studio brethren, particularly Rock Hudson (with whom he was linked romantically), Jeff Chandler and Tony Curtis. His early work included the cult sci-fi "classic" Robot Monster (1953) before he hit his stride in superior product such as Six Bridges to Cross (1955) and Away All Boats (1956). As his career faded he turned to TV and later moved to Europe, where he was successful as FBI agent, Jerry Cotton, in a series of West German films. He retired in 1974 and took up writing, his most famous novel being the gay science fiction novel Chrome (1978). His partner, Mark Miller, was Rock Hudson's personal secretary for more than a decade.

†Prolific songwriters Evans (1915–) and Livingston (1915–2001) had three Academy Award–winning songs: "Buttons and Bows" from The Paleface (1948), "Mona Lisa" from Captain Carey, U.S.A. (1950), and "Que Sera Sera" from The Man Who Knew Too Much (1956). They were also nominated for a Tony Award for their Broadway musical Oh, Captain! (1958) starring Tony Randall.

‡Kitty Kallen (1921–) had started out with the big bands of Jack Teagarden, Jan Savitt, Jimmy Dorsey and Harry James, before a solo career which included the million sellers "Little Things Mean a Lot" and "In the Chapel in the Moonlight," both 1954.

With Rall, Ellis and The Midwesterners, the dance routines in *The Second Greatest Sex* are standout scenes; only Rall's drunken dance with a mannequin is somewhat perfunctory.

Also in the cast were a plethora of popular singers of the era: Kitty Kallen making her one big screen feature appearance, Sheb Wooley,* best remembered for his monster smash hit song "The Purple People Eater" which he wrote and recorded in 1958, and Jimmy Boyd,† who had a pop hit with "Tell Me a Story" dueting with Frankie Laine. Keith Andes had a beautiful baritone voice that served him well on stage in *The Chocolate Soldier* (1947) and later opposite Lucille Ball on Broadway in *Wildcat* (1960), but as a member of the Universal charm school he was shoehorned into the beefcake mold that included Jeff Chandler, George Nader and Tony Curtis. It came as a surprise to many that he could sing although he never appeared in another musical. Cousin Emmy,‡ known as "the first hillbilly to own a Cadillac," is wasted in a thankless role.

Rounding out the singing cast is Bert Lahr, whose hiatus from Hollywood had ended the year before with another western musical, *Rose Marie*. For that he was told he would have to ride a horse. According to his son John Lahr,

Birdie Snyder (Mamie) sits with other dejected womenfolk of the town devoid of men (they're off fighting in the County wars) in *The Second Greatest Sex* (Universal, 1955).

*Sheb Wooley (1921–2003) had a long career in film (especially westerns) beginning with Rocky Mountain *(1950)* and encompassing High Noon *(1952)* and the teleseries Rawhide.
†Jimmy Boyd (1939–) appeared in Platinum High School *(1960)*, High Time *(1960)*, Inherit the Wind *(1960)* and Norwood *(1970)* before finding a home on the TV series The Electric Company *from 1971–77*.
‡Cynthia May Carver (1903–80) billed herself as Cousin Emmy in a number of musical westerns including Swing in the Saddle *(1944)* and Under Western Skies *(1945)* and was a folk and blues singer of renown.

Bert replied: "Riding? I get dizzy sitting on a foot stool. I don't want to get on one of those things. I don't know how to steer 'em." But the studio insisted. "When I got to the back lot, the cowboy in charge kept me on the horse for a full two hours. Well, I have a fear of heights, you know. When I got off, I could hardly walk. I came home and my posterior was completely raw from saddle sores."* The next day he told director Mervyn LeRoy: "I can't get up on a horse. The only way I'll do it is if you get me foam rubber and put Malibu tights on me so I can sit on the horse without getting sore." Lahr became the first member of the Canadian Mounted Police to have foam-rubber underwear. The experience must have been to his liking as there is no sign of discomfort in *The Second Greatest Sex* in which he spends a fair amount of time in the saddle.

But if it was more comfortable for Lahr, it was much less so for Mamie who was feeling unwell each morning when she reported for work. When she started bleeding on the set, she went to her doctor and was told she'd had a miscarriage. At that time she was seeing bandleader Ray Anthony: "The miscarriage itself did not leave a lasting impression on me. But afterward, the potential consequences of the pregnancy frightened me. Pregnancy, even more than marriage, and particularly pregnancy *without* marriage, was a surefire way to screw up one's future at U-I. I couldn't afford it. Ray would have to do what my other lovers had done — wear a rubber."†

REVIEWS: "What Aristophanes started 2,400 odd years ago with *Lysistrata*, Universal has now finished in grand style in its *The Second Greatest Sex*, a gay, carefree musical with all 'round appeal. In color and CinemaScope, it's an ambitious production that looks good for a hefty payoff. Film is actually a western operetta, with the accent on songs, dancing and the kind of home-spun humor that should go over big particularly in the smaller situations. Production by Albert J. Cohen benefits from a budget splurge (this is one of U's most expensive undertakings) and a well-kept balance of action vs. music which keeps things rolling along at a merry clip ... [The dancing is] plenty lively and the production numbers come through with strong impact ... Mamie Van Doren as the blonde who has her sights set on the Rev. Peter Maxwell, played by Keith Andes, is cute and attractive. Period costumes don't exactly hide her figure." *Variety,* October 5, 1955

"In a light, rollicking comedy-with-music, Jeanne Crain and George Nader duet appealingly ... But the featherweight plot is less important than the gay songs and dances and the romances, teaming Jeanne with George, coquette Mamie Van Doren with preacher Keith Andes, canary Kitty Kallen with hoofer Tommy Rall, spinster Edna Skinner with travelin' man Paul Gilbert." *Photoplay,* January 1956

"It might not be a classic. But it's fun — with some mighty fine, lively songs and dances all done up in CinemaScope and color..." *New York Times,* February 1, 1956

"On the whole only moderately entertaining, it offered some first-class acrobatic dancing ... and a lively cast..." Clire Hirschhorn, *The Universal Story*

"A tuneful, toe-tapping, entertaining musical with a western setting. The stars ... acquit themselves well." Gene Blottner, *Universal-International Westerns*

Running Wild • Universal-International, 1955 [*aka* The Girl in the Cage]

The Stark Brutal Truth About Today's Lost Generation!

CREDITS: *Director:* Abner Biberman; *Producer:* Howard Pine; *Screenplay:* Leo Townsend, from a novel by Ben Benson; *Music Supervision:* Joseph Gershenson; *Photography:* Ellis W. Carter; *Film Editors:* Edward Curtiss, Ray Snyder; *Art Direction:* Alexander Golitzen, Robert Boyle; *Set Decorations:* Russell A. Gausman, John P. Austin; *Costumes:* Bill Thomas; *Hair Stylist:* Joan St. Oegger; *Makeup:* Bud Westmore; *Sound:* Leslie I. Carey, John Kean;

---

*John Lahr, Notes on a Cowardly Lion: The Biography of Bert Lahr.
†Mamie Van Doren, Playing the Field, 115.

Assistant Director: George Lollier; B&W; 81 minutes.

SONG: "Razzle Dazzle" (Charles Calhoun) *Bill Haley and the Comets.*

CAST: William Campbell (*Ralph Barton*); Mamie Van Doren (*Irma*); Keenan Wynn (*Ken Osanger*); Kathleen Case (*Leta Novak*); Jan Merlin (*Scotty Cluett*); John Saxon (*Vince Pomeroy*); Walter Coy (*Lt. Newpole*); Grace [Grayce] Mills (*Osanger's Mother*); Chris Randall (*Arkie Nodecker*); Michael Fox (*Delmar Graves*); Will J. White (*State Trooper*); Richard Castle (*Herbie*); Otto Waldis (*Leta's Father*); Sumner Williams (*Monty*); William Boyett; Pat Cortland; Leo Curley; Johnny Duncan; Tim Johnson; Karen Kadler; Dorothy Martinson; Helen Mayon; June McCall; Jerry Mickelsen; Ken Miller; Jacqueline Park; Nancy Quinn; Felice Richmond; Lennie Smith; Lou Southern; Robert Williams.

PLOT: Tough guy Ralph Barclay blows into town and hustles for a job as a mechanic at Ken Osanger's garage, making hired help Scotty Cluett suspicious. At The Cove, a soda fountain for the "fast" crowd, he meets flirtatious Irma and Osanger's morose girlfriend Leta. Ralph deliberately picks a fight with Scotty and is taken away by the police. Back at the station it's revealed that Ralph is an undercover cop trying to infiltrate a network of car thieves. Ralph's subterfuge is further helped when a nervous young car thief, Vince, thinks he recognizes him from somewhere bad, and Ralph helps him escape suspicion for an attempted car theft in The Cove's car park. Osanger offers him a mechanic's job at the garage

Irma (Mamie) tries to seduce new boy in town Ralph Barton (William Campbell), little realizing he is an undercover cop in *Running Wild* (Universal, 1955).

and on his first day on the job Vince turns up and reveals he knows Ralph is a cop and wants to cut a deal to get out of the racket. He asks Ralph to meet him that night but, not surprisingly, Vince turns up dead.

The chink in Osanger's armor is Leta; Barclay is ordered by the police hierarchy to work on her to get her to spill the beans. Ralph meets Leta's dad who has lapses of memory because of his incarceration in a Polish concentration camp. Leta reveals she stays with Osanger only because he's blackmailing her with the knowledge that her father is in the country illegally.

Ralph is invited along on a car heist and is taken to Osanger's farm where he is shown the car drop in the barn. Scotty catches him phoning the police and they shoot it out inside the house; Scotty is killed. Osanger escapes the police net and Ralph stays to guard Leta's house believing Osanger will return to exact revenge. Five nights later he turns up, hidden in the back of a TV antenna van, breaches security and catches Leta and Ralph. In the subsequent shoot-out Ralph is hit and Osanger is killed. At the hospital it's revealed Leta and her father have moved to the city, she has a good job, and the governor has personally petitioned Congress to allow Leta's father to stay. Now all Leta needs is a good man: Ralph.

NOTES: On a darkened and near-deserted street, a man emerges from a shop and after locking the door gets into his car as an elderly woman crosses the road with her groceries. She drops them and the Good Samaritan gets out of his car to help. A thief jumps into his vehicle and drives off after running down the car's owner. His body is thrown onto the pavement. The old woman watches as the stolen car disappears. She hurries away seemingly in shock, leaving the man's sprawled body and her groceries. Much later the audience will be introduced to the criminal old lady as Osanger's mother who is involved in the stolen car racket and who is as venal as her son.

With its eerie black-and-white photography and the driving beat of title music, *Running Wild* gets off to an explosive start and never lets up. A little later, in a wrong-side-of-the-tracks soda fountain (this is the '50s after all and even bad guys didn't drink underage), Mamie's first words are "Hey, flip that Haley comet's Razzle Dazzle," and then explodes in a jitterbug before being flung across the counter, head back, bullet bra standing at attention. So hot was the dancing that Universal issued a set of black-and-white stills of the dance routine featuring Mamie and her partner, Lou Southern. Rock 'n' roll and Mamie Van Doren were a marriage made in Hollywood heaven.

As Andrew Dowdy wrote: "Mamie was gum chewing, hip talking, and city tough. Beginning with *Running Wild* (1955) the rock and delinquency cycles fused in a series of strange pictures in which Mamie faced a cruel world armed mostly with a body she had learned to use the way a hunter uses a steel trap."*

All this in a project she thought initially was a step down from her previous films. For a start it was in black-and-white. Secondly, she would be the "bad" girl, the predatory girlfriend of car thief Scotty Cluett (Jan Merlin), who delights in being the cause of fistfights. Here Mamie meets hedonism head on. The actress and the character collide and there followed a series of variations on a theme. Mamie would carve out a niche for herself in roles that are as distinctive to her as the tough women of Bette Davis or the brittle virgins of Annette Funicello.

In some respects Irma is Susie Ward, her character in *All American*, gone wild. And a role model to ape. Mamie is hedonism personified but she never falls pregnant, rarely smokes and rarely drinks alcohol. She's the purest bad girl around. What Irma is after is a good time and if that means being involved with a car thief, then so be it.

But Irma has little in the way of redeeming features. Apart from tears over the body of her dead boyfriend, Mamie never lets any humanity shine through Irma's armor of brazen opportunism. With her ponytail and jeans and her rocket-shaped breasts, Mamie becomes a beacon for adolescent (and not-so-adolescent)

Movies Are Better Than Ever: Wide-Screen Memories of the Fifties, 198–99.

fantasies. *Running Wild* was to be Universal's answer to the success of *Blackboard Jungle* which was sending shock waves through the community because of its then-perceived-realistic portrayal of juvenile unrest and its use of Bill Haley's "Rock Around the Clock" on the soundtrack. It was a clarion call to disenchanted young filmgoers, and Universal, like all astute studios, wanted teenagers' money.

William Campbell plays the undercover cop with just the right combination of swagger and sneer and with a little more realism than the later variation by Russ Tamblyn in *High School Confidential!* It was his first starring role at Universal and he found Mamie to be "a doll, and she was tough.... She was a sensational person.

"She had a great bod, and she had dimples. She was more beautiful than any of the Marilyn Monroe pretenders... But Mamie had a better body than Marilyn. The difference between Van Doren and Monroe is that Van Doren was nobody's fool. Mamie knew exactly where she was with everybody. She knew what she was about, and she was a lot of fun to be around."*

The movie was based on a novel, *The Girl in the Cage*, by Ben Benson† who had created an anti-hero cop figure, Ralph Lindsey, for a series of crime thrillers. Lindsey, whose name was changed to Ralph Barclay for this film, is a member of the Massachusetts State Police. Marvin Lachman describes Benson's style and the personality of Lindsey: "Benson was especially good at depicting young people, and the immaturity and vulnerability of his rookie State trooper, Ralph Lindsey, adds to the interest of this series. He is quick to lose his temper and become emotionally involved with suspects.... He is occasionally rebellious against authority.... But he is always brave and dedicated, willingly posing as a juvenile delinquent in *The Girl in the Cage* to get evidence against a brutal young gang."‡ For *Running Wild*, Ralph not only had a change of name but a change of location (to California) and a change of status.

Leo Townsend, who cut his teeth on Deanna Durbin films and late in his career penned vehicles for Annette Funicello, filled the script with sharp, cynical dialogue.

For instance, when Ralph turns up at Osanger's Garage looking for work as a mechanic:

OSANGER: What are you asking?
RALPH: Eighty-five a week.
OSANGER: I get guys for sixty-five and they kiss me for it.
RALPH: I get eighty-five. No kissin'.

Later at the boarding house, when the landlady is fussing about showing Ralph the room:

LANDLADY: You'll like this room, it's one of my nicest. View and all. It's real homey once you get settled.
RALPH: How much?
(*She is sizing him up*)
I said, how much?
LANDLADY: Only ten a week and the bathroom's right across the hall. Oh, I don't often have such a nice room vacant.
RALPH: Must be my lucky day. I'll give you six.
LANDLADY: Why, you've never seen a room like this for six dollars.
RALPH: I've never seen a room like this period. Okay, I'll make it eight.
LANDLADY: Well, okay, but there's some rules. No cooking in the rooms and no girls.
RALPH: I can't cook.
LANDLADY: And no girls.
RALPH: Look, I just got into town. I don't know any girls.
LANDLADY: (*She knows his type*)
Humph. You will.
RALPH: Oh, that's nice. Where would a guy go to meet them?
LANDLADY: Well, there's a nice soda fountain on Main Street, right next to the movie house.
RALPH: That's where they live it up around here? At a soda fountain?

---

*William Campbell, Filmfax #74
†Ben Benson (1915–59) was creator of crime series characters Trooper Ralph Lindsey and Det. Inspector Wade Paris. His novels include *Alibi at Dusk* (1951), *Lily in Her Coffin* (1952), *The Silver Cobweb* (1955), *The Affair of the Exotic Dancer* (1958), *and* The Blonde in Black *(1958).*
‡*Twentieth-Century Crime and Mystery Writers*, edited by John M. Reilly, St. Martin's Press, New York, 1980.

Irma (Mamie) in a wild dance sequence in *Running Wild* (Universal, 1955).

LANDLADY: Well, there's a place outside town called The Cove but it's an awfully fast crowd that goes there.
RALPH: Let's say, like Scotty Cluett and his crowd?
LANDLADY: You know Scotty Cluett?
RALPH: Yeah, met him at Osanger's. Might go to work there
LANDLADY: (*With finality*) The room will be ten dollars.
RALPH: Oh now ...
LANDLADY: In advance!

Later at The Cove, Scotty, Osanger's head mechanic, precipitates a fight with Ralph by goading him:

SCOTTY: Hi ya, hot rod.
RALPH: Hi.
IRMA: Who's hot rod?
SCOTTY: He's a rough, tough mechanic from the big city. Very rough and very tough.
OSANGER: He sure don't like you, does he, Ralph? (*Offering Ralph a drink*) Have a suck.
RALPH: No, no. I got a malt working at the fountain.
SCOTTY: Malted milk. You drink it straight or with a straw?
(*Ralph walks away*)
IRMA: That's kind of an insult. You'd think he'd kind of resent it.
SCOTTY: Yeah, but hot rod's kind of chicken.

On another occasion at The Cove, Irma makes a play for Ralph, who begs off. She's not to be dissuaded. "When I want something, I want it now," she pouts. When Scotty intervenes she walks away, blaming Ralph for the attempted pick-up. Irma's a girl interested only in instant gratification. And Mamie plays her to the hilt.

Abner Biberman was the ideal director for the material and he gives the film a gritty immediacy which made him a natural to go on to helm some of the most popular television series of the '60s (*The Twilight Zone*, *Ben Casey* and *The Outer Limits*). On *Running Wild* he is aided immeasurably by the crisp, atmospheric photography of Ellis W. Carter. The supporting cast which included Keenan Wynn as Osanger and Kathleen Case, who had appeared in the earlier Mamie vehicle *The Second Greatest Sex*, as Leta, added class to this superior B film. And Grace Mills was a forbidding Mrs. Osanger. A young John Saxon played Vince.

Jan Merlin, who played tough guy Scotty Cluett, remembers: "It was among the earliest films I made at Universal Studios in the middle of the last century, and Mamie Van Doren was another upcoming 'Marilyn Monroe type' Hollywood bombshell. At the time we worked in the film, I believe she was married to handsome Ray Anthony, the well-known orchestra leader.

"The only amusing recollection I have of that film engagement took place during a late night shoot on the back lot hills of Universal, a cold and damp location, even in summer. A number of us had small, comfortably furnished trailers in which to relax during the long hours spent up there. Between setups and filming brief scenes, Mamie suddenly had a yen for a pizza. She asked Ray, who was visiting the set, to get one, and he reluctantly drove his sporty topless convertible off the lot to hunt for a pizza parlor. Mamie retired to her cozy trailer to wait, while many of us hung about to chat with her, no doubt expecting to share a warm slice upon his return.

"Ray was gone for a great length of time, and when the poor guy returned with a large box of pizza, he was roundly scolded by Mamie for bringing back a barely tepid one. I wondered where he found any place open in the Valley area after midnight, and was sorry for the poor devil. Mamie and Ray were a nice-looking couple. But like many celebrity marriages, theirs wasn't to last."*

Adhering to the adage that a little hyperbole never hurt anyone, let alone the box office receipts, the radio ad campaign proclaimed: "*Running Wild* will jolt you with an explosion of teenage terror — the story of organized juvenile gangs; the hot car racket they run; the wanton murders they commit; and the girls who run wild in a jukebox jungle ruled by rock 'n' roll rhythms." In some cities the film went out on a double bill with *Tarantula*.

REVIEWS: "Howard Pine production makes use of a rock 'n' roll type of musical background to further enhance juve appeal. Several jukebox hot spot scenes are also in keeping. Cast capably performs what is asked of it by Abner Biberman's direction ... Abetting the overall youthful tone are Mamie Van Doren, tough blonde girl friend of equally tough Jan Merlin, Wynn's right-hand man." *Variety*, November 2, 1955

"In this mild melodrama are some rock 'n' roll numbers (featuring Mamie Van Doren) in a jump and jive joint. Notwithstanding Miss Van Doren's tempestuous Terpsichore, the customers at *Running Wild* are more likely to grunt and groan." *New York Times* November 12, 1955

"Aimed largely at the teenage rock 'n' roll market, *Running Wild* was a programmer ... [with a] hand-me-down plot." Clive Hirschhorn, *The Universal Story*

"Though William Campbell turns in an effective performance, this cops-and-robbers yarn isn't likely to give his career much of a boost ... Jan Merlin and, opposite him, Mamie are gang members." *Photoplay*, January 1956

Star in the Dust • Universal-International, 1956

The legend of Bill Jorden who took the short end of the most desperate gamble the West has ever known and staked his courage against the fury of a town — to save it from itself!

CREDITS: *Director:* Charles Haas; *Producer:* Albert Zugsmith; *Screenplay:* Oscar Brodney, *based on the novel* Law Man *by* Lee Leighton; *Music:* Frank Skinner; *Music Supervision:* Joseph Gershenson; *Photography:* John L. Russell Jr.; *Technicolor Color Consultant:* William Fritzsche; *Film Editor:* Ray Snyder; *Art*

---

*Letter to the author, March 24, 2006.

Direction: Alexander Golitzen; Alfred Sweeney; *Set Decorations:* Russell A. Gausman, John P. Austin; *Costumes:* Jay A. Morley Jr.; *Hair Stylist:* Joan St. Oegger; *Makeup:* Bud Westmore; *Sound:* Leslie I. Carey, Corson Jowett; *Assistant Director:* Frank Shaw; Technicolor; 80 minutes.

SONG: "Sam Hall" (Terry Gilkyson, adapted from traditional material) Terry Gilkyson.

CAST: John Agar (*Sheriff Bill Jorden*); Mamie Van Doren (*Ellen Ballard*); Richard Boone (*Sam Hall*); Coleen Gray (*Nelly Mason*); Leif Erickson (*George Ballard*); James Gleason (*Orval Jones*); Randy Stuart (*Nan Hogan*); Terry Gilkyson (*The Music Man*); Paul Fix (*Mike MacNamara*); Harry Morgan (*Lew Hogan*); Stuart Randall (*Jess Ryman*); Robert Osterloh (*Rigdon*); Stanley Andrews (*Ben Smith*); John Day (*Jiggs Larribee*); Stafford Repp (*Leo Roos*); Lewis Martin (*Pastor Harris*); Renny McEvoy (*Timothy Brown*); Jess Kirkpatrick (*Ed Pardee*); James Parnell (*Marv Tremain*); Anthony Jochim (*Doc Quinn*); *Uncredited*: Clint Eastwood (*Tom*); Kenneth MacDonald; Kermit Maynard; Frank Mills; Chuck Hamilton; Jack Ingram; Mike Bataran; Jim Brandt; Scott Lee; Rankin Mansfield; Paul McGuire; Rickey Murray; Erik Nielsen; Stephen Wootton.

PLOT: The town of Gunlock is preparing for the hanging of Sam Hall, found guilty of killing sheepherders who trespassed on cattlemen's land. But the town is tense. The townspeople believe that the man, identity unknown, who hired the gunslinger should also swing. Bets are being taken on whether Hall will hang or be sprung by the cattle barons, led by the town banker, George Ballard, the chief suspect as Hall's employer. Adding to the complications, Sheriff Bill Jorden is engaged to Ballard's sister, Ellen. The town does not believe he is as good a lawman as the previous sheriff, his dad, who would have hanged Hall immediately to save a confrontation. Bill, however, believes in the letter of the law. Sam Hall will hang at sundown and not a moment sooner.

As the day progresses, the town becomes eerily quiet. The farmers are forming a lynch mob to mete out rough justice and the cattlemen are equally determined to spring the killer. Hall has a lover, Nelly, who smuggles two letters from his prison cell. One letter, his contract of employment, offers a

Mamie in her first "conventional" role as a western sheriff's love interest in *Star in the Dust* (Universal, 1956). It was also her last role under contract to the studio.

$1000 bounty for every farmer he kills north of the river. The second is a letter he received during his trial, assuring that even if he is found guilty of the murder of a farmer's boy, he will never hang. The letters are not signed but Hall believes they are from Ballard and tells Nelly to take them to the sheriff if he is not freed by sundown. At Ballard's ranch, Nelly confronts Ellen and Ballard but the banker denies everything. He warns Ellen that it would be preferable for the sheriff to be out of the jailhouse in the afternoon and tells her to lure him away.

The head of the cattlemen, Jeff Ryman, pulls a gun on the sheriff and is locked in the cell next to Sam Hall, who boasts that the man he killed was not on the cattlemen's property but that he shot him south of the river and dragged the body north to claim the reward. Nelly tries to affect a rescue but it goes awry when the town drunk apprehends the escaped killer.

As the death hour approaches, Ballard's handwriting is identified on the incriminating letters and Ellen confronts her brother. In a struggle over his rifle, she is knocked out. The cattlemen burn the gallows but the sheriff decrees that Hall will be hanged from a tree. Ryman steps in to avert a gun battle by revealing Hall's treachery. In the turmoil that follows, Ballard atop a building overlooking the gallows, rifle in hand, is caught up in a life-and-death struggle with Ellen, who has clambered up after him. One of the cattlemen shoots him and he falls to his death. This spooks the horse on which Hall is seated, his neck in the noose. The killer is hanged right on time.

NOTES: This taut psychological western, with a screenplay by studio workhorse Oscar

Demure Mamie played a "good girl" to the town "bad guy" in *Star in the Dust* (Universal, 1956).

Brodney from a novel by award-winning western writer Wayne D. Overholser* under the *nom de plume* Lee Leighton, opens with a lengthy tragicomic set-up.

Close-up of a sign that says: WELCOME TO GUNLOCK. Then close-up of six-shooters and a sheriff's badge and the camera pans back to reveal the sheriff on his bed. Sound of a wagon in the street below. The sheriff gets up and looks out of his hotel window. We watch the wagon come down the street and then the camera pans up to a prisoner behind bars. The wagon is bringing the timber to build his scaffold.

ORVAL: Good a spot as any.
HELPER: Well now, I don't know. I think you ought to move it up the street a mite.
ORVAL: No. Right here. Then the folks from the casino can watch. All right, let's get unloaded boys.
HELPER: Orval, if you ask me this is just a waste of time and money. In the old days we didn't build no scaffolds for no hangin'.
ORVAL: These ain't the old days. Since Bill Jorden's been sheriff, everything's got to be done legally.
HELPER: A tree was good enough for my pappy and I reckon it's good enough for me.

The Music Man wanders on and decides to watch. He sits under a tree and sings the film's exposition. We learn the man in the prison is Sam Hall, who is due to hang at sundown for the killing of three men. The Music Man, played by singer-songwriter Terry Gilkyson,† is an affectation that is used throughout the film to comment on the action. It foreshadows similar characters played by Nat "King" Cole and Stubby Kaye in *Cat Ballou* (1965).

It's a classy opening for a classy film and sets the pace. The laconic, not-to-be-hurried sheriff, is played effectively by John Agar, who made a career out of westerns and B science fiction movies. His nemesis is Sam Hall, a vicious killer who expounds on the virtues of Delmonico's, Shakespeare and cultured things from the East. It's this posture of culture that makes Richard Boone's portrayal so chilling. And, even at the last, as he sits astride his horse, his hands fastened, the hangman's noose around his neck, he refuses the blindfold, saying, "The sun's setting for me, it'd be a shame to miss a minute of it."

Mamie's role as clean-living Ellen Ballard is one of the most conventional she ever played (the others being in *The Big Operator* and *You've Got to Be Smart*). Here she is taking on the Grace Kelly–like role in yet another "answer" film, this time to the Gary Cooper *High Noon* (1952), and she carries it off with aplomb. She looks magnificent strapped into her western bodice designed by Jay A. Morley Jr.,‡ who had done the same for her in her previous western outing, *The Second Greatest Sex*, and stoicism becomes her as well as the gum-chewing and tough-talking teens that were to follow. But Mamie's Ellen is not just a passive western heroine. She actively engages in saving her intended from certain death even if the morality of what she is doing is somewhat awry and even if she must struggle with her own brother atop a two-story building.

Mamie was chosen for the role by producer Albert Zugsmith, who would go on to produce or direct some of Mamie's most enduring films. At this stage, however, he was discouraged by

---

*Wayne D. Overholser (1906–96) was a multiple Golden Spur Award winner from the Western Writers of America. He also wrote as Lee Leighton, John S. Daniels, Mark Morgan, Wayne Roberts, Dan J. Stevens, and Joseph Wayne. He began writing for pulp western magazines before his first novel, Buckaroo's Code, was published in 1948; he won his first Golden Spur Award for Law Man (sometimes given as Lawman), on which Star in the Dust is based, in 1953. He also won Best Novel again the following year under his real name for The Violent Land and in 1969 for Best Juvenile Fiction with Lewis Patten for The Meeker Massacre. Another of his novels was filmed as Cast a Long Shadow (1959) starring Audie Murphy. His novels were noted for their psychological insights and his knowledge of the history and customs of the American frontier, particularly Colorado and Oregon.

†Terry Gilkyson (1916–99) was a successful singer-songwriter probably best known for the Dean Martin hit "Memories Are Made of This" (with Rich Dehr and Frank Miller) as well as a number of songs for Walt Disney movies of the 1960s. His "The Bare Necessities" for The Jungle Book (1967) was Oscar-nominated in the Best Song category.

‡Jay A. Morley Jr. (1918–97). Prolific designer between 1949–57, mainly at Universal, where he turned his skills to films as diverse as The Glenn Miller Story (1954), Abbott & Costello Meet the Keystone Kops (1955) and The Deadly Mantis (1957).

the studio (Universal did not see Mamie as a good girl). But Zugsmith insisted she test for the role and she won it. "I had first met Albert Zugsmith in the Universal commissary," Mamie recalled. "The straightest arrow I have ever known in the movie business, Zuggy was always absolutely candid and truthful in his dealings. And he was far too original for Universal's management. Thankfully he has a nose for what the public wanted *and* he saw possibilities for me that no one else did."*

During the exhausting five-week shoot, Mamie was frantic over her relationship with Ray Anthony, who was going cold on the idea of marriage even though Mamie was several months pregnant and suffering from morning sickness. "I was sick every morning and during the day I was cinched tightly into an eighteen-inch-waist dress by a corset that became my sworn enemy. I would throw up before they laced me into it, then pray that I could keep from throwing up again afterward."†

On the two male leads: "John Agar was very kind, very sweet. He always had a crush on me. Richard Boone was not a very friendly actor. He was very intense and he was one of these types of actors that meditated and would get into the mood [for his role]."‡

Among the other actors who brought their considerable talents to the project were Leif Erickson as Ballard, Paul Fix as the irascible deputy, Coleen Gray as the movie's bad girl Nelly, James Gleason as the gallows humor, and Clint Eastwood in an uncredited stroll-on as a

Sheriff Bill Jorden (John Agar) and Ellen Ballard (Mamie) in Universal's answer to *High Noon*, *Star in the Dust* (1956).

rancher who engages the sheriff in a discussion on the odds of Sam Hall hanging.

REVIEWS: "A superior B Western, this is one of the best of a number of Westerns that set lawmen against the people they were elected to protect...." *The Western: The Arum Film Encyclopedia*

"Action and suspense are mixed in good proportions ... As a western, it fits the bill ... a good script by Oscar Brodney ... Charles Haas' direction works up the varying angles that dress the basic plot, and time is taken to develop an assortment of divergent characters ... Mamie Van Doren, the banker's naïve sister and

---

*Mamie Van Doren, Playing the Field, *124.*
†Ibid., *125.*
‡Being Mamie, *an interview with Mamie on the DVD extras on* Voyage to the Planet of Prehistoric Women.

sheriff's fiancée, is okay..." *Variety*, April 18, 1956

"Intriguing cast is wasted in this trite tale..." *Leonard Maltin's Movie & Video Guide*

"Directed by Charles Haas with a sturdy grip on the material..." Clive Hirschhorn *The Universal Story*

"The entire cast, which includes Clint Eastwood in a bit part, are all satisfactory portraying characters with escalating emotions." *The Motion Picture Guide*

"There's a strong, low-key undercurrent of violence developed by director Charles Hass with satisfactory performances from the supporting cast [Coleen Gray, Harry Morgan, Randy Stuart, Paul Fix, James Gleason]. [E]ven usual film sexpot Mamie Van Doren is creditable. A nice touch is added by street balladeer Terry Gilkyson who keeps adding verses to 'Sam Hall' ... as the film progresses." Boyd Magers, *The Old Corral*

"Interesting, psychological western ... Mamie Van Doren gives an adequate performance as the sister of villain Leif Erickson who is forced to choose between her brother and her lover and almost ruins her chance at happiness." Gene Blottner, *Universal-International Westerns*

Untamed Youth • Warner Bros, 1957

Youth Turned Rock-N-Roll Wild — and the "House of Correction" That Makes 'em Wilder!

CREDITS: *Director:* Howard W. Koch; *Producer:* Aubrey Schenck; *Screenplay:* John C. Higgins, *Story by* Stephen Longstreet; *Music:* Les Baxter; *Choreographer:* Joe Lanza; *Photography:* Carl Guthrie; *Editor:* John F. Schreyer; *Art Director:* Art Loel; *Set Decorator:* Frank Miller; *Makeup Supervisor:* Gordon Bau; *Assistant Director:* Tommy Thompson; *Sound:* Robert B. Lee; B&W; 80 minutes.

SONGS: "Rolling Stone" (Les Baxter, Lenny Adelson) *Mamie Van Doren*; "Cottonpicker"* (Les Baxter) *Eddie Cochran*; "Oobala Baby" (Les Baxter; Lenny Adelson, Eddie Cochran, Jerry Capehart) *Mamie Van Doren*; "Salamander" (Les Baxter) *Mamie Van Doren*; "Go, Go, Calypso" (Les Baxter) *Mamie Van Doren*

CAST: Mamie Van Doren (*Penny Lowe*); Lori Nelson (*Jane Lowe*); John Russell (*Ross Tropp*); Don Burnett (*Bob Steele*); Eddie Cochran (*Bong*); Lurene Tuttle (*Judge Cecilia Steele Tropp*); Yvonne Lime (*Baby*); Jeanne Carmen (*Lillibet*); Robert Foulk (*Sheriff Mitch Bowers*); Wayne Taylor (*Duke*); Jerry Barclay (*Ralph*); Keith Richards; Valerie Reynolds (*Arkie*); Lucita (*Margarita*); Glenn Dixon (*Jack Landis*); Wally Brown (*Pinky, the Cook*); The Hollywood Rock and Rollers; *Uncredited*: Kenner G. Kemp (*Bailiff*); Stanley Andrews, Terry Frost, John Veitch (*Farmers*); Michael Emmet (*Doctor at Hospital*); Alex Montoya (*Morales*); William Henry (*TV Announcer*); Les Baxter; Jim Canino; Leon Tyler.

PLOT: Penny and her sister Jane are hitchhiking their way to Los Angeles to break into big-time show business but are arrested as vagrants by sheriff Mitch Bowers when he catches them naked, cooling off in a lake outside town. Judge Cecile Steele sentences them to 30 days in the county jail or as agricultural workers on a farm to get back "their self respect." The cotton (and potato) farm is run by martinet Russ Tropp as a front for cheap farm labor. The "slave" labor receives 75 cents a day and if anyone attempts to escape the $200 reward for the recapture is deducted from the other laborers' wages. Russ is hoping to corner the labor market to force the other cotton farmers in the area out of business and buy up their farms cheap.

Judge Steele's son, Bob, fresh out of the navy, turns up on the farm, which belonged to his family until his mom sold it. Looking for work, he is taken on as a harvester driver. When local farmers beg Tropp for help to harvest their cotton because of a labor shortage, he demands sixty percent of their crop in exchange for supplying pickers. They have no choice but to comply. Tropp is secretly married to Judge Steele and financed her re-election campaign as well as paying to have an ordi-

---

*The title of the song is variously given as two words but the film credits list it as a one-word title.

Penny (Mamie) sings "Cottonpicker" in the women's dorm on the prison farm in *Untamed Youth* (Warner Bros., 1957).

nance changed so prisoners could be used on his farm.

Tropp invites Penny for a private meeting at the house after the prison farm cook, Pinky, hears her singing and reveals that Tropp has investments in the local TV station and he might find her a job on it. At the same time, Bob is snooping and has discovered that the prison workers are being fed dog food. He arrives in the nick of time to save Penny from Tropp's savage dogs which have been sicced on to her after she spurns his advances and runs from the house.

The poor conditions at the farm are further revealed with the collapse of young inmate, Baby, who is rushed to a hospital but dies of a hemorrhage from a miscarriage brought about by the punishing conditions on the farm. Bob confronts his mother with the activities on the farm but she does not believe him and reveals her relationship with Tropp. Bob tells her about Tropp's attempted assault on Penny. Stung by his infidelity, Judge Steele sends for Jane to confirm what Bob has told her.

Back on the farm, Bob and Margarita overhear a plot by Tropp to employ illegal Mexican labor. They are caught and are about to be bundled across the border to their deaths when Penny and her fellow farm inmates turn up for a showdown. As the stand-off degenerates Judge Steele arrives with Jane; forged permits are found in Tropp's pocket. Judge Steele tells the farm workers to appear in court the next day at which time she will commute sentences to time served and that it will be her last task as a judge. All ends well with Bob and Jane in domestic bliss watching Penny perform on a television variety show.

NOTES: This is one of Mamie's iconic movies and one of her own personal favorites.

It's not hard to see why. Top-billed, below the title, Mamie gets to show off her assets, physical and vocal, in this above-average teen melodrama that fed the paranoiac fantasies of disenfranchised youth. There's not a sympathetic major adult character in this film which opens atmospherically with a rock beat on the soundtrack over the visuals of a male teen runaway zigzagging across dusty fields pursued by two police cars. This gives way, after the credits and the arrest of the escapee, to the titillation of the Lowe sisters, played by Mamie and Lori Nelson skinny-dipping before being apprehended for vagrancy by a leering sheriff. The skinny-dipping is a tease because while the sheriff's attention is distracted the sisters emerge and dress in conspicuous modesty. The real titillation comes later when Mamie, decked out with pony tail and bullet bra, swings her booty like no other major star of the era. To top it all, she has her first musical number on her bunk bed in a slip while removing her stockings and burnishing her legs with them.

The film was part of a two-picture deal Mamie signed with producer-director Howard W. Koch. "I really liked Howard Koch a lot. He was then part of Koch-Schenck Productions. They were just a little production company starting out and he later on, of course, became a big producer in Hollywood and head of Paramount Pictures." But there was a squabble over top billing: Both Mamie and Lori Nelson claimed it. Lori, who had appeared in *All American* (Mamie's first released picture at Universal), was cast as Mamie's younger but more world-savvy sister, Jane. "We had both left Universal and were freelancing, and both of us wound up in this picture," Lori told Marty Baumann. "Howard wanted to give her first billing because she was really a hot item about that time. She wouldn't do it unless she had star billing. I said, 'No. I'm a bigger star than she is.' And he begged and pleaded and begged and pleaded and finally he said, 'Look, I'll give you an extra bonus.' I said, 'No, I don't think so.' He said, 'I'll throw in a TV.' I said, 'Oh, Howard, if you want to that bad, go ahead and do it.' It really didn't make that much difference to me and I got some perks out of it."*

Despite the slight friction over billing, the two actresses sparked off each other in the film. Ms. Nelson brought a maturity to the caring June that contrasted well with Mamie's impulsive and petulant Penny — nowhere better than in the scene in which Penny is keen to visit prison farm boss, Tropp, at his house, to audition for the local TV station in which he has an investment.

JANE: What do you intend to do?
PENNY: Do? Don't be square. I'm going up there and sing his ears out right now.
JANE: Now wait a minute, kid. Let's talk this over.
LILLIBET: Yeah, think about it. He'll probably give you that corny pass about being his housekeeper.
PENNY: At least I'll be out of the fields.
LILLIBET: Yeah, right out of the cotton into a bed of thorns.
JANE: Are you crazy?
PENNY: No. I've got ambition, that's all. Bye, Janie.
JANE: You're not going up there to his house.
PENNY: I certainly am.
JANE: You heard what Lillibet said.
PENNY: Sour grapes. She got tossed out of the nest.
JANE: And what are you? The next candidate?
PENNY: Don't be dirty-minded. Pinky got me this chance and I don't think Mr. Tropp's that kind.
JANE: Wow.
PENNY: I can take care of myself.
JANE: Yes, you can take care of yourself like a kitten can scare off a pack of hounds. Oh, Penny, kid ...
PENNY: (*Stamping her foot*)
Stop calling me kid. I'm older than you and besides...
JANE: Yes, in one way. You were born before I was. Listen, Penny, don't be a sucker. The only way to get a booking is through an agent or a producer or somebody like that. Oh, forget this, will you! Look, we still got our thirty days and then we go on to Hollywood like we planned.
PENNY: You listen. Will you stop trying to keep me under an umbrella? I'm going to make it to the top. I know I've got what it takes and if Mr. Tropp can help get things started, so much the better. You can trust me, Janie. I'm not gonna make any nasty bargains no matter what. When you've got ability, you don't have to.

---

*Baumann, The Astounding B Monster, *158*.

Prison farm boss Tropp (John Russell) gets rough with Penny (Mamie) when she won't "put out" in *Untamed Youth* (Warner Bros., 1957).

JANE: Oh, I trust you, listen, you know that. I trust your intentions but when a sharpie gets to working on you, you never see through it. You think all men are dear little Cub Scouts.
PENNY: That's what you think I think. Well you're not interfering this time.
(*She storms off*)

The screenplay, from film noir stalwart John C. Higgins* from a story by writer-artist Stephen Longstreet,† was punchy and dramatic and played to every stereotype imaginable, especially the random nature of adult law used to curb victimless "criminal" behavior in young adults. But the conditions on Tropp's prison farm look like nothing so much as a retro *Porky's* with peek holes between the boys' and girls' showers and the opportunity for a lot of singing and dancing. Not a bad life if you could put up with the dog food for dinner and the grueling days of back-breaking labor in the cotton fields. But this is a sanitized prison farm: There are no African-American or Hispanic inmates; they were more likely to have been incarcerated in the "big house."

This is a hormone-laden prison that sublimates its sex drive in the throbbing music of rock. The only throbbing organ is that of lecherous boss Tropp, and the one pregnant single mother-to-be is dispatched via terminal hemorrhage in a warning against promiscuity. The film is a tease, a voyeur's delight with Mamie is various states of coy undress and the titillation of peephole fantasy. It's all harmless, disingenuous and loads of fun. If the songs weren't top-of-the-line rock 'n' roll they were serviceable enough and within Mamie's range. Although Eddie Cochran got a mere single number, it was the superior "Cottonpicker" which Mamie tried to persuade the powers-to-be that *she* sing. She lost and was saddled with nonsense like "Oobala Baby" which required the talents of Les Baxter, Lenny Adelson, Eddie Cochran and Jerry Capehart to write. Her best song was "Rollin' Stone. The moviemakers inserted a calypso song as the penultimate production number when Penny appears on TV. Harry Belafonte‡ had made it big in 1956 with the Jamaican folk song "Banana Boat Song" and became the first person to sell over one million copies of an LP, his Capitol album *Calypso*. Anticipating another trend, studios began a calypso cycle which petered out quicker than it began. *Untamed Youth* decided to butter its bread on both sides.

The soft rock songs included in the movie led to a rift in relations between Mamie and Ray Anthony. "He hated it because it was rock 'n' roll. The very thing that was making me successful was ruining his whole scene. He was into that Glenn Miller sound and I really wasn't into that."** What made it more galling for Anthony was Eddie Cochran's turning up at the house to rehearse. But, according to Cochran's son Bobby, it was Jeanne Carmen who was the subject of Eddie's attentions and that during one of the film's dance sequences "they chose to move toward the back of the set. As all the other couples earnestly danced for the camera, Ed and Jeanne did a dance of their own, grinding pelvises for pure pleasure. They didn't care if they wound up with any screen time or not—they were horny, plain and simple, and that took precedence."††

Bobby also admits: "My mom said there

John C. Higgins (1908–95) penned a number of top screenplays in his 37-year career including the film noir classics He Walked by Night *(1948) and* Border Incident *(1949).*

†*Stephen Longstreet (1907–2002) was a highly regarded artist and fiction writer as well as a scriptwriter. His movie scripts include* The Jolson Story *(1946) and* The Helen Morgan Story *(1957) plus* Stallion Road *(1947) and the Errol Flynn starrer* Silver River *(1948), both based on his own novels. His semi-autobiographical novel* The Sisters Liked Them Handsome *was adapted into the Broadway musical* High Button Shoes *(1948).*

‡*Harry Belafonte (1927–), the New York-born singer-actor-activist, was educated in Jamaica and, almost single-handedly, was responsible for the calypso craze that swept the world. He appeared in* John Murray Anderson's Almanac *on Broadway, for which he won a Tony Award as Best Featured Actor in a Musical, and went on to star in a number of top-grossing films including* Carmen Jones *(1954) and* Island in the Sun *(1957). He became a Kennedy Center honoree in 1986 and was awarded the American National Medal of the Arts by the National Endowment of the Arts in Washington D.C. in 1994.*

**Baumann, The Astounding B Monster, *205.*

††*Bobby Cochran with Susan Van Hecke,* Three Steps to Heaven, *65.*

Penny (Mamie) sings "Go, Go, Calypso" on television in the musical finale of *Untamed Youth* (Warner Bros., 1957).

was definitely a mutual attraction and some hint of hanky panky between Eddie and Mamie Van Doren."*

Joe Lanza[†] is credited as choreographer on the film and it's easy to see his influence in the "Go, Go Calypso" number as he would later create a short-lived dance craze, the bossa nova, to accompany the popularity of the musical style of the Latin America music in the late 1950s. Mamie maintains she created her own choreography for the rock numbers: "Howard [Koch, the director] took me aside and asked me if I knew how to rock 'n' roll. I said 'Sure'

because I'd already done it in *Running Wild* and I could boogie woogie and I loved dancing when I was little. So I basically choreographed my own dances with a little bit of help. I based it on Elvis and the swivel he got in his hips."[‡]

REVIEWS: "A juvenile (in all senses of the word) melodrama ... The script ... was of no consequence at all, but then nothing much in director Howard W. Koch's film was, except, possibly, the way Miss Van Doren uses her body as an accompaniment to Les Baxter's music." Clive Hirschhorn, *The Warner Bros Story*

"A combination of melodramatics, sex

---

*Ibid.

[†]*Joe Lanza (1923–) appeared as an onscreen dancer in* Rock Around the Clock *and* Don't Knock the Rock *(both 1956) as well as* High School Confidential! *(1958). His only other acknowledged screen choreographic credit is for* Virgin Sacrifice *(1959). He danced in upwards of 80 films (usually uncredited) and television shows and is a prolific writer on dance.*

[‡]*Phone interview with the author, March 25, 2006.*

and rock-and-roll gives *Untamed Youth* good commercial prospects ... The entire setup is slanted at the younger filmgoers and they will be attracted, even if some may suppose the moral tone isn't the best for this particular group. Driving beat of the music, four r&r pieces and one calypso, holds the footage together more so than the actual story development. Numbers are well staged within the plot framework, even though director Howard W. Koch tends to overflaunt Mamie Van Doren's physical attributes and her bodily gestures ... Miss Van Doren sounds real good on [her songs, and] does okay by her story portions..." *Variety*, March 27, 1957

"A mélange of mediocre melodrama, Mamie Van Doren and rock 'n' roll routines ... Miss Van Doren renders such exotic numbers as 'Oobala Baby,' 'Salamander' and 'Cotton Picker' to a variety of torrid gyrations that are guaranteed to keep any red-blooded American boy awake. Nothing else in this picture can make that claim." *New York Times*, May 11, 1957

"Side-splitting camp masterpiece ... you know something's wrong when Mamie sings four songs and Cochran only one..." *Leonard Maltin's Movie & Video Guide*

"As a lurid melodrama it ranks with the best of them. Les Baxter's score is appropriately sleazy and the love scenes between Russell and Tuttle are exquisitely ridiculous." Mark Thomas McGee & R.J. Robertson, *The J.D. Films*

"Yes, it's Eddie Cochran walkin,' talkin' and singin' on film! A youth prison farm where the inmates jitterbug to the 1950s rock 'n' roll beat! ... No one has ever looked sexier in a tight sweater than Mamie Van Doren! Va Va Voom!" *The Video Beat*, thevideobeat.com

"Mamie has called this her favorite film, and little wonder: top-billed in a tale of two gorgeous girls (with Lori Nelson) who are tossed in a prison farm for hitchhiking, she gets to belt out four songs (often clad in a clinging slip) and established herself as the first female movie star associated with rock 'n' roll. Mamie says ... that she copies Elvis' hip wiggles in her performance here, and their impact is seismic. The ads didn't exaggerate when they proclaimed her 'the girl built like a platinum powerhouse!'" Steve Sullivan, *Va Va Voom!*

The Girl in Black Stockings • United Artists, 1957 [aka Black Stockings; Wanton Murder]

She's every inch a teasing, taunting "Come-on" Blonde.

CREDITS: A Bel-Air Production. *Director:* Howard W. Koch; *Executive Producer:* Aubrey Schenck; *Script:* Richard Landau, *from the story* "Wanton Murder" *by* Peter Godfrey; *Music:* Les Baxter; *Photography:* William Margulies; *Editor:* John F. Schreyer; *Production Designer:* Jack T. Collis; *Set Decorator:* Clarence Steenson [Steensen]; *Women's Clothes by* The Pink Poodle; *Wardrobe:* Wesley Jefferies, Angela Alexander; *Hair:* Mary Westmoreland; *Makeup:* Ted Coodley; *Assistant Director:* Don Torpin; *Sound:* Charles Cooper; *Special Photographic Effects:* Jack Rabin, Louis DeWitt; B&W; 73 minutes.

CAST: Lex Barker (*David Hewson*); Anne Bancroft (*Beth*); Mamie Van Doren (*Harriet Ames*); Ron Randell (*Edmund Parry*); Marie Windsor (*Julia Parry*); John Dehner (*Sheriff Jess Holmes*); John Holland (*Norman Grant*); Diana Vandervlis [Van der Vlis] (*Louise Miles*); Richard [H.] Cutting (*Dr. Aitkin*); Larry Chance (*Joe*); Gene O'Donnell (*Felton*); Gerald Frank (*Frankie*); Karl MacDonald (*Deputy*); Stuart Whitman (*Prentiss*); David Dwight (*Judge Walters*); Dan Blocker (*Bartender*);*Uncredited*: Norman Leavitt (*Amos*); Mark Bennett (*Brackett*); Mickey Whiting (*Deputy Hib*).

PLOT: At a motel resort in Utah, the body of Marsha Mason is discovered hideously slashed across the jugular vein, eyes and lips in a frenzied pattern of disfigurement. This is no ordinary killing and the denizens of the motel, all of whom seem to have guilty secrets, fall under suspicion. The resort owner, Edmund Parry, is paralyzed from the neck down and has to be cared for by his sister Julia and a nurse, Beth.

Also on hand is a precocious model, Harriet Ames, who is making a play for has-been actor Norman Grant; David Hewson, a lawyer who has left the big city to clear his head; young hothead Frankie, who was keen on the dead girl; and Joe, who is brought in with the murder weapon but can't remember how he got it because he suffers mental blackouts when he drinks. It's up to the sheriff, Jess Holmes, to sort out motives and killer.

A nosy stranger checks into the motel; after he turns up dead in the swimming pool the next morning, they learn he was a private detective. Chasing down a hunch that Frankie is not telling all he knows, the sheriff goes to the lumber mill to question him but Frankie panics and backs into a mechanical saw and is killed. At a dinner party in the motel that night, a drunken Harriet flings her arms around and kisses Parry to thank him for the wonderful time she's having. After she is led away, Parry curses her with "In nature's plan for the survival of the fittest, creatures like that will one day be as extinct as the dinosaur." Harriet is found carved up and her arms slashed after she and Norman are attacked while rehearsing a new script. A suspicious David breaks into Parry's house and confronts him, insisting that his sister is responsible for the killings because she is jealous and possessive of any woman who pays attention to him. On his drive back to town, David sees Julia's car parked beside the road and discovers Beth leaning over an unconscious Julia with a knife in her hand. The sheriff arrives and Beth begs David not to let them take her. Beth has escaped from a psychiatric establishment in Pittsburgh after having been placed their by her concerned husband.

NOTES: This is a superb, complex murder thriller with *film noir* overtones that rewards multiple viewings. The dense script by Richard H. Landau from a short story by award-winning South African mystery writer Peter Godfrey* moves the setting of the original story, "Wanton Murder," from the Atlantic resort town of Muizenburg in the Cape's False Bay, to a spa resort in Utah. The same power that director Howard W. Koch brought to Mamie's earlier vehicle *Untamed Youth* is evident here.

It was her first movie since the birth of son Perry. She'd been dropped by Universal as motherhood did not suit the image they had mapped out for her so she signed a two-picture deal with producer-director Koch. *Untamed Youth*, the second of the films to be shot, was released first. For *The Girl in Black Stockings* Mamie had to travel to Kanab, Utah. "Right in the middle of Mormon country. We couldn't get a coffee, or alcohol or cigarettes. We had to go across the border. And it was there I heard rock 'n' roll for the first time. On a jukebox. It was 'Blue Suede Shoes' and the music got to me. I knew it was my sort of music."[†]

Mamie's Harriet, a professional model and (probably) professional gold digger, who attaches herself to aging movie idol on the skids Norman Grant (John Holland), is little more than set up for the penultimate murder. Mamie does her best with the character and it's the ambiguity of whether she is an opportunist or genuinely fond of Grant that lends added complexity. But it's the other "inmates" at Parry's Motel who fascinate and resonate long after the movie's conclusion.

Lex Barker's[‡] square-jawed, flawed hero's perfect beefcake physique is juxtaposed against the wheelchair-bound quadriplegic Parry, played by Ron Randell. It's one of the outstanding performances of Randell's career; his bitterly misogynistic character is psychosomatically paralyzed from the neck down after his fiancée ran out on him on the eve of their wedding, and he spits out his disgust at women and the world and himself. Told of the callous

---

[*]Peter Godfrey (1917–92), South African–born writer, playwright and broadcaster in the 1950s, with over one thousand published stories to his credit, was a three-time winner of the Ellery Queen Award for crime and mystery fiction and was once rated by The New York Times as one of the top ten thriller writers in the world. He went into exile in London because of his staunch opposition to apartheid and worked as a journalist on the Times of London.
[†]Phone interview with the author, August 3, 2006.
[‡]Lex Barker (1919–73) rose to stardom in Tarzan's Magic Fountain (1949) and went on to make another four Tarzan films before becoming a western-adventure film hero. When work in Hollywood dried up, he headed to Europe (he spoke five languages) and became popular, particularly in Germany. Among his five wives were Lana Turner and Arlene Dahl.

Harriet (Mamie) plays up to has-been movie star Norman Grant (John Holland) in *The Girl in Black Stockings* (United Artists, 1957).

murder that opens the film, he doesn't seem unduly unhappy about the occurrence: Parry's character is summed up in his outburst: "Unhappy? Romance on the gold standard. Common creature whose every word, every breath, every gesture was a show of an empty, shallow promise. Miss Morgan was an example of a completely justifiable homicide."

The role of his sister, Julia is beautifully delineated by Marie Windsor. Julia's "everything to him except a wife; she stays to feed him, clothe him and wipe his nose, through feelings of guilt and, it's implied, incestuous impulses. When she offers to make him some hot milk to help him sleep, Randell says with such venom and self-loathing: "Milk? I'd like to get so drunk I'd look in a mirror and spit in my own face." Later he admits that he is "tired of being surrounded by lipstick and love. And women's flesh that turns to jelly at the sight of a man." Parry is not only crippled physically but also emotionally, psychologically and spiritually. He is dependent on others, mainly women, for all his needs and he watches all that goes on around him and finds the human race, particularly women, vile. In an outburst of exuberance, Harriet hugs and kisses him because she has found happiness at his motel as muse to Norman; he condemns her with "It's Nature's plan for the survival of the fittest. Creatures like that will one day be as extinct as the dinosaur." And within hours the prophecy comes to pass.

But if most of the major characters are crippled in some way, John Dehner's sheriff stands as a beacon of unperturbed common sense and normality who refuses to be fazed by any eventuality or the strange characters who inhabit the town. When Parry snaps at him to "be brief and to the point," the sheriff replies,

"Folks around say I couldn't talk less without being dead." As befits a sheriff with the name Holmes, his character is methodical and thorough albeit, to some people in the town, plodding.

Director Koch, ably abetted by William Margulies' noirish black and white photography, fills the movie with a dark and brooding sense of isolation, dreams unfulfilled and a dangerous cancer eating at the soul of modern society.

And *The Girl in Black Stockings* is replete with symbolism and clues. For example, cigarettes feature prominently before each murder. In the film's opening moments the first murder victim is discovered as a result of the lighting of a cigarette.

Beth and David are dancing near a pool.

DAVID: You breathing this hard because of me or the altitude?

BETH: It could be because I love being held in your arms. Then again it could be the altitude.

He offers Beth a cigarette but she refuses because she doesn't smoke. When David flicks his lighter for his own cigarette, Beth sees the mutilated body of Marsha Norman in the bushes. This motif is continued through the film.

Ronald Godfrey, son of the original story's author, remembers,

> At the time of filming, I know that my dad was in close touch with Anne Bancroft, who sought his help in her characterization of Beth Dixon. But he had little contact with Mamie, whose role was vivid but savagely short as the victim of a psychopathic killer. Cue for lurid pre-publicity stories showing Mamie's stockinged corpse cut with hundreds of oozing wounds under the headline "Sliced Meat *a la* Maniac!"
>
> But I believe that Mamie played the part

Sheriff Jess Holmes (John Dehner) questions Harriet (Mamie) and Norman (John Holland) about a brutal murder in *The Girl in Black Stockings* (United Artists, 1957).

of Marcia Brown*— in the short story a curvy visitor to my hometown of Muizenberg, a popular seaside resort at the Cape in South Africa (shown as Kanab, Utah spa town in the film). My dad starts off by describing how sleepy little Muizenberg blooms into a thriving, sweltering holiday destination in the summer months in December and introduces Marcia thus:

The girl called Marcia Brown, blatantly flirting with young Gerry Reynolds in the triangular section of beach called by residents The Snake Park, thought only of having a good time. She tossed her soft hair back when she laughed, and moved her magnificently lithe body in the sand, and drew admiration from Gerry's eyes over her like a garment, and laughed again.

Someone thought: What are you lingering there for, Marcia? Why don't you get up, get dressed, get your baggage from the hotel and catch the first train before it gets dark? Go back to your house or flat or room in Johannesburg— and go now while the sun is still shining. Because things can happen to you in the dark. Things can happen to those eyes that lure, those lips that hint, that body that promises... A hand in that soft hair from the back; a sharp knife... Go now, Marcia. Go now.

If you've seen the film you'll know who it is has murderous intentions (successfully followed through!) and you'll also detect the same sinister mood that defines my dad's story.[†]

REVIEWS: "Could top an all-suspense bill with ease ... Miss Van Doren has little to do but get murdered. Richard Landau's well-developed screenplay has received good direction from Howard W. Koch, and the various technical contributions all measure up." *Variety*, October 2, 1957

"Interesting, little known thriller, similar to Hitchcock's *Psycho*. But pre-dating it by three years." *Videohound*

"Obviously David Lynch caught this on late-night TV and planned *Twin Peaks* the next morning. What a movie! What hateful dialogue! ... Mamie Van Doren ... is fine as the sexy young mistress of a washed-up movie star." *The Psychotronic Video Guide*

"Tolerable murder mystery." *Halliwell's Film & Video Guide*

"Minor murder mystery with some nice touches and good performances..." *Leonard Maltin's Movie & Video Guide*

Jet Pilot • Universal-International, 1957

Earth-Shaking! Sky-Shattering! The greatest air spectacle of the Jet Age!

CREDITS: *Director:* Josef von Sternberg; *Producer:* Howard Hughes; *Producer-Screenplay:* Jules Furthman; *Music:* Bronislau Kaper; *Music Conductor:* Mischa Bakaleinikoff; *Photography:* Winton C. Hoch; *Technicolor Color Consultant:* Francis Cugat; *Editors:* Harry Marker, William M. Moore; *Sound:* Earl Wolcott, Terry Kellum; *Art Direction:* Albert S. D'Agostino, Feild Gray; *Set Decoration:* Darrell Silvera, Harley Miller; *Costumes:* Michael Woulfe; *Assistant Director:* Fred A. Fleck; *Makeup:* Mel Berns; *Hair:* Larry Germain; *Assistant to the Producer:* Brig. Gen. Clarence A. Shoop; *Supervision of Aerial Sequences:* Philip G. Cochran; *Project Pilot:* Captain J.S. Nash; *Aerial Stunts:* Chuck Yeager; Technicolor; 112 minutes.

CAST: John Wayne (*Col. Jim Shannon*); Janet Leigh (*Lt. Anna Marladovna/Olga*); and the United States Air Force; Jay C. Flippen (*Maj. Gen. Black*); Paul Fix (*Maj. Rexford*); Richard Rober (*FBI Agent George Rivers*); Roland Winters (*Col. Sokolov*); Hans Conried (*Col. Matoff*); Ivan Triesault (*Gen. Langrad*); *Uncredited:* Paul Frees (*Lt. Tiompkin*); Gene Evans (*Airfield Sergeant*); Lois Austin (*Saleswoman at Palm Springs Dress Shop*); John Bishop (*Maj. Sinclair*); Alan Dinehart III (*Fresh Kid at Palm Springs Dress Shop*); Ruth Lee (*Mother*); Perdita Chandler (*Georgia Rexford*); Joyce Compton (*Mrs. Simpson*); Denver Pyle (*Mr. Simpson*); Phil Arnold (*Bellboy*); Tom Daly (*Hotel Clerk*); Paul Bakanas, James Dime (*Russian Security Men*); Vincent Gironda, Armand Tanny (*Musclemen*); Smoki Whitfield (*Henry*); Carleton Young (*Tech. Sgt. in Palmer*

---

*Mamie's character's name in the film is changed to Harriet Ames and is less the tease and more the young model attracted to the older man on the skids.

[†]Email from Ronald Godfrey, September 10, 2006.

Field Air Control Tower); Gregg Barton, Jack Shea (*MPs*); Elizabeth Flournoy (*WAF Captain*); Joan Jordan (*WAC Sergeant*); Nelson Leigh, Herbert Lytton (*FBI Agents*); Michael Mark (*Russian General*); Richard Norris, David Ormont (*Russian Interrogators*); Gene Roth (*Sokolov's Batman*); Barbara Freking (*WAF Private*); Allen Mathews (*Head Waiter*); Mike Lally, Al Murphy, Theodore Rand, Joey Ray (*Waiters*); Keith McConnell (*Bartender*); Ruthelma Stevens (*Saleswoman*); Joan Olander [Mamie Van Doren] (*Soviet WAF*); Billy Vernon (*Drunk*); Dorothy Abbott; Jane Easton; Janice Hood; Sylvia Lewis; Joan Whitney; Wendell Niles; Fred Graham; Don Haggerty; Darrell Huntley; John Morgan; Jack Overman; Bill Erwin; Harry Lauter; Jim B. Smith; Kenneth Tobey; Biff Yeager.

DVD: GoodTimes Home Video, widescreen format (2000)

PLOT: Lt. Anna Marladovna defects to the U.S. by landing her Soviet jet in Alaska claiming she escaped to avoid being shot by the authorities. She is assigned Colonel Jim Shannon as her control and his task is to introduce her to the luxuries of capitalism and pry secrets of Soviet air strength from her; she reveals nothing. Washington is about to jail her when Shannon, who has fallen prey to her charms, marries her only to discover later that she is a spy and has married him for any military secrets he may have. Shannon plans his revenge and convinces her that he wants to defect to the Soviet Union to be with her as she is about to be imprisoned. Back in Russia she realizes she does, in fact, love Shannon and the two of them escape to the U.S. in a stolen plane pursued by Soviet fighter jets.

NOTES: Mamie began her film career in this high-octane jet wannabe version of *Ninotchka* with one of the industry's most acclaimed directors, Josef von Sternberg,* although at 16 she didn't know who he was. Landing a contract with RKO through her meeting with Howard Hughes, she was cast as an extra.

Mamie remembers her first time on a movie set: "*Jet Pilot* was my very first time in front of the camera and I had to climb up this tower and it must have been a hundred ... oh, it was so high and only somebody really young would have had the nerve to go up on this ladder. And von Sternberg, he said 'You, you go up the ladder,' so I go up the ladder and I didn't dare look down." Mamie climbed to the top of the lookout. "He said, 'When I tell you, you say "Look!"' So I did, but it never showed up on the screen. It was cut."†

She spent two days filming on location at an Air Force base near Las Vegas. "I felt like I had at least made some kind of a start in the movie business. Hopefully, it would just be a matter of time until the larger roles came along."‡

Begun in December of 1949 and completed May the next year, *Jet Pilot* was Howard Hughes' attempt to duplicate the success of his aerial combat masterpiece *Hell's Angels* (1930) but his obsessive compulsive behavior kept it shelved until 1957 when it was released by Universal. In that time the Cold War had heated up and advances in jet technology rendered the film obsolete, not to mention the unsettling sight of John Wayne and Janet Leigh looking years younger than they had in their roles in the previous few years. Hughes could not stop tinkering with the film and ordered new aerial footage, re-takes, re-edits as well as a new music score by Bronislau Kaper. The list of directors and second unit directors hired and

---

*Josef von Sternberg (1894–1969) began his cinema apprenticeship in New Jersey around 1916 before helming a number of well-regarded American films including The Last Command *(1928). But it was with* Der Blaue Engel (The Blue Angel) *(1930), made in Germany starring the unknown Marlene Dietrich, that he was catapulted to world fame. He steered Dietrich through a number of her best films:* Morocco *(1930);* Shanghai Express, Blonde Venus *(both 1932) and* The Scarlet Empress *(1934). But his reputation as a martinet, the lackluster financial performance of the films and, finally, loss of artistic control led to a deterioration in quality and he essentially disowned any movie he made after the Dietrich-starring* The Devil Is a Woman *(1935).*

†Being Mamie, *an interview with Mamie Van Doren on the RetroMedia Entertainment DVD of* Voyage to the Planet of Prehistoric Women.

‡Mamie Van Doren, Playing the Field, *36.*

fired from the project included Josef von Sternberg, Don Siegel, Paul Cochrane, Byron Haskin, von Sternberg (again), and finally the film's screenwriter, Jules Furthman.

When Universal finally unleashed it on the public in 1957, the final film to carry the Howard Hughes credit, no one cared.

REVIEWS: "It oscillates between light comedy-romance and melodrama with one not complementing the other ... Aerial photography is short of expectations, which is a curious shortcoming in view of Hughes' kinship with aeronautics ... Josef von Sternberg's direction and the writing of Jules Furthman ... are reminiscent of old-fashion cops-and-robbers cinema ... performances are okay." *Variety*, September 25, 1957

"Wars have been fought and airplane designs have been improved since *Jet Pilot* ... went before the cameras in 1949. Likewise, John Wayne, the hero, has grown grayer; Janet Leigh, the heroine, has become more blonde, and a good many better motion pictures about jet pilots have gone over the dam. These are realizations that a sensitive viewer will find popping into mind as he watches this nigh-on two-hour color picture drone its weary way across the screen. He may also find himself wondering — if he does know how long it's been lying in the can — why, at this late date, they bother to release it. It is that silly and sorry a film." Bosley Crowther, *New York Times*, October 5, 1957

Teacher's Pet • Paramount, 1958

CREDITS: *Director:* George Seaton; *Producers:* William Perlberg, George Seaton; *Script:* Fay and Michael Kanin; *Music Score:* Roy Webb; *Songs:* Joe Lubin; *Photography:* Haskell Boggs; *Editor:* Alma Macrorie; *Assistant to the Producer:* Ric Hardman; *Art Direction:* Hal Pereira and Earl Hedrick; *Process Photography:* Farciot Edouart; *Set Decoration:* Sam Comer and Robert R. Benton; *Costumes:* Edith Head; *Makeup Supervision:* Wally Westmore; *Hair Style Supervision:* Nellie Manley; *Assistant Director:* Francisco Day; *Sound:* Hugo Grenzbach and Winston Leverett; *Technical Advisor:* Norton Mockridge; B&W; VistaVision; 120 minutes.

SONGS: "Teacher's Pet" (Joe Lubin) *Doris Day (over opening credits)*; "The Girl Who Invented Rock and Roll" (Joe Lubin) *Mamie Van Doren*; "Teacher's Pet Mambo" (Joe Lubin)

CAST: Clark Gable (*James "Jim" Gannon*); Doris Day (*Prof. Erica Stone*); Gig Young (*Dr. Hugo Pine*); Mamie Van Doren (*Peggy DeFore*); Nick Adams (*Barney Kovac*); Peter Baldwin (*Harold Miller*); Marion Ross (*Katy Fuller*); Charles Lane (*Roy*); Jack Albertson (*Guide*); Florenz Ames (*J.L. Ballentine*); Harry Antrim (*Lloyd Crowley*); Vivian Nathan (*Mrs. Kovac*); *Uncredited*: Army Archerd, Joe Hyams, Erskine Johnson, Paine Knickerbocker, Frank P. Quinn, Vernon Scott, Sidney Skolsky (*Themselves*); Terry Becker (*Mr. Appino*); Cyril Delevanti (*Copy Man*); Sandra Gould (*Tess*); Elizabeth Harrower (*Clara Dibney*); Norton Mockridge (*Harry*); Margaret Muse (*Miss Gross*); Frank Richards (*Cab Driver*); Steffi Sidney (*Book Store Girl*); Merritt Smith (*Mr. Cory*).

DVD: Paramount 05716

PLOT: Jim Gannon, city editor of the *New York Evening Chronicle*, is invited to lecture to the journalism class of Prof. Stone. Dismissive of any sort of college teaching when it comes to newspapers, Gannon is an old-time tough-guy reporter who preaches learning through experience. But his boss insists he attend and, on overhearing the professor reading out his letter of refusal and discovering Prof. Stone is an attractive unmarried female, he enrolls in her class as a student. Impressed by his first assignment, Prof. Stone encourages him to pursue his journalism while his thoughts are merely of pursuing her. A problem is the discovery that she is romantically involved with egghead author Dr. Hugo Pine. An alpha male competition ensues for Prof. Stone's affections with Hugo winning all but a drinking competition. Erica and Gannon are falling for each other but his secret identity is blown when Prof. Stone turns up at his newspaper office to canvas a job for her star pupil. She is devastated by his deception and rejects his advances, convinced it was all done to humiliate her. Gannon seeks solace from Hugo and admits he feels stupid and uneducated because he

Lobby card of Peggy DeFore (Mamie) and Jim Gannon (Clark Gable) in a scene cut from the finished print of *Teacher's Pet* (Paramount, 1958).

never graduated high school until he reads old copies of *The Eureka Bulletin*, Erica's father's award-winning newspaper only to discover the paper is full of folksy hokum and small-town esoterica. He reminds Erica that her father won the Pulitzer Prize for one of his editorials which Gannon admits are top notch but he challenges Erica to read the rest of the newspaper dispassionately and judge it by the standards of a big city newspaper which relies for its existence on the income from advertising. Erica decides to take up the challenge and in a flurry of reconciliation invites Gannon to lecture her journalism class. He won't be paid but he will become a member of the faculty.

NOTES: Mamie doesn't appear until almost an hour into the film. Then she makes the most of her few scenes as a singer at the Bongo Club and Clark Gable's rather attractive but bubble-headed girlfriend. She is chattering away while Gable is distracted over his attraction to Doris Day's Prof. Stone.

PEGGY: These days a girl's gotta know all about deductibles, capital gains, things like that, or she can wind up working for the government.

Gannon, who is preoccupied watching Erica Stone with psychologist Dr. Hugo Pine, grunts.

PEGGY: What do you think?

Gannon grunts again.

PEGGY: Huh.

GANNON: What?

PEGGY: Never mind, you've been thinking enough today

A short time later Gannon is still fuming over Erica and Dr. Pine.

GANNON: So he's got more degrees than a thermometer. So he speaks seven languages. So he's read every book. So what? The important thing is, he's had no experience. He didn't start at the bottom and work up; it's the only way you can

Peggy (Mamie) bumps and grinds her way through "The Girl Who Invented Rock and Roll" in *Teacher's Pet* (Paramount, 1958).

learn.

PEGGY: You're so right, Jimsy, where would I be if I just read books?

The club's entertainment, a harpist and bongo performer, finish their set.

PEGGY: Well, I gotta go get undressed.

With that, Mamie flounces off—her blonde bimbo character set but yet to dispatch the *coup de grace*. Weighing up Peggy's attributes against those of the educated Erica Stone,

Gannon finds his busty girlfriend wanting. He goes over and joins Erica and Hugo at their table.

After an awkward pause...

ERICA: Where's your ... friend?
GANNON: Who? Oh, you mean Miss DeFore. She had to go backstage. She sings here.
ERICA: Ohhhh. She's very pretty.
GANNON: Very talented, too
ERICA: I'm sure.
GANNON: Really a delightful, unassuming, wonderful person.

Naturally, Peggy comes on to bump and grind her way through "The Girl Who Invented Rock and Roll," to Gannon's extreme discomfort.

ERICA: (*bemused*)
Say, she *is* talented.

And Mamie's show-stopping role is at an end. Her only other scene, in which Clark Gable visits her in her dressing room at the club, ended up on the cutting room floor.* This led, over the years, to a small fracas between Mamie and Doris Day. Mamie accused Ms. Day of jealously having the scene excised and Doris retaliated with some invective of her own.

But Mamie has since thought better of it. "I think now it had nothing to do with Doris Day. It was just that I was so young and he looked so old in the scenes with me. I guess people thought it didn't look good. Clark was in his late fifties and I was in my early twenties, so he was worried about his age. We had to shoot our scenes very early in the morning while his face was tight."†

Teacher's Pet gave Mamie her major foray into an A picture and she makes the most of it, aided immeasurably by Joe Lubin's witty song which has become her unofficial anthem as well as the title of an album and a CD of Mamie's songs. "That number wasn't really rock 'n' roll. They kept it more subtle because Seaton and Perlberg wanted everything subtle and smooth. Very middle of the road."‡ Mamie is strikingly dressed in an outfit designed by Edith Head which invites comparisons with a similar dress worn by Marilyn Monroe in *Gentlemen Prefer Blondes*. In giving one of her strongest screen performances, Mamie was also sealing her fate. Even though she is portraying a *character* who is a cut-rate Monroe, her performance is so effective that some people blur the line between the character and the actress. This was something that would come back to bite her when she appeared in *Slackers*.

REVIEWS: "There is rich new life and liveliness and even fresh approach with humor and heartiness in Fay and Michael Kanin's original screenplay. Clark Gable and Doris Day give it solid star appeal ... Miss Van Doren is seen briefly but importantly ... Joe Lubin has written two good songs, 'The Girl Who Invented Rock and Roll' (a novelty) and 'Teacher's Pet,' both of them woven ingeniously into the musical background by Roy Webb." *Variety*

"Also on hand is Mamie Van Doren, who renders 'The Girl Who Invented Rock 'n' Roll' in a night-club interlude. Miss Van Doren really throws herself into the song and she has the heft to subdue it." John McCarten, *New Yorker*

"Gable romps home an easy winner in the best comedy Hollywood has given us in years, and lucky Miss Day and Mr. Young are right up there with him. Mamie Van Doren, Nick Adams and Vivian Nathan add a touch of beauty, comedy and drama in lesser roles..." *Cue Magazine*

"It has dazzling and curvaceous Mamie Van Doren in a brief but hilarious sequence as the strip-singer girl friend of Gable who grinds and bumps out 'The Girl Who Invented Rock and Roll,' to his public and agonized embarrassment." Kay Proctor, *Los Angeles Examiner*

"Mamie Van Doren ... has the opportunity to display her charms, and to sing one ditty

---

*Interestingly, the Teacher's Pet *lobby card set included one of Mamie and Gable in the deleted scene. Part or all of the scene still exists, although it is not issued as an extra on the DVD. However, a short snippet appears on the documentary* Hollywood Rocks and Rolls *(Passport International Productions, 1998).*

†*Phone interview with the author, March 25, 2006.*

‡*Femme Fatales, February, 1997, 19.*

Peggy (Mamie) and her boy friend Jim Gannon (Clark Gable) cozy up in the nightclub in *Teacher's Pet* (Paramount, 1958).

that contains some snappy lyrics and rock 'n' roll rhythms." *New York Times*

"Slightly lengthy newspaper comedy with many fine moments ... The story doesn't much matter as it has little surprise. The details are what make this film funnier than the plot. Van Doren does a striptease [sic] and sweet, virginal Day emulates her in an apple pie fashion that sets Gable's temperature rising ... The major problem with the film is Gable's overdone performance ... Gable mistook mugging for acting and was almost a parody of himself ... The movie screamed to be in color ... It's really a one-joke premise, but the Oscar-nominated script by Fay and Michael Kanin and the amiable acting by most of the cast make this funny enough to watch late at night on TV when the only other movie on is anything by Brian de Palma." *The Motion Picture Guide*

"A pleasant experience ... a sensible, funny, sometimes fresh and trenchant diversion." *New York Times*

"For all its discussion of modern journalism, the use of the profession for a romantic comedy recalls works of earlier decades, and *Teacher's Pet* would be one of the last significant films to deal with traditional aspects of the working press for several years." Richard R. Ness, *From Headline Hunter to Superman*

High School Confidential! • MGM, 1958
[Aka *Young Hellions*]

Not since Blackboard Jungle *such a shattering drama of the tough, troubled teenagers of our time!*

CREDITS: An Albert Zugsmith Production. *Director:* Jack Arnold; *Script:* Lewis

Meltzer and Robert Blees, *Screen Story* by Robert Blees; *Photography:* Harold J. Marzorati; *Editor:* Ben Lewis; *Art Directors:* William A. Horning and Hans Peters; *Set Decorators:* Henry Grace, Arthur Krams; *Makeup:* William Tuttle; *Assistant Director:* Joseph E. Kenney; *Musical Material:* Mel Welles. CinemaScope; B&W; 85 minutes.

SONG: "High School Confidential" [sometimes listed as "Boppin' at the High School Hop"] (Jerry Lee Lewis & Ron Hargrave) *Jerry Lee Lewis*

CAST: Russ Tamblyn (*Tony Baker/Mike Wilson*); Jan Sterling (*Arlene Williams*); John Drew Barrymore (*J. I. Coleridge*); Mamie Van Doren (*Gwen Dulaine*); Jerry Lee Lewis (*Himself*); Ray Anthony (*Bix*); Jackie Coogan (*Mr. A.*); Charles Chaplin Jr. (*Quinn*); Diane Jergens (*Joan Staples*); Michael Landon (*Steve Bentley*); Burt Douglas (*Jukey Judlow*); Jody Fair (*Doris*); Phillipa Fallon (*Poetess*); James Todd (*Jack Staples*); Lyle Talbot (*William Remington Kane*); Robin Raymond (*Kitty*); William Wellman Jr. (*Wheeler-Dealer*); Texas Joe Foster (*Henchman*); Irwin Berke (*Morino*); Diana Darrin (*Gloria*); Carl Thayler (*Petey*); *Uncredited:* Kim Chance (*Waitress*); Della Malzahn (*Woman at Race*); Gil Perkins (*Police Sergeant*); Pierre Watkin (*David Wingate*); Joe Lanza (*Dancer*); Norman "Woo Woo" Grabowski (*Flat Top*); Paul Frees (*Narrator*); William Smith; Mel Welles.

PLOT: A Chicago transfer student, Tony Baker, arrives at Santa Bello High and sets out to make an impression. He carries a knife, wads of cash, and antagonizes J.I. Coleridge, the head of the Wheeler Dealers, the wild crowd at the school. He is invited to a party held at the home of the wealthy socialites, the Stapleses, thrown by their pot-smoking daughter, Joan, who

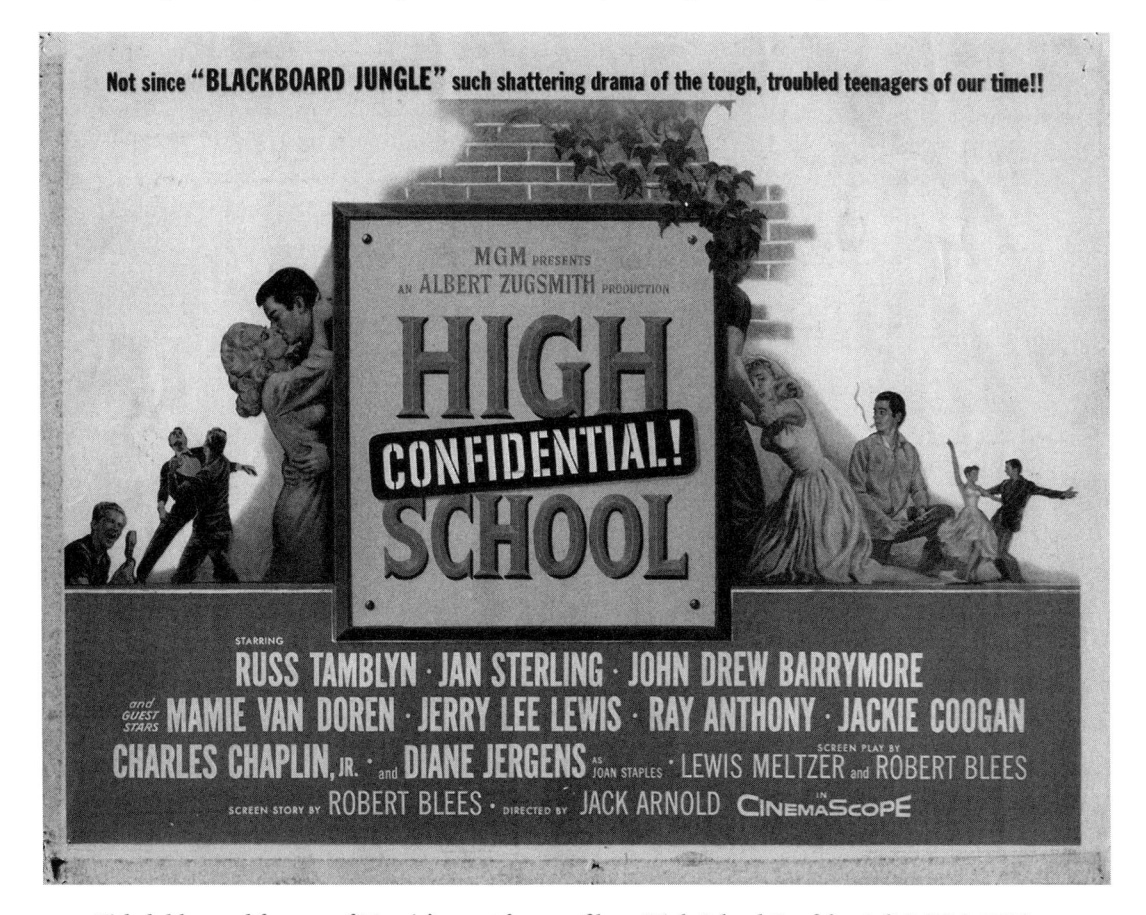

Title lobby card for one of Mamie's most famous films, *High School Confidential!* (MGM, 1958).

needs money for weed. Tony says he has the money but not the contacts and Jukey Judlow is pointed out as the source. Tony later approaches Judlow but it's penny ante stuff (he keeps his "sticks" in a magnetic box under his car). Judlow can't supply the hard drugs or the quantity Tony wants and tells him he'll arrange a meeting with the "boss."

Tony's teacher, Miss Williams, wants to give him after-school coaching but he's more interested in taking Joan drag racing in her dad's car. There he meets his contact for drugs and it turns out to be J.I. who sells him 100 sticks but not "coke, H and goof balls." Tony puts the stash behind the front wheel hubcap but during the drag race it comes loose and the police find it when they raid the track. He's taken to the police station but is bailed by a top lawyer, Kane, who works for the mysterious Mr. A. A meeting is arranged. Mr. A. turns out to be the owner and band leader at the club where the high school kids hang out. To prove his bona fides, Tony has to shoot up but while Mr. A's attention is distracted Tony pumps the drug into a rubber ball wedged in his elbow. Satisfied Tony is not a narc, Mr. A. offers to sell half a kilo of heroin but Tony won't part with the cash until he sees the goods. Mr. A. says he will arrange it.

Tony goes back to his room and plays his wire but Joan is lying on his bed in the dark. Her behavior threatens to blow his cover so he phones Miss Williams to baby sit but matters get complicated when first Aunt Gwen arrives home drunk with a pick-up and then J.I. comes looking for Joan, who reveals all to him. J.I. and his buddy beat up the three women. Joan, realizing what she has done, finds a reefer but also finds the strength to break it in half to symbolize her break with her drug habit.

Back at the club, Tony is taken into the kitchen and shown the goods hidden behind a brick in the wall. Before the trap can be sprung, a phone call comes through from J.I. revealing the set-up. Tony is about to be killed when one of the club's waiters, a police plant, comes to the rescue with the aid of the high school clean skins, The Rangers. The film ends happily with Mr. A. and Bix apprehended.

NOTES: This is the quintessential Mamie Van Doren movie but it is neither her best role nor her biggest; in fact, her character is superfluous to the plot and perhaps that's why it stands out. Mamie is listed as a "guest star" in the movie that many consider her ultimate cult classic and it is usually Mamie's full-on performance as Gwen Dulaine, "aunt" to undercover cop Russ Tamblyn, that is singled out for special mention. Aunt is usually enclosed in quotes because the actual relationship between the two characters is blurred. The film does make quite clear it is a relationship of convenience though a touch of attempted incest may have made *High School Confidential!* even more "surreal," as many film historians and critics like to label it. In fact, there's nothing surreal about the film at all. The film's opening with Jerry Lee Lewis and band on the back of a flat-bed truck driving around the high school campus (were high schools ever so Ivy League?) belting out the film's title song* was a clever way to get immediate audience attention. Instead of Jerry Lee Lewis on the soundtrack, he was placed center screen and the excuse, as if one were needed, is that he's selling records off the back of the truck at wholesale prices. A great marketing ploy. Nothing surreal about it. And indicative of the attention-grabbing openings of most of Zugsmith's films as producer or director.

In his perceptive article on Zugsmith, C. Jerry Kutner[†] sums up Hollywood's reigning view (then and now) of the producer-director: "Hollywood preferred to view Zugsmith as an exploitation filmmaker, one who was all too willing to capitalize on unwholesome subject matter — miscegenation, drug abuse, disturbed sexuality — in a word, the FORBIDDEN. In those days the arbiters of taste rarely considered that sleaze could coexist on the same plane

---

*The words "high school confidential" never appear in the lyrics; they seem more preoccupied with "boppin' at the high school hop,"
[†]"Albert Zugsmith's Opium Dreams." Bright Lights, #20, November, 1997.

It's afternoon already and Gwen (Mamie) is just getting out of bed to attempt another seduction of Tony (Russ Tamblyn) in *High School Confidential!* (MGM, 1958).

as visual fluency and high artistic expression. Indeed, what can one say about a producer who voluntarily made no less than seven films with Mamie Van Doren? Only, as Dietrich says at the end of *Touch of Evil*, that he was 'some kind of man.'"

Knowing that he was handling explosive cinematic material, Zugsmith went on the defensive and attempted to justify the film in an interview with the movie trade press. He even cited the cooperation of the narcotics committee of the Los Angeles County Medical Association and named areas in the country where marijuana was peddled in schools, calling the situation "a cancer that can spread like wildfire." He then went on to perpetuate the domino theory of drug taking, highlighted in the film itself, that juveniles smoking marijuana cigarettes almost invariably go on to heroin, and must be made to understand that. He made no apologies for the fact that *High School Confidential!* was a crusade film and, in a swipe at the competition, he is reported to have said that unlike *Blackboard Jungle*, it has a clear-cut moral lesson and it shows only a few juveniles as delinquents as contrasted with a whole class.

Lest anyone watching the film outside the U.S. think that American teenagers were a mob of delinquent brain-dead addicts, he told the press that the British and Commonwealth version was to have a prologue spoken by "an authority" to dispel any belief that juvenile use of marijuana was a common problem in the U.S. and to make the point that drug abuse in schools was a "threat" rather than a widespread menace. In the end, virulent anti-marijuana campaigner and Commissioner of the Federal

Bureau of Narcotics informed MGM that the movie would be in trouble if it didn't portray more graphically the connection between the "evil weed" and its dire consequences.

With the advantage of hindsight, Zugsmith revealed decades later that *High School Confidential!* was a "well-researched, realistic study of marijuana ... We felt that the subject of pot should be analyzed and handled in a realistic manner and that we should not take sides on it ... We tried to make the best, most realistic picture we could under the circumstances, but the narcotics people raised too much hell ... unfortunately I didn't have final control."* He also revealed that he gained insight into the material by going to Venice Beach coffee houses frequented by pot smokers and by attending private pot parties.

It is common for director Jack Arnold to be credited with much of *High School Confidential!*'s success. But Arnold, whose reputation rests on a number of classy Universal science fiction classics such as *Creature from the Black Lagoon* (1954), *Tarantula* (1955) and *The Incredible Shrinking Man* (1957), is probably the least interesting stylistically of all the major Albert Zugsmith-Mamie Van Doren collaborators. Perhaps this was because of his antipathy to the material although he jumped at the opportunity to direct it when he found out it was to be released through MGM. "I didn't know anything about dope. I had to assume the script was right. Now I know it wasn't, and that the business about marijuana leading to heroin is silly."†

Jack Arnold's wife, Betty, remembers, "He thought it was a very lightweight, nothing picture but he did the best he could do with it."‡

The film's heavy-handed editorializing was forced upon it. As initially released, the film opened with a voiceover introducing Dr. Stewart Knox, chairman of the narcotics committee of the Los Angeles County Medical Association, intoning: "How many parents are awake to the temptations facing their children?

I do not mean petty infringements. I refer to the terribly dangerous traffic which this film exposes. The story takes place in America but could happen anywhere, which is why police throughout the world have special divisions in close international cooperation to deal with this modern problem. *High School Confidential!* will shock you and, I hope, alert you."

This introduction is missing from the modern DVD recording and one wishes it had been included as an extra. But still on the film's soundtrack is ponderous narration intoned by an uncredited Paul Frees, over climactic footage of Russ Tamblyn in his car with Jan Sterling and Diane Jergens in the front seat while Mamie cavorts with her till-then-vacationing husband in the back seat. Frees provides an update on the all-too-obvious outcome of what has preceded it: "You have just seen an authentic disclosure of conditions which unfortunately exist in some of our high schools today. But now Arlene will teach in a school that has cleansed itself of its ugly problem. Joan confines her smoking to ordinary cigarettes. Gwen's problem is also solved, her husband came home. For some of the people in our story it didn't have a happy ending. Mr. A. and Bix are serving five years to life. J.I. and his boys are in reform school. But the job of a policeman like Mike Wilson will not be finished until this insidious menace to the schools of this country is exposed and destroyed."

Made for a little over half a million dollars, it grossed $8 million in its initial release and has been a consistent cult favorite since, aided to a large extent by Mamie's extravagant performance and her jazzy dialogue. For example, when we first meet Tony's Aunt Gwen, it's afternoon and she's just out of bed, munching an apple like Eve tempting Adam. Tony is drinking milk and Gwen offers him something stronger—coffee.

Later she attempts to kiss him. When he remains resolutely close-mouthed she says: "Stop treating me like a stranger. With Vic out

---

*Los Angeles Free Press, *October 24–30, 1975.*
†Reemes, *directed by Jack Arnold,* 115.
‡*Filmfax* #37, 94.

of town, it's lonely. Relatives should always kiss each other hello and goodbye polite like."

And when Miss Williams turns up at her house, she squelches the mousy teacher with her perceptive appraisal of character and her ability to cut to the crux of the matter.

GWEN: Look, Miss Dimple Toes, if you people at the school think Vic and me — Vic is my husband and he's out of town on a job — if you think we're raising a juvenile delinquent, say it.

MISS WILLIAMS: No, Mrs. Dulaine, we...

GWEN: Don't double-talk me. You've got me pegged as a no-good relative.

MISS WILLIAMS: The only reason I came here...

GWEN: Come on, honey, don't draw diagrams with me. I'm no idiot child. I just don't believe all that stuff the papers said about wild reefer parties and fates worse than death in the bushes at night. I know Tony even if he's only been living here a short while. He's practically a grown man who wants to get a bang out of life just like you or me.

MISS WILLIAMS: I think if Tony's interests were channeled then...

GWEN: There's nothing to channel. He's healthy and normal and full of fun. You know what I mean, too. Don't tell me you never rode a hot rod or had a late date in the second balcony.

(*Looking her over*)

... Or maybe you haven't.

As if that's not enough, the screenplay also takes a poke at beats, something of a bugbear to Zugsmith as he used the idea again in *The Beat Generation*, although he is careful to mix his satire with affection. First high school pupil J.I. tells the story of Christopher Columbus and his voyage to the New World in jive while the class teacher is out of the room; later, Phillipa Fallon recites beat poetry to musical accompaniment at Mr. A.'s club. The poetry, penned by special consultant Mel Welles, was apposite:

Schoolteacher Arlene Williams (Jan Sterling) comforts pot addict Joan (Diane Jergens) while Gwen (Mamie) looks on in *High School Confidential!* (MGM, 1958).

> My old man was a bread-stasher all his life;
> He never got fat.
> He wound up with a used car, a seventeen-inch screen,
> And arthritis.
> Tomorrow is a drag, man.
> Tomorrow is a king-size bust.
>
> They cried, "Put down pot,
> Don't think a lot."
> For what?
> Time, how much, and what to do with it.
> Sleep, man, and you might wake up
> Digging the whole human race,
> Giving itself three days to get out.
> Tomorrow is a drag, Pops.
> The future is a flake.

The lines would have resonated then with a generation under the threat of nuclear annihilation. The lines were probably meant to satirize the idea of obscure or pretentious beat poets in coffee shops in much the same way as Audrey Hepburn's scene in *Funny Face* (1957), but this time they speak directly to the audience at which the movie is aimed while being sufficiently obfuscatory as to confuse non-hip viewers. Much the same can be said about the teachers at the high school. The headmaster and his staff are "progressive" and proudly so. Their actions would be looked on today as enlightened in their treatment of their students but under the heavy-handed moralizing of the narcotics authorities they are shown to be out of their depth. They are meant to be figures of ridicule as are Joan Staples' wealthy parents who extol the virtues of their drug-of-choice, alcohol.

Time has been kind to *High School Confidential!* The many facets of the plot are as relevant today as they were in the 1950s: teenage drug addiction, pushing in schools, gang warfare, and prostitution. It's marred only by the excessive use of the domino theory of drug addiction (marijuana inevitably leads to heroin inevitably leads to prostitution) as personified by Doris (Jody Fair), and the ease with which addiction is broken as symbolized by Joan Staples (Diane Jergens) tearing a joint in half. And by the visual portrayal of withdrawal symptoms, portrayed with such melodramatic over-emphasis that, as McGee and Robertson note, "The harm in this sort of propaganda lies in the possibility that once the kids realize that what they have been told about marijuana is false, they might be more inclined to believe that the scare tactics against the really dangerous drugs, like heroin, is just more of the same."*

The film top-billed MGM contract player Russ Tamblyn. He was about to be called up for army service so the studio rushed him into *High School Confidential!*

"They literally picked me up from the airport [Tamblyn was returning from making *tom thumb* in England] and drove me straight to the studio. We started shooting the day I got back. To tell you the truth, I hated it at the time. My agent and I both thought the script was terrible, and he tried to get me out of it, but the studio threatened suspension if I didn't do the picture."†

But during the shoot, Tamblyn's profile rose dramatically when he was nominated for a Best Supporting Actor Oscar‡ for *Peyton Place* (1957) which had been released the previous year.

"What's still very strange to me is that *High School Confidential!* has become a very popular 'cult' film while *Peyton Place* has been completely forgotten ... *Peyton Place* was a class-act movie and nobody cares about it, while *Confidential*, a 'B' movie with dumb lines and a silly plot, has continued to grow in popularity.

"I mean, in the film some girl is sitting in the cafeteria, shaking because she didn't get her marijuana. It was stupid! Just a really silly film. And no one has ever figured out what Mamie Van Doren's character was. She's my aunt? It was weird."**

---

*The J.D. Films, 89.

†"*Russ Tamblyn Before* Twin Peaks— *The Artist as a Young Man*," interview by Sharon Lind Williams, Filmfax #27, June-July 1991.

‡*Tamblyn's fellow nominees that year were Arthur Kennedy, also for* Peyton Place, *Vittorio de Sica (*A Farewell to Arms*), Sessue Hayakawa (*The Bridge on the River Kwai*), and the recipient, Red Buttons (*Sayonara*).*

**"*Russ Tamblyn Before* Twin Peaks— *The Artist as a Young Man*," Filmfax #27, June-July 1991.

Mamie echoes the sentiments. "*High School Confidential!* was one of my favorites. It was my first movie at MGM. I met the leading man Russ Tamblyn, I met him the same morning I had a kissing scene with him. It's not easy to walk into a scene early in the morning just up from bed and you walk in and you've got this very passionate sexy scene with your nephew. Supposedly he was my nephew in the movie. I don't know who was looking at the movie and let that go by."*

REVIEWS: "A must for midnight movie fans thanks to high camp values, 'hep cat' dialogue and the gorgeous Van Doren as Tamblyn's sex-crazed 'aunt.'" *Videohound*

"An engagingly silly period piece..." *Halliwell's TV & Video Guide*

"From the opening with Jerry Lee Lewis singing the title song while pounding the keys of a piano on the back of a flat-bed truck to the absurd happy ending, this teen-dope-ring movie is a classic of its kind." *The Psychotronic Encyclopedia of Film*

"A sensational account of pills, marijuana and narcotics among the high school set. A good cast ... does a capable job of projecting the sad and sordid aspects of this kind of story. Although the presentation seems to 'exploit' to the fullest every facet of this evil situation, it does so skillfully and with compelling effect ... The screenplay is well-constructed ... and faithfully told in the special language of today's juniors ... Mel Welles has contributed two pieces of special material, one of which, an existentialist poem recited by Phillipa Fallon, is a standout ... Jack Arnold's direction is well-paced and draws some believable and sharp characterizations. *Variety* May 28, 1958

"*High School Confidential!* ... sought to cash in on the teenage affluence that was beginning to attract both Hollywood and the recording industry in the late Fifties. A publicity still captioned 'Sleazy Aunt Gwen tries to seduce her milk-drinking nephew' tells half the story. The other half is not worth mentioning, but for those with a taste for sublimely awful movies it is definitely worth looking at." George Robert Kimball, *The Movie* #55

"When will Mamie grow up? ... She's the girl most likely to try *anything* to prove she's still Hollywood's blondest, zippiest sexpot. Eye-popping pin-up publicity; a shot at cabaret at Las Vegas; a string of films with uninhibited titles ... even a spin as a disc star. Now Mamie tries a new gimmick. Acting ... And MGM claims it [*High School Confidential!*] is her first serious dramatic role. All grown-up? This time Mamie might mean it." *Picturegoer,* May 17, 1958

"Why sandwich in ... the extremely shapely Mamie Van Doren as Mr. Tamblyn's aunt? (That's right — aunt.) What, exactly, have her attempts at his seduction to do with the price of beans — or dope? As an actress she also manages to coil herself around a refrigerator like a python." Howard Thompson, *New York Times* May 31, 1958

"*High School Confidential!* was sold to the public as a hard-hitting expose of the tragic drug abuse running rampant in U.S. schools. The teenagers who went to see this film in droves knew better. The film is high camp, tongue-in-cheek fun on a par with the cult classic *Reefer Madness* ... This is not to say that the problems of drug abuse are played for laughs. The film's treatment of these scenes is fairly straightforward ... The amusement derives from 20/20 hindsight and the thought that a major studio (MGM) tried to address the horrors of drug addiction in a film that obviously panders to the rebellious attitudes of the very people to whom the 'message' is aimed." *The Motion Picture Guide*

"Grotesque melodrama involving juvenile delinquency, drug addiction, Rock 'n' Roll and hot-rod racing." David Meeker, *Jazz in the Movies*

"The film has intentionally sleazy elements. And it has the inimitable Van Doren strutting her stuff. It's worth the price of admission to watch her walking around in semi-obscene outfits (you'll dig her cashmere

---

Being Mamie, *an interview with Van Doren on the RetroMedia Entertainment DVD of* Voyage to the Planet of Prehistoric Women.

sweater), rolling around Tamblyn's bed as if she were a cat in heat, biting into his apple with thoughts of Eden in her naughty head, drinking herself into a stupor, even being slapped around in the manner of cheap dames with gangster boyfriends. Her verbal dual with Jan Sterling is not to be missed." *Box Office*

"Is the film exploitable? Strictly to sensation seekers. There is loads of jive talk but overall the film produces an effect of excess and, finally, disbelief." *Motion Picture Herald*

"A delirious mix of intergenerational miscommunication, heavy petting, and furtive dope use that's also the greatest 'teen' movie ever made ...This is Mamie's signature film: When she bites into the apple Tony is holding and coos 'You looking for excitement?' you're witnessing her ascendancy into screen legend." David J. Hogan, *Filmfax* August-September 1996

"This can only be described as a marvelous camp classic. The plot careens wildly, and often unbelievably, the lingo is totally gonesville, and Mamie Van Doren, as a seductive aunt(!), just about punctures the screen." Alan Betrock, *I Was a Teenage Juvenile Delinquent Rock 'n' Roll Horror Beach Party Movie Book*

"Spiffed out in a white cashmere sweater at least four sizes too small, Mamie tells a super straight young schoolteacher 'Don't tell me you never rode in a hot rod or had a late date in the balcony.' It is one of the finest moments in the history of teen-age flicks, and indicative of Zugsmith's modus operandi. It is also what made Mamie so appealing to teenagers of the period, who made up the majority of the audience for Zugsmith movies. She was one of them. She understood. Not enough can be said to recommend this farfetched tale of high schoolers and the evil weed. A cameo appearance by Jerry Lee Lewis (doing the title tune), a script loaded with jive talk, some great drag racing scenes, and memorable performances by the entire cast, especially Barrymore and Coogan, make the film a classic in the genre. Zugsmith at his exploitative finest." Richard Staehling, *Rolling Stone*, December 27, 1969

"Aunt" Gwen (Mamie) tells a reluctant Tony (Russ Tamblyn) that relations should kiss more often in **High School Confidential!** (MGM, 1958).

"Infused with hepcat jive talk and a thrill-seeking spirit, it managed to capture the myth and urgency of the times in a raw and sensational—if hardly realistic—fashion. Even though it punished the bad guys in formalistic style and promulgated the official mythologies (marijuana-leads-to-heroin-leads-to-promiscuity-leads-to-tragedy), it also attacked the hypocrisy of insensitive school administrators and 'juice-head' parents, and generally weighed in to its subject matter with an unhinged exuberance that no studio A-picture could muster." Jack Stevenson, *Addicted: The Myth and Menace of Drugs in Film*

"Were this anti-social film merely a poverty-row amorality made by fast-buckers for the titillation of morons and would-be criminals, *Films in Review* would take no notice of it. Instead, it was made for, and distributed by, a reputable company; and its producer, Albert Zugsmith, protests it is an exposé of social evil. The film itself is a social evil." *Films in Review*

Born Reckless • Warner Bros., 1958

She's Every Big-Time Rodeo Prize Rolled Into One ... pair of tight pants!

CREDITS: *Director:* Howard W. Koch; *Producer:* Aubrey Schenck; *Screenplay:* Richard Landau, *Story by* Richard Landau and Aubrey Schenck; *Music:* Buddy Bregman; *Photography:* Joseph F. Biroc; *Choreography:* Jack Baker; *Film Editor:* Joseph F. Schreyer; *Art Director:* Jack T. Collis; *Set Decorator:* Jerry Welch; *Costumes:* Marjorie O. Best; *Western Clothes:* H Bar C Ranchwear, California Ranchwear; *Makeup Supervisor:* Gordon Bau; *Assistant Director:* William Kissell; *Sound:* Stanley Jones; B&W; 80 minutes.

SONGS: "Born Reckless" (Buddy Bregman, Stanley Styne) *Johnny Olenn and His Group*; "Home Type Girl" (Buddy Bregman, Stanley Styne) *Mamie Van Doren*; "Song of the Rodeo" (Buddy Bregman, Stanley Styne) *Tex Williams*; "Something to Dream About" (Charles Singleton & Larry Coleman) *Mamie Van Doren*; "Born Reckless" (Buddy Bregman, Stanley Styne) *Mamie Van Doren*; "A Little Longer" (Buddy Bregman, Stanley Styne) *Mamie Van Doren*; "You Lovable You" (Buck Ram) *Johnny Olenn and His Group*; "Separate the Men from the Boys" (Buddy Bregman, Stanley Styne) *Mamie Van Doren*

CAST: Mamie Van Doren (*Jackie Adams*); Jeff Richards (*Kelly Cobb*); Arthur Hunnicutt (*Cool Man*); Carol Ohmart (*Liz*); Tom Duggan (*Wilson*); Tex Williams (*Himself*); Donald Barry (*Okie*); Nacho Galindo (*Papa Gomez*); Orlando Rodriguez (*Manuel*); Johnny Olenn and His Group (*Themselves*); Allegra Varron (*Mama Gomez*); Jim Canino (*Jose*); Jovon Monteil (*Dolores*); Jack Loomis (*Mayor*); Asa Maynor (*Trailer Camp Girl*); Jeanne Carmen (*Rodeo Girl*); Doye O'Dell (*Rodeo Official*); Ann Staunton (*Eve*); Ed Hinton (*Spade*); Ray Beltram (*Grandfather*); Jack Welden, Malcolm Roselle (*Rodeo Announcers*); Yvonne Vasquez (*Lola*); Christina Vasquez (*Chiquita*).

PLOT: Rodeo trick rider Jackie Adams is saved from the clutches of a lecherous sports writer, Mark Wilson, outside the Cattlemen's Hall by Kelly Cobb when a free-for-all breaks out. Kelly and his rodeo sidekick, Cool Man, make their getaway fast with a stowaway on board—Jackie. She tags along with the two bachelors and obviously develops feelings for Kelly, who tours the rodeo circuit attempting to raise money for a ranch he intends to buy. At the Little River Rodeo, Kelly manages to win but the takings are stolen by one of the organizers. Broke, Jackie gets a job singing at a local bar in exchange for their dinner. She's a success and is offered a permanent gig but the deal comes with provisos and, again, Kelly and Cool Man have to bail her out. Jackie is beginning to fall in love with Kelly but Cool Man attempts to warn her off.

Kelly takes Jackie to meet his friend Papa Gomez but their dreams of buying land to raise cattle is looking more dicey as Kelly is sending back winnings and then borrowing most of it back again. The three of them register for the big rodeo in Panamint but Kelly gets sidetracked by rich girl Liz. The next day at the rodeo, Kelly turns up exhausted and fails in all four events. Cool Man reprimands him when he gets duded up for his second visit to Liz, and

Kelly knocks him down. Jackie goes after him, not realizing that Kelly is there to give Liz the brush-off. Jackie pushes Liz in the pool and then kisses Kelly passionately before pushing him in as well.

The next day Jackie is missing but Kelly goes on to win his events and finally rides a bull that had never been defeated before. At the Panamint Rodeo Dance that night, Jackie is attempting to make Kelly jealous and plays up to Mark Wilson, the newspaperman who Kelly beat up to save Jackie when they first met. She gets into trouble again and Kelly goes to her rescue — again. After Kelly sends his winnings to Papa, he, and Kelly, Jackie and Cool Man head out for the rodeo circuit once again. But the next time they return to the ranch, it will be permanent.

NOTES: Corny? Cheesy? Sentimental? All of these? Most definitely. And yet *Born Reckless* features Mamie's most iconic costume from any of her films: the Capri pants; glittering sequined blouse barely holding in the bullet bra; and the cowgirl hat which is the image Quentin Tarantino chose to immortalize in *Pulp Fiction*. It is as identifiable with Mamie as any iconic movie costume is identified with its wearer — Dorothy's ruby slippers, for example. *Born Reckless* also lays claim to being the source of perhaps Mamie's most realized major role and perhaps her most charming. Charming is not a word normally associated with the good-bad girl but here Mamie's Jackie is a good girl who gets herself into scrapes because she can't help her good looks and her obvious physical assets (although it does make you wonder how she's survived for so long without a male protector in the male-dominated world of rodeo).

And Mamie plays "good girl" to perfection. She's done it before, notably in *Star in the Dust*, and although there's little or no back story to Mamie's Jackie (the concentration is on Kelly and his buddy Cool Man), Mamie is the springboard for all the action in *Born Reckless*. She shines in this film even though she, and the rest of the cast, is saddled with cheesy dialogue that would have the greatest of actors hard-pressed to make it work. But Mamie and Jeff Richards* manage an insouciance that helps underscore the emotion rather than point up the stilted words they have to mouth.

When Jackie and Kelly have their first real talk in a deserted rodeo ring:

JACKIE: It's like an empty battlefield out there.
KELLY: Yeah, sometimes you take a little blood, leave a little.
JACKIE: I saw you ride the other day.
KELLY: Yeah, I guess I did eat a mouthful of dirt at that.
JACKIE: For a minute I didn't think you'd walk away from that Brahma.
KELLY: Neither did I. It's like each time I walk away a little slower.
JACKIE: Why do you, Kelly?
KELLY: Why do I what?
JACKIE: Stay in it?
KELLY: Ah, lots of reasons I guess.
JACKIE: Name one that's worth getting buried for.
KELLY: I'd sort of be unhappy if I got buried with my pockets empty. It'd hurt my pride.
JACKIE: It'd hurt your pride a lot more if they couldn't bury you all in one piece.
KELLY: Well, to tell the truth, I figure I got three, maybe four, more good years left in me. So one day I don't walk away from a bull or a horse. I end up like Cool Man. Twisted ribs, broken bones, a hole big enough to stick your fist in from a steer's horn. But when that happens I want to have enough put away so I can let my aching body rest on a nice piece of land I got picked out. Yeah, I got me a real sweet piece of land all picked out.
JACKIE: If you live that long.
KELLY: I'll live that long.

Later, Cool Man (a beautifully understated performance by Arthur Hunnicutt, the lean character actor who specialized in wizened but worldly-wise offsiders) realizes Jackie is falling for Kelly, and he philosophizes while they are camped around a fire:

---

*Jeff Richards (real name: Richard Mansfield Taylor) (1922–89) was a professional baseball player turned actor who graced the screens, large and small, from 1948 to 1961 but never graduated to true stardom. He was usually cast in rugged he-man roles and had his own short-lived TV series, Jefferson Drum *(1958–59) in which he played a widower (with a young son) who starts a newspaper in the Wild West. There is some dispute as to whether he died in 1989; Maria Ciaccia in her book* Dreamboats: Hollywood Hunks of the '50s *suggests he was still alive in 1992.*

COOL MAN: You got a fire burning for Kelly almost as hot as this one. Kelly, he's not like ordinary people. It takes a wild man to ride a wild horse. He's no different when it comes to women. I know, it's like I raised him from a colt. Just when you think he might get the peaceful notion of going the route ... Yeah, when Kelly unseats them, they hit that ground harder than any bronco. Sometimes that kind of hurt can last a long time.

But the relationship between rodeo trick rider Jackie and tough man Kelly has to be toughened by fire before the obligatory happy ending. And it's Mamie singing of her heartbreak that is one of the loveliest screen moments she ever had. Almost perfectly still, framed by a post at the ranch where she has been deserted by the man she loves for a rodeo floozy, she sings the haunting ballad "A Little Longer." The scene's stillness sets it apart from the rest of the action in what is essentially a modern western intercut with real rodeo footage. It's an oasis of calm before the action leading to the climax and is marred only by the insertion of a heavenly choir supporting Mamie's song. It's an unnecessary intrusion.

Later, Papa Gomez attempts to cheer up Jackie with some home-spun philosophy.

Rodeo cowboy Kelly Cobb (Jeff Richards) and rodeo trick rider Jackie Adams (Mamie) in *Born Reckless* (Warner Bros., 1958).

PAPA GOMEZ: You dream the same dream as Kelly maybe.
JACKIE: How do you dream dreams with your eyes open, Papa?
PAPA GOMEZ: Sometimes it is the best way. You can see what you want in your dream. I dream someday all this [ranch] belong to Kelly and I. I save hard to put away my share.
JACKIE: And Kelly?
PAPA GOMEZ: I know he wants it too. But sometimes his eyes are shut too tight.
JACKIE: Not the way he went off with that little dream today. His eyes weren't shut.
PAPA GOMEZ: He will wake up.
JACKIE: You didn't see this dream, Papa. Right out of a bedtime story, but not for children. I don't know, Papa, with me I get whistles and propositions from all the wrong characters. From Kelly all I get is protection. What haven't I got that low-down saddle rat wants?
PAPA GOMEZ: You wait. Kelly will open his eyes and then ...
JACKIE: And then it can be too late. I don't want the man I marry in this business. I know, I'm in it. I'm not on the outside looking in where all the Kellys look glamorous. I've seen too many of them hit the dirt and lay there and never get up.
PAPA GOMEZ: Not Kelly.
JACKIE: Who says, Papa? I want Kelly in one piece. I want him to enjoy the kind of life I can give him. I don't want him living it in a wheelchair.
PAPA GOMEZ: Kelly's indestructible. One of the iron men.
JACKIE: Like Cool Man.

PAPA GOMEZ: Maybe after tomorrow and Kelly wins, maybe we will come closer to our dreams.
JACKIE: Maybe, Papa. Maybe

The rockabilly songs by Buddy Bregman and Stanley Styne are, in many respects, superior to most of the songs she had throughout her film career, and are much more carefully integrated into the action. The songwriting team also penned the strong numbers for her next outing, *Guns, Girls and Gangsters*. She has five numbers, the remainder done by Tex Williams* and Johnny Olenn and His Group.† Director Howard W. Koch seemed to bring out the best in Mamie and elicited two of her best performances on screen in *Untamed Youth* and *Born Reckless*.

When asked what quality it was Howard Koch saw in her that he used her in three movies, Mamie's answer was succinct: "Money!"‡

REVIEWS: "*Born Reckless* blends enough romance, rodeo action and bouncy song numbers to come off as very acceptable divertissement for the program trade. With name of Mamie Van Doren to serve as lure specially for the younger audiences, film may be exploited for good returns... Miss Van Doren ... socks over five numbers for good effect ... Miss Van Doren lends an enticing presence throughout pic, and is given some rather breathtaking (or holding) rodeo costumes which probably will bring whistles from the audience. Her singing is pleasant and she

Jackie (Mamie) is peeved as she watches her man drive off with another woman in *Born Reckless* (Warner Bros., 1958).

---

*Tex Williams (1917–85), popular western swing bandleader and singer, made a number of musical shorts in the 1940s and 1950s. His biggest hit, and the first million seller for Capitol records, was "Smoke, Smoke, Smoke (That Cigarette)." Ironically, he died of lung cancer.
†Johnny Olenn was born in 1936 and began his career in the early 1950s playing steel guitar in the band of Eddie Dugosh and the Ah-Ha Boys before forming his own band, The Jokers, in 1954. He appeared in The Girl Can't Help It *(1956)* but his career slowed down shortly after Born Reckless. He continued to play gigs but his career really took off again when he toured Europe in the 1980s to tremendous success.
‡Phone interview with the author, September 20, 2006.

Jackie (Mamie) is the bar entertainment who spins a mean lasso in *Born Reckless* (Warner Bros., 1958).

knows how to handle a song." *Variety*, April 8, 1959

"Hardly a bucking bronco of a plot…" Clive Hirschhorn, *The Warner Bros Story*

"Not bad enough to be funny … Van Doren shows an incredible lack of talent while singing several tunes." *Videohound*

"Hear Mamie sing the title song for a steak dinner. Koch didn't direct again for 14 years." *The Psychotronic Encyclopedia of Film*

"A third-rate Marilyn Monroe clone, Van Doren plays a rodeo star in love with aging rider Richards, who couldn't care less… The musical numbers aren't bad, but throughout her career Van Doren displayed a stunning lack of talent." *Motion Picture Guide*

The Big Operator • MGM, 1959 [Reissue title: *Anatomy of the Syndicate*]

Vice-violent drama of today's new jungle of crime!

CREW: An Albert Zugsmith Production. *Director:* Charles Haas; *Producer:* Red Doff; *Script:* Robert Smith and Allen Rivkin, based on a *Cosmopolitan* story by Paul Gallico; *Music:* Van Alexander; *Photography:* Walter H. Castle; *Editor:* Ken Lewis; *Art Directors:* Hans Peters, Preston Ames; *Set Decorators:* Henry Grace, Jack Mills; *Makeup:* William Tuttle; *Costumes:* Kitty Mager; *Assistant Director:* Ridgeway Callow; *Dialogue Coach:* Jackie Coogan; CinemaScope; B&W; 92 minutes.

CAST: Mickey Rooney (*Little Joe Braun*); Steve Cochran (*Bill Gibson*); Mamie Van Doren (*Mary Gibson*); Mel Tormé (*Fred McAfee*); Ray Danton (*Oscar Wetzel*); Jim Backus (*Cliff Heldon*); Ray Anthony (*Slim Clayburn*); Jackie Coogan (*Ed Brannell*); Charles Chaplin Jr. (*Bill

Title lobby card for Albert Zugsmith's brutal look at workplace relations in *The Big Operator* (1959).

Tragg); Vampira (*Gina*); Billy Daniels (*Tony Webson*); Ben Gage (*Bert Carr*); Jay North (*Timmy Gibson*); Lawrence Dobkin (*Phil Cernak*); Leo Gordon (*Danny Sacanzi*); Donald Barry (*Detective Sergeant*); Ziva Rodann (*Alice*); Joey Forman (*Ray Bailey*); [Norman "Woo Woo"] Grabowski (*Lou Green*); Vido Musso (*Picket Leader*); *Uncredited*: Bobi Byrnes; Stephen Ellis; Frederick Ford; Gary Hunley; Robert Hunter; Aram Katcher; Larry Kent; Peter Leeds; Carey Loftin; John P. Melfi; Hugh Sanders; Joe Schneider.

PLOT: A Senate Committee which is examining labor rackets is concerned that 32 of the 34 unions that makeup the umbrella union are run by men with criminal records. Little Joe Braun takes the Fifth Amendment 17 times in violation of his own union's rules and William Tragg, a witness against Braun, fails to show up at the hearing; he has been disposed of in a cement truck by thug Oscar Wetzel, also known as The Executioner. Braun denies knowing Wetzel and is charged with perjury. Watching the news on TV, a family man and precision tooler, Bill Gibson, realizes that he and his work buddy, Fred McAfee, saw Braun talking to Wetzel outside a union meeting. Braun attempts to buy their silence by offering them high-paying jobs with the union. They both refuse.

The Labor Federation expels Joe Braun but through a series of stand over tactics and blackmail he gets the workers a fifteen percent pay raise. Fred, a hot head, complains about the tactics and physically attacks Braun. Later that night Fred is flung out of a car after being beaten and set alight. Fred accuses the union boss but Braun counterclaims the burns are as a result of Fred's arson attempt on his house. In disgust, Bill goes to the Labor Federation and they, in turn, contact the district attorney. Bill is prepared to testify against Braun, but Braun learns of it through a plant he has at the union and has Bill kidnapped. Bound, and with tape over his eyes, Bill is threatened and tortured but insists that he will testify the next day. Braun has his henchmen kidnap Bill's son Timmy and tells Bill that the boy will be killed if Bill takes the stand and tells the truth. Bill is taken back to his home blindfolded and released.

When Bill's wife Mary learns what has happened, she wants to call the police. But Bill thinks he can retrace his journey and rescue Timmy. With the help of investigators who have been waiting at his home to go over his testimony, he laboriously makes his way back to the house where Timmy is held captive. While Mary goes to phone the police, Bill and his group break into the house and a brawl erupts. The police arrive and arrest the gang but there is no sign of Timmy or Braun until they are discovered behind the false back of a closet. Braun is led away in handcuffs. The family unit is back together

NOTES: Tense and absorbing, *The Big Operator* deftly juxtaposes middle-class American family life against murder and corrupt labor practices. And, unusually, Mamie, as Mary Gibson, is on the side of the angels. She and husband Bill are the almost-too-perfect family unit with their young son Timmy, a wonderful performance from Jay North who would go on to stardom as television's Dennis the Menace. Well meaning and well intentioned, the Gibsons sometimes stand back to allow others to battle on their behalf instead of getting involved. For example, Bill watches from the sidelines as his son fights with his best friend. Later he remains on the sidelines and watches as his best friend takes on the corrupt union boss. After Fred is thrown out of a union meeting, Bill warns him not to be such a hothead.

BILL: How do you think you'll look without teeth?
FRED: A lot better than I'd look without guts.

It's a warning to a complacent America: be ever vigilant and don't stand by passively and let the next guy take the fall. Direct intervention is the answer. Bill doesn't learn this until his comfortable middle-class world is threatened, indirectly by his best friend being bashed and set on fire and later, directly, with his own kidnapping and the subsequent kidnapping of his son. Family life is sacrosanct and when this cornerstone of the American Dream is threatened, Bill comes out fighting although it sometimes seems his allies are an ineffectual bunch who seem to believe that doing the right thing for its own sake is its own reward and damn the personal consequences. Bill, once spurred into action, is possessed and becomes the avenging angel. In the car on his way home after his kidnapping, Bill is vigilant although still blindfolded and attempts to map the route via street sounds measured against the rate of his pulse. It's his grit and determination that propels him back to the gang's hideout to free his son. Director Charles Haas, helped by a fine atmospheric jazz score from Van Alexander, ratchets up the tension to screaming point. Earlier he has set the violent landscape with a darkly gripping murder in which the body is disposed of in a cement truck. And he's already teased the audience with a faux Jimmy disappearance that makes the real kidnapping all the more harrowing.

Mamie's adoring wife, Mary, is in some respects the banal hysterical housewife who goes to pieces when her child is abducted but she doesn't allow her despair to incapacitate her and rallies in support of her husband, even joining the fray against the kidnappers when it becomes necessary. Even as a wife and mother, Mamie is no passive wallflower. It's a touching performance and one most people would never have associated with Mamie.

The Big Operator is an unattractive look at labor corruption in the U.S. which has always had a love/hate relationship with the union movement. The script, which doesn't shy away from brutality, is from a short story by Paul Gallico (1897–1976), the prolific wordsmith most noted for *The Snow Goose* (1940), *The Poseidon Adventure* (1969) and the creation of the London charwoman Mrs. 'Arris. *The Big Operator* is based on *The Adventures of Joe Smith, American,* a short story which appeared in *Cosmopolitan* and was filmed

Mary Gibson (Mamie) and Bill Gibson (Steve Cochran) in a moment of happiness before a corrupt union boss tears their lives apart in ***The Big Operator*** (MGM, 1959).

originally as *Joe Smith, American* in 1942. Robert Young then played the average Joe, Joe Smith, an aircraft factory worker during World War II who is kidnapped and tortured for the secret to a radical new bombsight by enemy agents. The story was adapted to the screen by Allen Rivkin for the 1942 film and he was given the same chores on the 1959 version which turned Joe Smith, aircraft worker, into Bill Gibson, precision tooler. Rivkin, with co-screenwriter Robert Smith, fashioned a script which remained true to the original by creating a family unit, a symbol of America itself, fighting the evil forces, in this case not that common 1950s bugbear communism but corrupt union bosses a la Jimmy Hoffa.* This threat of violence makes it more immediate than the threat of an ideology, like communism, would have.

It's a tough film and it has tough performances. Mickey Rooney in particular is superb as union dictator Little Joe Braun, ably supported by Steve Cochran in one of his best-ever performances (tough and resilient under torture while sympathetically instilling courage in his young son who is under threat of death), Mamie and Jay North as the idealized nuclear family, and by the effective performance of Mel Tormé as Fred McAfee. The cast is rounded out by the usual reliable Zugsmith repertory company that includes the irreplaceable Jackie Coogan, Ray Anthony, Ziva Rodann, Vampira, Charles Chaplin Jr. and the underrated (and under-utilized) Norman Grabowski.

REVIEWS: "Unpleasant gangster exploitation melodrama from the bottom of the barrel." *Halliwell's Film & Video Guide*

"*The Big Operator* marked a departure for Mickey Rooney, cast as a sadistic gang leader ... Mamie Van Doren [is] good as a housewife..." John Douglas Eames, *The MGM Story*

"Suspense is high and so is the violence ... Smith and Rivkin respected the Gallico story and provided cast and crew with a no-nonsense, tense story that never flags. When the film community begins to appreciate that it all begins with the word and that no star will triumph over bad material, movies will be a lot better off." *Motion Picture Guide*

"Another labor-racketeering movie ... cheerfully exploitative treatment..." *The Gangster Film*

"A walloping labor rackets melo with enough stamina to carry it through the general market to hefty grosses ... [It] packs highly topical exploitation potential ... Mamie Van Doren, as Cochran's wife, lands excellent distaff interest..." *Variety*, August 5, 1959

"A characteristic Zugsmith production, purporting to expose American labor rackets while dwelling with relish on scenes of torture and violence." David Meeker, *Jazz in the Movies*

"Mr. Zugsmith has specialized in taking the stories that scream from the headlines—teen-age dope addiction, miscegenation, labor racketeering—and turning them into lurid, sensational, utterly superficial melodramas. Obviously turned out for the fast buck, they seem specifically designed to exacerbate the tensions of our society. *The Big Operator* is no exception. ... Every scene, every violent incident seems designed to shock, not to enlighten. And the only solution to the problems raised is the kind of slam-bang, knockdown fight that has served the Western in good stead since the days of William S. Hart. It is just possible that labor racketeering demands action somewhat less direct." Arthur Knight, *Saturday Review*, September 26, 1959

"For the first 30 minutes of this exposé of the labor rackets, we had the crazy notion that executive producer Uncle Albert Zugsmith had turned respectable and was going to let his exploitation fans down. Fortunately for them (and unfortunately for us), Uncle Albert comes good (or goes bad, depending on your point of view) and the film turns out as piously sadistic as any unhealthy extrovert could wish. Still,

---

James Riddle "Jimmy" Hoffa (1913–75?) was a labor leader with ties to crime syndicates. He wielded considerable power as the president of the International Brotherhood of Teamsters for a decade from the mid–1950s to the mid–1960s. He was jailed in 1964 for attempting to bribe a member of a grand jury but his 15-year sentence was commuted to time served by Richard Nixon. Hoffa disappeared, presumed murdered, in 1975.

Bill (Steve Cochran) and Mary (Mamie) with neighbor Fred McAfee (Mel Tormé), who has been bashed and burned by thugs in *The Big Operator* (MGM, 1959).

Van Doren as an incongruous hausfrau is unintentionally amusing ... Haas has directed with punch, the music score is suitably wild, and the sets show the expert hands of art directors Hans Peters and Preston Ames." *Film Index* #49

Guns, Girls and Gangsters • Imperial Pictures, 1959

A Cheating Blonde ... A Crazed Con ... The Biggest Armored-Car Robbery in History!

CREDITS: *Director:* Edward L. Cahn; *Producer:* Robert E. Kent; *Script:* Robert E. Kent, *Story by* Paul Gangelin and Jerome Sackheim; *Music:* Buddy Bregman; *Musical Director:* Emil Newman; *Choreographer:* Jack Baker; *Photography:* Kenneth Peach; *Editor:* Fred Feitshans; *Art Director:* William Glasgow; *Set Decorator:* Morris Hoffman; *Wardrobe Man:* Einar Bourman; *Wardrobe Woman:* Vou Lee Giokaris; *Makeup:* Layne Britton; *Assistant Director:* Jack R. Berne; *Sound:* Jack Solomon; B&W; 82 minutes.

SONGS: "Anything Your Heart Desires" (Buddy Bregman, Stanley Styne) *Mamie Van Doren*; "Meet Me Half Way, Baby" (Buddy Bregman, Stanley Styne) *Mamie Van Doren*

CAST: Mamie Van Doren (*Vi Victor*); Gerald Mohr (*Chuck Wheeler*); Lee Van Cleef (*Mike Bennett*); Grant Richards (*Joe Darren*); Elaine Edwards (*Ann Thomas*); John Baer (*Steve Thomas*); Paul Fix (*Lou Largo*); Carlo Fiore (*Tom Abbott*); Beal Wong (*Mr. Wong*).

PLOT: Chuck Wheeler stands atop a hill overlooking the highway, armed with a rifle. He is waiting for a car with black marketeer Joe Darren as a passenger to pass on its way to Los Angeles. Wheeler shoots out the front tire and the car careens to a stop outside the Stage Coach Inn, the third such incident in two weeks. Darren's girlfriend, entertainer Vi Victor, is surprised to find a stranger in her dressing room after her show that night. It's Wheeler with a message from her husband, with whom Wheeler recently shared a cell at San Quentin. He slaps her. That's her husband's answer to her request for a divorce. He asks her to set up a meeting with Darren, and she refuses. Wheeler tells her next time she sees him to ask about the blown tire and also reveals he is staying at Huggin's Trailer Court. To make sure she mentions it, he makes a pass at her. Angry, she calls Darren and tells him and he tells her he'll take care of it.

Wheeler is outside waiting for Vi; he forces her into his car and drives out to the trailer park. The ruse has worked and Darren is waiting for him but he turns the tables by asking him to join in a plan to rob an armored car of $2 million. Darren is definitely interested in the plan that has been hatched by Wheeler and Mike Bennett while in prison but is shocked to learn that Mike is due for release in three months. Also involved is Lou Largo, who has created a radio that picks up the police frequency and also that of the armored car command.

Vi wants nothing to do with the scheme but is persuaded when Darren tells her he is dumping her in fear of her husband's imminent release and that her employment will be terminated. It's Darren's task to find a fence for the stolen money. He finds Mr. Wong, who runs a Singapore syndicate and into whose Los Angeles warehouse the money will be delivered.

Vi drives behind the armored car towing a horse trailer in which Wheeler is hidden, recording the coded radio check-ins between the armored car and their base. She then checks into the Stage Coach Inn and requests a front room which will enable her to check out any car and truck movements at the garage-motel. She becomes friendly with the young married couple, Ann and Steve, and they invite her to their New Year's Eve party.

Her husband Mike escapes from prison and beats and kills Lou Largo after he reveals Vi's whereabouts. Then he waits in hiding to force Darren at gunpoint to drive him to her hotel. Darren attempts to overpower the armed Mike but is shot and killed, his body dumped beside the highway. At the motel, Wheeler asks Vi to go with him to Mexico after the heist is pulled. She agrees but Mike is waiting for them back at her cabin. The men declare a truce for the benefit of the job but acknowledge only one of them will live to spend the pickings.

The next day all goes according to plan but Mike kills the armored car guards and is

Mamie is nightclub singer Vi Victor in the gritty heist drama, *Guns, Girls and Gangsters* (Imperial Pictures, 1959).

about to kill Ann and Steve when Vi gets hysterical. Mike knocks her out and Wheeler takes the couple away from the highway to shoot them with a silencer. Vi is bundled into the armored car which heads toward Los Angeles and success. Using the tape recording of the coded messages Wheeler has made, they radio the base at the next checkpoint but the dispatchers know something is up because the code has been changed for the new year. The police are notified but the robbers hear it on the police radio frequency and head back to the Stage Coach Inn where they will reload the sacks of cash into Wheeler's car and head across the desert. But the police arrive before they can make their escape and Mike is shot down and Wheeler machine gunned. Vi is taken away but Ann and Steve appear and tell the arresting officers their survival is due to Vi's pleading and Wheeler's firing in the air. The narrator intones:

> "There can't be a tomorrow for those who live only for today."

NOTES: Even though Mamie took *Guns, Girls and Gangsters** for the money, she has mellowed in her view of it over the years: "It was a gun moll, Jean Harlow–type of role. There was no comedy in that at all. It was a straight dramatic role. I had to work my butt off in that. You didn't think about anything except your acting, which had to be really good. I kind of liked that role."[†]

And it's a good role in a good film, marred (but not fatally) by its portentous voiceover which does give the film the trappings of tragedy and inevitable retribution. It adds a certain tension and verisimilitude in the same way Walter Winchell would in the successful television gang drama, *The Untouchables* (1959–1963). But the film would have been better without it.

Mamie is top billed as a world-weary nightclub singer whose husband is in jail and who is the lover of the nightclub owner. But she is merely another of his chattels. Although her character, snarls out the line "Nobody owns me now, nobody's going to. No muss, no fuss," she really is beholden to the men who surround her. Seeking a divorce from her jailbird husband, she is subsequently dumped by the nightclub owner who essentially forces her to take part in the armored car robbery against her better judgment. But she needs money to escape the life she finds herself in and it's the only ready cash she can lay her hands on. And the mastermind of the robbery, Chuck Wheeler (Gerald Mohr[‡]), is eager to get his hands on Vi.

In her dressing room after she's been forced by circumstances to join the robbery, Wheeler is persistent in his attentions, and wants her to quit her singing job.

WHEELER: When are you quitting here?
VI: As soon as you let me know about getting the information you want.
WHEELER: I should know by tonight what the first move will be.
(He puts his hands on her shoulders)
VI: Seems to me you're already making it.
WHEELER: I'm waiting for you to stop me.
VI: *(Breaking out of his grip)* The red light just went on.
WHEELER: You waited too long.
VI: I meant what I said. I'm out strictly for little old Vi now. Remember that, it might give you something else to think about.
WHEELER: I don't mind waiting as long as I'm first in line.

This is the land of the hard-boiled criminal and the equally hard-boiled dame. But in the case of the dame, she has a soft center and during her stay with the financially struggling newlyweds, the Thomases, she has a glimpse of what life could have been like and, perhaps,

---

**Although usually listed as* Guns, Girls and Gangsters, *the title in the film's credits has no comma.*
[†]Femme Fatales, February 1997, 17.
[‡]*Gerald Mohr (1914–68) landed a . job as a CBS staff broadcaster, and that led to work with Orson Welles' Mercury Theatre. He made his Broadway debut in* The Petrified Forest *as a gangster in the play that kick-started Humphrey Bogart's career. On radio extensively in the 1940s in* The Adventures of Philip Marlowe *and* The Whistler, *Mohr was named Best Male Actor on Radio. In film he passed relatively unnoticed until* Lady of Burlesque *(1943) with Barbara Stanwyck but he was unable to escape the trenchcoat typecasting on film and TV. He died of a heart attack, aged 54, while filming the pilot of a new TV series,* Private Entrance.

Vi (Mamie) sings "Meet Me Half Way, Baby" at a New Year's Eve celebration at the motel where she is staying in *Guns, Girls and Gangsters* (Imperial Pictures, 1959).

could still be like. They go out of their way to be friendly and Vi is knocked unconscious when she intervenes to save their lives. She is not totally rotten, nor is Wheeler who eventually breaks down her resistance to his advances. He spares the couple.

Mamie's performance is one of her very best. She gets a nightclub production number, "Anything Your Heart Desires," and a more uptempo number to jukebox accompaniment, "Meet Me Half Way, Baby," at the Thomases' New Year's Eve party. Both were penned by Buddy Bregman and Stanley Styne, who also supplied the numbers for *Born Reckless*. Her basically decent girl gone bad is matched by Gerald Mohr's low-key performance. A Humphrey Bogart lookalike, his career never reached the heights of his doppelganger but here his laconic but vicious performance (tinged with enough humanity to make him salvageable and enough of a rough gentleman to make him appealing to Vi) grounds the eye of the criminal hurricane that eventually leads to tragedy. As the murderous psychotic who brings about the gang's downfall, Lee Van Cleef* is chillingly effective.

It's little wonder this movie has popped up on the *film noir* festival circuit in the past decade. It's a superior heist movie that has the inevitable moral ending given the times. Director Edward L. Cahn was the perfect director, having cut his teeth on B-crime melodramas

---

Lee Van Cleef (1925–89) began his professional career on stage where he was noticed and cast in the non-speaking but important role of Jack Colby in the classic western High Noon *(1952). A series of villain roles followed before his cult following from Sergio Leone's spaghetti western* Per qualche dollaro in più/For a Few Dollars More *(1965) made him a cult anti-hero and an international star.*

in the 1930s, graduating to the inevitable rock movies and science fiction films of the 1950s with the "classic" *Creature with the Atom Brain* (1955), *Shake, Rattle & Rock* (1956), and *Dragstrip Girl* (1957). His spare, no-nonsense style works to perfection with this morality tale. He would go on to direct Mamie in *Vice Squad*, another gritty melodrama about the prostitution racket, released a year later. But by this time the television crime drama was becoming the market mainstay for this type of material.

Mamie dominates the proceedings as the singer drawn into the robbery by circumstances and she has a nice line in stoic self-preservation, matched by Mohr as the "romantic" lead and by Grant Richards* as the sleazy and cowardly opportunist who dumps her and blackmails her at the first sign of trouble. This is one of the best of Mamie's films.

REVIEWS: "Vicious and cynical, it's convincing on the robbery, but not in its characters." *Picturegoer*, November 29, 1958

"Van Doren lends her voluptuous blonde self to this crime tale ... Van Doren's the only reason to watch and it's surely not for her acting or singing." *The Motion Picture Guide*

Vi (Mamie) cradles her dead boyfriend, Chuck Wheeler (Gerald Mohr), after the heist goes badly wrong in *Guns, Girls and Gangsters* (Imperial Pictures, 1959).

B-picture stalwart Grant Richards (1916–63) did voiceovers for the popular 1930s radio series Gangbusters *and became a regular in movie and television westerns and crime series.*

The Beat Generation • MGM, 1959

The wild, weird world of the Beatniks! ...Sullen rebels, defiant chicks...searching for a life of their own! The pads...the jazz...the dives... those frantic "way-out" parties... beyond belief!

CREW: An Albert Zugsmith Production. *Director:* Charles Haas; *Script:* Richard Matheson, Lewis Meltzer; *Music Conductor:* Albert Glasser; *Choreographer:* Hamil Petroff; *Photography:* Walter H. Castle; *Art Direction:* William A. Horning, Addison Hehr; *Set Decoration:* Henry Grace, Jack Mills; *Paintings:* John Altoon; *Assistant Director:* Ridgeway Callow; *Editor:* Ben Lewis; *Makeup:* William Tuttle; *Sound:* Franklin Milton; *Women's Costumes:* Kitty Mager; *Dialogue Coach:* Jackie Coogan; CinemaScope; B&W; 95 minutes.

SONGS: "The Beat Generation" (Walter Kent; Tom Walton) *Louis Armstrong and His All-Stars*; "To Whom It May Concern" (Nat "King" Cole, Charlotte Hawkins) *Nat "King" Cole (on soundtrack)*; "Love" (Ralph Blane, Hugh Martin) *Cathy Crosby*; "Someday You'll Be Sorry" (Louis Armstrong) *Louis Armstrong and His All-Stars*; "I'm Off to the Moon" (Lewis Meltzer, Albert Glasser) *Dick Contino*; "I've Got the Real Gone Nothing Blues" (Lewis Meltzer, Albert Glasser) *Dick Contino*; "The Beat Is Ours" (Lewis Meltzer, Albert Glasser) *Dick Contino, Beat Club Patrons*; "Speed, Speed, Speed" (Lewis Meltzer, Albert Glasser) *Dick Contino, Beat Club Patrons*

CAST: Steve Cochran (*Detective Sgt. Dave Culloran*); Mamie Van Doren (*Georgia Altera*); Ray Danton (*Arthur Garrett/Stanley Belmont/Stan Hess*); Fay Spain (*Francee Culloran*); Louis Armstrong and His All-Stars (*Themselves*); Maggie [Margaret] Hayes (*Joyce Greenfield*); Jackie Coogan (*Jake Baron*); Jim Mitchum (*Art Jester*); Cathy Crosby (*The Singer*); Ray Anthony (*Harry Altera*); Dick Contino (*Singing Beatnik*); Irish McCalla (*Marie Baron*); Vampira (*The Poetess*); Billy Daniels (*Dr. Elcott*); Max ["Slapsie Maxie"] Rosenbloom (*Wrestling Beatnik*); Charles Chaplin Jr. (*Lover Boy*); [Norman "Woo Woo"] Grabowski (*The Beat Beatnik*); Paul Cavanagh (*Mr. Hess*); *Uncredited:* Anne Anderson; Bobi Byrnes; Regina Gelfan [Carrol]; Gerry Cohen; Phyllis Douglas; Fred Engelberg; Diane Fredrick; Melody Gale; Paul Genge; Fred Hansen; Shirley Haven; Darlene Hendricks; Carolyn Hughes; Nancy Kay; John Melfi; Sid Melton; Gil Perkins; Hamil Petroff; Kathy Reed; William Schallert; Cole Simpson; Phyllis Standish; Guy Stockwell; Larri Thomas; Renata Vanni; William Vaughn; Camille Williams.

PLOT: A serial rapist, The Aspirin Kid, inveigles his way into married women's homes on the pretext that their husbands have loaned him money and he is there to pay it back. Once inside he pretends to have a headache and asks for a glass of water, overpowering the woman when she returns from the kitchen. He then bashes and brutally rapes them, leaving a small container of aspirin as his calling card. On the case is cynical and misogynistic Detective Srgt. Dave Culloran, who has been desensitized by his three years on the vice squad, and his partner Jake Baron. Culloran bullies the victims and his partner warns him he is the mirror image of The Aspirin Kid in his treatment of women. Victim Joyce Greenfield helps an artist create a composite of the attacker; a young beach bum, Art Jester, is picked up as matching it but he is released when The Aspirin Kid rings the station and sets up an appointment to meet the two cops. It's merely a ruse to enable the attacker to assault Culloran's wife. Culloran becomes even more obsessed with tracking down the assailant after the rapist rings him gloating.

Art Jester is The Aspirin Kid's protégé and he's sent out to rape the next victim himself. His target is Georgia Altera but he is thwarted when her estranged husband lets himself into her home at the pivotal moment. When he finds tell-tale aspirin on the floor, the police are called. Culloran is disgusted by Georgia's attitude and lack of cooperation. His home life is suffering because of his inability to cope with his wife's obvious psychological problems resulting from the attack, and it's plunged deeper into crisis when she reveals she is pregnant and it could be the rapist's child. She toys with the idea of abortion but Culloran's automatic response is that abortion is against the law. He

Posed publicity shot of Steve Cochran and Mamie for *The Beat Generation* (MGM, 1959).

can't find it in himself to comfort his distressed wife. The cop is convinced one of the victims will be contacted again and continually harasses the women in an effort to find out which one. In particular, he stalks Georgia until she finally breaks down and admits she has set up a date with Art. When he doesn't show, she rings him and, after admitting to The Aspirin Kid that he gave her his phone number, she is invited to the beat club the rapist owns. Georgia turns up in her car with Culloran hidden in the back seat but when he attempts to arrest Art he is overpowered and both he and Georgia are tied up in rooms at the back of the club. While the Kid is entertaining in his club, Georgia persuades Art to let them go. A cat-and-mouse pursuit follows until The Aspirin Kid dons diving gear and attempts to escape with Culloran in hot pursuit. An underwater fight results in The Aspirin Kid's capture. Francee Culloran, who has rejected the idea of abortion after speaking with a neighborhood priest, gives birth to a baby girl and she and her husband are reconciled.

NOTES: The title has very little to do with the content of this extremely cynical crime film in which the hero and the criminal are from the same mold. The beat aspect is merely background coloring, a color producer Zugsmith seemed to like. Garrett (he has various names throughout the film), aka The Aspirin Kid, is an opportunist who is using the beat movement as a moneymaking exercise. Perhaps a little like MGM which copyrighted the title even though Jack Kerouac had used it previously on one of the early drafts on what would become *On the Road* (1951) and an unproduced three-act play he had written in 1953 (the third act was filmed in 1958 but with the title *Pull My Daisy*). The script for *The Beat Generation* was by famed science fiction-horror author Richard Matheson* and Lewis Meltzer, who had co-written the Mamie vehicle, *High School Confidential!*

Mamie plays the potential target of the serial rapist although he sends his protégé, Art Jester (Jim Mitchum), as proxy for practice. But Mamie's Georgia Altera, separated from a jealous husband, warms to the young man. Even after being warned of the dangers, she pursues her would-be attacker. The sexual politics of the film are fascinating. The investigating detective, played by Steve Cochran (with whom Mamie was romantically involved during filming), is almost as much a woman hater as his quarry, in part because of his bitter first marriage. But this bitterness carries over into his job (where he humiliates and bullies the victims) and into his home life, especially after his wife becomes a victim, and he finds it difficult to touch her physically and emotionally. He is impotent to help in the face of her suffering and sublimates his anger in an obsessive pursuit of the perpetrator.

Tucked away in the film is the subtle implication of a homoerotic relationship between Garrett and Jester. While Georgia is a prisoner at the back of the beat hang-out, watched over by Jester, she attempts to win her freedom. "Art, I thought you liked me. You know I like you. Look, you're in a real jam but you don't have to be. You don't have to be a pigeon for that guy. You can still get out of this. If you don't do the right thing real quick, there's gonna be a murder and you'll be going to the gas chamber with your boy friend." After he's kissed her, she asks, "Would you rather be dead with him or alive with me?" The answer is a no-brainer. Art is awkward with women but doesn't have the hatred toward the gender that Garrett or Culloran have. And he's a polite boy; he says *please* even to his prisoners. Culloran later takes up the theme of homosexual attraction or, in this case, rape when he gets Garrett in a headlock and, pressing against his back, says, "This the way you did it to Arthur, huh? Was it fun?" Homosexuality was not a theme Zugsmith tackled in his moral melodramas and the lines above only hint at that hoary old misconception that gay men hate women so much they rape them.

Richard Burton Matheson (born 1926) is a prolific short story writer and novelist as well as screenwriter. Many of his novels and short stories have been turned into movies including Duel, The Shrinking Man, Hell House, *and* I Am Legend. *He has also written for many TV series including* The Twilight Zone, Thriller *and* Star Trek.

Georgia (Mamie) is saved from almost certain sexual assault when her estranged husband, Harry (played by her real-life husband Ray Anthony), makes a timely arrival in *The Beat Generation* (MGM, 1959).

Mamie's Georgia is a woman too long constricted by conventional society and she's looking to break out: out of an unhappy marriage, out of her loneliness, and out of stuffy conventionality. That she is the personification of that outdated clichéd woman who is "asking for it" is to misunderstand her attraction to the young Art Jester. She reacts intuitively to another dysfunctional soul, albeit one that she little realizes is being manipulated by an arch woman hater. As played by Jim Mitchum with just the right combination of eager puppiness and psychological dependence with an edge of danger, it's obvious why a woman like Georgia would be attracted to him.

It's these psychological permutations which led critics to label the film as sleazy and unsavory. Zugsmith jumped to the defense of his film in *Life* magazine, justifying the subject matter as "a terrific exposé against criminal rape. My pictures are moral essays. I don't make movies without a moral, but you can't make a point for good unless you expose the evil." But, whether by choice or accident, the film is much more than that. The serial rapist, played with icy malevolence by Ray Danton,* is a Schopenhauer sprouting pseudo beat. Pseudo because he fakes it for the money, the contacts and, particularly, as a cover for his perverse sexuality. He hates women, calls them "filth" and does not like to be touched or touch. He dons rubber gloves before he assaults the women and bashes them. When the film opens, a female friend is bemoaning the fact she has to leave the city and him. He responds:

GARRETT: Hey, hey. Play it cool, chick, now play it cool. You've got to go. Everybody's gotta move. You can't stand still and wait for the next mushroom cloud now, you dig?
WOMAN FRIEND: As soon as I cut out, you'll forget me.
GARRETT: Oh, man, you're the most. But there's no tomorrow, not while the sky drools radiation gumdrops. I mean, you've got to live for kicks. Right here and now. That's all there is.

And his kicks are of a particularly cold-blooded kind. His attitude toward beats is little different from that of Culloran who calls them "a bunch of fawning pseudo-intellectuals jumping on the gravy train of rebellion. I guess we've always had them. Fake bohemia. I don't know, maybe I'm getting old, Jakey, but they bore me." Both the cop and the rapist are cynical and cruel and when the cop's wife becomes a victim he is psychically bereft and unable to help her, instead mouthing platitudes when she reveals she is pregnant and it could be the rapist's child. Here the cop is confronted with real pain and all he can tell his wife is that abortion is against the law. Zugsmith's clever answer to the dilemma is to introduce a priest who, like the others, is unable to touch women, and who mouths the banalities that abortion is murder just as Francee's husband mouths similar banalities. Perhaps it's convenient filmic shorthand to get on with the rest of the plot and allow Francee a moment's anguish before she decides to keep the baby. Abortion was, and still is, a subject fraught with controversy. It was a controversy not within the scope of *The Beat Generation*.

Charles Haas, again, blends the elements of *noir* and crime thriller: jazz, beat satire, perverse sexuality and, surprisingly, comedy, with a skill unmatched by most of his contemporaries. If the sermonizing occasionally becomes heavy-handed, at least it is over quickly and the quirky and perceptive exploration of social alienation and existential paranoia returns to dominate this extraordinary film from the 1950s.

REVIEWS: "The beatniks of Albert Zugsmith's *The Beat Generation* are not angry young men, at all, but Freudian cases who impersonate statues and gaze moronically at Vampira reading a jingle on how to loathe one's parents. They constitute little more than atmosphere within the framework of an average cop-and-culprit yarn, but it's an atmosphere

---

*Ray Danton (1931–92) was a good-looking leading man who excelled at oily bad guys but was equally at home as a good guy. Married to Universal star Julie Adams, he successfully made the transition to television before heading to Europe for a number of movies in Spain and Italy between 1964 and 1969. On his return to the U.S. he began directing; his first film was AIP's *Deathmaster* (1972). His most memorable screen roles were in *The Rise and Fall of Legs Diamond* (1960), *Portrait of a Mobster* (1961), *The George Raft Story* (1961) and *The Longest Day* (1962).

"THE BEAT GENERATION"

The Aspirin Kid (Ray Danton) is about to assault Georgia (Mamie) in a room at the back of his "beat" club in *The Beat Generation* (MGM, 1959).

that is entertaining and off-beat enough to back up the exploitable title ... The screenplay often is obvious but just as often is exciting ... Mamie Van Doren looks her sexy self, plays her sexy self and is wholly believable." *Variety*, July 1, 1959

"*The Beat Generation* is enough to make any member or non-member walk outside the theatre and butt his head against the wall. This excruciating and tasteless little entertainment package arrived at neighborhood showcases yesterday, courtesy of Metro-Goldwyn-Mayer — if courtesy is the right word ... [T]he first reel of this Albert Zugsmith production has the potentials of a snug little thriller ... The mess that ensues, however, is downright embarrassing... [The] climax involves one battle in that beatnik den and another one under water. It's hard to tell the difference." Howard Thompson, *New York Times*, October 22, 1959

"An enervating mixture of slapstick, religiosity, psychological hokum and grubby sensationalism." *Monthly Film Bulletin*

"*The Beat Generation* is little more than a title that some executive thought would get the patrons away from the TV sets and into the theatre." *Motion Picture Guide*.

"Mamie Van Doren almost gave her all for cinema art at frequent intervals, as Albert Zugsmith productions kept zugging. In *The Beat Generation* she generated a beat in Ray Danton..." John Douglas Eames, *The MGM Story*.

"*The Beat Generation* is actually a compelling character study of indifferent cops and callous youth." *Film Noir*

"Any similarity between this Al Zugsmith tale and the artists/beatniks of the 1950s is purely coincidental ...The raunchy sets, lurid plot, and jive talk make the whole thing eminently palatable though, and Mamie is there to keep interest up when all else fails." Richard Staehling, *Rolling Stone*, December 27, 1969

Le Bellissime Gambe di Sabrina/The Beautiful Legs of Sabrina • Produzione Generale Cinematografica — Cei Incom, 1959

CREDITS: *Director:* Camillo Mastrocinque; *Producer:* Nino Crisman; *Screenplay:* Piero Pierotti, Vittorio Metz, Edoardo Anton, Marcello Fondato, based on a story by Piero Pierotti; *Music:* Lelio Lattazzi; *Photography:* Alvaro Mancori; *Editor:* Roberto Cinquini; *Set Decorators:* Mario Bedoni, Alberto Boccianti, Franco Fontana; *Costumes:* Gaia Romanini; *Assistant Director:* Carlo Lastricati; *Sound:* Guido Del Grande, Raffaele Del Monte; B&W.

SONG: "Don't Fool Around Sabrina" (Y.K. Broady, Lelio Luttazzi) Mamie Van Doren

CAST: Mamie Van Doren (*Sabrina*); Antonio Cifariello (*Teo*); Rossana Martini (*Toni*); Raffaele Pisu (*Mario*); Enrico Viarisio (*Il Commendatore*); Irene Aloisi; Mario Ambrosino; Willy Birgel; Lola Braccini; Guido Celano; Renzo Cesana; Mario De Simone; Adrian Hoven; Alice Kessler; Ellen Kessler; Donatella Mauro; Michele Riccardini; Bibi Socali; Edoardo Toniolo.

PLOT: "One night in Paris, there is a sensational burglary in a jeweler's shop, right under the nose of the night-watchman, who has his attention taken by a marvelous pair of feminine legs. In Rome, in an atelier where they are preparing an exhibition of jewelry, that magnificent pair of legs appears again, on a staircase that leads to a terrace: and a pair of hands appears too that take an imprint of the lock on the French window of the atelier.

"Those legs, the wonderful legs of the model Sabrina, are the bait used by her uncle, the false count Goffredo, the international thief that nobody can catch. Sabrina, a model, will be among the girls appearing at a fashion parade at the atelier. She will be one of the people wearing the jewelry, for which the capacious pockets of her uncle are all ready. But Ted, a young photojournalist, gets in the way.

"A stocking manufacturer has set up a competition with a first prize of millions for a photograph of the world's most beautiful legs to advertise his product, and Ted thinks of nothing else but those millions. Sabrina, on the other hand, thinks only about the jewelry, and doesn't want to know about the competition.

"To make things more complicated, Sabrina and Ted fall in love at first as a joke but it becomes real. Meanwhile, Toni, who works at the photo agency, is in love with Ted, and the stocking manufacturer is in love with Sabrina. As Sabrina's uncle is about to scoop up the jewels, she begins to have scruples. But Toni wins the beautiful legs competition and finds romantic consolation with Mario, another member of the photo agency, Ted gets Sabrina and a share of the prize money, and Uncle Goffredo gets the jewelry and goes abroad forever."*

NOTES: Although Mamie and the producers of this Italian-German co-production expected a backlash from Catholic Italy over her recently announced separation from husband Ray Anthony, she was mobbed by fans everywhere she went. And, as solace for her separated status she began a torrid affair with her co-star Antonio Cifariello. "He taught me that when in Rome, do [it] as the Romans do. And we did it a lot. I have a copy of *The Beautiful Legs of Sabrina*. It's in Italian, but it's a hot picture."†

A body double was used for the leg and ass shots. "The movie starts off with a scene similar to the one of Marilyn in *The Seven Year Itch* where her skirt is blown up. But you only see the legs. And they're not my legs. They like their women more voluptuous in Italy. Like Sophia Loren. A few more curves than American women have. But, at least, from the waist up, I had everything the average Italian male could possibly want. And more."‡

---

*Quoted from fractured English-language publicity material.
†Email to the author, July 4, 2006.
‡Phone interview with the author, July 8, 2006.

French-German poster for Italian movie *The Beautiful Legs of Sabrina* (1959).

Girls Town • MGM, 1959

Last Stop on the Road to Nowhere!

CREDITS: An Albert Zugsmith Production. *Director:* Charles F. Haas; *Script:* Robert Smith, *Story by* Robert Hardy Andrews; *Music:* Van Alexander; *Photography:* John L. Russell; *Editor:* Leon Barsha; *Art Directors:* Hans Peters, Jack T. Collis; *Set Decorators:* Henry Grace, Hal Gausman; *Makeup:* William Tuttle; *Assistant Director:* Ridgeway Callow; B&W; 90 minutes.

SONGS: "Girls Town" (Paul Anka) *Paul Anka, Mamie Van Doren* (over titles); "I Love You" (Paul Anka) *Cathy Crosby*; "Hey, Mama" (Paul Anka) *Mamie Van Doren*; "(I'm Just a) Lonely Boy" (Paul Anka) *Paul Anka*; "Wish It Were Me" (Buck Ram) *The Platters*; "It's Time to Cry" (Paul Anka) *Paul Anka*; "Ave Maria" (Franz Schubert; Sir Walter Scott) *Paul Anka*; "Girls Town" (Paul Anka) *Mamie Van Doren* (over end credits)

CAST: Mamie Van Doren (*Silver Morgan*); Mel Tormé (*Fred Alger*); Ray Anthony (*Dick Culdane*); Maggie [Margaret] Hayes (*Mother Veronica*); Paul Anka (*Jimmy Parlow*); Cathy Crosby (*Singer*); Gigi Perreau (*Serafina Garcia*); Elinor Donahue (*Mary Lee Morgan*); Gloria Talbott (*Vida*); Sheilah Graham (*Sister Grace*); Jim Mitchum (*Charley Boy*); Dick Contino (*Stan Joyce*); Harold Lloyd Jr. (*Chip Gardner*); Charles Chaplin Jr. (*Joe Cates*); The Platters [Tony Williams, Herb Reed, Paul Robi, David Lynch, Zola Taylor] (*Themselves*); Peggy Moffitt (*Flo*); Peter Leeds (*Michael Clyde*); [Norman "Woo Woo"] Grabowski (*Skin*); Jody Fair (*Gloria Barker*); Nan Peterson (*Carhop*); Karen von Unge (*Sister Agnes*); Susanne Sidney (*Carlie*); Wendy Wilde (*Sister Magdalene*); Gloria Rhoads (*Matron*); Nancy Root (*Jaguar Girl*); Bobi Byrnes (*Dolores*); Phyllis Douglas (*Eleanor*); *Uncredited:* Audrey Saunders; Carla Alberghetti; John Brennan; Alan Callow; Jack Carr; Robert S. Carson (*Chip's Father*); Bill Couch; Dick Dial; Claire Du Brey; Charlene Glazer; Fred Lerner; William Smith; Bruce Tegner; Kay Windsor.

PLOT: Fred and his girlfriend are making out in their car near the Jaguars clubhouse when there is a scream and they see a blonde girl in a scarf struggling with their buddy Chip. Later, after they see her running from the scene, they find Chip's body at the bottom of a cliff. Identification of the fleeing girl revolves around a lipstick engraved with the name Silver found at the site. Silver, who had a date with Chip, is actually out with Stan Joyce and the Dragons at Lake Malibu. When Fred turns up to confront her, a rumble breaks out but is broken up by the police. At the police station, Serafina, one of the girls from the local convent school for girls who has had problems with the law, has been apprehended in the hotel room of pop sensation, Jimmy Parlow, wearing only a lace nightie. Silver is sent to this same girls' school after Chip's dad wants her charged with murder even though there is only circumstantial evidence she was involved.

At the "home" Silver is forced to bunk with the disturbed Serafina and tough girl Vida and her doting henchwoman, Flo. Silver makes little effort to fit in although she lackadaisically attends dressmaking and typing classes. She starts up a relationship with the only male available, delivery man Dick Culdane, but drops him when she realizes he is a private detective hired by Chip's dad to get the goods on her. Silver is roughed up by a kangaroo court convened by the girls to enforce discipline on uncooperative inmates and Serafina goes into a rage of jealousy when Jimmy turns up at the school to sing and is friendly to other girls. She takes an overdose and is cared for by Silver and Mother Veronica. Meanwhile, Culdane is questioning Silver's younger sister, Mary Lee, about Chip's death and is getting close to the truth. She flees with Fred, who also has stumbled across the truth as she is wearing the same scarf that he saw the night of the accident. He blackmails her into participating in a drag race in which a boy is killed and she is apprehended by the police. Frightened that Mary Lee will squeal on him as the driver of the other car in the accident, Fred kidnaps her and is attempting to raise one hundred dollars to send her south to Mexico to work as a "hostess or something." She escapes and confesses all to Silver but is again kidnapped and taken to the Jaguars' hideout. Silver persuades some of the

Title lobby card for the cult classic *Girls Town* (MGM, 1959).

girls at the school and one of the nuns that her sister is in real trouble and they set out in pursuit leading to a confrontation in which Fred and his gang are apprehended. Silver is "released" from Girls Town just in time to hear the news that Serafina is to join the "sisterhood."

NOTES: This movie has everything. Paul Anka singing "Ave Maria" at the bedside of a girl who has taken an overdose because of her unhealthy adoration of him, Mamie as a hip-swiveling, gum-chewing bad girl, nuns the likes of which you won't find outside Hollywood fantasy, lesbian subtext (particularly between Vida and her acolyte Flo), and Mamie praying tearfully to St. Jude the patron saint of lost causes, all tied up with a ribbon of convenient pop psychology, mawkish religious piety, rock music and the deft production values of Albert Zugsmith and the vastly underrated directorial skill of Charles Haas. This movie is near perfect in cult movie status. The Zugsmith moral, embedded in all his movies, is so saturated in teen (especially heterosexual male) predilections as to be overpowered. The Catholic hierarchy saw through Zugsmith's ruse and insisted a scene of Mamie singing in the shower, filmed from the armpits up, be excised or cooperation would be withdrawn. "They cut the scene out. Cardinal Spellman didn't approve. Paul Anka wrote a song for me to sing while I was taking a shower and nothing showed. Only my head and arms while I was soaping up. Because it took place in a Catholic home for bad girls, it had to have Spellman's approval. I asked Zuggy to go tell him that even bad girls had to take a shower but it didn't do any good. It was cut."*

*Phone interview with the author, August 3, 2006.

Mamie's Silver, who is often erroneously described as taking the rap to protect her little sister when, in fact, she does not know of her sibling's involvement until long after her incarceration, aggressively asserts her individuality in a closed society that promotes uniformity as suggested by the almost expressionistic scenes in the typing school where the girls are merely automatons churned out by the well-meaning nuns as secretarial fodder. In providing the girls with a means to escape their poor socio-economic background and the cycle of juvenile crime, they are also crushing their individuality. Mamie's Silver emerges triumphant at the film's end with a new respect for the sisters but basically unchanged in outlook and fashion. The pony tail wins out over the wimple. But you can only wonder what's in store for the sexually repressed Serafina, who has offered herself willingly to an unreceptive pop idol for sexual gratification when she sublimates her natural inclination even further to join the convent.

There's much gratuitous criticism of teenagers, to the extent you begin to wonder if Zugsmith actually liked his target audience. Mother Veronica opines that teenagers are like lemmings which is a bit rich coming from a woman whose mode of dress and thinking is bent to regimentation and conformity dictated by the religious fashion of the day. But the cartoon piety blanketing the film is leavened somewhat by offbeat humor: When Silver asks what holy water is, she's told, "It's plain ordinary water with the hell boiled out of it." Silver calls Mother Veronica "ma" and when asked to call her "Mother" replies, "You mind if I call you something else? That's a dirty word to me." Parents are usually dirty words in Zugsmith movies: They are either weak, unsavory, uncaring or indulge in odious habits while criticizing their offspring for similar misdemeanors. (In *High School Confidential!* parents extol the virtues of booze while their kids are addicted to pot; in *College Confidential* the father has a collection of smutty magazines in the attic that are worse than the sex survey a college professor is conducting.)

But, if an audience is not attuned to the more subversive elements of the film, it can still be enjoyed as a camp classic for its all-female setting which wallows in the heterosexual male/lesbian fantasy world of a girls' prison where the inmates mete out a brutal form of justice. As if to reinforce the cult status of the film, a stage musical version was presented Off Off Broadway in May, 1999, at the Actors Playhouse, adapted from the film by Robie Carrigan. Anita Gates in *The New York Times* said the stage version "makes the movie look like art. It completely fails in its attempt to capitalize on the film's camp."[*] Mamie's character, renamed from Silver to Rusty to reference the actress's red hair, was played by Billie Madley, "whose acting ability consists of looking pleased with herself for having a nice body (nothing remotely resembling Ms. Van Doren's, however)."

Mamie is superb as Silver, the role fitting the actress like a pony tail. She is matched by Elinor Donahue[†] in the role of younger sister Mary Lee, who did not want to make the movie. "*Father Knows Best* was on hiatus and I was tired and looking forward to some relaxing time at home with my one-year-old son, Brian. My manager, Tillie Messenger, who brought the offer to me, said, 'You can't just turn it down. Here is what I'll do. I'll come back and ask them for a lot of money. It's a low-budget picture and they'll never agree to it — and you won't have to do it!' I agreed, and put it out of my mind, and continued filming the remainder of our television season. A week or so later she called me back. 'Well [long pause], guess what? They agreed to your salary without blinking an eye. So you have to do the movie.'

---

[*]The New York Times, *May 18, 1999.*

[†]*(Mary) Elinor Donahue was born in 1937 and as a child began appearing on radio and in vaudeville. Signed to Hollywood she made her first (uncredited) screen appearance at age five in, ironically,* Girls' Town *(1942). A series of younger sister roles followed over the next decade until stardom on TV as Betty "Princess" Anderson, the oldest daughter, of Robert Young and Jane Wyatt in* Father Knows Best *(1954–60). In 1998, she published her memoirs,* In the Kitchen with Elinor Donahue, *which also included 150 of her recipes.*

Silver (Mamie), a bad girl, smokes even when the nuns tell her not to in *Girls Town* (MGM, 1959).

"Why he [Zugsmith] had wanted me is a mystery. I am a brunette, I needed to be blonde. My measurements at that time were 34(A)-22-34, I needed to be busty. My barefoot height is a tad under 5'5", my 'big sister' Mamie Van Doren is petite. But we pressed on with the preparations.

"Of course, my first visit was to the hair and makeup department at MGM. It was a homecoming of a sort, as I had spent my happiest childhood years there as a contract player from late 1946–49. And I had been made blonde before. In 1951 for *Her First Romance* with old friend Margaret O'Brien, and immediately after kept the color to be in *Love Is Better Than Ever*, a Stanley Donen movie starring Elizabeth Taylor. So, I was looking forward to my transformation from Betty Anderson and her ponytail.

"Becoming blonde was a snap, but it was deemed I didn't have the tresses of a glamour girl's sister. The easy decision was for me to wear a 'fall,' a hair piece. They are very comfortable and I liked them. Of course the figure part was easy. Just put on the old padded bra, and away we go.

"There was only one thing to do about my height and that was to put me in ballerina flats in all my scenes. As it was, I seemed to tower over the size-challenged cast members. Mel Tormé, Dick Contino, Ray Anthony and the itty-bitty Paul Anka, not to mention the star herself, Miss Van Doren, were (let's face it) short. Even my good friend from our child actress days, Gigi Perreau, was little. Only model Peggy Moffit, Gloria Talbott and probably a few others were as tall as I, but I had no scenes with them.

"On my first day of shooting on MGM's back lot, the actors' trailers were all lined up in a row. We finished on schedule, fighting the light, and I was thrilled to be able to get to my house at a reasonable time. I'd got a few admiring looks from crew members that day, and I was waved goodbye as I ran to the trailer. Off came the long, blonde fall, off came the padded bra, on went my favorite work jeans and comfy plaid shirt and after grabbing my purse and script bag, I flung open the door to the smiling faces of those few crew members and watched as their faces fell in horror as their 'sexy' teen emerged a very ordinary young woman.

"I didn't learn to drive a car until I was 18 or so. Because the only time I could take a lesson was on my lunch hour from *Father Knows Best* and we shot in the middle of Hollywood at Columbia Pictures-Screen Gems (the traffic on Sunset Blvd. being very scary), I learned with the new automatic shift rather than bother with the stick or manual transmission. However, in *Girls Town* I was to drive—hysterically running away—and I mentioned to someone that I could only drive with an automatic. 'Oh—yeah—don't worry about it. No problem,' I was told by this person, so I put it out of my mind.

"Comes the day to shoot it, I strode confidently into the outdoor set. The car (an MG, I think, but a cute sports car anyway) was parked, the camera and lights already in place directly in front of the car. I was given directions and told my moves and we began a rehearsal. I was to hurriedly get into the seat, crying, turn on the car and gun it past camera left. There was only one problem. It was a stick shift. I didn't have any problem at all crying, because I was scared to pieces. It was the last shot of the day in Malibu, the sun was rapidly sinking and I had to drive this blankety-blank car. Mercifully, they got it in one take. I don't think the crew would have let the director call for another one, because after the hurried instruction on gas, clutch, pedal, etc., I nearly ran over the crew as the car leaped out of frame. Everyone screamed as I slammed on the brakes and lurched to safety. It's funny now, not so funny then.

"It was a pleasant shoot, as I recall now. I certainly didn't have to work every day, and probably because it was low-budget, the schedule was very well organized without a lot of sitting-around-doing-nothing for long stretches of time, which can happen on bigger-budget movies.

"I remember one day between set-ups seeing Ray Anthony and Miss Van Doren having a private talk—way off to the side, away from

Silver (Mamie) and her nemesis Vida (Gloria Talbott) in *Girls Town* (MGM, 1959).

any other people. There were rumors going around that they were not getting along. That the role for him had been written into the script so that he could keep an eye on her. Or maybe it was so she could keep an eye on him. I didn't know. I didn't care.

"But what struck me that day was how perfect they looked together. He was so darkly handsome and she was such a golden beauty. They were both perfectly formed and looked like dolls. Their expressions that day were somber and somewhat sad. No anger. No waving of arms. But very serious. I'd hoped what I'd heard was untrue, but apparently the rumors were correct, because the marriage didn't last much longer.

"I have an anecdote which I am hesitant to write, because it sounds so bitchy. But when it happened I found it amusing, of course, but also endearing. No one ever expected Mamie Van Doren to be the reincarnation of Sarah Bernhardt. Mamie was professional, knew her lines, followed direction. What more can be asked? Near the wrapping of the movie it was decided to write an added scene for the two of us to play. I'd already left the production (mercifully, I'd not yet dyed my hair back to its natural color) and was brought in just for this one short bit.

"The crew, the director and I were ready to rehearse on the camera set-up, but no Mamie appeared. Calls were made and we waited some more. She arrived finally, breathless and apologetic, and we began the scene. She was tentative, at best, and seemed lost. She knew her lines, but kept 'fluffing' them. The director took her

Silver (Mamie) and Mother Veronica (Maggie Hayes) try to keep Serafina (Gigi Perreau) awake after her suicide attempt in *Girls Town* (MGM, 1959).

aside, though in the small space they couldn't go far, or out of earshot of everyone. He was very frustrated, because, as usual, time was of the essence, and he said basically, 'What is the matter?!'

"And she, in her sweet, soft voice, said, 'I don't know. When I'm in a scene all by myself I'm fine, but when there's someone else ... [shrug].' It took a few tries, but we got it, and that was my very last day on *Girls Town*."*

REVIEWS: "This is merely another badly-executed, cheaply made (in black-and-white) exploitation item from Albert Zugsmith ... The inane plot and grade 'Z' (for Zugsmith) acting is compensated for by the unusual array of personalities trapped into this misadventure ... It was a sad sight to have the once mighty Metro-Goldwyn-Mayer ... release this stinker." James Robert Parish, *Prison Pictures from Hollywood*

"Typical bad girls and drag racing '50s flick." *Videohound*

The screenplay of the film is as flimsy as a G-string, and designed for somewhat the same purpose. There are ... disturbing scenes or approaches to scenes. The party scene which opens the film, for instance, is clearly intended to be as stimulating carnally as is possible. Scenes of Miss Van Doren in the tightest of costumes exchanging badinage with nuns are in dubious taste, to say the least. *Variety*, September 30, 1959

"In the correctional institution [Mamie] looks for the real culprit. Was it Mel Tormé? Paul Anka? Ray Anthony? The Platters? What are they all doing in a female lockup?" *The Psychotronic Encyclopedia of Film*

"A host of popular stars of the time helped sell this one at the box office, but its tawdriness lingers to embarrass them all." *The Motion Picture Guide*

"The marketing campaign said, 'This sexually explicit, low-budget film makes no pretensions about being anything other than offensive.' Sounds like a 'must see' film to me! ... Mamie is hot!" *The Video Beat!*, thevideobeat.com

"When the dykes haul [Mamie] before a mock court, she tells the most repulsive of them, 'Why don't you go bingle your bongle?'" Andrew Dowdy, *Movies Are Better than Ever*

Vice Raid • United Artists/Imperial Pictures, 1960

Syndicate Owned Sin-Center Smashed! Phony model agency exposed as B-girl headquarters!

CREDITS: *Director:* Edward L. Cahn; *Producer:* Robert E. Kent; *Script:* Charles Ellis; *Music:* Paul Sawtel, Bert Shelter; *Photography:* Stanley Cortez; *Editor:* Grant Whytock; *Art Director:* William Glasgow; *Set Decorator:* Morris Hoffman; *Property Master:* Max Frankel; *Wardrobe Man:* Einar Bourman; *Wardrobe Woman:* Rudy Harrington; *Hair:* JoAnn [Joan] St. Oegger; *Makeup:* Monty Westmore; *Assistant Director:* Herbert S. Greene; *Sound:* Al Overton; B&W; 70 minutes.

CAST: Mamie Van Doren (*Carol Hudson*); Richard Coogan (*Whitey Brandon*); Brad Dexter (*Vince Malone*); Barry Atwater (*Phil Evans*); Carol Nugent (*Louise Hudson*); Frank Gerstle (*Capt. William Brennan*); Joseph Sullivan (*Ben Dunton*); Chris Alcaide (*Eddie*); George Cisar (*Marty Heffner*); Nestor Paiva (*Frank Burke*); *Uncredited*: Jeanne Bates (*Marilyn*); Juli Reding (*Gertie*); Russ Bender (*Drucker*); Paul Bryar, George Eldredge (*Internal Affairs Hearing Officers*); Lester Dorr (*Malone's Receptionist*); Alex Goda (*Hennessy*); John Hart (*Thug*); Jack Kenney (*Leo Dempsey*); Nelson Leigh (*Louise's Doctor*); Tom McKee (*Whitey's Doctor*); Shepherd Sanders (*Mugsy*); John Zaremba (*Sidney Marsh*).

PLOT: Mugsy is apprehended at the bus station in Los Angeles transporting someone other than his wife across the state line, a federal offense that will land him in prison for five years. If he reveals who employs him, the cops will give him a head start before making an arrest. While Brandon is putting the girl back on the bus, Ben Dunton takes Mugsy to the police car. He tells him to run and then shoots him in the back.

Vince Malone is the kingpin behind the prostitution racket that uses phony modeling

---

*Letter from Elinor Donahue, May 17, 2006.

agencies as a front. He's feeling the pinch from the police clamp-down and gets a girl sent from the Detroit branch of the syndicate to help frame Brandon. Beautiful blonde Carol turns up and Malone promises to take real good care of her if she succeeds. He sets her up in an apartment as a struggling model. She's not impressed with the surroundings: "Great decorating job. Probably early Skid Row." At the apartment, Malone's henchman Phil Evans makes a play for Carol but she rejects it.

Brandon turns up at the Star Agency pretending to be a photographer looking for a model. He is recognized and paired up with Carol, who turns up at his hotel room that night to model in swimwear. He arrests her but she counterclaims he tried to extort money from her. The DA drops the case and police internal affairs is called in to investigate. Carol's testimony and that of his corrupt partner are enough to have him found guilty. Whitey confronts Dunton outside and learns he's been in Malone's pay for six years. Carol is rewarded by being put on Malone's personal payroll and is set up in a new apartment. Her young sister Louise turns up to stay for a few weeks. Brandon also turns up to confront Carol and pushes her around but she makes the mistake of denying she knows anyone named Malone. Alone in the apartment and trying on Carol's clothes, Louise is interrupted by Phil Evans, who promises to look out for a modeling position for the teenager.

Now a civilian, Brandon sets up in direct competition with Malone and is wildly successful (he has better contacts because of his police background). He has the unofficial backing of Captain William Brennan. The police raid Malone's agencies and all other agencies except Brandon's and even Carol is swept up in the busts. To show his power, Brandon organizes it so he is the only one who can bail her out. Evans makes another pass at her, thinking that the syndicate will soon move in and replace Malone with himself. Carol slaps him hard. Dunton, Brandon's former partner, is sent to kill him but he can't do it and instead makes an appointment to confess everything. But he is gunned down as he leaves Brandon's apartment.

Evans lures Louise to his apartment on the pretext of a modeling job and brutally assaults and rapes her. Carol is called to the hospital and Brandon waits for her and says he'll help if she gives him a list of Malone's contacts. She tells him she only wants Evans, not Malone. But Malone is unwilling to give up his henchman and Carol agrees to conceal a recording device in her handbag during the visit of the syndicate bigwigs to Malone's office to sound out Brandon. They reveal everything but Malone discovers the wire when he goes to Carol's handbag to get a cigarette. In the ensuing mêlée the syndicate bosses flee and Malone is machine gunned on the fire escape attempting to flee. Carol and Louise go back home to Middle America.

NOTES: Another tough girl role for Mamie. The film was released as the bottom half of a double bill with director Cahn's *Inside the Mafia* (1959), also produced by Robert E. Kent. What differentiates *Vice Raid* from television fare is the depiction of the ruthlessness of organized crime and corrupt police and, particularly, the severe physical aftermath of the brutal rape. The unflinching depiction of the brutalized young woman in the hospital is a shock tactic that works. Television was, at that stage, unable to explore the subject of prostitution and rape with the same intensity as that seen on film and Edward L. Cahn's *cinéma vérité* style, used expressively in the earlier *Guns, Girls and Gangsters*, is again effective albeit on a lesser story.

Mamie, who was back and forth between teen and adult roles at this stage, garnered good reviews. Her cynical hard-boiled dame for hire, knows enough to sleep with the boss and reject the advances of the hired help. Here's a dame who can take care of herself but is broken by her inability to take care of her young and impressionable sister. Mamie keeps a tight lid on the steely determination of Carol Hudson and heads a cast of (mainly television) heroes and villains including Brad Dexter, Richard Coogan, and Frank Gerstle. There's a strong supporting performance from Carol Nugent as her wide-eyed and envious younger sister, Louise. But it is Barry Atwater as the amoral

Phil Evans (Barry Atwater) propositions his boss's girlfriend, Carol Hudson (Mamie), and she's not impressed in *Vice Raid* (Imperial Pictures, 1959).

Phil Evans who matches Mamie in on-screen strength. His portrayal of the unrepentant rapist and girl basher made this film strong stuff for its day.

REVIEWS: "Except for the prostitute angle, there's not much difference between the Imperial Pictures production and television's 30-minute cops-'n'-robbers yarns ... Miss Van Doren has a few moments of rather believable acting..." *Variety*

"Capitalizing on the current wave of headline exposes and sex — which is always strong box-office bait, this low-budget ordinary program melodrama unfolds along standard lines but comes equipped with a number of exploitable possibilities. Foremost is the title, promising more than is actually delivered..." *Harrison's Reports*

"Another uneventful outing for Van Doren ... Van Doren showed more talent in this picture than usual, giving a fairly convincing portrayal of a call girl." *The Motion Picture Guide*

College Confidential • Universal-International, 1960

No Film Ever Dared Touch This Theme Before

CREDITS: *Producer-Director:* Albert Zugsmith; *Script:* Irving Shulman, *Story by* Albert Zugsmith; *Photography:* Carl Guthrie; *Music:* Dean Elliott; *Art Direction:* Alexander Golitzen, Malcolm F. Brown; *Set Decorations:* Julia Heron; *Editor:* Edward Curtiss; *Sound:* William G. Watson, Frank H. Wilkinson; *Makeup:* Bud Westmore; *Assistant Directors:* Ralph Black; 90 minutes.

Louise (Carol Nugent) tries to stop ex-cop Whitey Brandon (Richard Coogan) from slugging her sister, Carol (Mamie), the woman who set him up in *Vice Raid* (Imperial Pictures, 1959).

SONGS: "College Confidential" (Randy Sparks) *Randy Sparks*; "College Confidential Ball" (Conway Twitty) *Conway Twitty*; "Playmates" (Randy Sparks) *Randy Sparks*

CAST: Steve Allen (*Professor Steve Macinter*); Jayne Meadows (*Betty Duquesne*); Walter Winchell (*Himself*); Mamie Van Doren (*Sally Blake*); Mickey Shaughnessy (*Sam Grover*); Herbert Marshall (*Henry Addison*); Cathy Crosby (*Fay Grover*); Conway Twitty (*Marvin*); Randy Sparks (*Phil*); Pamela Mason (*Edna Blake*); Rocky Marciano (*Deputy Sheriff*); Sheilah Graham (*Herself*); Earl Wilson (*Himself*); Louis Sobol (*Himself*); Elisha Cook [Jr.] (*Ted Blake*); Ziva Rodann (*GoGo Lazlo*); Theona Bryant (*Lois Addison*); Nancy Root (*Sweet Young Thing*); William Wellman Jr. (*Bob*); [Norman] Woo Woo Grabowski (*Skippy*); Robert Montgomery Jr. (*Second Boy*); Stuart Randall (*Sheriff*).

PLOT: Small-town Collins College has been rocked by a sex scandal unleashed by the lies of one of the students, Sally Blake, who blames her sociology professor, Steve Macinter, for keeping her out until 2:45 in the morning answering his sex questionnaire. Her father, Ted, confronts Professor Macinter the next day and is shocked to find his office locked and a young female student with him. The professor's girlfriend, Lois Addison, the daughter of the head of the sociology faculty, wants him to give up his survey and, when he refuses, she walks out on him. To make matters worse, journalist Betty Duquesne is snooping after receiving an anonymous letter accusing Macinter of corrupting the college students. She meets him when he is filming college behavior, albeit the girls and boys in their swimwear, and is invited to a party at his place the following Friday when he will screen the film footage he has been shooting.

At the party, Macinter seems inebriated although the fruit punch is non-alcoholic. When he puts on the student film, spliced into it is a "pornographic" movie. As the students leave in disgust, the police, alerted to a "wild" party and "dirty" movies, arrive and arrest the professor. He is charged with corrupting the morals of minors. Bailed out, he leaves town but not before a lecture from journalist Betty, who has turned on him as easily as the students. On the day of the court case, the magistrate Sam Grover is distributing photographs of his star-struck daughter to the nation's press royalty, all of whom are there to see the trial that will "rock the education system." The court is shocked by some of the revelations but the magistrate finds that the survey, although not to everyone's moral liking, is supported by the college and is a legitimate field of study. What's more, the sex component is only two pages of the twenty. Further, on examination, the "obscene" film contained no nudity, the cast wore flesh-colored tights, and there was no sexual activity. Although Macinter is not allowed to defend himself, Sam dismisses the charges. The professor stands and lets loose with a barrage of criticism of the town "dirty-mindedness" and the repercussions of such behavior for the future of America. As he is leaving, an accident reveals that Sam was responsible for inserting the dirty movie in the professor's reel in order to get national press coverage for his daughter to break into the movie industry and escape the drudgery of small-town life. Macinter and Betty Duquesne walk away together.

NOTES: From the vantage point of fifty years on, the morality of *College Confidential* is quaint and the closed small-town "dirty-mindedness" horrifying, especially with the rise of Christian fundamentalism in the U.S. After he has the charges dismissed, Professor Macinter's final summation of the town's vendetta is apposite: "You know I was lucky. There are a lot of scientists engaged in studies and some group, through ignorance or fear or bigotry or whatever, is going to hound these men to inflame the passions of the mob until the people attack the very men who represent knowledge." And Macinter sees this as an attack on the very foundation of the U.S. However, his behavior toward his students, filming them in swimming costumes, giving them free access to his house when he's not there, and having student parties for them, would severely compromise him today.

For much of its running time the film is an engrossing time capsule of mid-twentieth century mores and the sexual behavior of young adults, changing much too fast and too liberally for the adult population. With the Kinsey Report* and its explosive revelations just over a decade old and the incidence of adolescent sexual experimentation leading to increasing teen pregnancies and sexually transmitted diseases, *College Confidential* attempts to tackle the subject head on. But screenwriter Irving Shulman,† working from a story by Albert Zugsmith, fudges the issues.

The film begins strongly and promisingly with the Blakes (Elisha Cook Jr. and Pamela Mason) worried because their teenage daughter Sally (Mamie) has not returned home and it's almost 3 A.M. When she does a few minutes later, she is unceremoniously dumped by a speeding car and she walks into a storm of questions and abuse. The prolonged argument between Cook's Ted and Mamie's Sally (with Mason's Edna sidelined and conflicted in her loyalties) is one of the movie's strongest scenes and is conducted mainly

---

American biologist Alfred Charles Kinsey (1894–1956) who founded the Institute for Research in Sex, Gender and Reproduction at Indiana University in 1947 and thereafter shocked bourgeois America with a series of reports beginning with Sexual Behavior in the Human Male *(1948), following up with* Sexual Behavior in the Human Female *(1953). Although his methods of collecting data were controversial, most of his theories on human sexual behavior have been accepted.*

†*Among Irving Shulman's (1913–1995). handful of screen outings was his adaptation of the iconic* Rebel without a Cause *from a story by Nicholas Ray.*

Sally Blake (Mamie) and Marvin (Conway Twitty) whoop it up in *College Confidential* (Universal, 1960).

in the claustrophobic space on the stairs, meaning it all takes place at close quarters, making the shouting all the more aggressive. Mamie's Sally, realizing she is caught in a trap of her own making, sits down on the step and is filmed through the stair railings as if behind bars. The image is reinforced by the dialogue that has preceded it. After Ted tells his daughter she would be forced to knuckle down to a more disciplined life if she was at a boarding school ...

SALLY: It just so happens I'm living at home though you do your best to make it into a jail.

TED: Oh, I make it into a jail. Well, what are your complaints, miss prisoner? Matching skirts and cashmere sweaters? A cell that costs more to furnish than any room in this house? A guard who ... who makes your bed and cleans up your daily mess?

SALLY: Even a warden hasn't got the right to go snooping in other cells.

TED: No? Who's got a better right?

SALLY: Before your screaming broke my eardrums, I heard you. You said, "Who's got a better right," correct?

TED: I'm gonna make this house really into a jail if you don't answer my original question

Where were you until 3 o'clock ... almost 3 this morning? Sally, I'm gonna ground you but good if you don't answer me. I'll see to it you go to your room after meals and you don't go anywhere on weekends.

SALLY: Mom, make him leave me alone.

TED: You'll go to none of the college affairs and instead of that formal your mother's asking me for, I'll use the money it would have cost to put bars on your windows and a time lock on your door.

SALLY: Why don't you put me to work in the yard breaking rocks? It'll make quite a sight for the neighbors.

The scene is well written and realized. The psychological nuances of a young girl caught out (she first attempts to divert attention from her misdemeanor by questioning her father's timekeeping, his impotent screaming jag caused by concern and relief, and the mother's cowering passiveness in the face of the verbal onslaught) are superb. It's a measure of the strength of the actors and director Zugsmith's control and placement that make the scene so

Fay Grover (Cathy Crosby) discusses the professor's sex quiz with a cynical Sally (Mamie) on campus in *College Confidential* (Universal, 1960). That's Randy Sparks in the background with the guitar.

effective. Sally, realizing her diversionary tactics to protect her boyfriend's identity are not working, changes from a dominant position (on the staircase standing up to, and over, her father) to the more subservient one of sitting on the stairs. She changes tack and plays the teen girl in danger but safe because of the way her parents have brought her up. The about-face works and the parents buy it. It's masterly film work. This work is matched later by Steve Allen's strong central performance as the humiliated but unbowed Professor Macinter who despairs of what is happening to his country which knows "more about sex than it does about love." He gives his tormentors a tongue-lashing which is a wake-up call for civilized societies and a wake-up call which is as valid today as it was in 1960.

But the film pulls its punches, never daring to transgress the morality it is, in part, criticizing. The questionnaire is rather preciously described in academese as "a social study of college-age youngsters and their reactions to a mechanistic environment that's poised with one foot in space and the other on the brink of nuclear destruction" (yet again promoting nuclear annihilation paranoia, a thread running through many Zugsmith films). Macinter justifies his survey on the grounds that "I thought it important to know what young people, the ones we refer to as our future leaders, thought about a world that's been at war since 1914." And, in one of the more ludicrous pleas for understanding, he says the source of the questions is the Bible plus the works of all great thinkers whose works bring us closer to God. He even goes on to quote *Hamlet*. The college kids never get to partake of the spiked fruit punch at the professor's party. Macinter imbibes freely himself; it's a plot point as he's a reformed alcoholic, but the kids are kept away from the cocktail so they are not corrupted by the filmmakers; the "dirty" movie they witness and to which they have an aggressive (and totally unbelievable) aversion turns out to be fake. That's because the film's "villain" is really only a sad little man who wants the best for his daughter.

Mamie's Sally Blake is one of the most unsympathetic characters she ever played and at the film's end she remains unrepentant. She's manipulative and demanding although the boyfriend she has been protecting is unworthy of her attention and treats her woefully. Mamie makes the most of it although after her initial strong dramatic scene she has little to do but look and sound badly done by. She's one of those middle-class brats who populate a number of 1950s juvenile delinquent movies and, although not a JD herself, is the spoiled offspring of World War II. Mamie doesn't sing in *College Confidential* (those chores are allocated to Randy Sparks[*] and Conway Twitty[†]) because the dramatic content doesn't really allow for musical numbers except when the students, who never seem to attend classes, are partying or at play.

In one of the film's worst jokes, Walter Winchell, one of a bunch of real journalists that appears vulture-like in the college town for the small-time court case, describes Sally Blake as "the Mamie Van Doren type." In many respects, *College Confidential* is the dramatic reverse of *Beach Party* (1963) in which Robert Cummings plays the surfside equivalent of Steve Allen's Prof. Steve Macinter.

REVIEWS: "Steve Allen and Jayne Meadows are such personable, alert performers that it is truly painful to find them co-starring in a piece of movie claptrap like *College Confidential* ... a picture best described as punk ... The students ...apparently never touch a book, continually grasp each other instead, or slither around mouthing a kind of steamy, beatnik jargon. The leaders are Ziva Rodann, Conway Twitty ... and that pneumatic leftover from

---

[*]*Singer-songwriter Randy Sparks (born 1933) appeared in a small number of films including* Thunder Road *(1958),* The Young Land *(1959) and* The Big Night *(1960) before going on to found the New Christy Minstrels, for whom he also acted as musical director, in 1962.*

[†]*Conway Twitty (real name: Harold Lloyd Jenkins) (1933–93) was a hugely successful pop singer elected to the Country Music Hall of Fame in 1998. He had between 41 and 53 number one hits depending on whose charts you believe.*

High School Confidential!, Mamie Van Doren." Howard Thompson *New York Times,* August 22, 1960

"Tinpot exposé of a highly dubious kind." *Halliwell's Film and Video Guide 2000*

"The producer of *High School Confidential!* steps out and directs the inevitable sound-alike follow-up. This time the small-time scandals involve sex instead of drugs..." *The Psychotronic Encyclopedia of Film*

"A courtroom finale (in a grocery store) attended by such journalists as Earl Wilson, Sheilah Graham, Walter Winchell and Louis Sobol promised more than it delivered. So did a cast that included Jayne Meadows, Mamie Van Doren, Cathy Crosby, Herbert Marshall..." Clive Hirschhorn, *The Universal Story*

"Walter Winchell, Earl Wilson and other members of the fourth estate show up in court to demonstrate their shortcomings as actors..." *The New York Herald Tribune* August 22, 1960

Sex Kittens Go to College • Allied Artists, 1960 [Aka: *The Beauty and the Robot*]

Never Before Has the Screen Had So Much Fun with the Student Body!

CREW: A Photoplay Associates Picture. *Director-Producer:* Albert Zugsmith; *Associate Producers:* Martin Milner, Robert Hill; *Script:* Robert Hill, *Story by* Albert Zugsmith; *Music:* Dean Elliott; *Choreographer:* Jack Baker; *Photography:* Ellis W. Carter; *Editor:* William Austin; *Set Decorator:* John Sturtevant; *Hair:* Elenore [Elenor] Edwards; *Makeup:* Monte [Monty] Westmore; *Assistant Director:* Ralph [E.] Black; B&W; 94 minutes.

SONGS: "Sex Pots Go to College" Mamie Van Doren; "Mamie's Song" Conway Twitty; "Baby" Mamie Van Doren

CAST: Mamie Van Doren (*Dr. Mathilda West*); Tuesday Weld (*Jody*); Mijanou Bardot (*Suzanne*); Mickey Shaughnessy (*Boomie*); Louis Nye (*Dr. Zorch*); Pamela Mason (*Dr. Myrtle Carter*); Marty [Martin] Milner (*George Barton*); Conway Twitty (*Himself*); Jackie Coogan (*Wildcat MacPherson*); John Carradine (*Prof. Watts*); Vampira (*Etta Toodie*); Allan Drake (*Legs Raffertino*); [Norman] Woo Woo Grabowski (*Woo Woo*); Irwin Berke (*Prof. Towers*); Jody Fair (*Bartender*); Arline Hunter (*Nurse*); Buni Bacon (*Night Club Hostess*); Babe London (*Miss Cadwallader*); John Van Dreelen; *Uncredited*: Charles Chaplin Jr. (*Fire Chief*); Harold Lloyd Jr. (*Policeman*).

PLOT: THINKO, a giant robotic computer at Collins College, selects Dr. Mathilda West, who has 13 college degrees and speaks 18 languages, as the new head of the science department. When the curvaceous blonde arrives on campus she causes consternation and envy among the women and lust among the male students and teachers. Also on the train that brought Dr. West are gangsters Legs Raffertino and Boomie, who have been sent by their boss to do away with THINKO, who is just a little too canny in picking horse race winners. They enlist the help of a French exchange student, Suzanne, who is researching her book *How American Men Make Love*; she promises to take them to what they believe is a rival racketeer.

Woo Woo, the captain of the college football team, gets hot flashes and faints around Dr. West much to the consternation of his girlfriend, Jody, while the college public relations director, George Barton, is trying to keep the lid on the disruptive blonde. Things get worse when the college benefactor, Wildcat MacPherson, turns up unexpectedly and Barton and the dean of the college, Dr. Myrtle Carter, attempt to hide Dr. West from him, fearing he will curtail his philanthropy if he finds a blonde sexpot running the science department. But when he meets her at the local night spot, The Passion Pit, he falls for her. The two gangsters recognize her as Tassels Monclair, the former Tallahassee Tassel Tosser, and expose her identity.

Dr. West realizes her childhood dream of being a teacher is folly and that she cannot escape her past but Barton is forgiving and asks her to marry him, thus leaving the coast clear for Jody and Woo Woo. Wildcat has fallen for the charms of Dean Carter and proposes. To top it all off, THINKO is cured of his gambling addiction and the gunmen leave town happy.

NOTES: Mamie never looked better than she did around her most prolific filmmaking period and her entrance stepping off the train

Tuesday Weld, Mijanou Bardot and Mamie on the set of *Sex Kittens Go to College* (Allied Artists, 1960).

at the small university town makes the most of it. But if her beauty was in the ascendant, the vehicles for showing it off weren't. This supremely silly farce would have done a campus beach party movie proud. Top-billed Mamie also sang "Sex Pots Go to College," which had been the film's original title, over the credits. The film had undergone a number of identity changes from *Teacher Was a Sexpot* to the final *Sex Kittens Go to College* before another identity crisis for television where it was renamed the more prosaic and more acceptable *The Beauty and the Robot*. The robot in question was the Westinghouse-constructed Elektro which was constructed in 1937 and displayed at the New York World's Fair in 1939. He was modified for the film by the insertion of a speaker square in his chest. The original now resides in the Mansfield Memorial Museum in Ohio.

Norman Grabowski* remembers working with Mamie because, as the college jock who faints whenever girls come near him, she kisses him. "Kissing on film is not like kissing for real and Mamie only gave me a peck which is what the script called for. I got the impression, working with her, she was unhappy because she hadn't become a big star like Marilyn and she wanted to."†

Albert Zugsmith came up with the story from which his house writer Robert Hill fashioned a singularly unfunny comedy. Hill had also penned the Zugsmith *Female on the Beach* (1955), *Raw Edge* (1956), and *The Female Animal* (1958), again from Zugsmith's story. There's something ad hoc and improvisational about this sluggish film as if the players are feeling their way as it unfolds. The cast may be having fun but most of the audience isn't. Even the added bonus, in the European print, of a sequence involving four strippers, ostensibly the dream fantasy of THINKO, is limp and likely to leave all but the most undiscerning male that way too. The reviews were scathing. Those that didn't attack it for tastelessness attacked it for being boring.

But Mamie made a friend on the set: "I met a young actress that reminded me of myself. Tuesday Weld was eight or nine years younger than me but we immediately became friends. She was a wild youngster, always looking for excitement. Tuesday and I zoomed around Hollywood on the Vespa motor scooter I had brought when I came back from Italy. We went to Palm Springs and spent a few days hitting the Racquet Club and other 'in' spots of the Hollywood week-end crowd."‡

REVIEWS: "Some big names can't save this farce about beauty and brains ... Strutting their stuff in tight sweaters along with Doren [sic] are Weld, Bardot (Brigitte's sister) and Vampira." *The Motion Picture Guide*

"Mr. Chips, if he could have seen *Sex Kittens Go to College*, would be very grateful to have said good-bye to the world of education when he did." *Los Angeles Times*

"One expects to see such people as Jackie Coogan, John Carradine and Louis Nye in garbage like this—but how did Tuesday Weld get talked into participating? And wait till you see that nightclub number performed by Conway Twitty." Hal Erickson, *All Movie Guide*

"Zugsmith strikes again! This time with a really lame story about strippers, robots, and college ... Theater owners were mixed on this one. One said: 'Used for late shows on Saturday night for the teenagers. They loved it!' Another one reported: 'The poorest picture we have had since *Top Banana* several years ago. Eighteen walked out the first hour, all teenagers, and five of them asked for their money back.' For the dedicated only." Alan Betrock, *The I Was a Teenage Juvenile Delinquent Rock 'n' Roll Beach Party Movie Book*

"Let's face it; with a title like *Sex Kittens Go to College* and a director like Albert Zugsmith,

---

*Norman Woo Woo Grabowski, actor and custom car designer (he designed Edd "Kookie" Byrnes' car in 77 Sunset Strip) was one of the stalwarts of the Albert Zugsmith repertory company, appearing in the Mamie vehicles High School Confidential! (1958), The Big Operator (1959), The Beat Generation (1959), Girls Town (1959), and College Confidential (1960). He retired from the business in the early 1980s to concentrate on his custom cars.

†Phone interview with the author, March 25, 2006.

‡Mamie Van Doren, Playing the Field

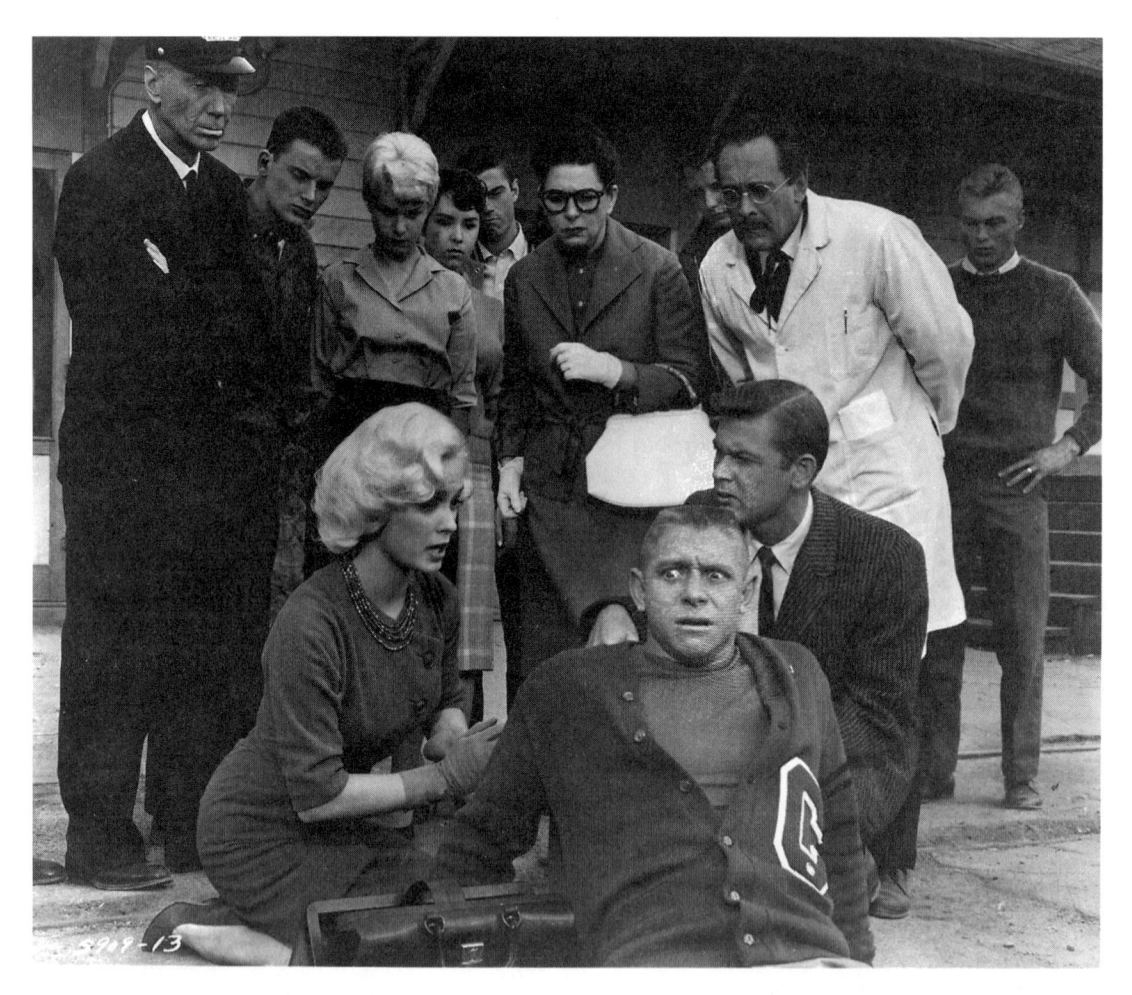

Dr. Mathilda West (Mamie) and George Barton (Marty Milner) go to the aid of Woo Woo (Norman Grabowski) after he has an adverse reaction to Dr. West in *Sex Kittens Go to College* (Allied Artists, 1960).

you won't be expecting anything along the lines of *Citizen Kane* ... and there are several things here I that I won't forget. Such as—

• Seeing Jackie Coogan engaging in a W. C. Fields impersonation.

• Watching Brigitte Bardot's sister Mijanou coming on strong to a gangster called Legs Raffertino in order to do scientific research.

• Watching John Carradine do the Charleston with Mamie Van Doren.

• Watching John Carradine do the tango with Mamie Van Doren.

• Watching John Carradine, Louis Nye, Jackie Coogan and Irwin Berke engaging in the same sexy dance moves being used by Mamie Van Doren which ends with a kick line on top of the bar." Dave Sindelar, scifilm.org

"Albert Zugsmith strikes again! ... Classic line from curvy nymphet Tuesday Weld, gazing at Mamie's tight-sweatered form: 'Why do you have to be so darned much of a woman?'" Steve Sullivan, *Va Va Voom!*

"Typical of producer Albert Zugsmith's movies, the cast is marvelously eclectic, ranging from oldtimers to budding sexpots to wives-, sons- and sisters-of-stars, but all flounder in a crude, slapstick sex comedy movie that *looks* like a cheap television variety show skit directed (badly) by a former Keystone Cop." Tom Weaver, *John Carradine: The Films*

The Private Lives of Adam and Eve •
Universal-International, 1960

CREDITS: *Directors:* Albert Zugsmith, Mickey Rooney; *Producer:* Red Doff; *Script:* Robert Hill; *Music:* Van Alexander; *Photography:* Phil Lathrop; *Art Direction:* Alexander Golitzen, Richard Riedel; *Set Decorations:* Russell A. Gausman, Oliver Emert; *Sound:* Waldon O. Watson, Frank Wilkinson; *Production Manager:* Ralph Black; *Assistant to the Producer:* Russell F. Schoengarth; *Editor:* Eddie Broussard; *Makeup:* Bud Westmore; *Assistant Directors:* Phil Bowles, Carl Beringer; *Costumes:* Frederick's of Hollywood; B&W/Garden of Eden sequences filmed in Spectacolor; 86 minutes.

SONGS: "The Private Lives of Adam and Eve" (Paul Anka) *Paul Anka*; "Rock of Ages" (Thomas Hastings, Augustus Toplady) *Cecil Kellaway*

CAST: Mickey Rooney (*Nick Lewis/Devil*); Mamie Van Doren (*Evie Simms/Eve*); Fay Spain (*Lil Lewis/Lilith*); Mel Tormé (*Hal Sanders*); Martin Milner (*Ad Simms/Adam*); Cecil Kellaway (*Doc Bayles*); Tuesday Weld (*Vangie Harper*); Paul Anka (*Pinkie Parker*); Ziva Rodann (*Passiona*); Theona Bryant, June Wilkinson, Phillipa Fallon, Barbara Walden, Toni Covington (*The Devil's Familiars*); Nancy Root, Donna Lynne, Sharon Wiley, Miki Kato, Andrea Smith, Buni Bacon, Stella Garcia (*Satan's Sinners*).

PLOT: The bus to Reno stops over in Paradise, Nevada, where a microcosm of society is waiting. Nick, the casino owner, and his wife Lil are heading to Reno for a divorce. Also on board is Evie, the wife of the garage mechanic, Ad, also heading to divorce so she can hook up with the more flashy Nick Lewis. Just as the bus is about to depart, a phone call comes through of a flash flood and a bridge out. Nick, fearing

Eve (Mamie) emerges from the water in the Garden of Eden, her bosom discreetly covered by her hair, in *The Private Lives of Adam and Eve* (Universal, 1961).

that if Ad gets on the bus Evie will back out, insists that Doc, the driver, take off. Adam goes after the bus in Pinky's jalopy but Nick, who has grabbed the wheel of the bus, runs Adam off the road. The jalopy goes off the cliff and explodes but Adam is thrown clear. Warned of the dangers ahead, the bus turns back but is swept off a bridge but not before the driver and passengers escape and find refuge in a church which is slowly filling with water from the swollen river.

Evie and Ad fall asleep and dream they are back in the Garden of Eden. Adam experiments with walking, eating, etc., but seems to have no interest about what's under his loincloth. He can speak and begins naming the animals and insects in alphabetical order. He meets and names the hip-talking Lilith* who is working for the Devil. Lilith tempts him with an apple but God intervenes and tells him he has a surprise and creates Eve. He explains that she can eat everything except apples and the two settle into a form of childish married life. Eve (who has yet to be named) complains that God never talks to her and gets impatient when Adam is always going off to work naming the animals. Surprisingly, even though animals remain unnamed, fruit seems to have sprung miraculously branded. The Devil turns up as a snake and tempts her to eat an apple. Adam rushes to her side and in support takes a bite as well. They are cast out of the Garden and become just another squabbling suburban couple, living in a cave watched over by the Devil, who is knitting booties. Eve sets about redecorating their cave which leads to a domestic argument and, ultimately, makeup sex.

The Devil arrives and introduces himself to Eve as a neighbor, and sows dissension by making her dissatisfied with her lot. Meanwhile, Lilith is introducing Adam to the joys of alcohol. The Devil gets Evie to cut her hair and she suddenly has a bikini top. Lilith reveals she has invented the bed and gets Adam to try it out but Eve catches them and runs off saying she wants to be alone. Lilith attempts to stop him but Adam goes after Eve as a thunderstorm rages. Eve stumbles wet and bedraggled and begs God's forgiveness for eating the apple. The rain stops as Eve clutches her stomach and Adam turns up.

Back in the church, the storm is over, the flood has passed, and Adam and Eve reveal they both had the same dream. The stranded passengers pair off, leaving Nick alone. As they head to a nearby farm to try to get some breakfast, Evie has a craving for a dill pickle.

NOTES: *The Private Lives of Adam and Eve* is notable for a number of reasons, not least of which is its fatuous piety which earned it a "C" (Condemned) rating by the National Legion of Decency, the first awarded by the Catholic censorship group to a movie made by major studio since 1956. They labeled it "blasphemous and sacrilegious in its presentation of man's sex life as the invention of the devil,[†] rather than as the handiwork of God. This unconscionable offense to religion is compounded by the treatment in which the filmmaker resorts to indecencies and pornography." As a sop to the moralists, the filmmakers recalled all 150 prints in circulation for alterations and re-editing to make the film more obviously a dream fantasy.

So now the film opens with a number of titles telling us

This is a pipe dream.
This is a fantasy.
This is a fable.
Once upon a time, not too many years from now, eight very different people embarked on a bus to Reno.
There was the teenager running away from home —
The traveling salesman with the wandering eye —
The husband chasing his bride —
The bride getting a divorce —
The gambler making a mockery of decency —
The gambler's wife trying to save a bad marriage —

Lilith, in early mythology a demon, is sometimes believed to be the first wife of Adam and sometimes thought to be one of Satan's lovers.
†*The film actually suggests that the discovery of sex is made as a result of Adam and Eve eating from the Tree of Knowledge and being expelled from the Garden of Eden. The Devil merely helps it along on the road to adultery.*

The young boy seeking his fortune —
And the kindly old bus driver.
The Floods came and death was very real.
The buffoon tried to make jokes about life itself and the beginnings of mankind.
In his terror he ridiculed God.
The religious prayed, each in their own way —
And two people named Adam and Eve dreamed a fantasy —
Composed of their own wishes and desires and needs —
Distorted into a crazy-quilt —
Of laughter and tears — like all dreams.
Fade into the Universal-International logo.

Robert (*Sex Kittens Go to College*) Hill penned the screenplay for this mess, from a story by George Kennett. The central premise has more than a passing similarity to Mark Twain's *The Diary of Adam and Eve*—reinterpreting Adam and Eve as a "typical modern couple" but in prehistoric times. It was only marginally amusing when a master storyteller like Twain wrote it, and it didn't get any better in the intervening hundred years or so. But if the retelling of the Adam and Eve myth is feeble, the surrounding modern story is nauseating. When the bus passengers are stranded in a church that is rapidly filling with flood waters and Vangie, the teenage runaway, gets hysterical, Doc smugly placates her and the others, as well as squelching the cynical Nick, with:

Doc: Place your trust in God. Remember God is in his Heaven all is right with the world.
Nick: That's very touching, preacher.
Doc: What would you know of such things?
Nick: Believe it or not, I read the good book once. It's on the bestseller list.

Eve (Mamie) is tempted by The Devil (Mickey Rooney) in a dream sequence in *The Private Lives of Adam and Eve* (Universal, 1961).

Doc: You may have read it, but you didn't get the message.

It's hard not to warm to Nick's more realistic appraisal of their predicament but the writers have stacked the deck against his character because we've just seen him attempt to run Adam off the road to prevent him from reclaiming his wife. But the homilies just keep on coming. As the flood worsens, instead of trying for higher ground, Doc is content to let the good book rescue them.

Nick: I suppose the book could save us?
Doc: It can. He's our father, we're His children. He created us just the same as He created everything else. It says so here. "In the beginning God made the heaven and the earth..."
Eve: Oh, Ad, has God abandoned us because we've sinned?
Adam: The original Adam and Eve sinned. He didn't abandon them.
Eve: Didn't He? I never read the Bible.
Adam: Don't be scared, Evie. God's with us and I'm with you just as Adam was with Eve.
Eve: Oh, Ad, take me back to our paradise.
Adam: Shh, sleep Evie, go to sleep. We'll go back to Paradise.

Cue for some pretty ordinary special effects of the solar system, comets, oceans and lightning and a portentous voiceover which intones: "This is the dream of two people about the battle of selfishness and lust."

And the film bursts into "spectacular" Spectacolor until Adam and Eve eat the forbidden fruit and are cast out of the Garden into the horrors of black and white.

Surprisingly, most of the bus passengers don't appear in the Garden of Eden sequence. Only the two divorcing couples become characters. Nick, naturally, becomes the Devil, Lilith becomes the mythical Lilith and sometimes reputed first wife of Adam, and Adam and Eve become, well, Adam and Eve. Paul Anka, Tuesday Weld, Mel Tormé, and kindly old bus driver Cecil Kellaway (did they consider using him as the voice of God or was that a blasphemy too far?) disappear for half the movie. The mythology is muddled and is merely an excuse for the satirical husband-and-wife bickering as Lilith and the Devil attempt to turn the couple against each other and claim them for "the dark side." In this film, "the dark side" has tons more charm than the other.

But reality was never this film's strong suit. In the long shots of the bus trying to force Adam and the jalopy off the road, it is obvious there are no passengers. And when the flood survivors leave the church the next day to seek out breakfast at a nearby farm, the soil that was until hours earlier underwater is completely dry and the farm, seen in the distance, is lower on the hill and therefore would have sustained more damage from the flood.

Mamie gets to parade about as the Biblical Eve is a bikini bottom and long blonde hair strategically covering her breasts while Adam prances about in a loincloth that is even briefer than Tarzan's, all contrary to the Bible. This couple is embarrassed by their bodies right from creation. Mamie remembers, "Universal's censors required that my breasts be covered by flesh-colored balloon rubber with hair extensions glued over them. If you look closely at the movie today, you'll see Marty Milner eyeing two enormous mounds of hair on my chest. And, because the censors fretted over the sight of my belly button, the makeup department glued my fig leaf slightly north of its traditional location. Marty's navel, of course, was there for all to see."* Later, after the Devil gets her to cut her hair, Eve appears with a bikini top which matches the bottom.

Mamie's Eve is a nag and feminist nightmare, ordering Adam to move rocks like furniture, claiming he doesn't pay enough attention to her, and that he never gets her nice things. This Eve is a harridan. The modern-day Eve is little better. She's leaving Ad because for their fifteen months of marriage she's actually had to do a bit of work to build up the business. She thought marriage meant she could be a housewife. She's the male nightmare, the castrating bitch, and intends to marry Nick, the sleazy casino operator, though it's hard to

---

*Mamie Van Doren, Click: Becoming Feminists

understand why once we get a glimpse of Martin Milner's tight little body in his loincloth.

Her retort to her distraught husband is a classic.

ADAM: You can't just walk out on a marriage like walking out of a phone booth.
EVE: I'm tired of putting coins in the slot. Besides I kept getting the busy signal.

But the absolute highlight of this Albert Zugsmith–Mickey Rooney–directed disaster which makes it a must-see for Mamie aficionados is the fabled sequence of Mamie, fallen in the rain and mud in the midst of a thunderstorm, bosom heaving, cleavage to the camera, soaked better than any wet T-shirt competition, begging God to forgive her for eating the apple. This sequence is a masterpiece of camp cinema.

"That scene was shot on what we called the pneumonia stage at Universal. I spent hours rolling around in the mud and the rain trying to deliver my lines. I thought I was going to drown."*

REVIEWS: "Aside from Mickey Rooney, who sometimes overplays, there is little evidence of talent." *The New York Daily News*

"Tacky soap opera with bizarre tinted fantasy sequence in the Garden of Eden ... It was condemned by the Catholic Legion of Decency but it's real harmless stuff..." *The Psychotronic Encyclopedia of Film*

"Perfectly awful fantasy ... Rooney chews the scenery as the Devil." *Leonard Maltin's Movie & Video Guide*

Possibly [the Garden of Eden dream] was meant to show them all the error of their ways. What it actually showed was the error of scenarist Robert Hill's way with words, and the unfocused direction of Mickey Rooney and Albert Zugsmith ... " Clive Hirschhorn, *The Universal Story*

"A tasteless, if harmless farce ... [T]he film, an obvious parody, is less morally objectionable than artistically chaotic ... Mickey Rooney makes a puckish Satan, Mamie Van Doren a naïve Eve, Marty Milner a Tarzanesque Adam, Fay Spain a torrid temptress..." *Variety* January 18, 1961

"Rooney plays the Devil! (What would Judge Hardy say?) ... [A] chaotic and ultimately dumb tale..." *The Motion Picture Guide*

"Mickey Rooney's Devil is truly painful to behold at times ... Mamie Van Doren is fetching and fairly good as Eve, but she is given little worthwhile material in the script." Charles P. Mitchell, *The Devil on Screen*

Una Americana en Buenos Aires/The Blonde from Buenos Aires • Argentina, 1961

CREDITS: *Director:* George Cahan; *Music:* Waldo de los Rios; *Photography:* Americo Hoss; *Editor:* Vicente Castagno; B&W; 80 minutes

CAST: Mamie Van Doren; Jean-Pierre Aumont; Carlos Estrada; Catherine Zabó; Juan Carlos Mareco; Nathán Pinzón; Guido Gorgatti; Chela Ruíz.

NOTES: Mamie traveled to Argentina, where her popularity was as strong as ever, for this film in which she co-starred with Jean-Pierre Aumont and Carlos Estrada, with whom she had a brief romance during filming. One of the lures for the making of the film was that Mamie held the English-language rights although the film has never been released in the U.S. and she has never seen it. It's one of Mamie's "lost" movies.

She does remember, however, one occasion during which she feared for her life. "It was one night when Jean-Pierre Aumont escorted me to a movie premiere. I was a little naïve and didn't realize he leaned to the left and the film he took me to was a 'communist' film. Argentina was going through political turmoil and the fascists were in power. Argentina had a new president every few years. After we took our seats, these armed men burst in and told us all to vacate the theatre. Jean-Pierre refused to budge and these men threatened him and me telling us there was a bomb under the seat. I was ready to go but Jean-Pierre said, 'Stay where you are, Mamie, it's a trick to get us

---

*Phone interview with the author, August 3, 2006

out of the theatre. There is no bomb.' But I'd had enough and I left."*

The Candidate • Cosnat Productions, 1964 [aka: *Party Girls for the Candidate, the Playmates and the Candidate*]

My bed is not for sale! Scenes behind the political scandal ... Gals, fast talking Guys, Sex, Blackmail, and Payoffs for personal Power!

CREDITS: *Director:* Robert Angus; *Producer:* Maurice Duke; *Screenplay:* Joyce Ann Miller, Quenton Vale, Frank Moceri; *Music:* Steve Karmen, Sid Robin; *Photography:* Frank Cortez; *Editor:* William Martin; *Art Director:* Archie Bacon; B&W; 84 minutes.

CAST: Mamie Van Doren (*Samantha Ashley*); June Wilkinson (*Angela Wallace*); Ted Knight (*Frank Carlton*); Eric Mason (*Buddy Barker*); Rachel Romen (*Mona Archer*); Robin Raymond (*Attorney Rogers*); William Long Jr. (*Fallon*); John Matthews (*Senator Harper*); Herb Vigran (*Dr. Endicott*); Art Allessi (*Psychiatrist*); Phil Arnold (*Plumber*); Carol Ann Lee, Joyce Nizzari, Beverly St. Lawrence, Susan Kelly, Sharon Rogers, Suzzanne Hiatt (*Party Girls*).

NOTES: One of the "missing/lost" films of Mamie Van Doren, *The Candidate* concerns an investigation by a U.S. Senate committee into the moral fitness of Buddy Barker (Eric Mason) to continue as Congressional coordinator. His "social secretary," Samantha Ashley (Mamie Van Doren) is called to give evidence and the tale unfolds in flashback.

She reveals she met Buddy when she was a hostess in a Miami hotel and was quickly persuaded to set up house in his apartment in Washington, D.C. Part of her official duties: being on call 24 hours a day and being "nice for a price" to New England Senatorial candidate Frank Carlton (Ted Knight).

On the Boston campaign trail with Frank, Samantha persuades an acquaintance, English girl Angela (June Wilkinson), to play up to Frank. He likes her and she gets herself a new sugar daddy. Buddy and Samantha throw a fundraiser party for Frank's campaign which degenerates into a free-for-all during which Frank[†] has it off with a good-time girl, Mona Archer (Rachel Romen). Samantha is called upon to help out when Mona realizes she is pregnant and arrangements are made for an abortion by respected Washington physician Endicott (Herb Vigran), but while Mona is under sedation the doctor rapes her.

Mona is brought before the committee to testify but, in the middle of all the sleaze, Frank and Angela have fallen in love and plan to marry. At the Senate committee hearings, in front of a packed session of important congressmen, a "stag reel" of Angela is shown and this precipitates a fatal heart attack for Frank and the ruination of Buddy's career. Even the loyal Samantha walks away from him in disgust.

The film premiered in Dallas on October 7, 1964, and has been little seen since. TV producer Robert Angus directed with Mamie starring alongside fellow screen siren June Wilkinson and Ted Knight a decade before his success as Ted Baxter on *The Mary Tyler Moore Show* (1970–75).

Mamie remembers *The Candidate* as "the story of Lyndon Johnson's pal Bobby Baker[‡] and his shenanigans with Washington corruption. It starred Ted Knight in a serious role. It was a good script and I was excited about doing a role that was a departure for me. I played a senator's secretary who was a Washington party girl working her way up, rather than the all-too-typical dumb blonde."**

---

*Phone interview with the author, August 3, 2006.
[†]Some sources credit Buddy Barker as Mona's sex partner.
[‡]Robert "Bobby" Baker (1928–) was alleged to be a Capitol Hill wheeler dealer. At the age of 14 he got a job as a page in the Senate, working his way up to become assistant secretary to the Democrats and, in 1961, secretary to the Democrats. He was close to then Senate Majority Leader Lyndon B. Johnson. Allegations arose over his supposed involvement with casino operations in the Dominican Republic and with vending machine fraud with underworld figures. His closeness to Johnson led to an investigation by Attorney-General Robert Kennedy even though it was alleged Baker was used to procure women for John F. Kennedy. By October, 1963, the allegations were gaining momentum and Baker resigned his Senate position as secretary to the majority.
**Mamie Van Doren, Playing the Field, 187–188.

Samantha Ashley (Mamie) addresses the Senate Committee in her "missing" film, *The Candidate* (Cosnat, 1964).

English-born June Wilkinson, known as The Bosom because of her 44DD-23-36 figure, made her uncredited screen debut in Russ Meyer's *The Immoral Mr. Teas* (1959) and followed up with forgettable film roles in *Thunder in the Sun* (1959), *Career Girl* (1960) and *Macumba Love* (1960). She appeared with Mamie in *The Private Lives of Adam and Eve* (1960); they became great friends during the shoot.

"She's been a friend of mine since I was 24 years of age and I like Mamie very much," says June. "We're still friends. We meet up at the Playboy Mansion all the time. She goes to Hugh Hefner's parties and so do I so we always sit down and chat and catch up. Mamie's one of the good old broads. She's a terrific lady."*

There was no competition between the two stars and June feels Mamie was secure in her status. "Mamie has her own niche. She's not in competition with the younger girls. She's only in competition with herself. I think Mamie is a fascinating lady. She's vibrant and she's very much with it today. She's not one of those sitting in a rocking chair, she's out there and with it."

As to the film itself: "Mamie and I cannot get a copy of that one. We'd love to. I would love to see that movie again. I have no idea what happened to the film and it's really a shame; there's a big market for those films now. I have no idea why it hasn't shown up any place."

In light of the frequent sex scandals that swamp Washington in general and the particular sex scandal involving Representative Mark Foley in late 2006, *The Candidate* seems ripe for revival. If only it could be found.

*All quotes from June Wilkinson are from a phone interview with the author, August 3, 2006.

Samantha (Mamie) with sleazy Congressional coordinator Buddy Barker (Eric Mason) in *The Candidate* (Cosnat, 1964).

REVIEWS: "Really sleazy tale of political corruption ... bottom of the barrel." *The Motion Picture Guide*

"[S]uper-sleazy political drama." *New York Times*

3 Nuts in Search of a Bolt • Harlequin International Pictures, 1964

The Screwiest Comedy of the Year!

CREDITS: *Director:* Tommy Noonan; *Produced and Written by* Tommy Noonan, Ian McGlashan; *Music Composed and Conducted by* Phil Moody; *Choreography:* Ward Ellis; *Photography:* Fouad Said; *Production Manager & Assistant Director:* William Magginetti; *Supervising Editor:* William Martin; *Production Designer:* Carrol Ballard; *Miss Van Doren's Coiffures:* Don Morand; *Wardrobe:* Vou Lee Giokaris; B&W/Eastman Color; 80 minutes.

SONG: "I Used to Be a Stripper Down on Main" (Phil Moody; Pony Sherrell) *Mamie Van Doren*

CAST: Mamie Van Doren (*Saxie Symbol*); Tommy Noonan (*Tommy*); Ziva Rodann (*Dr. Myra Von*); Paul Gilbert (*Joe Lynch*); John Cronin (*Bruce Bernard*); Peter Howard [Howard Koch] (*Dr. Otis Salverson*); T.C. Jones (*Henry*); Charles Irving (*R.L. Katz*); Alvy Moore (*Sutter T. Finley*); Marjorie Bennett (*Mrs. Barkley-Kent*); Phil Arnold (*Television Technician*); Arthur E. Gould-Porter (*Mr. Blyth*); Ray Dannis; Damon Knight; Pat Noone (*Miss Frisbee*); Frank Kreig (*Bartender*); Leslie Snyder; Robert Kenneally (*Lennie*); Loyal T. Lucas; Jennie Lee (*Miss Griswald*); Kathy Waniata (*School Teacher*); Curt Mercer (*First Crook*); Richard Normoyle (*Second Crook*); *Uncredited*: Anthony Eisley (*Himself*); Pat O'Moore (*Edwards*); Jimmy Cross (*Drunk*).

Saxie Symbol (Mamie) singing "I Used to Be a Stripper Down on Main (But Now I'm the Main Attraction on the Strip)" in *3 Nuts in Search of a Bolt* (Harlequin, 1964).

DVD: VCI Entertainment KPF-538 (Widescreen; *Bonus Features*: Interview [approximately 45 minutes] with Mamie Van Doren; On-Set Photo Gallery; Actor Biographies; "Hot" and "Cold" Theatrical Trailers)

PLOT: At the unemployment office, stripper Saxie Symbol runs into Tommy Noonan and invites him back to her home where she lives with Joe, a car salesman, and Bruce, a male model. They share the rent and now they want to share a psychiatrist. All three suffer from some sort of neurosis but can't afford the cost of therapy with world-famous psychiatrist, Dr. Myra Von. They are after someone with a good memory and, because he's an actor, they hire Tommy to front the psychiatrist and relate their symptoms in turn, changing character every twenty minutes, and then report back on the doctor's analysis. Thus the three will be paying for one consultation rather than three.

So Tommy can get to know their problems intimately, they take turns talking to him about their lives. As a result, Tommy's portrayal of their mannerisms and problems is so effective that Dr. Von believes she has a patient with a split personality. Seeking fame and fortune, she offers a free three-hour session the next day although, unbeknown to Tommy, she sets up a closed circuit broadcast of the next session to be beamed to the world's top mental health experts. But a mechanical problem beams the consultation to the world's television sets and it becomes a ratings winner, catapulting Dr. Von to prominence. She even sells the film rights to R.L. Katz, an exploitation filmmaker whose seminal work is *The Four Faces of Adam*.

Rival psychiatrist Dr. Otis Salverson discovers the truth and blackmails Dr. Von for part of her screen royalties and insists on being called in as a consultant, during which time he will perform a "miracle" cure on Tommy, thus ensuring his own fame. Meanwhile, Tommy is having a crisis of conscience and admits the scam to Katz. Rather than being upset by the news, Katz thinks the story now has even greater box office potential. During a bar stickup, Tommy is slugged and when he regains consciousness he has taken on the housemates' personalities. However, because of his brief time as a psychiatric patient, and having listened to the three housemates' stories in detail, he analyzes their problems and cures them. Saxie's problem is that she is a virgin who has repressed her sexual feelings and merely needs a good man—Tommy, in fact.

NOTES: This is one of Mamie's best-known films although it is far from her best. It's a rather labored comedy, boringly directed by Tommy Noonan,* who had a career of sorts as the milquetoast hero opposite a number of 1950s blonde bombshells: Marilyn in *Gentlemen Prefer Blondes* (1953), Sheree North and Betty Grable in *How to Be Very, Very Popular* (1955), and Jayne Mansfield in *Promises! Promises!* (1963).

"I always thought he was a terrific comic," Mamie recalls, "but I turned down his first offer *Promises! Promises!* which Jayne and Marie McDonald ended up doing. It was such a hit that when he presented me with another script he found called *3 Nuts in Search of a Bolt* I thought the title was really crazy and I read it and I liked it and I did it for a percentage of the profits."†

The film opens with a color sequence of Mamie in front of a gold curtain in a silver lamé dress, singing and stripping to "I Used to Be a Stripper Down on Main" by Phil Moody and Pony Sherrell, the songwriters who'd penned the majority of the numbers for *The Second Greatest Sex*. The sequence was filmed at Ciro's Nightclub on the Sunset Strip; a pack of male journalists was invited to watch the shoot to add ambience for Mamie to play to and, predominantly, to whet the press's appetite to publicize the film. "I learned how to strip from a couple of really well-known strippers in those days so I did the best I could. It came off pretty well. I think."

Alas, after this great credit sequence the film goes into free fall although the basic premise is ripe with promise. But Noonan and fellow writer-producer Ian McGlashan don't manage to come up with any other good ideas, and resort to padding with feeble jokes. Perhaps the

---

*Tommy Noonan (1922–68) was originally a stage actor with his half-brother, John Ireland. Noonan's career was interrupted by service in the Navy during World War II, after which he was signed by RKO and went on to secure top-notch supporting roles in class vehicles such as *A Star Is Born* (1954), as Judy Garland's pianist, and *The Girl Most Likely* (1957). He was also the straight man in the comedy duo Noonan and Marshall with Peter (The Hollywood Squares) Marshall. By the late 1950s his heyday was over and he resorted to a number of sex farces with Jayne Mansfield and Mamie.

†All quotes by Mamie are from a phone interview with the author, August 3, 2006.

Saxie Symbol (Mamie) in the famed nude beer bath scene from *3 Nuts in Search of a Bolt* (Harlequin, 1964).

most inspired padding, is Mamie's fabled beer bath, 53 minutes into the film, which was added after the film was completed.

"I'd already told Tommy I didn't want to do any nudity but at the end of the film he came to me and said, 'You've got a do a beer bath scene. You own two percent of the movie and a beer bath scene will make you more money, so why not?' So I said okay if it will make me more money. And it was tied in with a layout for *Playboy* and I was on the cover in June of '64. *Playboy* did very well and the movie did very, very well. But I didn't see much money out of it. And the beer bath scene took forever. We shot it in a house up in the Hollywood Hills. But the foam wasn't beer. They used shaving foam to make it look good but it stung my pussy. I loved the openness of it when I did it. It was liberating and I just really enjoyed doing it. I had a lot of fun on the set. Jayne was the one who really opened the way for that kind of nudity in movies back then. I was skeptical at first about taking my clothes off but then they offered me more money the second time around. That clinched it."

One thing that didn't please Mamie, however, was Tommy Noonan's use of outtakes and footage of on-set shenanigans that included swearing and goofing off. He attempted to release it, to the chagrin of the cast. "I didn't like that. I didn't think it was cool of him to try it."

REVIEWS: "Nudie exploitation picture suitable only for specialty art houses that play nudie films. Poorly written, but suitably cast ... There are apparently enough specialty houses catering to the customers who like to see a pretty girl take her clothes off ... In this case it's Mamie Van Doren who shows almost every inch of her delectable physiognomy in scenes from a nude beer bath to a torrid strip that bumps and grinds as far as the screen could possibly allow ... *Nuts* is supposed to be a comedy and there are some genuinely funny moments in it ... Where *Nuts* is completely lost is in the dull, unbelievable and careless dialog in which the story is couched." *Variety*, June 17, 1964

"Is this film dumb? You bet — it even switches between black-and-white and color with no rhyme or reason. But it is funny in a nicely stupid way, with some genuinely amusing performances including Tommy Noonan as the actor and T.C. Jones as the psychiatrist's effeminate male secretary. Mamie Van Doren plays the stripper and she's quite the dish — sexy, sassy, and she even indulges in a bit of a nipple display during a bathing sequence. Tits ahoy, Mamie!" Phil Hall, *Film Threat*, filmthreat.com

"Highball meets highbrow in this underrated little onscreen romp that plays off of an energetic premise, a little naughtiness, and the all-but-lost art of ribald humor. [It's] like an 80-minute vintage *Playboy* cartoon, or a barely offensive 1960s 'adult humor' comedy album come to life. It's a witty little exploitation flick that gently chides all manner of 1960s pop-cult obsessions like gentleman's clubs, psychiatry, women's rights, and a manly cocktail intake. Unfortunately, the film has trouble maintaining its comedic momentum, especially as the plot turns its attention to dealing with Noonan's accidental celebrity. Even then, there's still the lingering promise of Van Doren's nude scene that would have kept viewers glued to their seats, even if the jokes, for all intents and purposes, stop hitting their mark. Unlike Jayne Mansfield in Noonan's earlier film, however, Mamie wasn't fully ready to take it all off on the big screen (though she did in a *Playboy* pictorial to promote the film), so instead, she keeps her back to the camera during the film's legendary beer bath sequence, in which she rolls around in a big tub o' suds. Other scenes, in which she sings and strips on stage while singing bawdy ballads, are equally demure, as she's clad in panties and pasties. Interestingly, the film is shot in black and white, but switches to color for all of Van Doren's potential flesh-baring scenes." Paul Corupe, *DVD Verdict* dvdverdict.com

"Working from an unpromising idea, Noonan and his co-writer Ian McGlashan make 78 minutes seem like forever. That the film is poorly directed means little when the jokes are so unfunny, and the best Noonan can do to compensate is to concentrate on Ms. Van Doren's perplexing exhibitionist act. The basic

B&W story is interrupted with color inserts: Mamie sings (after a fashion) a song while stripping, and tells her troubles to Tommy in a hot-cha episode cavorting in a spa bathtub. Obviously self-conscious, she keeps looking at the camera and flashing a pixie smile to mask her feelings. There are only about ten seconds of nudity in the film and none of it is particularly sexy, as Saxie Symbol's overdone personality is hard to take, clothed or un-. There is barely any human contact in the picture. The rules with 'nudie films' were probably the same that applied to 'adult entertainment' on the nightclub circuit: Nudity could dodge the vice squad only if it were free of any overt sexual context." Glenn Erickson, DVD Savant

"Starring Mamie Van Doren modeling the Frederick's of Hollywood catalog, including a production number (!) with the Queen of the Drive-In in a silver-sequin spaghetti-strap spill-it-all-out hip-hugger evening gown. Starring, directed, written, produced by the little weenie Tommy Noonan, the drive-in Jerry Lewis (and Mamie's husband at the time).* ... Very sixties. One of Mamie's best." Joe Bob Briggs, *Joe Bob's Ultimate Movie Guide*

Freddy und das Lied der Prärie/The Sheriff Was a Lady • Avala Film/CCC Filmkunst GmbH, 1964 [Aka *In the Wild West; The Wild, Wild West*]

CREDITS: An Arthur Brauner Production. *Presented by*: Walter Manley Enterprises, Inc. *Director:* Sobey Martin; *Producer:* Arthur Brauner; *Executive Producers:* Willy Egger, Bosko Savic; *Script:* Gustav Kempendonk; *Music:* Lotar Olias; *Photography:* Siegfried Hold; *Editor:* Walter Wischniewsky; *Production Designers:* Veljko Despotovic, Heinrich Weidemann; *Art Director:* Slobodan Mijacevic; *Costumes:* Irms Pauli; *Assistant Directors:* Fritzi Ostermann, Charles Wakefield, Dusan Zega; *Sound:* Ancona Films Inc.; *English Version:* Bellucci Productions Inc.; Color; 101 minutes.

SONGS: "Black Bill" *Unknown Off-screen Singer*; "Riding On" *Freddy Quinn*; "Who Knows Where?" *Freddy Quinn*; "I'm Here to Stay" *Mamie Van Doren*; "The Wild, Wild West" *Freddy Quinn*; "Traveling West (With the Sun)" *Freddy Quinn*; "Old Joe" *Freddy Quinn;* "Give Me Your Word" *Freddy Quinn*

CAST: Mamie Van Doren (*Olivia*); Freddy Quinn (*Black Bill/John Burns/Freddy*); Rick Battaglia (*Steve Perkins*); Beba Longar (*Anita/Betty Wilson*); Trude Herr (*Joana*); Carlo Croccolo (*Sheriff*); Klaus Dahlen (*Harry*); Vladimir Medar (*Murdoch*); Mavid Popovic [Milivoje Popovic-Mavid], Stojan Arandjelovic, Mirko Boman (*Bandits*); Josef Albrecht (*Ted*); Otto Waldis; Ulrich Hüls; Bruno W. Pantel; Mariona; Desa Beric; Janez Vrhovec, Karl Dall.

DVD/VIDEO: Something Weird Video #6555

PLOT: Black Bill has been riding the West in search of his parents' killers for ten years. During that time he has gained a reputation for killing bad guys and leaving a plugged silver dollar at the scene. Returning to the ranch of his childhood sweetheart, Anita, he is told she has gone in pursuit of her father's kidnappers who want him to reveal the location of huge gold deposits. Anita arrives in the lawless town of Moon Valley, lorded over by the unscrupulous Steve Perkins, the town's corrupt judge, banker and Last Chance Saloon owner. She assumes the name Betty Wilson and takes on the job of deputy to Moon Valley's drunken and ineffectual sheriff in an effort to find her dad. Black Bill rides in to town as John Burns, pretending to search for gold but also looking for the kidnapped man, Ted Daniels, who is a prisoner in the saloon's cellar.

Olivia, the Last Chance Saloon's top entertainer, fears for her life because she has discovered that her boyfriend, Perkins, is the leader of the outlaws who are responsible for killings and other lawlessness in the town. She befriends Black Bill. Ted won't disclose the whereabouts of the gold but eventually succumbs to delirium when he is deprived of water and reveals the map is in his fob watch. Realizing Perkins is the killer of his parents as well as Ted's kidnapper, Black Bill lures him and his

---

*Mamie was never married to (or even dated) Noonan, or Jerry Lewis for that matter.

henchmen out of town by stealing the stagecoach. Olivia has stowed away and Black Bill tells her to take his horse and escape and she in turn reveals the whereabouts of Ted Daniels. But Anita, and a posse from the town, doesn't recognize her childhood love and arrests him though the mistake is revealed at the jail. Ted's rescue is effected and Black Bill and Steve Perkins face each other in a shoot-out in Moon Valley's main street. Perkins is killed. But Black Bill is too restless to settle down and heads off for more adventures, making Anita promise she will wait for him. Olivia watches his departure hidden from view among the trees.

NOTES: Mamie looks radiant as saloon singer-dancer Olivia in this mediocre western musical. Although she is top-billed, it's essentially a vehicle for famed Austrian-born singing star Freddy Quinn, one of the German-speaking world's top recording artists. Quinn was catapulted to fame with his hit recording "Heimweh" ("Homesick"), a Germanized version of Dean Martin's "Memories Are Made of This" (Terry Gilkyson, Richard Dehr & Frank Miller), the same year he represented Germany at the Eurovision Song Contest in Switzerland. He had ten number-one singles on the German charts over the next decade. He was also a popular stage actor and appeared in *Charley's Aunt*, *Die Fledermaus*, and *The King and I* (as the king). From 1954 he began appearing in movies, in many of which his character's name was Freddy. He adopted the character of the rootless lone wanderer not quite ready to settle down.

And *The Sheriff Was a Lady* was no exception. Freddy's character is chaste as well as chased — by Mamie in particular — and even though she is the subject of his gallantry as he saves her from the unwanted attentions of western rowdies and helps her escape the clutches of her bandit boyfriend, Freddy's philosophy is: "A woman's worse than a gun. A well-aimed shot can kill a feller all right but if you fall in love, that can pain you for a lifetime." And when Olivia goes to kiss him he stops her with: "Good night, Olivia, and stop looking at me like that. I have a lot of things I gotta take care of."

In this pseudo-west, Mamie's hair is piled so high she'd have trouble walking under a lamp, but her body-hugging, cleavage-revealing dresses show her off to major advantage. However, she is saddled with dialogue such as "Oh Steve, oh Steve, I love you. Give up the life you're leading, Steve. Some day in Moon Valley there'll be law and order. I've seen enough people dangling from the trees." Worse yet, the English-language print is poorly dubbed. So Mamie can do little to enliven the sluggish proceedings apart from look beautiful. In the DVD version currently available, Mamie sings only one number (the prophetic "I'm Here to Stay") as part of the saloon entertainment.

Fourth-billed Belgrade-born beauty, Beba Loncar, is the lady of the film's title, not Mamie, and is, in fact, merely the deputy sheriff. She spends most of the film chasing the bandits who kidnapped her father and only belatedly realizes that the man she has arrested is the boyfriend she not seen since she was eight. Not that Freddy recognizes her either. It doesn't auger well for their future happiness. Their slightly incestuous and pedophile relationship is never explored. Beba's Anita fares little better than Mamie's Olivia in the romance dept. as Freddy's Black Bill rides off into the sunset with two men seeking further adventure, telling his neglected sweetheart she should wait for his return.

In this German-Yugoslav co-production, Mamie delivered her lines in English and was later dubbed for the German-language version. After a three-week shoot in studios in Berlin, the company moved to Dubrovnik (then in Yugoslavia, now in Croatia) for exteriors. "The three weeks in Dubrovnik were hell," Mamie recalls. She found the political climate oppressive and considered every waiter, porter or hotel maid a potential spy for the secret police. "We couldn't wait to get out of there. And the food was terrible. I couldn't eat it. I lost about 10 pounds during my stay."*

But for all the hardships Mamie endured

---

*Van Doren, Playing the Field, *196.*

filming outside Dubrovnik, the wide-open vistas surrounded by mountains give the film an authentic western air. Not so the German accents. "It was amusing to watch European actors and crew tackling something as apple-pie American as a western. Freddy Quinn did a passably good job, but there were moments—like the time-honored street shoot-out—when the guttural German phrases Freddy hurled at the bad guys seemed laughably out of place."*

But she liked Freddy. "He was supposed to be Germany's answer to Elvis. Everybody is always an answer to somebody else. But he was a real man of the people. They loved him."[†] Of course, it always helps if you're good-looking and wear your western gear so tight it looks as if you've had to be poured into it. But, neither the charms of her co-star nor those of the "gorgeous" Yugoslav men could keep Mamie in the country a moment longer than she had to be there.

REVIEWS: "I fully expected Mamie to be tacked on (*a la* Raymond Burr in *Godzilla*), but nope, there she is on location as a swinging, singing saloon girl, deliriously dubbed along with the rest of the lager-bellied cast. The lead character in this mind-ripper is 'the German Elvis Presley,' namely Freddie [sic] Quinn as 'Black Bill,' who shoots holes through silver dollars and saves the day every 15 or 20 minutes by breaking into a soul-searing song. Try to picture Tex Ritter and Johnny Horton song knock-offs, filmed in excruciating close-ups, horribly dubbed (not lip-synced) by a teen idol Judd Hirsch look-alike." Johnny Legend, Notes on the *Something Weird Video* release

"Talk about making a German spectacle out of itself! This European sagebrusher is unlike anything you've ever seen before, a tale of Black Bill (German Elvis-wannabe Freddie [sic] Quinn), a singing Teutonic cowpoke in search of his parents' killer, and Anita, the sexy female sheriff searching for those same creeps, who also swiped her father's gold. Mamie Van Doren is also featured. Wow!" *Movies Unlimited* website

Las Vegas Hillbillys • Woolner Brothers, 1966

Jayne Swings! Mamie Sings!... in the wildest romp since Pa blew the still!

CREDITS: *Director:* Arthur C. Pierce; *Written and Produced by* Larry E. Jackson; *Executive Producer:* Bernard A. Woolner; *Music Composed and Directed by* Dean Elliott; *Country Music Supervision:* Audie Ashworth; *Photography:* William de Diego; *Sound:* LeRoy Robbins; *Wardrobe Mistress:* Sara Anderson; *Chief Makeup Artist:* Mark Snegoff; *Supervising Editor:* Roy V. Livingston; *Assistant Director:* Edgar G. Stein; *Associate Editor:* Holbrook N. Todd; *Sound Effects Editor:* Frank Baldridge; *Special Effects:* Harry Woolman; *Music Editor:* Edward Norton; Pathécolor; 90 minutes.

SONGS: "White Lightning Express" *Ferlin Husky*; "Down Yonder" (Gilbert) *Junior Carolina Cloggers, The Po Boys*; "Bright Lights and Country Music" *Bill Anderson, The Po Boys*; "Nobody But a Fool" *Connie Smith*; "I Feel Better All Over" *Ferlin Husky*; "Yippee-i-o-ay Las Vegas" *Chorus on Soundtrack*; "Fresh Out of Lovin'" *Mamie Van Doren*; "Baby, Sweet Sweet Baby" *Mamie Van Doren*; "Dixie" *Band*; "Money Greases the Wheel" *Ferlin Husky*; "Baby, Sweet Sweet Baby" *Wilma Burgess*; "What Makes a Man Wander?" *Sonny James*; "I'll Be Holding On" *Sonny James*; "That Makes It" *Jayne Mansfield*; "True Love's a Blessing" *Sonny James*; "I Don't Believe You Love Me Any More" *Roy Drusky*; "Belles of the Southern Bell" (Del Reeves) *Del Reeves*; "Women Do Funny Things to Me" (Del Reeves) *Del Reeves*; "Money Greases the Wheel" *reprised by Ferlin Husky*

CAST: Ferlin Husky (*Woody*); Jayne Mansfield (*Tawny*); Mamie Van Doren (*Boots Malone*); *Country Music Stars*: Sonny James; Roy Drusky; Del Reeves; Bill Anderson; Connie Smith; Wilma Burgess; Duke of Paducah; Jr. Carolina Cloggers; The Jordanaires; *Co-Starring*: Don Bowman (*Jeepers*); Louis Quinn; Billie Bird (*Clementine*); Richard Kiel (*Moose*);

---

*Ibid.
[†]*Phone interview with the author, August 3, 2006.

Arlene Charles; Helen Clark; Christian Anderson; Theodore Lehmann; John Harmon; Bennett King; Chuck Harrod; Larry Barton.

DVD: VCI Home Video #8233 (no extras)

PLOT: Woody lives in Johnson's Corner, Tennessee, with a big ambition to be a country-western singer, and his best friend Jeepers wants nothing more than to be his manager. So when Woody's uncle dies and he inherits a Las Vegas club, the Golden Circle Casino, it looks like the beginning of a beautiful career move. On the way to Vegas, the boys help out a stranded singer, Tawny, by pushing her pink convertible to the nearest gas station. It seems she's the biggest star in Vegas and is also paying the repair bills on the boys' casino.

Naturally, the Golden Circle Casino is a dump awaiting foreclosure and the boys arrive as manager Boots Malone is singing at the wake for Woody's uncle. Jeepers cuts off the free drinks and is all for dumping the place and going home whereas Woody sees potential. He'll turn it into a hillbilly bar with gambling and entertainment. He's determined to show Las Vegas something they've never seen before.

With creditors closing in, Tawny takes over the casino gambling tables because it was Woody's uncle Woodrow who gave her a start in the business. Woody's Aunt Clem also turns up to lend a hand. She's taken her savings out of the hog jar and called in a few favors from her pals in Nashville. They, of course, turn out to be Nashville headliners. The casino is going great guns until the chief creditor turns up with his goon. A pie fight ensues, the creditor is thwarted in true movie-fantasy style, and everything ends happily with Woody and Boots in a lip lock.

NOTES: A perfunctory storyline, a variation on *The Beverly Hillbillies*, is merely an excuse to highlight country singer Ferlin Husky in an acting job he's simply not up to. Husky, born in 1927, became a successful singer, guitarist, songwriter and comedian creating, among others, the popular hayseed character Simon Crum. He began as a radio DJ under the name Terry Preston because he thought his real name sounded phony and he created Simon Crum to add variety to his announcing chores. The character became so popular he was first signed to a recording contract for his comedy, only later progressing to "legit" country songs as Terry Preston; he had a number one hit with "Dear John," dueting with Jean Shepherd. He began recording under his own name later that same year. During the 1950s and 1960s his albums and singles were consistent best-sellers and it was only natural he would appear in movies. His first vehicle *Country Music Holiday* (1958), about a country singer's rise to fame, featured Zsa Zsa Gabor, June Carter Cash, Rocky Graziano, and Patty Duke.

Las Vegas Hillbillys also highlights a number of then-popular Nashville names in obviously interpolated sequences which stop the feeble plot stone dead. While Mamie has the lion's share of the female acting, she is billed as a "Special Guest Star" below Jayne Mansfield, but gets to sing two songs to Jayne's one. Her blonde bombshell co-star Jayne looks heavier than normal swathed in pink. There were reports of animosity between the two; they share just one scene, in which Mamie arrives at the club as Jayne is departing. "Jayne was a little on the heavy side, having just had a baby, so there was a little jealousy there. And while we did have problems over billing, there were no fights. We were standoffish."*

Although Mamie got on well with Husky, there is no onscreen chemistry between the two. Husky is ill-at-ease in front of the camera and never seems to know what to do with his hands or his body. Mamie is in fine voice as she warbles her way through her two numbers but, ultimately, the film is aimed squarely at a specialist audience, country music fans, and was a showcase for popular performers of the genre in an age before MTV. It's a hillbilly equivalent of AIP's popular *Beach Party* movies. A year later Husky would appear in the execrable follow-up *Hillbillys in a Haunted House* with Joi Lansing, John Carradine, Basil Rathbone and Lon Chaney Jr.

REVIEWS: "A pair of country-singing

---

*Van Doren, telephone interview with author, Oct. 23, 2005.

hillbillies inherit a saloon in Las Vegas and enjoy, wine, moonshine, and song, These two make the Clampetts look like high society." *Videohound*

"Jayne Mansfield and Mamie Van Doren together! ... Both Mamie and Jayne (who plays a famous star) sing and dance ...It's really unfair that Northerners were denied the opportunity to see these cheap star oddities at the time of the original release." *The Psychotronic Encyclopedia of Film*

"A strange cast and a strange idea." *The Motion Picture Guide*

"This movie has four great things about it...Mamie Van Doren and Jayne Mansfield! There's also a ton of great 60s hillbilly and country music! ... More hillbilly pickin' and singin' than you can shake a durn burn crooked stick at! Terrific bouffants and pompadours plus lots o' cool sequined duds! Wild scene where a local motorcycle gang raids the club while a go-go version of 'Dixie' is played! We see guys and dolls doing The Twist, The Watusi and The Mashed Potato!" *The Video Beat!* Thevideobeat.com

The Navy vs. the Night Monsters • Standard Club of California Productions/Realart Pictures, 1966 [U.K. Title: *Monsters of the Night*]

Beware of the Night Crawlers...their clutches will disintegrate you!

CREDITS: A Jack Broder Production. *Director:* Michael A. Hoey; *Producer:* George Edwards; *Associate Producer:* Madelynn Broder; *Screenplay:* Michael A. Hoey, based on a novel [*Monster from Earth's End*] by Murray Leinster; *Music:* Gordon Zahler; *Music Editor:* Igo Kantor; *Photography:* Stanley Cortez; *Supervising Editor:* George White; *Production Manager:* Richard Dixon; *Art Director:* Paul Sylos; *Set Decorator:* Clarence Steensen; *Special Effects:* Edwin Tillman; *Costumer:* Patrick Cummings; *Makeup Artist:* Harry Thomas; *Hair Stylist:* Jean Austin; *Sound Effects Editor:* Del Harris; *Assistant Director:* Wyott Ordung; *Special Photographic Effects:* Modern Film Effects; *Script Supervisor:* Wandra Ramsey; DeLuxe Color; 87 minutes.

CAST: Mamie Van Doren (*Nora Hall*); Anthony Eisley (*Lt. Charles Brown*); Bill Gray (*Petty Officer Fred Twining*); Bobby Van (*Ensign Rutherford Chandler*); Pamela Mason (*Maria, a Scientist*); Walter Sande (*Dr. Arthur Beecham*); Edward Faulkner (*Spalding*); Phillip Terry (*Doctor*); David Brandon; Del West; Kaye Elhardt (*Diane*); Biff Elliot (*Commander Simpson*); Taggart Casey (*Holly*); William Meigs; Russ Bender (*McBride*); Garrett Myles; Mike Sargent; Paul Rhone; Charles Kramer; Red West.

VIDEO: EPI 2005

PLOT: A plane from McMurdo Sound is heading for Gow Island, an American military base in the Pacific, carrying a cargo of scientists plus a precious collection of plant ("undernourished cactus") and animal life found in a 300-square mile Eden in the heart of the Antarctic ice pack (an area heated by underground lakes). The unique vegetation has been there since before the first ice age.

On Gow Island itself, a stir crazy civilian meteorologist, Spalding, is anxiously awaiting the plane as his ticket off the island. The harassed Lt. Charles Brown has taken over duties while Commander Simpson is in Washington on a top-secret mission. Both men are in love with Nora, the cool-headed nurse with a yen for Brown and outlandish nurse's attire.

The incoming plane is cleared for landing but sounds of an on-board struggle and gunshots are heard over the radio. The gooney bird corrects its course and comes in for a crash landing. When Brown and Dr. Beecham search the disabled plane, they discover the traumatized pilot is the only one on board. In the infirmary the pilot's heartbeat is that of a man in mortal terror. The mystery deepens when eight bullet holes are discovered in the plane's cabin. There are no signs of blood although the doctor does find traces of a liquid which is corrosive enough to have eaten into the plane. He takes a sample to his lab for analysis.

Concerned the scientific specimens will die, Dr. Beecham has them replanted near the island's warm springs. Since their arrival, strange things have been occurring on the base and a body, believed to be one of the missing scientists from the plane, is discovered. The trees begin producing spores as more and more of the base's personnel disappear and a siege mentality kicks in.

In Washington, Commander Simpson receives a report from Gow that animal-like plants are moving about on root-like tentacles. The admiral places the island in quarantine and commands the nearest Navy destroyer to head there. Dr. Beecham reveals his theory that the spores are the young of the trees, reproduced through the leaf stalks, and that the ripe ones fall off when a plant is burned. He warns that the trees are omnivorous, and their peculiar habits are a result of the six months of darkness in the Antarctic. They had to move to survive and find sustenance. During sunlight they behave like ordinary plants but in the dark ... And in the darkness of the plane hold, they sprang back to life as they do on the island at night.

In Washington, Simpson demands that a fighter squadron be sent to the island to napalm the monsters. He is flown back to his command to watch as the fighter jets drop their lethal cargo. Brown and Nora go into a clinch and the narrator intones: "Gow Island. In the past virtually unknown to the rest of the world; today a famous landmark in Man's struggle with the unknown, another step forward in the march of science."

The only thing missing is a question mark after THE END.

NOTES: *The Navy vs. the Night Monsters* is a frustrating experience. It's a 1950s B-sci fi thriller with overtones of *The Thing from Another World* (the Arctic environment) and *The Day of the Triffids* (walking vegetation) that was actually made in 1966. Mamie is top-billed as Nora, Gow Island's blonde bombshell nurse whose taste in uniforms runs to Lt. Charlie Brown's but not to wearing the usual Navy-accredited garb herself. As Mamie said: "I think everyone went to that movie to see my uniforms or to see my yellow sweater."*

Director Michael A. Hoey explained to

Poster for what many consider one of Mamie's worst-ever movies, *The Navy vs. the Night Monsters* (Standard Club of California/Realart, 1966).

*Phone interview with the author, August 3, 2006.

interviewer Tom Weaver the origin of Mamie's outfits: "Mamie was supposed to be a Navy nurse. When it came time to do the costuming, the wardrobe person [Patrick Cummings], George Edwards* and I got together and we looked at pictures of Navy nurse uniforms and said, 'That's fine.' Then I got a phone call from George saying Mamie wanted us to come to the house 'cause she'd like to discuss wardrobe. Okay, fine, up we go—and Mamie has had all these costumes made. And they look like pinafores! She came out in this one outfit with these deep pockets on this pinafore and she said, 'See, it's very functional. I can keep all my thermometers in here.' I was biting my tongue. I was not angry, I was absolutely ready to burst into laughter! It got to a point where she said, 'I will not wear the uniform.' So we eventually arrived at a compromise where I said, 'We'll make her a civilian.' I wasn't a fool, so I put her in a tight sweater and a pair of slacks for about 50 percent of the time. Actually, Mamie tried very hard. We worked hard on a couple of the scenes, to try to get a performance out of her, and she was terrific. She certainly did everything that I asked her to do."†

Director Hoey was the force behind the film being made and there are shreds of what it could have been had there been no outside interference. London-born Hoey, the son of character actor Dennis Hoey, began in the film industry as an editor. In the late 1950s, he read *The Monster at Earth's End* by Murray Leinster‡ and noted the similarities with a film he admired, the classic *The Thing from Another World* (1951). He optioned the rights to Leinster's novel and set about writing the screenplay, then titled *The Nightcrawlers*.

Producer George Edwards liked the pitch and handed director's duties to the fledgling writer. As Hoey told Tom Weaver: "The whole 'package' for the screenplay and my services as a director, I think, came to $10,000. Four thousand went to Murray Leinster, $2000 went to the Directors Guild, another thousand went to my agent. I didn't exactly get fat on it!"**

While Hoey has nothing but praise for George Edwards, he is less than enamored of executive producer Jack Broder who changed the film's name to *The Navy vs. the Night Monsters*. Worse was to come. Hoey completed what he thought was a taut, psychologically potent 78-minute low-budget B sci-fi movie. But Broder wanted 90 minutes, a running time he felt would make the movie more attractive to television programmers.

"When I left the picture, he had Arthur Pierce, the director of *Women of the Prehistoric Planet*, come in and shoot added scenes. Well, what Arthur did was not just shoot scenes, but change the whole premise. He added all those scenes of those Navy officers in that base on the mainland. It completely ruined the premise of what I had in mind."††

What also ruined the claustrophobic little chiller were the special effects. With a budget of $178,000, a union crew and a 10-day shoot, there was little money available for the omnivorous trees. From the start, Hoey had wanted his trees to blend in as much as possible with normal vegetation, thus making them all the more terrifying.

"The only tree that I worked with was the one that had the guy in it manipulating the limbs, which is the one that has the fight with the pilot. We shot it in pretty low-key light,

---

*George Edwards (1924–91) produced a number of cult movies in the 1960s and 1970s including Voyage to the Prehistoric Planet (1965), Queen of Blood (1966), Women of the Prehistoric Planet (1966), What's the Matter with Helen? (1971), Frogs (1972), and The Killing Kind (1973).
†Tom Weaver, The Astounding B Monster, www.bmonster.com.
‡Murray Leinster (1896–1975) was the nom de plume of William Fitzgerald Jenkins, who began writing adventure stories and mysteries before graduating to science fiction and winning the Hugo Award for his novelette Exploration Team in 1965. He was a Hugo nominee in 1960 for his novel The Pirates of Zan. His story The Purple Hieroglyph, written as Will F. Jenkins, has been filmed three times: as The Purple Cipher (1920), Murder Will Out (1930), and Torchy Blane in Chinatown (1939). His novel The Wailing Asteroid was filmed as The Terrornauts (1967).
**Tom Weaver, The Astounding B Monster, www.bmonster.com.
††Ibid.

Dr. Beecham (Walter Sande), Spalding (Edward Faulkner), Nora (Mamie) and Diane (Kaye Elhardt) await the planeload of scientists from Antarctica in *The Navy vs. the Night Monsters* (Standard Club of California/Realart, 1966).

to try to hide as much of it as we possibly could."*

A number of the characters meet their grisly demise in the trees' embrace, including Bill Gray, a cult favorite for his appearance in *The Day the Earth Stood Still* (1951), who has his arm ripped off.

"Yea, talk about A to Z!!" Bill wrote. "The only thing I remember [about *Night Monsters*] is having an ear syringe full of 'blood' in the armpit of my 'good arm.' the one not devoured, that I caused, by rhythmic squeezing, to pulsate several gushing streams of crimson gooey liquid from the shredded vessel end of the severed limb. It was so effective, that it was cut (too gory) for the TV version."†

If that tree had a certain panache, that's more than can be said for the stumps which attack the base and are napalmed into oblivion by the Air Force. Laughably inept, they were yet more added footage, shot this time by actor Jon Hall, who had his own production company. These marauding stumps are about as threatening as sea anemones and the dispro-

---

*Ibid.
†*Bill Gray (1938–), formerly Billy Gray, had a long screen career which included a string of childhood appearances uncredited until he played Doris Day's younger brother, Wesley, in the nostalgic* On Moonlight Bay *(1951) and* By the Light of the Silvery Moon *(1953) and Bud on the popular television series* Father Knows Best *(1954–60).*

portional firepower brought in to destroy them must have tweaked some audiences to the parallels to what was occurring in Vietnam where napalm was being used to denude the countryside and was having devastating effects on the civilian population.

The successful scenes, and they are the core of Hoey's vision, were created by the director and his cinematographer, Stanley Cortez.* They effectively create an atmosphere of a tense standoff between the Navy base, a little oasis of civilization, and the unknown and unseen dangers in the tropical jungle.

The leading man, and Mamie's love interest, was the stolid Anthony Eisley[†] who had appeared briefly and uncredited in the earlier Mamie flick *3 Nuts in Search of a Bolt*. He was not Hoey's first choice as he was angling for a bigger box office name. But when it became obvious the budget wouldn't stretch to a marquee name, Hoey was happy to go with the star of TV's *Hawaiian Eye*.

It was neither a high point in his career nor in Mamie's. In an interview with Marty Baumann, Mamie revealed, "I had fun doing it — but I thought I should have been eaten by the monster. I was looking forward to being gobbled up. I just took my money and ran. Now that *was* a 'B' movie!"[‡]

REVIEWS: "Fatuous science fiction adventure, woodenly acted and directed ... Its

Nora (Mamie) and acting base commander Lt. Charles Brown (Anthony Eisley) take time out from chasing acid-spewing vegetation in *Navy vs. the Night Monsters* (Standard Club of California/Realart, 1966).

only positive merit is Stanley Cortez's clean and sometimes atmospheric photography — but even this is thrown away by the meandering, obtusely talkative script." *Monthly Film Bulletin,* May 1967

"There is a certain silly pleasure to be derived from watching Mamie Van Doren being threatened by carnivorous vegetables, which hardly look a match for her..." *Halliwell's TV and Movie Guide 2000*

"A throwback to the type of sci-fi junk which had entertained moviegoers a decade earlier. Even the cast ...gave the movie the look of being a reissue rather than a new feature." James Robert Parish, *The Great Science Fiction Pictures II*

---

*Stanley Cortez (1908–97) garnered most of the good reviews for this film for his atmospheric photography and because of his connection to Orson Welles (Cortez was cinematographer on 1942s The Magnificent Ambersons).
[†]Anthony Eisley (1925–2003), a stalwart of television, was a star from his role as Tracy Steele in Hawaiian Eye (1959–62), the series which also catapulted Connie Stevens to TV superstardom. Eisley's film career was largely underwhelming although he appeared in cult favorites The Wasp Woman (1960), Journey to the Center of Time (1967), The Mummy and the Curse of the Jackals (1969), Dracula vs. Frankenstein (1971), and Monster (1979). He also appeared opposite Julie Andrews in Star! (1968).
[‡]Baumann, The Astounding B Monster, 209.

"A top must-see feature. The casting director deserves an award ... Acid-bleeding, walking plants are after the cast! The cast is after Mamie!" *The Psychotronic Encyclopedia of Film*

"1) Look at the title. 2) Examine the cast. 3) Be aware that plot involves omnivorous trees. 4) Don't say you weren't warned." *Leonard Maltin's 2006 Movie Guide*

"The good guys wipe out the nasty vegetation in the end. Of course, their obvious answer of simply destroying such creatures came from an era before the Environmental Protection Agency and recycling. Speaking of which, consider recycling any copies of this bomb you might come across." C.J. Henderson, *The Encyclopedia of Science Fiction Movies from 1897 to the Present*

"One of those films that is so bad you go and see it for the laughs instead of the chills." *The Motion Picture Guide*

"Van Doren breathes heavily to push the biggest night monsters of all against the thin material of her blouse, thereby revealing the roundness of the Gargantuas concealed beneath." John Stanley, *Creature Features*

"Civilization in the shape of Mamie Van Doren is threatened by man-eating plants from the Antartic; they don't stand a chance." Robin Cross, *The Big Book of B Movies*

You've Got to Be Smart • World-Cine Associates/Stage 19 Productions, 1967

C'mon to a hoe-down of happiness!

CREDITS: *Written and Directed by* Ellis Kadison; *Associate Producers:* Jack G. George, Jeb Gholson; *Photography:* Harry May; *Music:* Gerald Alters, Stan Worth; *Lyrics:* Ellis Kadison; *Music Arranger-Conductor:* Stan Worth; *Choreography:* Al Gilbert; *Editorial Supervision:* Douglas Robertson; *Production Manager:* Jeb Gholson; *Editor:* A.J. Cornall; *First Assistant Director:* Wingate Smith; *Second Assistant Director:* Leo Silver; *Assistant to the Director:* Aida Lioy; *Music Supervisor:* Bob Ballard; *Associate:* Lyle Murphy; *Art Director at Allied Studios:* Bill Tury; *Makeup:* Steve Lane; *Hair Stylist:* Cherie De La Mar; *Wardrobe:* Paul McCardle, Jean Merrick; *Miss Castillo's Wardrobe:* Gloria Miguel; *Models' Gowns:* Michael Novarese; *Special Hair Styles:* Don Moran; *Décor:* Ken Tolman; Color by Pathé; 108 minutes.

SONGS: "Him Who Loves Ain't Got Time to Hate" *The Bantams;* reprised by *The Bantams, Congregation;* "You've Got to Be Smart" *Unidentified singer over opening credits;* "Nothing But Sin" *Tom Stern;* "Why?" *Gloria Castillo;* "Look Before You Leap" *The Bantams;* reprised by *The Bantams and Gloria Castillo;* "You're Terrific (Mr. Harper)" *Gloria Castillo;* "(Turn to) The Reverend Methuselah Jones" *Choir;* "Restin' Time" *Gloria Castillo;* "You're Adorable (Miss Jackson)" *Roger Perry;* "Time Will Tell" *Gloria Castillo;* "Don't Look in Other Pastures" *The Bantams*

CAST: Tom Stern (*Nick Sloane*); Roger Perry (*Jerry Harper*); Gloria Castillo (*Connie Jackson*); Preston Foster (*D.O. Griggs*); Mamie Van Doren (*Lynn Hathaway*); George "Shug" Fisher (*Grandpa*); Hanna Landy (*Illona Griggs*); Phil Fenton (*Jerry Grayson*); Jeff Bantam (*Methuselah Jones*); Mike Bantam (*Zeb*); Fritz Bantam (*Noah*); William Scully; Chester Hayes; Crayton Smith; Kenneth Tolman; Sandra Marsh; Suzan E. Claude; Gilda Texter; Calvin Brown.

DVD: Something Weird Video #7843

PLOT: Nick Sloane is fired from his advertising job after being caught attempting to steal one of the agency's top-dollar accounts. While driving through Arkansas for no good reason other than plot contrivance, he finds himself in Platitude (population 238) at an open-air revival meeting overseen by the precocious Methuselah Jones, a young boy also known as The Reverend. Nick sees the potential of a money-making enterprise and convinces Methuselah and his two cousins, Zeb and Noah, to come with him to Los Angeles where he gets them a 15-minute television gig as *TV Tabernacle.*

Nick is aided and abetted by the dewy-eyed Connie Jackson, former secretary to D.O. Griggs, who fired Nick from the advertising agency. She is so in love with the scam artist she cannot see his faults while TV producer Jerry Harper, who pines for Connie, keeps his peace because he doesn't want to rock the boat. Nick begins a clandestine affair with Lynn Hathaway, a rich socialite, although he has asked Connie to marry him. The money-making enterprise begins to unravel when the IRS asks questions about the whereabouts of public donations and the Jones boys follow Nick and discover his secret assignation with Lynn.

At the subsequent IRS examination, Nick is exonerated of a fraud charge, although his skimming of management dollars from the contributions is considered a scam. Outside the court, Connie is confronted with Nick's perfidy when Lynn turns up to support him. Realizing she has been a fool, she turns to Jerry for solace. Nick and Lynn walk away a couple, and the Jones boys head back to the comparative innocence of Arkansas.

NOTES: Mamie, making a "Special Guest Appearance," plays an unusual role: a rich bitch. It's almost as if she's managed to wriggle from the working girl of *All American* to get what she wants most — money and power. Here she no longer has to use her sexual wiles to win her man; this time she uses her financial independence. And she power-dresses to prove it. This lady is not to be tangled with. And although the film is a musical, Mamie is, luckily, not encumbered with any of the trite songs.

Still glamorous, although her green outfit does her no favors, Mamie has little to do and the film, written and helmed by Ellis Kadison, pulls its punches as if he's afraid to make anyone too venal. Even Tom Stern's cad is not a total bounder; he's a small-time scam artist skimming enough from TV evangelism to make life comfortable while staying just within the law. And Mamie is not the rich bitch attempting to destroy a relationship because there's simply no real connection between Stern's Nick and Gloria Castillo's Connie. Mamie is a device to expose Stern's duplicity and, as such, has little to work with. The evenhandedness and lack of real spite and deviousness in the plot drags it into the mawkish. Instead of going for a satire on teleevangelism, not quite as prevalent back in 1967 as it has become today, Kadison presents Methuselah as a genuine, albeit somewhat naïve, child preacher. Although he may be winking at the audience by having the boys live in Platitude, Arkansas, the sheer unrelenting banality of The Reverend's sing-preaching such trite hymns as "Him Who Loves Ain't Got Time to Hate," "Look Before You Leap" and "Don't Look in Other Pastures" merely reinforces the shallowness of the treatment.

Kadison's directing career, which ended with *You've Got to Be Smart*, concentrated on family fare, especially movies about children,[*] and he's competent without being inspired. Gloria Castillo[†] is much too nice as Connie although she sings well on the numbers she has to warble. Roger Perry is a bland enough hero. The Bantams, Jeff, Mike and Fritz, are unrelentingly upbeat although their inexperience shows and they don't seem to have made any further forays into movies since. The film is notable as Preston Foster's second-to-last movie[‡] and for the appearance of George "Shug" Fisher[**] as the boys' grandpa.

---

[*]*Ellis Kadison (1927–88) was a writer-producer-director who helmed* The Cat *(1966), about a lost boy and a killer wildcat, and* Git! *(1965), about a runaway boy and a renegade hound. He was a writer on* Theatre of Death *(1966) and* The Gnome-Mobile *(1967) as well as a number of TV series.*

[†]*Gloria Castillo (1935–) was another in the long line of lurid teen movie stars. Her first big-screen appearance was as Ruby in Charles Laughton's solo stab at directing, the awesome* The Night of the Hunter *(1955). She then lurched into teen exploitation territory with* Runaway Daughters *(1956) as a troubled teenager whose mother is absent overseas divorcing her third husband. In* Reform School Girl *(1957) she is lusted after by her uncle (Jack Kruschen) and involved in a hit-and-run accident for which she's sent away to a school for girls. If that weren't enough, she's pursued by the disembodied hand of a space alien that she and her boyfriend have run over in their car in* Invasion of the Saucer Men *(1957). In* Teenage Monster *(1957), she becomes the lust object of a hormonal teen turned into a monster by the mysterious rays emanating from a meteor.* You've Got to Be Smart *was her last movie.*

[‡]*Preston Foster (1900–70), noted for his early tough-guy roles, finished his screen career with* Chubasco *(1968).*

[**]*George "Shug" Fisher (1907–84) began his career in radio and with country music bands such as the Hollywood Hillbillies and the Beverly Hill Billies before lasting fame as one of the Sons of the Pioneers (he joined in 1943) in Roy Rogers' highly profitable westerns. He appeared with the Sons of the Pioneers at New York's famed Carnegie Hall in 1951. He was also a regular on television and appeared as Shorty Kellums in the television series* The Beverly Hillbillies.

The movie is competently made but bland, and only for Mamie Van Doren completists.

REVIEWS: "A frighteningly bad picture ... This was the untalented Van Doren's final try at film acting." *The Motion Picture Guide*

"Well-made and insufferably upbeat — by his second or third song, you'll be praying someone beats Methuselah with a two by four..." Luther Heggs, *Something Weird Video*

Voyage to the Planet of Prehistoric Women • Filmgroup, 1968

Beware of the Night Crawlers ... their clutches will disintegrate you!

CREDITS: *Directors:* Derek Thomas [Peter Bogdanovich] [uncredited: Pavel Klushantsev]; *Producer:* Norman D. Wells; *Screenplay:* Henry Ney [Peter Bogdanovich] [uncredited: Aleksandr Kazantsev, Pavel Klushantsev]; *Music Composed and Conducted by* Keith Benjamin; *Production Manager:* Gilles de Turenne; *Photography:* Flemming Olsen; *Production Coordinator:* Polly Platt; *Special Effects:* Giovanni de Palma, Don Jones, Gary Kent, Walter Robles; *Art Director:* Vittorio Ferroni; *Costume Designer:* Alice Mitchell; *Editor:* Bob Collins; *Sound Editor:* Burt Campbell; *Costumes Executed by* Maureen of Hollywood; *Hair Styles:* Vergee; *Makeup:* Mary Jo Weir; *Special Props:* Wah Chang; *Production Designers:* V. Aleksandrov, M. Tsybasov; Color by Pathé; 78 minutes.

CAST: Mamie Van Doren (*Moana*); Mary Marr (*Verba*); Paige Lee (*Twyla*); Aldo Romani [Gennadi Vernov] (*Astronaut Andre Freneau*); Margot Hartman (*Mayaway*); Irene Orton (*Meriama*); Pam Helton (*Wearie*); Frankie Smith (*Woman of Venus*); James David [Georgi Tejkh] (*Capt. Alfred Kern*); Judy Cowart (*Woman of Venus*); Roberto Martelli [Vladimir Yemelyanov] (*Commander William "Billy" Lockhart*); Robin Smith, Cathie Reimer (*Women of Venus*); Ralph Phillips [Yuri Sarantsev] (*Astronaut Howard Sherman*); Murray Gerard [Georgi Zhzhyonov] (*Astronaut Hans Walters*); Adele Valentine (*Woman of Venus*); Peter Bogdanovich (*Narrator*).

DVD: RetroMedia Entertainment RMED 1053

PLOT: Two Earth astronauts, Sherman and Kern,* accompanied by a robot named John, lose radio contact with mission control when they land on Venus. Freneau, Lockhart and Walters are sent to rescue them. On Venus, the astronauts encounter lizard men, dinosaurs and giant man-eating anemones. While searching for the stranded astronauts, Freneau hears a woman's song — the song of the siren — and is convinced the planet is inhabited. As the rescue party closes in on their stranded countrymen, they are attacked in their space car by a pterodactyl which they kill. They next discover the remains of an advanced civilization under the ocean. Unbeknownst to them, they have killed Tera, a god to the women whose voices Freneau has heard. The women swear revenge on the invaders by calling forth the power of the Fire God. A volcano erupts, stranding Sherman and Kern. Robot John carries them to safety through the rivers of hot lava until his self-preservation mechanism instructs him to dump his human cargo; they disconnect his wiring just in time. The space car rescues them but Robot John, incapacitated, falls into the lava and is washed to the seashore where the women discover him. They think it's one of the "demons" that the Fire God has destroyed and sent to them to show his power. But they see the Fire God has not destroyed all the invaders as the astronauts return to their ship. They pray to Tera to destroy the remainder of the astronauts; even though heavy rains almost wash the ground from beneath the rocket they escape. Freneau discovered a sculpture of a humanoid face, proving the planet is inhabited. He vows to return. The women turn on Tera as a "false god" who is less powerful than the astronauts. They retrieve the charred and lava-coated remains of Robot John and set him up as their new deity.

NOTES: Long ridiculed and pilloried, *Voyage to the Planet of Prehistoric Women* is ac-

---

*The dubbed voices use Kern and Kerns interchangeably throughout the film.

tually a fine movie primarily because it's a redubbed version of a superior science fiction film called *Planeta Bur* [*Planet of Storms*] (1962) which Roger Corman bought and managed to turn into not one but two English-language movies. The first, *Voyage to the Prehistoric Planet* (1965), with interpolated scenes of Basil Rathbone and Faith Domergue, was "directed" by Curtis Harrington. Three years later, Corman tried again, this time with Mamie as the star, directed by Peter Bogdanovich (using the name Derek Thomas). He doubled as the scriptwriter under the name Henry Ney. Much has been made of Bogdanovich's use of a *nom de screen*; Curtis Harrington was also guilty and listed himself as John Sebastian on the other movie. It's implied Bogdanovich is embarrassed by the finished product but the reasons are far less complicated.

"I didn't put my name on *Voyage to the Planet of Prehistoric Women* because I only directed about 10 minutes of it. It was a Russian science fiction film and Roger tried to sell it to AIP but they didn't think it was viable because it didn't have any women in it. He'd given me this film to do which turned out to be *Targets* (1968) but he told me I had to do this first. It wasn't my film. I had nothing to do with the whole Russian side of it. That's why I didn't put my name on it. I didn't think I should take credit when such a small piece of it is mine."*

The Encyclopedia of Science Fiction entry on the original *Planeta Bur* says: "Cosmonauts land on Venus, accompanied by a robot that plays dance music (thus proving that funny robots are not peculiar to U.S. cinema). A well paced adventure story follows as they search for intelligent life. In an interestingly realized alien landscape they encounter dinosaurs, dangerous plants and a volcanic eruption, but the sole intelligent Venusian appears only at the end, watching unnoticed as the crew departs. By Western standards the film is a little slow and overtalkative (long conversations between the ground crew and the woman controlling the command ship), but it is always watchable. The best Russian sf film until the 1970s, it is ...stronger on production design than on plot."†

The technological quality of the original Russian film shines through; director Pavel Klushantsev was such a consummate futurist that variants on visual and plot ideas from his science fiction films, relatively unknown in the West, turned up later in movies including Stanley Kubrick's *2001: A Space Odyssey* (1968). Bogdanovich's task was to add women to the almost all-male environment of space. His solution was masterly. "There's a reference to the sirens in the Russian film but they're never seen so it was easy just to add them." What was not nearly as easy was making the idea work. Roger Corman dictated that there was not enough money for synchronized sound so "I directed my part and it was all silent. I remember meeting with Mamie, who Roger Corman wanted me to use, and she read through the script and said, 'There's no dialogue.' She was ready to walk out and I had to persuade her to do it by explaining the sirens communicated telepathically. I don't think she was really convinced but she signed up to do it. I guess I owe Mamie an apology for that."

The Russian actors were dubbed, most effectively, by American actors; Bogdanovich himself did the narration as Freneau and is listed on the film as doing so. But the sirens' footage remained silent until a test screening showed the audience was confused as to what was going on. Corman got another director to add voices to the soundtrack to explain the action and make it obvious the women were communicating telepathically. By this time Mamie was well gone and another actress dubbed her voice.

Mamie appears 33 minutes into the film, one of a bevy of long-haired blondes lounging on rocks near the seashore. They are wearing long white flared pants and shells as breast covers, in Mamie's case ridiculously large shells which not only look uncomfortable but look anything but sexy. Added to this was a ridiculous baker's hat she wears each time she adopts

---

*All quotes by Peter Bogdanovich are from a phone interview with the author, May 20, 2006.
†John Clute and Peter Nicholls, *The Encyclopedia of Science Fiction*, 934.

the guise of high priestess. "They couldn't get shells big enough for my breasts. I had these shells and they were huge and I had them strapped around my neck and all the other girls they had smaller little boobs and cute little shells but mine were so ugly and big old shells I wanted to rip them off."*

Both Mamie and Peter Bogdanovich admit there was conflict on the set. One flare-up involved a scene in which the sirens are called upon to eat fish. "We were all underwater and had to eat these raw fish. Well, sushi wasn't as popular then as it is now and these weren't, like, top quality fish. He wanted me to take a fish and bite its head off. I thought he was crazy and I said, 'You eat it!' The next day he brings this rubber fish and when I bite into it all this fake blood comes out."†

Further trouble arose when the cast and crew went out on a boat. "It was a terrible day," Bogdanovich remembers. "We were all seasick and Mamie wouldn't get in the water. I think she was scared of sharks. Even when we did scenes at the water's edge, Mamie was reluctant to get in the water. And she had her husband of the time, Lee Meyers, standing on the rocks out of camera range with a loaded rifle in case he had to come to her rescue."

Mamie recalls, "We shot it down in Malibu amongst these rocks, a lot of boulders, and we'd have to time the scene because the waves would come in at a certain time and we'd all have to run up and the waves would go back and I'd go 'God, here we go again.' I've got to admit this, I have never seen the [whole] movie, all I've seen is the scenes I did with these girls. Peter Bogdanovich took me out on this boat on Marina Del Rey one morning and I got on this boat and all these other girls were on this boat. He wanted me to get in the water. We went way out. The water was deep. It doesn't matter how deep the water is if you can't swim, right? I'm a pretty good swimmer but I said, 'This water is ice-fucking-cold, you know, and there's no way you're going to get me in that water.'"‡

For making do with a minuscule budget, Peter Bogdanovich has much to be proud of in his first effort at big-screen directing.** Of course, there are camp elements to the film: the prehistoric animals that seem to abound on Venus, and the stylistically different siren sequences. But overall it's a masterly cut-and-paste job. If it's not one of Mamie's great performances, it's not surprising given what she had to work with and it's doubtful even Marcel Marceau could have mimed his way out of it. Most of the kudos goes to the cast and crew of the original Russian film.

I Fratelli di Arizona/The Arizona Kid •
Premier Productions, 1971

CREDITS: A Cirio H. Santiago Production. *Director & Story:* Luciano Carlos; *Producer:* Cirio H. Santiago; *Script:* Lino Brocka, Luciano Carlos; *Music:* Restie Umali; *Lyrics:* Levi Celerio; *Editor:* Ben Barcelon; *Photography:* Felipe Sacdalan; *Sound Engineer:* Demetrio de Santos; *Sound Effects:* Tony Gosalves; Color by Premiere; 111 minutes.

SONG: "San Francisco" (Bronislaw Kaper, Gus Kahn) *Jazz band on soundtrack*

CAST: Chiquito (*Ambo*); Mamie Van Doren (*Sharon Miller*); Gordon Mitchell (*El Coyote*); Mariela Branger; Bernard Bonnin; Cass Martin; Dan van Heusen [Husen]; Víctor Israel; Ángel Aranda; John Mark; Felipe Silano; Gene Reyes; Tony Brandt; Vigente Poja; Pilar Vela [Velázquez]; Ramón Serrano; Zaido Moreno; M. Restilla; Modesto Dajarado.

VIDEO/DVD: Video Search of Miami #11033

PLOT: Ambo arrives in San Francisco from the Philippines in the early 1900s with a jar of bagoong†† for his uncle. Uncle has already

---

*Being Mamie, *an interview with Mamie on the RetroMedia Entertainment DVD of* Voyage to the Planet of Prehistoric Women.
†*Phone interview with the author, August 3, 2006.*
‡Being Mamie.
**The previous year he had directed a television documentary on Howard Hawks.*
††*Bagoong is a favorite Filipino fish paste or sauce delicacy, made from fermenting salted bonnet mouth fish sometimes with fragments of the fish intact. To non-aficionados, it has a smell similar to a sewer outlet.*

left for Mexico and, via a letter left at a Chinese tailors, asks Ambo to follow. The stagecoach on which Ambo is traveling is held up by Frank Darrow's gang and he's later dumped, penniless, in El Dorado. There he gets a job as a cook at the local cantina but Darrow's gang turns up again and shoots the cantina owner who, before dying, makes Ambo promise to protect his niece (his brother Don Miguel's daughter). At the burial, Ambo hears how the cantina owner had hired the Arizona Kid to rid Sierra Vista of El Coyote and his gang. Darrow and his men attempt to rough up Ambo and the niece to keep them quiet about the killing but the Arizona Kid turns up in the nick of time and rescues them.

The trio heads toward Sierra Vista, pursued by Darrow and his men. In a shootout, the Arizona Kid is killed, but Ambo and the niece are saved by her boyfriend, Undo. Continuing on their way, they save a lone woman, Sharon Miller, being threatened by Indians. She is en route to a cattle ranch she has bought outside Sierra Vista. That night Ambo feels the cold and Sharon tells him to put on the Arizona Kid's clothes to keep warm. Naturally, when the party arrives at Don Miguel's villa, Ambo is mistaken for the gunslinger. They decide the only real way to get the local ranchers to fight El Coyote is to go along with the pretext that Ambo is the Arizona Kid, and Sharon uses her wiles to seduce him into acquiescing. But while Ambo is out practicing target shooting, El Coyote comes by disguised as an old priest and Ambo confesses the ruse to him.

El Coyote takes his gang into the town to confront Don Miguel and the fake Arizona Kid but Undo arrives with the local ranchers. They rout the gang, and El Coyote is killed in a wrangle with Ambo. Now a hero, Ambo decides to continue on to Mexico to deliver his precious cargo to his uncle. And Sharon insists on going with him.

NOTES: Mamie is second-billed below the title after Chiquito, for whom this film was a vehicle. A famed comedian in the Philippines and throughout the Spanish-speaking world, he was born Augusto Valdez Pangan in Manila in 1928; so widespread was his popularity that the Philippines media called his 1997 death "the day the laughter died." He is reputed to have made over one hundred films and is credited in some sources as the first male to portray the comic strip superheroine Darna.* The plot is merely a framework on which to hang Chiquito's comic shtick. Enjoyment will be in direct proportion to a viewer's understanding of Filipino culture and language.

But, in any language, Chiquito's comic turn with the dreaded jar of bagoong in the crowded confines of the bouncing stagecoach, and his antics subverting the traditional Main Street shoot-out, are highlights. The most readily available version of the film is not subtitled, with dialogue mainly in Tagalog but also Spanish, English, and one of the Chinese languages.

Unfortunately, the post-dubbing on the film is atrocious and Mamie, who does not enter the film until just about the one-hour mark, is dubbed in a high-pitched, whiny, imitation–Jayne Mansfield voice that becomes increasingly irritating. Although it's interesting to note the women in this movie are dab hands with a gun and not the usual passive liabilities of westerns, Mamie has little to do but show ample cleavage and spend a lot of screen time kissing the movie's star. She has no songs while Chiquito has two at the cantina in El Dorado.

Mamie and Gordon Mitchell,[†] (El Coyote) are the U.S. contingent in a movie that is a virtual United Nations of acting talent with German, Italian, Spanish and Chinese rounding out the cast. This Filipino-Italian co-production was filmed mainly in Spain.

---

*The super heroine created by Mars Ravelo, made her first appearance in Bulaklak Magazine in July, 1947. The character underwent a name change in 1950 to Darna. Although she has superficial characteristics similar to Wonder Woman, her powers include flight, super strength, super speed and near-invulnerability. Chiquito played Darna in Terebol Dobol.

†Gordon Mitchell (1923–2003) (real name: Charles Allen Pendleton) began his entertainment career as a muscleman in Mae West's famed nightclub act and as a bit player in movies such as The Ten Commandments (1956), Li'l Abner (1959) and Spartacus (1960). He headed to Italy to appear in the popular peplum movies before graduating to spaghetti westerns.

That Girl from Boston • Moonstone Films, 1975

CREDITS: *Director/Executive Producer:* Matt Cimber; *Photography:* Dean Cundey; *Assistant Production Manager:* Don Behrns; *Camera:* Raymond Stella.

CAST: George "Buck" Flower (*Thirsty*); John F. Goff (*Gay Architect*); Alexandra Hay; Marius Mazmanian (*Pierre Grass*); Mamie Van Doren.

NOTES: One of Mamie's "lost" movies. "We shot in Lake Havasu and I have no idea about the plot. Not the best script. It was from a somewhat well-known novel, but I never read it. I never saw the movie and I don't think it was ever completed, much less released."*

That Girl from Boston is "a novel about the newest rules for the oldest game of all. Willa Starch has the most sought-after breasts and the fairest white backside in greater Boston. It's just a matter of time until someone finds the secret fuse that ignites the love bomb known as Willa Starch." Published in 1966, it was written by Robert H. Rimmer (1917–2001), the author of *The Harrod Experiment* (filmed 1973) and *Proposition 3*. He was also co-writer and co-cinematographer, with Wes Craven and Andrzej Kostenko, on *The Evolution of Snuff* (1978).

Matt Cimber was executive producer and director on the project. Cimber, born 1936, had been married from 1964 to 1966 to Mamie's competition, Jayne Mansfield, whom he had met during the road company tour of *Bus Stop* and *Gentlemen Prefer Blondes*,[†] both of which had starred Marilyn Monroe on screen. He guided her career until shortly before her death, directing her final screen outing, *Single Room Furnished* (1968). He would go on to direct a string of screen beauties such as Pia Zadora, Lola Falana, Laurene Landon and Millie Perkins. Many of his films featured George "Buck" Flower (1937–2004), one of the stars of *That Girl from Boston*.

Free Ride • A Kingston Production, 1986

Dan Got His Tuition the Easy Way — Unfortunately, Somebody Wants it Back!

CREDITS: *Director:* Tom Trbovich; *Producers:* Tom Boutross, Bassem Abdallah; *Executive Producer:* Moustapha Akkad; *Associate Producer:* M. Sanousi; *Written by* Ronald Z. Wang, Lee Fulkerson, and Robert Bell; *Story by* Ronald Z. Wang; *Music:* David C. Williams; *Photography:* Paul Lohmann; *Casting:* Dan Guerrero; *Art Director:* Daniel Webster; *Editor:* Ron Honthaner; *Costumer:* Barbara Scott; *Makeup:* Ali Greene; *Hair Dresser:* Leslie Lightfoot; *Production Manager:* John J. Smith; *Set Decorator:* Joe Mirvis; *First Assistant Director:* Robert Smawley; *Second Assistant Director:* Lawrence Lipton; *Sound:* Steve Nelson, Clark King; *Stunt Coordinator:* Ray Saniger; *Color Consultant:* Paul O'Driscoll; Color; 92 minutes.

SONGS: "I Want You" (Smile) *Smile*; "Free Ride" (Jeff Lantz, Joel Atkins) *Laura Martier*; "Young Dudes" *Mamie Van Doren*; "Funiculi Funicular" *Norman Panto*

CAST: Gary Hershberger (*Dan*); Reed Rudy (*Greg*); Dawn Schneider (*Jill Monroe*); Peter DeLuise (*Carl*); Brian MacGregor (*Elmer*); Warren Berlinger (*Dean Stockwell*); Mamie Van Doren (*Debbie Stockwell*); Babette Props (*Kathy*); Chick Vennera (*Edgar Ness*); Anthony Charnota (*Vinnie Garbagio*); Mario Marcelino (*Vito Garbagio*); Joseph Tornatore (*Murray Garbagio*); Ken Olfson (*Mr. Lennox*); Liam Sullivan (*Mr. Monroe*); Frank Campanella (*Old Man Garbagio*); Diana Bellamy (*Woman Guard*); Tally Chanel (*Candy*); Terresa Hafford (*Monique*); Karen L. Scott (*Stuck-up Girl*); Robert De Frank (*Bartender*); Jeff Winkless (*Waiter*); Vicki Seton (*Marie*); Mary Garripoli (*Girl in Slip*); Kevin Welch (*Brent*); Sasha Jenson (*Boy #1*); John Washington (*Boy #2*); Christina MacGregor (*Jill's Friend*); Robert Apisa (*Thug #1*); Michael Carr (*Thug #2*); Anthony S. Ragonese (*Valet*); Robert E. Bastanchury (*Cabbie*); Crystal Smart (*Vito's Girl Friend*); Norman Panto (*Accordion Player*);

---

*Email to the author, April 7, 2006.
[†]Mamie also appeared stage revivals of these two plays.

Elizabeth Cochrell (*Nude Girl #1*); Rebecca Lynne (*Nude Girl #2*); Millie Moss (*Lady in Disco #1*); Roberta Smart (*Lady in Disco #2*); Caroline Davis (*Lady in Disco #3*); Scott Waller (*Singer*); Tommy Girvin (*Lead Guitarist*); David Blade (*Bass Guitarist*); Mark Poynter (*Keyboardist*); Tony Pacheco (*Drummer*).

PLOT: College student Dan Garten steals a car to impress a girl but, unknown to him, there is a quarter of a million dollars in stolen mob money under the front seat. Dan is attending Monroe College, overseen by the martinet Dean Stockwell, whose wife is the college nurse. Naturally enough the Garbagio family goes after the stolen money, as does Dean Stockwell and the FBI. Dan hides the money up the butt of a statue on the grounds of a snooty girls' school run by the Totally Holy Sisters of Self Flagellation. It all culminates in a Rambo-style free-for-all at the girls' school when the mob, Dean Stockwell, and the film's heroes all turn up to claim the money.

NOTES: Gary Hershberger makes the most spectacular entrance to college since Russ Tamblyn in *High School Confidential!* and that's not the only similarity. Mamie here plays another of her predatory stock-in-trades. In the most cleavage-exposing uniform ever, Mamie as the school nurse oversees the annual student health check-up, a line of teenage boys she surveys as if they are her own personal harem.

NURSE STOCKWELL: You all look so healthy.
(*Looking Carl up and down*)
My, you've grown so much since last semester.
(*Cupping his balls*)
Cough.

After she's been along the line of studs, and made an appointment with the most promising, she snaps, "Pull 'em up and tuck 'em in."

Even though Nurse Stockwell does her best to seduce students, jumps into a car with a bound-and-gagged fellow teacher, and is taught that it's all in the wrist movement by the sisters, she still ends up with her rather mundane and inattentive husband.

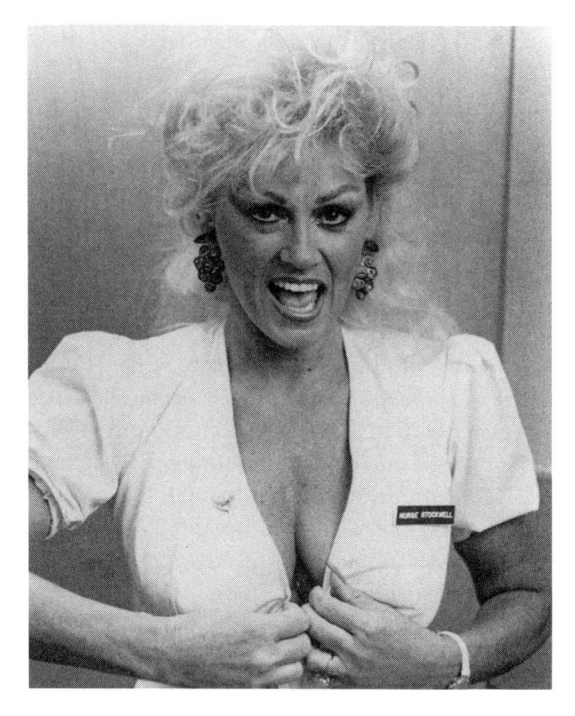

Nurse Stockwell (Mamie) in the most cleavage revealing nurse's uniform ever in *Free Ride* (Kingston, 1986).

This tepid gross-out teen comedy relies heavily on puns, sexual innuendo, pretty girls, pretty boys, hookers, nuns, the mob, stolen loot, gay and lesbian putdowns, drag, and jokes to do with anal passages and penises. But the mix is lackluster and the humor flaccid although Peter DeLuise* as the college suck-up registers strongly. Warren Berlinger is bombastic enough as the dean and Mamie is fun to watch as his randy wife in her all-too-few scenes.

REVIEWS: "On certain days videocassettes can be rented for 99¢ a day. If outlets reduce the price of some to 49¢, films like *Free Ride* might do a little business. Picture doesn't even qualify as sophomoric because even some silly films about teen antics can be amusing at some level — which this never is. Low-budget work lasting 82 tedious minutes... Whole production has the feel of being shot by a home movie camera in someone's backyard using props found in the garage." *Variety*

---

*Peter DeLuise (1966–), son of actor Dom DeLuise, is best remembered as Officer Doug Penhall opposite Johnny Depp in the TV series, 21 Jump Street. A trivia note: When DeLuise turns up in drag at the girls' school, his dress is torn at the back — but when he passes the security guard and goes through the gate the dress is undamaged.

Glory Years • Atlanta/Kushner-Locke, 1987

When you lose everything you have to win it all back.

CREDITS: *Director:* Arthur Allan Seidelman; *Supervising Producer:* Jonathan Debin; *Executive Producers:* Peter Locke, Donald Kushner; *Coordinating Producer:* Dawn Tarnofsky; *Associate Producer:* Thomas A. Bliss; *Creator-Producer-Writer:* Gary H. Miller; *Music:* Rocky Davis; *Musical Directors:* Dave Fisher, Rocky Davis; *Photography:* Stan Taylor; *Editor:* Janet Ashikaga; *Art Director:* Ninkey Dalton; *Set Decorator:* Tom Talbert; *Costumes:* Bernadene Morgan; *Makeup:* Donn Markel, Nina Kraft; *Hair Stylist:* Cheri Montesanto; *Stunts:* Joe Gilbride; *First Assistant Director:* Mack Bing; *Second Assistant Director:* Michael Smidt; *Second Second Assistant Director:* Ray Gomez; 150 minutes.

SONG: "Glory Years" (Dave Fisher, Rocky Davis, A.B. Clyde)

CAST: George Dzundza (*John Moss*); Archie Hahn (*Gerald Arkin*); Tim Thomerson (*Jack Sanders*); Tawny Kitaen (*Melinda*); *Guest Stars:* Michael Fairman (*Robert Murphy*); Tom 'Tiny' Lister Jr. (*Sal*); Sandy Simpson (*Stephen Rosen*); Beau Starr (*Joe Nelson*); Joey Bishop (*Sydney Rosen*); *Special Appearances by:* Al Bernstein (*Ring Announcer*); Dr. Joyce Brothers (*Dr. Karen Kugler*); Larry Holmes (*Ring Announcer*); Engelbert Humperdinck (*Himself*); Avery Schreiber (*Taxi Driver*); Mamie Van Doren (*Minnie*); Tony Longo (*Rizzo*); Donna Pescow (*Norma*); Franklyn Ajaye (*Wilson*); Gary Bisig (*IRS Agent*); Donna Denton (*Gina*); Chazz Palminteri (*Drummond*); Lew Palter (*Mr. Stein*); Geoffrey L. Rivas (*Juan Mojica*); Rick Telles (*Lupe Mojica*); Michael Aaron; Harley Akers [Akens]; Scott Beldin (*Unicycle Rider*); Rocky Davis, Dave Fisher, George L. Green, Leila Thigpen, Robert J. Walden (*Band at Reunion*); Joe Bellomo; Peter Bugel; Gloria Camden; Dean Casper; Burton Cohen; Linda Cohen; Dallas Cole; Johnny Dark; Pepper Davis; Frankie De Angelo; Robert Dulaine; Carmen Filpi; Greg Haugen; Chuck Hill; Victoria Hirsch; Jim Hodge; Charles Holman; Bobby Hosea; Vince Inneo; Mack Jackson; Roy Kieffer; Marco Lopez; Joe Mayer; Gary H. Miller; Nomi Mitty; Davey Pearl; Frank Perotti; Carme Petrillo; Penelope Reed; Leilani Sarelle; Cary Silver; Sly-Ali Smith; Bobbi Stevenson; Carol Wyand.

VIDEO: HBO Video 0033.

DVD: Hollywood Entertainment DH9115

PLOT: At the Coney Island High Class of 1966 20th reunion, three buddies meet up again: womanizer Jack Sanders, impotent alumni treasurer Gerald Arkin, and klutzy John Moss. Jack is in financial difficulties and needs $25,000, naturally the exact amount in the alumni fund. He has a scheme whereby a surefire bet on a fight in Las Vegas (the favorite will take a dive in Round 6) will not only earn back the alumni fund and enough to get him out of debt but also a $25,000 profit for Gerald. Like all such gamblers—they lose. They are pursued by the Mojicas (thugs hired by a Long Island millionaire whose daughter's advantageous marriage was thwarted by Jack), the daughter herself, the society girl's jilted fiancé, Jack's loan shark, and the IRS. When they are thrown out of their hotel after Jack is caught cheating at cards, they go to Minnie's Ranch, a brothel, to regroup and maybe help Gerald overcome his problem.

A series if misadventures follows during which the hapless trio endures a number of calamitous misfortunes including winning and losing the money a number of times, and a series of near-death experiences at the hands of the Mojica brothers, the Colombian Army, and the loan sharks. All ends happily with Jack and Melinda wed, Melinda pregnant and Daddy paying off Jack's debts. Gerald has found his tumescence, and klutzy John has found true love with klutzy waitress Norma.

NOTES: First broadcast on HBO, this fitfully amusing but frenetic romp through Las Vegas (much of it shot at the Dunes Hotel) and the surrounding desert, is notable for the performance of Donna Pescow as the bumbling waitress Norma who flirts with the equally clumsy John, played with nerdy panache by George Dzundza. Mamie plays it straight as the madam of Minnie's Ranch, a whorehouse in the desert. She has four short scenes (just after the 40-minute mark) in which she is swathed in a hip-hugging dark turquoise dress which shows her to her best advantage. She delivers the few lines she has with the no-nonsense assurance of a businesswoman who happens to run a brothel. It's a stylish performance made even more so by its restraint.

George Dzundza remembers Mamie "was still beautiful and quite sexy. And that the years had not ravaged her the way they have so many other ladies. She was extremely professional and I hope that she had some fun."*

The Vegas Connection • Pacific Films/Shooting Star Entertainment LLC/Suzanne DeLaurentiis Productions, 1999

CREDITS: *Director:* Lou Vadino; *Producers;* Suzanne DeLaurentiis, Serge Poupis; *Executive Producer:* Dennis Lanning; *Associate Producer:* George Engel; *Screenplay:* Dennis Lanning; *Photography:* Dwight F. Lay; *Art Director:* Renee Cash; *Costumes:* Matt Berger; *Makeup:* Jo Crowley; *Production Manager:* George Engel; *First Assistant Director:* Don Poquette; *Second Assistant Director:* Serge Poupis; *Sound Mixer:* Marty Kasparian; *Special Effects Coordinator:* Erich Martin von Hicks; *Stunt Coordinator:* Stephen R. Hudis.

CAST: Ashley F. Brooks (*Charlie*); Robert Carradine (*Matt Chance*); Mark Chaet (*Shifty*); Nicole Gian (*Jess*); Ed McMahon (*Al Ross*); Kathy Shower (*Gina*); Barry Sigismondi (*Blair Fessard*); Tom Smothers (*Himself*); Mamie Van Doren (*Rita*); Kelly J. Christopher (*Doll*); Kim Krentz (*Girlfriend*).

NOTES: This unreleased thriller top-lines Ashley F. Brooks[†] and Robert Carradine,[‡] who says, "It's never been released. The producer, Dennis Lanning, I heard had died. It was an action movie and I was the star. Ashley Brooks was one of his favorites. I was a private investigator called in to solve a big crime. I had a scene in a bar. We filmed it in the San Fernando Valley where, I think, [Mamie] was giving me some information. Working with her was a treat. She still had a presence that commanded attention. The whole room stopped to watch her."**

Liz Smith attempted to drum up interest in her column: "Mamie Van Doren, a '50s era blond bombshell who survived to tell the tale — and boy, does she have tales to tell!— has signed to do a TV pilot called *The Vegas Connection.* Mamie is cast as the proprietor of a topless bar. This is a given, yes? Van Doren's co-star is Bob Carradine. He's a crime buster, Mamie's his informant — and the proprietor of a topless bar. (We can't emphasize this enough!) Mamie's always had quite a lot of fun with her image and her career, which consisted mostly of B-movies involving teenage hormones run amok. This is Van Doren's first turn on the small screen. Given her moxie, I expect a *TV Guide* cover any minute."[††]

Slackers • Screen Gems/Alliance Atlantis/Destination Films/Original Film, 2002
Higher Education Just Hit a New Low

CREDITS: A Neal H. Moritz Production in association with Erik Feig Productions. A Dewey Nicks Film. *Director:* Dewey Nicks; *Producers:* Neal H. Moritz, Erik Feig; *Co-Producer:* Louis G. Friedman; *Executive Producer:* Patrice Theroux; *Co-Executive Producers:* Brad Jenkel, Mark Morgan; *Associate Producers:* Dawn Ebert-Byrnes; Carrie Cook, Shintaro Shimo-

---

*Email to the author, March 28, 2006.

[†]Irish-American actress Ashley F. Brooks was a finalist in the Miss Ohio heats of the Miss America competition and went on to become a model. She dabbled in the occasional movie, beginning with Open Fire *(1988)* and ending, so far, with Ella *(2002).*

[‡]Robert Carradine (born 1954) is from the talented Carradine clan that included dad John (1906–88), brother Keith (born 1949) and half-brother David (born 1936). After a series of small roles, particularly in teen movies such as The Pom Pom Girls *and* Revenge of the Cheerleaders *(both 1976). Robert, made it big as Louis Skolnick, the good-hearted fashion disaster de facto leader of the socially inept band of misfits in the remarkably funny* Revenge of the Nerds *(1984) and its less amusing sequels* Revenge of the Nerds II: Nerds in Paradise *(1987),* Revenge of the Nerds III: The Next Generation *(1992) and* Revenge of the Nerds IV: Nerds in Love *(1994).*

**Phone interview with the author, May 20, 2006.

[††]Liz Smith, New York Post, *September 10, 1999.*

sawa; *Screenplay:* David H. Steinberg; *Music Supervisor:* Amanda Scheer-Demme; *Music:* Joey Altruda, Venus Brown & Printz Board, Justin Stanley; *Photography:* James Bagdonas; *Editor:* Tara Timpone; *Production Designer:* William Arnold; *Set Designer-Art Director:* Sue Chan; *Set Decorators:* John Fraser Brown, Lisa K. Sessions; *Costumes:* Jennifer Levy; *Makeup for Ms. Van Doren:* Rebecca L. Deherrera; DTS/Dolby Digital/SDDS; Technicolor; 86 minutes.

SONGS: "Baba O'Riley" (Peter Townshend) *London Philharmonic Orchestra, Peter Scholes* (*conductor*); "Three Is a Magic Number" (Robert Dorough) *Blind Motion*; "Plucking the Strings" (David Snell); "Rock 'n' Roll (Could Never Hip Hop Like This)" Contains a sample of "On Fire" (Dan Nakamura, Paul Huston, Glenn Bolton, Arnold Hamilton, Martin Nemley, Leona Roman, Shjahid Wright) *Handsome Boy Modeling School*; "Lohengrin" (Richard Wagner); "No Hay Problema" (Jacques Marray) *Pink Martini*; "Holy Calamity" (John Davis, Dan Nakamura, Paul Huston) *Handsome Boy Modeling School*; "Oh Angela" (Jason Schwartzman) *Jason Schwartzman*; "SOS" (Charles Williams); "Pomp and Circumstance (Edward Elgar, John Fox); "The Sign" (Jenny Berggren, Malin Berggren, Jonas Berggren) *Occidental College Glee Club*; "Spongebath" (Justin Stanley) *Justin Stanley*; "Ethan's Song" (Jason Schwartzman) *Jason Schwartzman*

CAST: Devon Sawa (*Dave*); Jason Schwartzman (*Ethan*); James King (*Angela*); Jason Segel (*Sam*); Michael Maronna (*Jeff*); Mamie Van Doren (*Mrs. Van Graaf*); Joe Flaherty (*Mr. Leonard*); Leigh Taylor Young (*Valerie Patton*); Sam Anderson (*Charles Patton*); Laura Prepon (*Reanna*); Travis Davis (*Airborne Express Driver*); Jim Rash (*Head T.A. Philip*); Nat Faxon (*Karl, the Grad Student*); Don Michaelson (*Prof. Markoe*); Retta (*Bruna, the Office Manager*); Marilyn Staley (*Singing Waitress*); Jason Garner (*Singing Waiter*); Gedde Watanabe (*Japanese Proctor*); Heidi Kramer (*Hot Twin #1*); Alissa Kramer (*Hot Twin #2*); Michael [James] McDonald (*Economics Professor*); Charles Dougherty (*Astronomy Professor*); Robert B. Martin Jr. (*The Gimp*); Michael Swiney (*Long-Haired Hobo*); Shelley Dowdy (*Shelley*); Jonathan Kasdan (*Barry*); Japhet (J.P.) Coe (*Philip*); Howard Mungo (*Doctor*); Joanna Sanchez (*Nurse*); Melanie Deanne Moore (*Pissed-Off Co-Ed*); Cameron Diaz (*Movie Star*); Kim Stanwood (*Dave's Mom*); Wesley Mann (*Male Executive*); Mary Faulkner (*Female Executive*); Rick Dubov (*Security Guard*); Margaret Easley (*Receptionist*); Todd Giebenhain (*Stoned Test Taker*); Mickaella L. Agnello, Matthew Cody, Claire Seely Fedorux, Christa Gates, Joseph Guarascio, Paul Lakin, Renee Miller, Christopher Smith, Lisa Spencer, Matt Weitzman, Spencer Wright (*Choir*).

DVD: Columbia TriStar/Screen Gems 08084

PLOT: Dave, Sam and Jeff are scam artists who have lied and cheated their way through college. They expend more time on their scams than if they actually studied. All goes well until Dave humiliates fellow student Ethan at an exam but leaves incriminating evidence. Ethan threatens to expose the trio unless they hook him up with his dream girl, Angela. They set about the seemingly impossible task by massively invading her privacy to find out what makes her tick as their entire future careers depend on Angela falling for the socially inept Ethan. They burgle her dorm room, her parents' home, they steal her notebooks and they copy material on her computer. And, as he gets to know her better, Dave begins to fall in love. The feelings are reciprocated until Angela discovers that Dave has been attempting to set her up with Ethan. Ethan intends to get his revenge by exposing the trio as cheats. However, in an effort to win back Angela, Dave confesses all in front of a lecturer and a class full of students about to take an exam. The lovers are reconciled but Dave, Sam and Jeff are expelled. Not all is lost, though, as they've learned how to forge college diplomas.

NOTES: In her last big screen outing to date, Mamie received probably more review column inches per minute of screen time than for any previous film. Most of the references to her performance have been coarse, ageist or, simply, rude. For Mamie, at 70, plays an aging whore who comes on to "Cool Ethan" (Jason Schwartzman) as he attempts to impress the girl of his dreams, Angela (James King), by volunteering at the hospital. Mamie's Mrs. Van Graaf is an incredible old crone who propositions Ethan by miming her profession of giving blow jobs on the docks and feigning heat stroke so that her breasts need a sponge bath. Ethan is only too willing as Mrs. Van Graaf flashes her septuagenarian knockers in one of the film's funniest scenes.

Scripted by David H. Steinberg,* *Slackers* is not sufficiently gross to rival the best of the genre although it has its fair share of fart jokes, a talking penis covered with a sock, Super Glue as masturbation lube, and tits. But it seems that 70-year-old breasts are beyond the pale. The incredible concentration on Mamie's performance again blurred the distinction between the actress and the character. Some critics even accused Mamie of wearing prosthetic breasts.

"No, they are all mine. Julie Strain's husband[†] told me about the film a friend of his was making and said I should audition as the old whore who works the docks. So I turned up with *Ship Ahoy* written across my breast and when I opened my blouse I got the job straight away.

"I didn't even read the script. When I got to the set, they said I shouldn't even pay attention to it. This is unheard of, you know. I worked during a time when every word had to be 100 percent, everything had to be just the way it was in the book. If you changed one line, you would have had the writer on the set. But it's so different now, compared to when I was working in the movies, because everything is sort of improvised. It was exciting because it kept you on your toes and really made you do the best job you can do.

"Everyone writes about that scene. They say any publicity is good publicity but what they wrote about me is downright nasty. I was playing a role. I don't look like that. I went to Julie and said, 'Give me the ugliest wig you've got.' I look like an old whore. It's makeup. People think it's me but I'm playing a role. It's acting. It took hours in makeup to look like that."[‡]

Directed by fashion photographer Dewey Nicks, the film is a hotbed of attractive juvenile talent of both sexes** and it helped, or perhaps hindered, the careers of Devon Sawa, James (now Jaime) King and Jason Schwartzman, among others.

As her last film to date (as of October 2006), it's fitting that *Slackers* found Mamie causing as much, if not more, consternation in her 70s as she did at the height of her career in the 1950s and 1960s. One glance at the sampling of reviews below will confirm that Mamie is not only the girl who invented rock 'n' roll but she's the dame who put the big mama in mammaries.

REVIEWS: "*Slackers* is a dirty movie. Not a sexy, erotic, steamy or even smutty movie, but a just plain dirty movie. It made me feel unclean ...This film knows no shame ... [C]onsider a scene where Mamie Van Doren, who is 71 years old, plays a hooker in a hospital bed who bares her breasts so that the movie's horny creep can give them a sponge bath. On the day when I saw *Slackers*, there were many things I expected and even wanted to see in a movie, but I confess Mamie Van Doren's breasts were

---

*Steinberg's initial career was in law (he earned his degree from Duke University) but after four years of entertainment law in Atlanta and New York, he abandoned his legal career and subsequently graduated from USC School of Cinema-Television (1998). He and Adam Herz wrote the story for American Pie 2 (2001) before Slackers became Steinberg's first solo screenplay credit. Other screenwriting credits are After School Special (2003) and Puss in Boots (2008).

[†]Kevin Eastman (born 1962), the co-creator, with Peter Laird, of Teenage Mutant Ninja Turtles.

[‡]Phone interview with the author, May 23, 2006.

**Vancouver-born Devon Sawa (born 1978) began his career on Canadian TV before his breakout role as the human form of the ghost in Casper (1995), but a series of blandly juvenile roles followed. His best film to date is Idle Hands (1999). Jason Schwartzman (born 1980) burst onto the screen in Rushmore (1998); Slackers and I ♥ Huckabees are his career highs to date. The son of producer Jack Schwartzman and actress Talia Shire, he formed the band Phantom Planet when he was 14 but left the group in 2003. James (now Jaime King) is one of the world's top fashion models and has been voted one of the world's sexiest women by a number of magazines. She appears in the cult movies Sin City (2005) and Sin City 2 (2009) as well as Cheaper by the Dozen 2 (2005).

not among them." Roger Ebert, rogerebert.com, February 1, 2002

"[In the sponge bath scene,] the 70-year-old former bombshell oohs and ahs in a state of arousal. The scene isn't particularly amusing, but it does remind us why clothes were invented." Mick LaSalle, *San Francisco Chronicle*, February 1, 2002

"No movie with an extended Mamie Van Doren topless scene ... is lacking in nerve to plumb fresh sources for comic shock value. There are laughs here, but easily as many groans...Somehow, a first-time director has pulled some casting strings, starting with that revealing look at Van Doren in a hospital..." Mike Clark, *USA Today*, January 31, 2002

"While *Slackers* does feature a sampling of solid giggles and is a better film than many of the other recent teen flicks, there's simply not enough there to make it worth a trip to the cinema. If you simply must see this year's most shocking scene (in which the 70-year old Mamie Van Doren unleashes her massive old hooters) just wait for the DVD. Something that disturbing should be viewed in the privacy of your own home." Scott Weinberg, apolloguide.com

"Just when you'd expect of a film full of commando-style, test-taking shell games and classroom cons, however, the film falls back on the same old formula of teen sex, outrageous pranks and scenes designed to push the envelope of bad taste for laughs. ... The apex of this brand of humor occurs when guest star Mamie Van Doren flashes her naked torso and coos a come-on to Schwartzman, who calmly obliges her by sponging, fondling and finally kissing her ... sorry, it's not an image I really want to recall. There's no punch line to the gag, just an attempt to shock a laugh out of the audience." Sean Axmaker, *Seattle Post-Intelligencer*, February 1, 2002

"Did I mention that this film shows the fake breasts of a 70-year-old woman? Jason Schwartzman's character gives a sponge bath to a grandmother who has the breasts of a porn star because they're obviously fake — I can only surmise that they were added in preparation for the day when a part would call for a grandmother to demonstrate that the plastic surgery industry has finally gone too far. I would have been more aroused if the doctors had sewn the decapitated heads of two different zoo animals to this woman's chest." Mr. Crankey, mrcrankey.com

"*Slackers* goes for the gutter and misses. Its random rock 'n' roll sex fantasy sequences are lame and obnoxious. A man in Speedos and a young woman with a vibrator are no longer uproariously shocking, they're yawns. A 71-year-old Mamie Van Doren exposing her chest for a sponge bath is morbidly repulsive." Rasheed Newson, *Flak Magazine*

"Nicks peppers his cast with some fun cameos including Gina Gershon, Cameron Diaz, and ... 1950s sex bomb Mamie Van Doren, who in a deeply courageous move — considering the picture's core demographic of teenagers — provides the film's only nudity." Brian Orndorf, Modamag.com

"With cameos from Mamie Van Doren (still baring her breasts at 70, bless her), Cameron Diaz, and Joe Flaherty, *Slackers* has its moments, to be sure, but it's too interested in jerking off in all its Byzantine incarnations to bother pleasuring its audience." Walter Chaw, filmfreakcentral.net

"Uninteresting, annoying characters. Awkward plotting, and the requisite ton of sophomoric, sexual and gross-out humor, including a gratuitous septuagenarian sponge bath." *Videohound*

"Repellent excuse for a comedy, even by 21st-century teen-movie standards. A couple of surprise movie-star cameos add nothing to the mix, though Van Doren's scene is memorable — for all the wrong reasons." *Leonard Maltin's 2005 Movie Guide*

"Nicks may have cracked the 'slackers' genre with a tightly scripted, eccentric and at times insane tale ... It's undoubtedly a lads' film (the implausible romantic stuff feels like an afterthought), though the laughs are almost entirely at their expense. If it's unlikely to stimulate the brain cells, it will almost certainly make you laugh out loud." *Time Out Film Guide*

"Crude, anything goes comedy with some

moments to embarrass the audience, if not the cast; it is best to look away when Mamie Van Doren is on screen." *Halliwell's Film & TV Guide*

"I laughed until I was thoroughly ashamed of myself." Joe Leydon, *San Francisco Examiner*

Television Appearances

This is a partial list of television programs on which Mamie has appeared over the years.

Dramas, Situation Comedies and Soap Operas

The Bob Cummings Show "Bob Creates a New Mamie Van Doren" • NBC, February, 1959; Season 5, Episode 18

CAST, SERIES REGULARS: Bob Cummings (*Bob Collins*); Rosemary DeCamp (*Margaret MacDonald*); Ann B. Davis (*Charmaine "Schultzy" Schultz*); Dwayne Hickman (*Chuck MacDonald*); Lyle Talbot (*Paul Fonda*); Nancy Kulp (*Pamela Livingstone*); Lisa Gaye (*Collette DuBois*); Joi Lansing (*Shirley Swanson*); Tammy Marihugh (*Tammy Johnson*). GUEST STARS: Mamie Van Doren (*Herself*); Rose Marie.

So she won't be bothered while she prepares for a new movie role, Mamie works in disguise in Bob's office.

Award Theater "Girls About Town" • NBC, November 2, 1959

The Comedy Spot "Meet the Girls" • CBS, August 30, 1960; Pilot Episode

CREDITS: *Director:* Charles Barton; *Producer:* Harry Sauber; *Writer:* Roger Clay.

CAST: Virginia Field (*Charlotte "The Brain" Dunning*); Gale Robbins (*Lacey "The Face" Sinclair*); Mamie Van Doren (*Maybelle "The Shape" Perkins*).

The Dick Powell Show "No Strings Attached" • NBC, April 24, 1962; Season 1, Episode 29

CAST: Dick Powell (*Mike Scott*); Don Beddoe (*Judge Bender*); Angie Dickinson (*Judy Maxwell*); Barbara Nichols (*Bunny Easter*); Leo Gorcey (*Billy Vale*); Mamie Van Doren (*Penny Nickels*); Buddy Lewis (*Andy Dugan*); John Litel (*Floyd Maxwell*); George Petrie (*Bunny's Attorney*); Paul Smith (*George*); Robert Strauss (*Danny Cannon*); Amzie Strickland (*Miss Talbot*); Herbie Faye (*Waiter*); Percy Helton (*Janitor*); Martin Walker (*Hood #1*); Sid Curtis (*Hood #2*).

The Real McCoys "The Farmer and Adele" • CBS, 1962

CAST, SERIES REGULARS: Walter Brennan (*Grandpa Amos McCoy*); Richard Crenna (*Luke McCoy*); Kathleen Nolan (*Kate McCoy*); Lydia Reed (*Hassie McCoy*); Tony Martinez (*Pepino Garcia*). GUEST STAR: Mamie Van Doren (*Adele Webster*). Grandpa Amos McCoy plots to get grandson Luke out of a long-term contract with a dance studio run by Adele Webster (Mamie Van Doren).

Valentine's Day "Yen Ku Horowitz" • ABC, November 13, 1964

CREDITS: *Creator-Executive Producer Writer:* Hal Kantor; *Director:* Jerry Hopper.

CAST, SERIES REGULARS: Tony Franciosa (*Valentine Farrow*); Jack Soo (*Rockwell "Rocky" Sin*); Janet Waldo (*Libby Freeman*); Mimi Dillard (*Molly*); Jerry Hausner (*O.D.*

204 Television Appearances

Grandpa Amos McCoy (Walter Brennan) learns a new dance step from instructor Adele Webster (Mamie) in an episode of *The Real McCoys* (CBS, 1962).

Dunstall); Eddie Quillan (*Grover Cleveland Fipple*). GUEST STAR: Mamie Van Doren.

The Adventures of Ozzie and Harriet
"The Housemother" • ABC, December 9, 1964

CAST, SERIES REGULARS: Ozzie Nelson (*Ozzie Nelson*); Harriet Hilliard (*Harriet Nelson*); David Nelson (*David Nelson*); Ricky Nelson (*Ricky Nelson*). GUEST STAR: Mamie Van Doren.

Burke's Law
"Who Killed 711?" • ABC, December 9, 1964; Season 2, Episode 12

CREDITS: *Producer:* Aaron Spelling; *Associate Producer:* Richard Newton; *Script*: Gwen Bagni, Paul Dubov; *Director*: Sidney Lanfield; *Production Supervisor:* Norman S. Powell; *Editorial Supervisor:* Bernard Burton; *Supervising Art Director:* Bill Ross; *Music:* Joseph Mullendore; *Theme:* Herschel Burke Gilbert; *Music Supervision:* Alfred Perry; *Photography:* George E. Diskant; *Production Manager:* Barry Crane; *Assistant Director:* Michael Salamunovich; *Story Editor:* Bud Kay; *Editor:* Desmond Marquette; *Set Decorator:* John Burton; *Sound:* Woodruff H. Clarke; *Music Editor:* Earle Dearth; *Sound Effects:* Norval Crutcher, Jr.; *Casting:* Betty Martin; *Mr. Barry's Wardrobe:* The House of Worsted-Tex; *Makeup:* Carlie Taylor; *Hairstylist:* Scotty Rackin; *Wardrobe:* Robert B. Harris.

Series based on characters created by Frank D. Gilroy.

CAST: Gene Barry (*Capt. Amos Burke*); Gary Conway (*Det. Tim Tilson*); Regis Toomey (*Det. Les Hart*); Leon Lontoc (*Henry*). GUEST STARS *(in alphabetical order):* Hans Conried (*Van Heller*); Broderick Crawford (*Tristram Corporal*); Dan Duryea (*Sam Atherton*); Rhonda Fleming (*Clarissa Benton*); Burgess Meredith (*Harold Harold*); Mamie Van Doren (*Aurora Knight*); Also: Lisa Seagram (*Ventura Jones*); Susanne Kramer (*Cindy*); Lou Krugman (*Man*); Allyson Ames (*Gal*); Marianna Case (*Glamorous Dame*); Buddy Lewis (*Cab Driver*); Eileen O'Neill (*Sergeant Ames*).

Mamie is one of the suspects when embezzler Buddy Jack Cook is killed in the elevator of a hotel.

General Hospital ABC, 1965

Mister Roberts
"In Love and War" • NBC, April 1, 1966

CAST, SERIES REGULARS: Roger Smith (*Lt. Douglas Roberts*); Steve Harmon (*Ensign Frank Pulver*); George Ives (*Doc*); Ray Reese (*Seaman Reber*); Richard Sinatra (*Seaman D'Angelo*); Richard X. Slattery (*Capt. John Morton*); Ronald Starr (*Seaman Mannion*); Robert Ivers (*Bob*). GUEST STAR: Mamie Van Doren (*Alice Blue*).

Vega$
"Serve, Volley and Kill" • December 20, 1978; Season 1, Episode 11

CAST, SERIES REGULARS: Robert Urich (*Dan Tanna*); Phyllis Davis (*Beatrice Travis*); Bart Braverman (*Bobby "Binzer" Borso*); Judy Landers (*Angie Turner*). GUEST STARS *(in alphabetical order):* Phil Abbott (*Harry Snyder*); Dave Burton; Red Buttons (*Tommy Cirko*); Nathaniel Christian; Lynda Day George (*Sandra Wells*); Don DeFore (*Sid Green*); Pamelyn Ferdin (*Katie Howard*); Christopher George (*Nicky Trent*); Randolph Mantooth (*Bobby Howard*); Gail Martin; Al Scaglione; Naomi Stevens (*Sgt. Bella Archer*); Mamie Van Doren (*Spa Manager*); Dawn Wells (*Millie Farmer*).

Fantasy Island
"Stripper/Boxer" • ABC, February 10, 1979; Season 2, Episode 17

CREDITS: *Director:* Lawrence Dobkin.

CAST, SERIES REGULARS: Ricardo Montalban (*Mr. Roarke*); Hervé Villechaize (*Tattoo*); Kimberly Beck (*Cindy*); GUEST STARS *(in alphabetical order):* William Beckley (*Barnaby Jeffers*); Michael Callan (*Russ McCoy*); Stacy Keach Sr. (*M.V. Banning*); John Lawrence (*Ernie Peevey*); Chuck McCann (*Whoopee Hoover*); Maureen McCormick (*Jennie Collins*); Ben Murphy (*Billy Blake*); Beverly Powers (*Betty*); Laraine Stephens (*Maureen Banning*); Forrest Tucker (*Jake Gordon*); Mamie Van Doren (*Sheba*).

Crime Story
"Flashbacks of the Good and Bad Times with Luca" • NBC, March 1, 1988

L.A. Law
"Rhyme and Punishment" • NBC, December 16, 1993; Season 8, Episode 9

Mister Roberts (Roger Smith) and Alice Blue (Mamie) in an episode of *Mister Roberts* (NBC, 1966).

CREDITS: *Director:* Gary Weis; *Written by* Julie Martin.

CAST, SERIES REGULARS: Richard Dysart (*Leland McKenzie*); Alan Rachins (*Douglas Brackman, Jr.*); Jill Eikenberry (*Ann Kelsey*); Corbin Bernsen (*Arnie Becker*); Michael Tucker (*Stuart Markowitz*); Larry Drake (*Benny Stulwicz*); Blair Underwood (*Jonathan Rollins*); John Spencer (*Tommy Mullaney*); A Martinez (*Daniel Morales*); Alan Rosenberg (*Eli Levinson*); Debi Mazar (*Denise Ianello*); Alexandra Powers (*Jane Halliday*); Lisa Zane (*Melinda Paros*); Sheila Kelley (*Gwen Taylor*). GUEST STARS *(in alphabetical order):* Teri Austin (*Morgan Farrell*); Norm Crosby (*Jack Tavelman*); Dann Florek (*David Meyer*); Marvin Katzoff (*Cowboy Joe*); Phil Lenkowsky (*Ira Mytelka*); William H. Macy (*Bernard Ruskin*); Hugh Maguire (*Lanny*); Frank Medrano (*Bobby Del Giotto*); Keith Mills (*Judge Walter Green*); Cristine Rose (*Attorney*); Susan Ruttan (*Roxanne Melman*); Raymond Singer (*Nat Pincus' Son*); Jerry Stiller (*Nat Pincus*); Mamie Van Doren (*Herself*).

Mamie is a guest at the firm's Christmas party.

Variety Shows

The Ray Anthony Show • ABC, 1956-1957

The Red Skelton Show • CBS, 1960

The Jack Benny Program "Death Row Sketch" • February 12, 1961; Season 11, Episode 17

CAST, SERIES REGULARS: Jack Benny (*Jack Benny*); Eddie "Rochester" Anderson (*Rochester Van Jones*); Don Wilson (*Don Wilson*); Dennis Day (*Dennis Day*). GUEST STARS: Gerald Mohr (*Harry*); Frank Nelson (*Warden*); Mamie Van Doren (*Herself*); Alan Dexter; Jeanette Eymann; Howard McNear; Ned Miller.

Documentaries

A Star Is Born *World Premiere* • NBC, September 29, 1954; 30 minutes.

CAST: Jack Carson, George Jessel, George Fisher, Larry Finley (*Hosts*); Desi Arnaz; Edward Arnold; Lauren Bacall; Lucille Ball; Suzan Ball; William Bendix; Ray Bolger; Joan Crawford; Tony Curtis; Doris Day; James Dean; Andy Devine; Clark Gable; Judy Garland; Greer Garson; Gloria Grahame; Jon Hall; Sonja Henie; Jean Hersholt; Hedda Hopper; Katy Jurado; Alan Ladd; Dorothy Lamour; Peggy Lee; Janet Leigh; Liberace; Richard Long; Sid Luft; Gordon MacRae; Sheila MacRae; Dean Martin; Virginia Mayo; Jimmy McHugh; Dennis Morgan; Louella Parsons; Debbie Reynolds; Edward G. Robinson; Cesar Romero; Ann Sheridan; Elizabeth Taylor; Claire Trevor; Sophie Tucker; Mamie Van Doren; Vera-Ellen; Jack L. Warner; Marie Wilson (*Themselves*).

Included on the DVD release of *A Star is Born* (1954), this is a live television broadcast of the world premiere. It was described by various participants as the biggest world premiere in memory, even bigger than the Academy Awards.

DVD: Warners Home Video

Hollywood Uncensored • Caidin Film Company, Castle Hill Productions Inc., 1987

CREDITS: *Director:* James Forsher; *Cinematography:* Paul Savage; *Editors:* Bill Botts, Tom Klemesrud; *Art Director:* Alan Jones; *Makeup:* Roberta Reitman, Palah Sandling; *Production Manager:* Charles "Skip" Newman; *Director (New York):* Anthony Potenza; *Sound:* David Sperling; *Second Sound:* Anne Rogers; *Researchers:* Leith Adams, Ladonna Conard, Mayra Linares, Felix Racelis, Michael Peter Yakaitis; B&W/Color; 75 minutes.

CAST: Douglas Fairbanks Jr. (*Host*); Peter Fonda: (*Host*); Carroll Baker; Ira Barmak; Charles Champlin; Don Murray; Sheree North; Hal Roach; Jane Russell; Martin Scorsese; Mamie Van Doren; Robert Vogel; Eli Wallach (*Interviewees*).

VIDEO: Lionsgate

Unseen Hollywood • Henninger Media Development, James Forsher Productions, 1998

CREDITS: *Writer-Director:* James Forsher; *Production Assistant:* Steve Hadden.

CAST: Sandra Dee (*Host*); Robert Duvall; John Saxon; Mamie Van Doren (*Interviewees*).

Hollywood Rocks and Rolls • Passport International Productions, 1998

CREDITS: *Director-Editor:* Kent Hagen; *Executive Producer:* Dante Pugliese; *Producers:* Steve Edwards, John L. Beale Jr.; *Written by* Troy Szebin; *Production Controller:* Jeanette Pugliese; *Musical Director:* Pat Britt; *Researcher:* Robert Weaver, B&W/Color; 44 minutes.

CAST: Michael Ochs; Mamie Van Doren; Tommy Sands; Jerry Lee Lewis; Dick Clark (*Interviewees*).

ARCHIVE FOOTAGE: Bill Haley & His Comets; Alan Freed; Chuck Berry; The Platters; Little Richard; Tuesday Weld; Frankie Lyman; Big Joe Turner; Elvis Presley; Jerry Lee Lewis; Fats Domino; Pat Boone; Ricky Nelson; Buddy Holly.

DVD: Passport Video DVD-9005. Extras

Mamie spins some platters on a portable record player in a publicity shot from the 1950s.

include an extended interview with Mamie and archive footage, including a brief glimpse of the missing scene with Clark Gable from *Teacher's Pet*.

Biography   "Jayne Mansfield" • A&E, 2001
CREDITS: *Writer:* Ed Singer; *Executive Producer:* Kevin Burns; *Co-executive Producer:* Kim Sheerin.
CAST: Army Archerd; Mickey Hargitay; Hugh Hefner; Jayne Mansfield; Mamie Van Doren (*Interviewees*).

Screen Tests of the Stars • Carlton Television, 2002
CREDITS: *Director:* Geraldine Dowd; *Producers:* Simon Harries, Mark Tinkler; *Executive Producer:* Nick Bullen; *Editor:* Mark Towns.

CAST: Paul O'Grady (*Host*); Jason Connery; Roger Corman; Daryl Hannah; Melissa Joan Hart; Tippi Hedren; Christine Keeler; Claire King: Martin Landau; John Landis; Stefanie Powers; Jane Russell; Emma Samms; William Shatner; Jennifer Tilly; Mamie Van Doren; Jon Voight; Robert Wagner; Denise Welch: Edward Woodward; Michael York (*Interviewees*).

Movie and television stars explain how they got their big breaks, and talk us through their screen tests. This show is a combination of TV studio interviews conducted by host Paul O'Grady, and pre-filmed interviews on location in London and Hollywood.

Cleavage • World of Wonder, 2002
CREDITS: *Writer-Producer:* David Story; *Co-producer:* Lisa Fancher; *Executive Produc-*

ers: Fenton Bailey, Randy Barbato; *Executive Producer (A&E):* Tamara Hacker; *Executive Producer (UK):* Jacquie Lawrence; *Associate Producer:* Tracy Hood; *Music:* Jeff Cardoni; *Editors:* A.J. Dickerson, Rob Lundy; B&W/Color; 100 minutes.

CAST: Carmen Electra (*Narrator*); Tyra Banks; Jeni Bartiromo; Dennis Bartok; Gillian Bentley; Miriam Bolber; Anna-Lise Breuning; Helen Gurley Brown; Deenie Castleberry; Keli Clark; Coop; Caroline Cox; Kelli Delaney; Norine Flores; Amanda Frank; Merle Ginsberg; Angela Harris; Greg Hildebrandt; Wendy Johnson; Doug Kappy; Bonnie-Jill Laflin; Crickett Lancaster; Natasha Lyonne; Louis Meisel; Monica Mitro; Samantha Monaco; Willy Mrasek; Lillian Müller; Colette Nelson; Dawn Nikithser; Chris Pellegrino; Alina Peralta; Sara Peters; Alina Ratta; Nicole Raught; Joan Rivers; Nina Rolle; Tony Romando; Frank Ryan, M.D.; Tura Satana; Maura Spiegel; Valerie Steele; Laurie Straub; Kate Valentine; Mamie Van Doren; Stacy Walker; Amy Wallace; The World Famous *BoB*; Jennifer Zmurk (*Interviewees*).

DVD/VIDEO: Available through A&E.

Celebrity Naked Ambition • Somethin' Else, 2003

CREDITS: *Producer-Director:* Bruce Hepton; *Writers:* Chuck Cartmel, Harry Harrold, Bruce Hepton; *Assistant Producer:* Harry Harrold; *Photography:* Ben Frewin; *Editor:* Chuck Cartmel; 105 minutes.

CAST: Nick Frost (*Presenter*); David Aaronovitch; John Beyer; Andrew Collins; Mike Fenton; Michael Forest; Jeanine Gearity; Haji; Hugh Hefner; Oliver James; Zalman King; Kitten; Randal Kleiser; Karen Krizanovich; Kathy Lloyd; Bibi Lynch; Scott Manson; Shelly [Shelley] Michelle; Paul Morley; Ken Russell; Brian Sewell; Eva Simpson; Jim Skin [Mr. Skin]; Pam St. Clement; Paul Verhoeven; Mike Walker; John Wilson (*Interviewees*)

ARCHIVE FOOTAGE: Keith Allen; Pamela Anderson; Julie Andrews; Tom Baker; Anne Bancroft; Brigitte Bardot; Kim Basinger; Alan Bates; Kathy Bates: Sean Bean; Lynda Bellingham; Elizabeth Berkley; Halle Berry; Helena Bonham Carter; Phoebe Cates; Kim Cattrall; Russell Crowe; Catherine Deneuve; Bo Derek; Farrah Fawcett; Tara Fitzgerald; Kerry Fox; Richard Gere; David Hasselhoff; Elizabeth Hurley; Angelina Jolie; Patsy Kensit; Nicole Kidman; Sylvia Kristel; Hedy Lamarr; Jennifer Jason Leigh; Lucy Liu; Ruth Madoc; Madonna; Jayne Mansfield; Helen Mirren; Demi Moore; Emily Mortimer; Oliver Reed; Denise Richards; Joely Richardson; Mickey Rourke; Mark Rylance; Anna Nicole Smith; Sylvester Stallone; Pam St. Clement; Sharon Stone; Mamie Van Doren; Barbara Windsor; Kate Winslet; Catherine Zeta-Jones.

TALK SHOW AND GAME SHOW GUEST APPEARANCES

The Colgate Variety Hour • NBC, April 17, 1955; Season 5, Episode 24

CAST: Gordon MacRae (*Host*); Guest Stars: Edgar Bergen and Charlie McCarthy; Sue Carson; The Treniers [Claude Trenier, Cliff Trenier, Milt Trenier, Gene Gilbeaux, Don Hill]; Ronny Graham; Leigh Snowden

PROMOTIONAL FOOTAGE: Piper Laurie, Mamie Van Doren, Dani Crayne (scene from *Ain't Misbehavin'*).

What's My Line? • CBS, March 24, 1957

Mamie appeared as the mystery guest.

The Steve Allen Show • NBC, 1956

The Steve Allen Show • NBC, 1957

The Steve Allen Show • NBC, 1958

Here's Hollywood • NBC, 1960

Talent Scouts • CBS, 1962

Guest Shot • Rick Spalla Productions, 1962

Stump the Stars "Clint Walker vs. Mamie Van Doren" • July 1, 1963

CREDITS: Host: Mike Stokey; Regular Panelists: Sebastian Cabot; Hans Conried; Beverly Garland; Stubby Kaye; Gisele MacKenzie; Ross Martin.

The Tonight Show Starring Johnny Carson • NBC, 1964

The Hollywood Squares • NBC, January 3, 1967
OTHER GUESTS: Mickey [Michael] Callan; Barbara Feldon; Noel Harrison.

The Tonight Shows Starring Johnny Carson • NBC, 1968

The Merv Griffin Show • Syndicated, 1968

The Merv Griffin Show • Syndicated, 1969

The Merv Griffin Show • CBS, 1969

The Merv Griffin Show • CBS, August 3, 1970
OTHER GUESTS: Jimmy Martinez; Jacqueline Susann.

The Tonight Show Starring Johnny Carson • NBC, September 2, 1971
OTHER GUESTS: Stanley Myron Handelman; Corbett Monica; Karen Morrow; Dennis Weaver.

The Tonight Show Starring Johnny Carson • NBC, March 5, 1973
OTHER GUESTS: Ace Trucking Company; Linda Hopkins; Jack Lemmon.

The Hollywood Kids • Cable, 1986

Photoplay • Channel 2, 1986

Sonya • CNN, October 5, 1987

The Oprah Winfrey Show • November 28, 1987

Night Watch • 1987

The Late Show with Arsenio Hall • 1987

E.T. • September, 1998
Leonard Maltin interviews Mamie about her web site.

E! • August, 2002
Mamie is interviewed about Doris Day.

Larry King Live • December 12, 2002
OTHER GUESTS: James Bacon; Steve Crist; Arlene Dahl; James Dougherty; Jane Russell.

Hollywood Confidential • BBC 4, 2003
Documentary written and directed by Angus Cameron for BBC Scotland about the rise and fall of the Hollywood scandal magazine, *Confidential*. Interviewee Mamie later boasted on her website "I gave them the lowdown on the evils of *Hollywood Confidential*, the grandmother of all gossip sheets!"

Recordings

SINGLES/EPs

"Salamander"/"Go Go Calypso" (Les Baxter) Capitol CAP 45-16701 F80446/Prep 100 (1957)

Untamed Youth: "Rollin' Stone"/"Salamander"/"Oobala Baby"/"Go, Go Calypso" Prep M 1-1 (1957)

"Something to Dream About"/"I Fell in Love" Capitol CAP 45-17774 (1957) Released a year later as a 45rpm in the UK with picture sleeve.

"Nobody But You"/"A Lifetime of You" Dot 15883 (1959)

"Beat Generation"/"I'm Grateful" Dot 15970 (1959)

"Bikini with No Top on the Top"/"So What Else Is New" [with June Wilkinson] Jubilee 5483 (1964).

"Mamie's a singer and I'm really not a singer," says Wilkinson. "So what Billy Strange did was, he had Mamie do hers and then he had me come in by myself and he made me do it over and over till I got it right and then put the two together. Mamie's certainly a much better singer than I am and Billy, knowing that I would be a little inhibited about singing, had it all recorded first and had me come in after it was recorded."*

"The Boy Catcher's Theme" (Gladys Shelley)/"Cabaret" (John Kander, Fred Ebb) Audio Fidelity AF 133 (1966)

"State of Turmoil" (Vocal 5'19")/"State of Turmoil" (vocal 3'50")/"State of Turmoil" (instrumental) (R.D. Simpson) Corner Stone Records CS/12-3003 8 (1984)

"Young Dudes" (extended dance mix)/"Young Dudes" (single version)/"Queen of Pleasure" Rhino RNPD 70513 (1986)

SOUNDTRACKS

Le Bellissime Gambe de Sabrina (Motion Picture Soundtrack) RCA Italiana 0736

The Candidate (Motion Picture Soundtrack) Jubilee 5029 (1964)

ALBUMS

Mamie (As in Mamie Van Doren) • Churchill Records 67232
1. "You and Me and Tonight"
2. "Rub It In"
3. "Guantanamera"
4. "You Talk Too Much"
5. "Ragtime Cowboy Joe"
6. "Lifetime Lover"
7. "When You're Smilin'"
8. "Alice Blue Gown"
9. "Never On Sunday"
10. "I Wanna Be Loved"

*June Wilkinson, phone interview with the author, August 3, 2006.

Mamie Van Doren: The Girl Who Invented Rock 'n' Roll • Rhino Records RNLP 70819 (1986)
1. "The Girl Who Invented Rock 'n' Roll" [sic]
2. "Something to Dream About"
3. "Salamander"
4. "Go Go Calypso"
5. "Rollin' Stone"
6. "Oobala Baby"
7. "Separate the Men from the Boys"
8. "I Fell in Love"
9. "The Beat Generation"
10. "I'm Grateful"
11. "Nobody but You"
12. "Lifetime of Love"

Mamie Van Doren: The Girl Who Invented Rock 'n' Roll • Marginal Records CD MAR 062 (1997)
1. "Nobody But You (Clark)"
2. "Rolling Stone (Baxter-Adelson)"
3. "Do Ba La Baby" (Baxter-Adelson-Cochran)
4. "The Beat Generation" (Kent-Walton)
5. "I'm Grateful" (Rogers-Corpora)
6. "Lifetime of Love" (Kent)
7. "Separate the Men from the Boys" (Robin)
8. "I Fell in Love" (Davis)
9. "The Girl Who Invented Rock 'n' Roll" [sic] (Smith)
10. "Something to Dream About" (Singleton-Coreman)
11. "Salamander" (Baxter)
12. "Go-Go Calypso" (Baxter)
13. "Cabaret" (Kander-Ebb)
14. "The Boy Catcher's Theme" (Shelley)
15. "The Bikini with No Top on the Top" (Robin) with June Wilkinson
16. "So What Else Is New" (Robin)

Note: While this CD shares the same title, cover art, album notes and most of the songs with the Rhino Records release of 1986, the tracks have been re-ordered and four new numbers have been added: "Cabaret," "The Boy Catcher's Theme," "The Bikini with No Top on the Top," and "So What Else Is New." "Rollin' Stone" is listed as "Rolling Stone" and "Oobala Baby" (often listed as "Oo-Ba-La Baby") is misspelled as "Do Ba La Baby."

Compilation Albums

Va-Va-Voom • Rhino Records RNTA 1985 (Re-released as a CD in 1999)
1. "That Makes It" (Jayne Mansfield)
2. "So Little Time" (Diana Dors)
3. **"Something to Dream About" (Mamie Van Doren)**
4. "You'd Be Surprised" (Marilyn Monroe)
5. "Baby Won't You Please Come Home" (Ann-Margret)
6. "Come By Sunday" (Diana Dors)
7. "Let Me Entertain You" (Ann-Margret)
8. "Love on the Rocks" (Jane Russell)
9. "Lazy" (Marilyn Monroe)
10. "I Surrender Dear" (Elke Sommer)
11. "When I Fall in Love" (Rhonda Fleming)
12. "River of No Return" (Marilyn Monroe)
13. "Crazy He Calls Me" (Diana Dors)
14. "When a Woman Loves a Man" (Jane Russell)
15. "Don't Take Your Love from Me" (Rhonda Fleming)
16. "She Acts Like a Woman Should" (Marilyn Monroe)
17. "You Know You Don't Want Me" (Elke Sommer)
18. "Almost in Your Arms" (Sophia Loren)
19. "Bing Bang Bong" (Sophia Loren)
20. "It's Too Late" (Diana Dors)
21. "I Just Don't Understand" (Ann-Margret)
22. "Little Things Mean a Lot" (Jayne Mansfield)
23. "Heat Wave" (Marilyn Monroe)
24. **"Separate the Men from the Boys" (Mamie Van Doren)**

Beat, Beat, Beat! Beatnik Rock 'n' Roll • Bongo 001 1988 (Re-released as a CD in 1993 Phantom Sound B00000E11J)
1. "Herman Munster Reads"
2. "Beat Generation" (Paul Evans)
3. "Like, I Love You" (Edd Byrnes)

4. "Beatnik" (The Royal Jokers)
5. "Benny the Beatnik" (The Untouchables)
6. "Beatnik Bounce" (The Beats)
7. "Beatnik Daddy" (Barbara Evans)
8. "Laffin Beatnik" (Johnny Beeman)
9. "Mama's Place" (Bing Day)
10. "Beatnik" (The Champs)
11. "Guy Lombardo's Back in Town" (The Hermit)
12. "Beatnik Baby" (The Bee Hives)
13. "Beat-Nik" (J.M. Van Eaton)
14. "Doin' the Beatnik Twist" (Huey Smith)
15. "Beatnik Bounce" (Paul Gayten)
16. "Teenage Beatnik" (Louis Nye)
17. "Beatnik Walk" (Rune Overman)
18. "Beatnik Bill" (Richard Pine)
19. **"The Beat Generation" (Mamie Van Doren)**
20. "Endsville" (The Wild Man of Wildsville)

Rockin' Boppin' Girls • Titanic TR-CD 5000 (1994)
1. "Under the Stars" (Carole King)
2. "Seven Minutes in Heaven" (Poni-Tails)
3. **"Nobody But You" (Mamie Van Doren)**
4. **"Rollin' Stone" (Mamie Van Doren)**
5. "Strolypso Dance" (Jackie Dee)
6. "I Really, Really Love You" (Jo-Anne Campbell)
7. "You-oo" (Jo-Anne Campbell)
8. "I Ain't Got No Steady Date" (Jo-Anne Campbell)
9. "Tell It Like It Is" (Jean Chapel)
10. "Chico's Girl" (Susan Barrett)
11. "24 Hours of Loneliness" (Bonnie Lou)
12. "No" (Dodie Stevens)
13. "Souvenirs" (Barbara Evans)
14. "The Tingle" (Jackie Weaver)
15. "Tintarella Di Luna" (Dorothy Collins)
16. "Nine Girls Out of Ten Girls" (Georgia Gibbs)
17. "Laughing at Me" (Lynn Conner)
18. "Don't Let Your Eyes Get Bigger Than Your Heart" (Sylvia Robbins)
19. "Silly Boy" (Lucy Campo)
20. "He Sends Me Presents" (Lucy Campo)
21. "The Pretty One" (Willis Sisters)
22. "Like the Honey for the Bee" (Barbara Russell)
23. "Kilindini Docks" (Peggy March)
24. "You Can Never Get Away from Me" (Georgia Gibbs)
25. "Mr. Principal" (Ruth Batchelor)
26. "Don't Remind Me of Tommy" (Barbara Jean)
27. "Don't Let the Hurt Show Through" (Karen Kelly)
28. "The Roll" (Evie Sands)
29. "Tabasco" (Amru San)
30. "Poor Little Boy" (Debby Worth)

Hollywood Hi-Fi • Brunswick Records B000004BNC (1996)
1. "Turn Me Loose on Broadway" (Bette Davis)
2. "What's This Generation Coming To" (Robert Mitchum)
3. "The Lurch" (Ted Cassidy)
4. "I'm Ready to Groove" (Raquel Welch)
5. "Got to Get You Into My Life" (Joe Pesci)
6. "That Makes It" (Jayne Mansfield)
7. "Ooh! Ooh!" (Joe E. Ross)
8. "Roaches" (Jack Larson)
9. "The Ask Not Waltz" (JFK)
10. "Wind Up Toy" (Jerry Mathers)
11. "59th Street Bridge Song" (Danny Bonaduce)
12. "Love Me Do" (Brady Bunch)
13. "John You Went Too Far This Time" (Sissy Spacek)
14. **"Bikini with No Top on Top" (Mamie Van Doren & June Wilkinson)**
15. "How's Your Sister" (Steve Allen)
16. "Chicken Mash" (Dennis Weaver)
17. "Your Cheating Heart" (Joey Bishop)
18. "What Is Love?" (Anthony Quinn)

Divas Exotica • Capitol B00000HY5W (1999)
1. "Let Me Entertain You" (Ann-Margret)
2. "Don't Touch My Tomatoes" (Josephine Baker-Jo Bouillon)
3. "Near You" (Marlene Dietrich)
4. "Teach Me Tiger" (April Stevens)
5. "Je Me Donne a Qui Me Plait" (Brigitte Bardot)
6. "Do Your Duty" (Billie Holiday)
7. "Since Me Man Has Done Gone and Went" (Maya Angelou)

8. **"Go, Go, Calypso" (Mamie Van Doren)**
9. "Let's Misbehave" (Eartha Kitt)
10. "That Makes It" (Jayne Mansfield)
11. "Jezebel" (Edith Piaf)
12. "Forbidden Fruit" (Nina Simone)
13. "Heatwave" (Marilyn Monroe)
14. "Goldfinger" (Shirley Basset)
15. "Mam Eu Quero" (I Want My Mama) (Carmen Miranda)
16. "La Molina" (Yma Sumac)
17. "Zoo Be Zoo Be Zoo" (Sophia Loren)
18. "Feeling Good" (Nina Simone)

Bibliography

Abbott, Karen. "Bombshells Away." salon.com, July 19, 2000.

Agan, Patrick. *Is That Who I Think It Is? Vol 1.* New York: Ace Books, 1975.

Baumann, Marty. *The Astounding B Monster.* New York: Dinoship, 2004.

Baxter, John. *Hollywood in the Sixties.* London: The Tantivy Press; New York: A.S. Barnes, 1972.

Betrock, Alan (compiled by). *Battle of the Blondes: Jayne Mansfield vs. Mamie Van Doren.* New York: Shake Books, 1993.

Betrock, Alan. *The I Was a Teenage Juvenile Delinquent Rock'n'Roll Horror Beach Party Movie Book.* New York: St. Martin's Press, 1986.

Billman, Larry. *Film Choreographers and Dance Directors.* Jefferson, NC: McFarland, 1997.

Blottner, Gene. *Universal-International Westerns, 1947–1963: The Complete Filmography.* Jefferson, NC: McFarland, 2000.

Brady, Barry. *Reelin' and Rockin': The Golden Age of Rock 'n' Roll Movies.* Australia: The Printing Place, 1982.

Brode, Douglas. *The Films of the Fifties.* Secaucus, NJ: Citadel Press, 1976.

Cocchi, John. *Second Feature: The Best of the "B" Film.* New York: Citadel Press, 1991.

Cochran, Bobby, with Susan Van Hecke. *Three Steps to Heaven: The Eddie Cochran Story.* Milwaukee, WI: Hal Leonard, 2003.

Cohn, Nik. *Awopbopaloobop Alopbamboom: Pop from the Beginning.* London: Paladin, 1973.

Doherty, Thomas. *Teenagers and Teenpics: The Juvenilization of American Movies in the 1950s.* Philadelphia: Temple University Press, 2002.

Dowdy, Andrew. *"Movies Are Better Than Ever": Wide-Screen Memories of the Fifties.* New York: William Morrow, 1973.

Essoe, Gabe. *The Films of Clark Gable.* Secaucus, N.J.: Citadel Press, 1970.

Fisher, Eddie, with David Fisher. *Been There, Done That.* New York: St. Martin's Press, 1999.

Ford, Ron. "Life Beyond the Camera. Jack Arnold. The Man Behind the Legend: A Conversation with Betty Arnold." *Filmfax* #37, February-March 1993.

Freedman, Evelyn. "Conversation with Mamie Van Doren." *Stallion*, n.d.

Hardy, Phil, ed. *The Gangster Film: The Overlook Film Encyclopedia.* Woodstock, NY: The Overlook Press, 1998.

_____, ed. *The Western: The Arum Film Encyclopedia.* London: Arum Press, 1991.

Haskell, Molly. *From Reverence to Rape: The Treatment of Women in the Movies.* New York-Chicago-San Francisco: Holt, Rinehart and Winston, 1974.

Hefner, Hugh, ed. "Mamie Van Doren Unadorned." *Playboy*, February, 1964.

_____, ed. "The Nudest Mamie Van Doren." *Playboy*, June 1964.

Henderson, Jan Alan. "William Campbell. You Know the Face, Now Meet the Man." *Filmfax* #74, August-September 1999.

Higham, Charles. *Howard Hughes — The Secret Life.* London: Sidgwick & Jackson, 1993.

Hirschhorn, Clive. *The Universal Story.* London: Octopus, 1983.

_____. *The Warner Bros. Story.* London: Octopus, 1979.

Hoekstra, Dave. "Film Fans to Honor Sexpot Mamie." *Chicago Sun-Times*, November 13, 1987.

Hogan, David J. "Sex and Thugs and Rock and Roll...Turgid Teens." *Filmfax* #23, November 1990.

Kashner, Sam, and Jennifer MacNair. *The Bad and the Beautiful: Hollywood in the Fifties.* New York-London: W.W. Norton, 2002.

Keeyes, Jon, ed. *Attack of the B Queens.* Baltimore, MD: Luminary Press, 2003.

Kimball, George Robert. "The Rise of the Bosom." *The Movie, The Illustrated History of the Movies* #55, 1981.

Krafsur, Richard P. *The American Film Institute Catalogue of Motion Pictures: Feature Films 1961–1970.* New York-London: R.R. Bowker, 1976.

Kutner, C. Jerry. "Albert Zugsmith's Opium Dreams." *Bright Lights* #20, November, 1997.

Lacy, Madison S., and Don Morgan. *Leg Art: Sixty Years of Hollywood Cheesecake.* Secaucus, NJ: Citadel Press, 1981.

Larsen, Peter. "Mamie Mia!" *The Orange County Register*, April 19, 2006.

Luijters, Guus, and Gerard Timmer. *Sex Bomb: The Life and Death of Jayne Mansfield*. Secaucus, NJ: Citadel Press, 1988.

Maltin, Leonard, ed. *Leonard Maltin's Movie Encyclopedia*. New York: Dutton, 1994.

Mann, May. *Jayne Mansfield*. London: Abelard-Schuman, 1973.

McCarthy, Todd, and Charles Flynn, eds. *Kings of the Bs*. New York: E.P. Dutton, 1975.

McGee, Mark Thomas, and R.J. Robertson. *The J.D. Films: Juvenile Delinquency in the Movies*. Jefferson, NC: McFarland, 1982.

Medved, Harry, and Michael Medved. *The Golden Turkey Awards*. New York: Perigee Books, 1980.

Medved, Harry, and Michael Medved. *Son of Golden Turkey Awards*. Sydney and London: Angus & Robertson Publishers, 1986.

Meeker, David. *Jazz in the Movies: A Guide to Jazz Musicians 1917–1977*. London: Talisman Books, 1977.

Mitchell, Charles P. *The Devil on Screen: Feature Films Worldwide, 1913 through 2000*. Jefferson, NC: McFarland, 2002.

Moline, Karen. "Put the Blame on Mamie." *Interview*. 1987, Vol. 17, No. 10.

Nash, Jay Robert, and Stanley Ralph Ross. *The Motion Picture Guide*. Chicago IL: Cinebooks, 1985.

Ness, Richard R. *From Headline Hunter to Superman: A Journalism Filmography*. Lanham, MD: The Scarecrow Press, 1997.

Parish, James Robert. *Actors' Television Credits 1950–1972*. Metuchen, NJ: Scarecrow Press, 1973.

_____, with Mark Trost. *Actors' Television Credits Supplement I*. Metuchen, NJ: Scarecrow Press, 1978.

_____, and Michael R. Pitts. *The Great Science Fiction Pictures II*. Metuchen, NJ: Scarecrow Press, 1990.

_____. *Pirates and Seafaring Swashbucklers on the Hollywood Screen*. Jefferson, NC: McFarland, 1995.

_____. *Prison Pictures from Hollywood*. Jefferson, NC: McFarland, 1991.

_____. *Prostitution in Hollywood Films*. Jefferson, NC: McFarland, 1992.

Parr, Jorie. "Mad About Mamie." *Desert Magazine*, January 2006.

Pascall, Jeremy, and Clyde Jeavons. *A Pictorial History of Sex in the Movies*. London: Hamlyn, 1975.

Peary, Danny. *Cult Movies 2*. New York: Dell, 1983.

Rosen, Marjorie. *Popcorn Venus: Women, Movies & the American Dream*. New York: Coward, McCann & Geoghegan, 1973.

Ross, Jonathan. *The Incredibly Strange Film Book: An Alternative History of Cinema*. London: Simon & Schuster, 1992.

Rothel, David. *The Great Show Business Animals*. San Diego-New York: A.S. Barnes, 1980.

Salemi, Dom. "The Amazing Life and Times of Mamie Van Doren: 'Teen Queen of the 1950s.'" *Filmfax* #23, November, 1990.

Sargeant, Jack, ed. *Naked Lens: Beat Cinema*. Creation Books, 2001.

Saxton, Martha. *Jayne Mansfield and the American Fifties*. Boston, MA: Houghton Mifflin, 1975.

Scapperotti, Dan. "Mamie Van Doren, '50s Blonde Bombshell." *Femme Fatales*. February, 1997, Vol. 5, No. 8.

_____. "Mamie Van Doren on the Web." *Femme Fatales*. August, 1999, Vol. 8, No. 3.

Schreiner, Gregory. "Marilyn Remembered." *Hollywood Studio Magazine*, May, 1987.

Scott, Willard, and friends. *The Older the Fiddle, the Better the Tune: The Joys of Reaching a Certain Age*. New York: Hyperion, 2003.

Shaheen, Jack G. *Reel Bad Arabs: How Hollywood Vilifies a People*. New York-Northampton: Olive Branch Press, 2001.

Shapiro, Marc. "Mamie Van Doren." *Femme Fatales*. September-October, 1991, Vol. 10, No. 4.

Silver, Alain, and Elizabeth Ward, eds. *Film Noir*. London: Secker & Warburg, 1980.

Staehling, Richard. "From *Rock Around the Clock* to *The Trip*: The Truth About Teen Movies." *Rolling Stone* #49, December 27, 1969.

Stevenson, Jack. *Addicted: The Myth and Menace of Drugs in Film*. New York: Creation Books, 1999.

Strait, Raymond. *The Tragic Secret Life of Jayne Mansfield*. Chicago: Henry Regnery, 1974.

Strodder, Chris. *Swingin' Chicks of the '60s*. San Rafael, CA: Cedco Publishing, 2000.

Sullivan, Steve. *Va Va Voom! Bombshells, Pin-Ups, Sexpots and Glamour Girls*. Los Angeles, CA: Rhino-General Publishing Group, 1995.

Tarantino, Quentin. *Pulp Fiction*. London: Faber & Faber, 1994.

Thomas, Tony. *Howard Hughes in Hollywood*. Secaucus, NJ: Citadel Press, 1985.

Tormé, Mel: *It Wasn't All Velvet*. London: Robson Books, 1988.

Tyler, Parker. *A Pictorial History of Sex in Films*. Secaucus NJ: Citadel Press, 1974.

Van Doren, Mamie. "The Great Debate: Is Bigger Better, or Is More Than a Handful a Waste?" *Glamour Girls: Then and Now* #14, February-March 1999.

_____. *I Swing*. Chicago: A Specialty Book, 1965.

_____. "My Life as a Decoration." *Click: Becoming Feminists*. Toronto: Macfarlane Walter & Ross, 1997.

_____. *My Wild Love Experiences*. Chicago IL: Specialty, 1965.

_____. "The Penis Master Debate Revisited." *Glamour Girls: Then and Now* #15, Fall-Winter 2000.

_____, with Art Aveilhe. *Playing the Field*. New York, G.P. Putnam's Sons, 1987.

_____, as told to Richard Bernstein and Robert J. Rhodes. *My Naughty, Naughty Life!* Hollywood: Century Publishing, 1964.

_____, as told to Carson Kerr. "I Try to Get Along with Women." *Liberty*, May 1958.

Walker, John (ed.). *Halliwell's Film & Video Guide 2000.* London: HarperCollins, 1999.

Wallenfeldt, Jeffrey H., editor-in-chief. *Sports Movies.* Evanston, IL: Cinebooks, 1989.

Weaver, Tom. "The Flora! The Flora!" *The Astounding B Monster*, www.bmonster.com/scifi22.html.

_____. *John Carradine: The Films.* Jefferson, NC: McFarland, 1999.

_____. "Mamie!" *Movie Club* #11, Summer 1997.

Weldon, Michael J. *The Psychotronic Video Guide.* New York: St. Martin's Griffin, 1996.

Williams, Sharon Lind. "Russ Tamblyn: Before *Twin Peaks*—The Artist as a Young Man." *Filmfax* #27, June-July 1991.

Wortley, Richard. *Erotic Movies.* London: Studio Vista, 1975.

PERIODICALS

Film Index
The Hollywood Reporter
Los Angeles Examiner
Los Angeles Times
Mamie Van Doren Fan Club Journal
Monthly Film Bulletin
The New York Times
Picturegoer
Variety

Mamie Van Doren Fan Club:
 Bob Bethia, President
 1067 Lake View Terrace
 Azusa, CA 91702, USA
 p422b@aol.com

www.mamievandoren.com

Index

Numbers in ***bold italics*** indicate pages with photographs.

Adams, Julia (later Julie) 21, 69n, 77n, 78, 144n
"The Adventures of Joe Smith, American" 132
The Adventures of Ozzie and Harriet 205
Agar, John 98–99
AIDS 10, 48, 51
Ain't Misbehavin' 9, 22, 25, 72n, 78–82, ***83***, 88, 209
"Ain't Misbehavin'" 79n
Alexander, Van 132
All American 21–22, 62–66, 68, 92, 102, 189
Allen, Steve 162, 209, 213
Una Americana en Buenos Aires 34, 171–172
Anderson, Pamela 52, 54, 209
Andes, Keith 9, 25, 35n, 82, 85, 88–90
Angus, Robert 172
Anka, Paul 149, 152, 155, 170
Ann-Margret 9, 37n, 212–213
Anthony, Perry Ray 26–27, 29, 34, 38, 42–45, 107
Anthony, Ray 23–27, 29, 31, 33–34, 90, 95, 99, 104, 133, ***143***, ***146***, 152, 155, 207
"Anything Your Heart Desires" 138
Apaka, Alfred 69
Aristophanes 85–86, 90
The Arizona Kid see *I Fratelli di Arizona*
Arnold, Jack 7, 120, 123
Atwater, Barry 156–157
Aumont, Jean-Pierre 171
Autry, Gene 41
Axelrod, George 25

Baker, Carroll 10, 207
Baker, Jack 29, 34
Ballard, Kaye 54
Bancroft, Anne 27, 109, 209
Bard, Ben 18, 20
Bardot, Brigitte 8, 209, 213
Bardot, Mijanou ***164***, 166

Barker, Lex 27, 107
Barris, George 55
Barrymore, John Drew 124
Baxter, Les 27, 104–106, 221
Beat, Beat, Beat! Beatnik Rock 'n' Roll 212–213
The Beat Generation 31, ***35***, 121, 140–146, 165n, 213
"The Beat Generation" 211–213
The Beautiful Legs of Sabrina see *Le Bellissime Gambe di Sabrina]*
The Beauty and the Robot 165
Belinsky, Bo 37, 39, 41–42
Le Bellissime Gambe di Sabrina 34, 39, ***50***, 146–147, 211
Benjamin, Phil 20, 67
Benson, Ben 25, 93
Berkeley, Busby 61
Berlinger, Warren 195
Bernstein, Richard 48
Biberman, Abner 94–95
The Big Operator 31, 98, 130–134, 135n
"Bikini with No Top on the Top" 211, 213
Bill Haley and the Comets 7, 25, 47, 92–93, 207
Billion Dollar Baby 16, 18
Bilson, George 57
Blackboard Jungle 7, 25, 93, 116, 119
Bliss Hayden Theater 20
The Blonde from Buenos Aires see *Una Americana en Buenos Aires*
The Bob Cummings Show 203
The Body, the Face and the Brain 33
Bogdanovich, Peter vii, 191–192
Bolger, Ray 57, 207
Boone, Richard 98–99
Born Reckless 29, 125–130, 138
"The Boy Catcher's Theme" 211–212
Boyd, Jimmy 89
Bracken, Eddie 61

Bregman, Buddy 128, 138
Brennan, Dr. George 51
Brennan, Walter ***204***
Broder, Jack 185
Brodney, Oscar 76n, 97–98
Brooks, Ashley F. 197
Brooks, Jack 34
Burke's Law 205
Burr, Raymond 58, 181
Bush, George W. 10, 54–55
Buzzell, Edward 81

"Cabaret" 211–212
Cahn, Edward L. 33, 138, 156
Calhoun, Rory 9, 65, 80, 81–82
Campbell, William 25, ***91***, 93, 95
The Candidate 4, 31, 172–174, 211
Captive Women 31
Carmen, Jeanne 104
Carradine, John 165–166, 182
Carradine, Robert vii, 197
Carrigan, Robin 150
Carson, Jack 18, 82, 207
Carson, Robert 80
Carter, Ellis W. 95
Case, Kathleen 25, ***86***, 95
Cash, June Carter 182
Castillo, Gloria 189
Celebrity Naked Ambition 209
Chandler, Jeff 22, 26, 71–74, 88n, 89
Chanel, Coco 16, 39
Chaney, Lon, Jr. 182
Chaplin, Charles, Jr. 31, 133
Chapman, Ben vii, 69
Chiquito 193
Cifariello, Antonio 34, 146
Cimber, Matt 194
Cleavage 208–209
Cobb, Lee J. 22, 74
Coca, Imogene 47
Cochran, Eddie 27, 47, 104–106
Cochran, Steve ***132***, 133, ***134***, ***141***, 142
The Colgate Variety Hour 209
College Confidential 31, 150, 157–163, 165n

Index

Come Back, Little Sheba 20, 67
communism 6, 10, 31, 133
Contino, Dick 152
Coogan, Jackie 31, 124, 133, 165–166
Coogan, Richard 156, *157*
Cook, Elisha, Jr. 159
Corday, Mara 77n
Corey, Danielle 16
Corman, Roger 191, 208
Cortez, Stanley 187
Cotten, Joseph 9,
"Cottonpicker" *101*, 104, 106
Cousin Emmy 86–88, 89
Crain, Jeanne 25, 82n, 86, 90
Crayne, Dani 80, *81*, 209
Creature with the Atom Brain 139
Crime Story 205
Crissman, Nino 34
Crosby, Bob 61
Crosby, Cathy 31, *161*, 163
Cummings, Patrick 185
Cummings, Robert (Bob) 45, 162, 203
Curtis, Tony 20–22, 49, *63*, 64–68, 77n, 88n, 89, 207
Cutler, Leslie B. 45

Daniels, William H. 67
Danton, Ray 144–145
Day, Doris 7, 9, 10, 29, 113, 115–116, 186, 207, 210
The Day of the Triffids 184
DeHaven, Gloria 61
Dehner, John 27, 108, *109*
DeLuise, Peter 195
Dempsey, Jack 17–18
Dexter, Brad 156
Diaz, Cameron 200
The Dick Powell Show 203
Dietrich, Marlene 16, 39, 66n, 111n, 213
Divas Exotica 213–214
Dixon, Thomas *2*, 46–47, 51–52
Domergue, Faith 191
Donahue, Elinor vii, 150, 152, 154–155
drag racing 31, 55, 118, 124, 155
Dragstrip Girl 139
Dru, Joanne 20, 67
drugs 29, 31, 39, 43, 118, 122–123, 133
Duke, Patty 182
Dzundza, George vii, 196–197

E! 210
Eastman, Kevin 199n
Eastwood, Clint 21, 77, 99–100
"Edge of Hollywood" 51
Edwards, George 185
Eichler, Alan 47, 52
Eisley, Anthony 187
Ellis, Ward 88
Erickson, Leif 99–100
Estrada, Carlos 171

E.T. 210
Evans, Ray 88
Ewell, Tom 9
Exotique Dancers' League 37

Fair, Jody 122
Falana, Lola 194
Fallon, Phillipa 123
Fantasy Island 47, 71, 205
Father Knows Best 150, 152, 186n
Fields, Dorothy 18
Fischetti, Charlie 16, 18
Fisher, Eddie 18
Fisher, George "Shug" 189
Fix, Paul 99–100
Flaherty, Joe 200
Fleming, Rhonda vii, 22, 71–72, 74, 205, 212
Flowers, George "Buck" 194
Footlight Varieties 15, 57–58
Forbidden 19, 20, 22, 66–68
Ford, Tom 10, 52
Forrest, Steve 9
Foster, Preston 189
Francis, Robert (Bob) 23
Francis Joins the WACS 22, 68n, 74–78
I Fratelli di Arizona 192–193
Freddy und das Lied der Prärie 39, 179–181
Free Ride 48, 194–195
Freeman, Devery 81
Frees, Paul 77n, 120
Funicello, Annette 9, 92, 93
Funny Face 122
Furthman, Jules 112

Gable, Clark 29, 113, 115–116, 207–208
Gabor, Zsa Zsa 182
Gallico, Paul 132–133
gangs 31, 95
Gardiner, Reginald 9, 82, *83*
Gaye, Lisa 68, 71, 203
Geisler, Jerry 24
General Hospital 205
Gentlemen Prefer Blondes (film) 115, 176
Gentlemen Prefer Blondes (stage) 43, 194
Gershon, Gina 200
Gerstle, Frank 156
Gilbert, Paul 88, 90
Gilkyson, Terry 98, 100, 180
The Girl Can't Help It 7, 27, 128n
The Girl in Black Stockings 27, 106–110
The Girl in the Cage 93
"The Girl Who Invented Rock and Roll" 7, 29, 51, *114*, 115
The Girl Who Invented Rock 'n' Roll (CD) 212
Girls Town 31, *33*, 49, 148–155, 165n
Gleason, James 99–100
The Glenn Miller Story 22, 98n

Glory Years 196–197
"Go, Go Calypso" 105, 211, 214
Godfrey, Peter 107
Godfrey, Ronald vii, 109, 110n
The Golden Turkey Awards 47
"A Good Man Is Hard to Find" 34
Grable, Betty 176
Grabowski, Norman "Woo Woo" 31, 133, 165, *166*
Graham, Sheilah 163
Granlund, Nils Thor 15
Grant, Johnny *2*, 52, 55
Grant, Lee 41
Gray, Bill vii, 186
Gray, Coleen 99–100
Graziano, Rocky 182
Guest Shot 209
Guns, Girls and Gangsters 33, *38*, 52, 128, 135–139, 156
Gutterman, Maurie 27, 29

Haas, Charles 99–100, 132, 135, 144, 149
Haley, Jack 57
Hall, Jon 68–69, 186, 207
Harrington, Curtis 191
Harrison, George 39
Hawaiian Eye 187
Hayes, Maggie *154*
Head, Edith 115
Hefner, Hugh vii, 16n, 48, 173, 208, 209
Hell's Angels 111
Hepburn, Audrey 10, 122
Her First Romance 152
Here's Hollywood 209
heroin 118–120, 122, 125
Hershberger, Gary 195
Hibbs, Jesse 21
Higgins, John C. 104
High School Confidential 5, 7, 9, 31, 55n, 93, 105n, 116–125, 142, 150, 163, 165n, 195
Hill, Robert 165, 169, 171
Hillbillys in a Haunted House 182
Hilton, Nicky 22, *23*
Hirsch, Clement 37
His Kind of Woman 15, 58–59
Hoey, Michael A. 184–187
Hoffman, Charles 85, 88
Holland, John 9, 107, *108*, *109*
Hollywood Confidential 210
Hollywood Flash-Back 49
Hollywood Hi-Fi 213
The Hollywood Kids 210
Hollywood Rocks and Rolls 115n, 207–208
The Hollywood Squares 176n, 210
Hollywood Uncensored 207
Hollywood Walk of Fame 10, 51
House Un-American Activities Committee 6, 41
How to Succeed in Business Without Really Trying 45

Howe, Andy 47
Hudson, Rock 21, 22, 88n
Hughes, Howard 14n, 15, 58n, 59, 111–112
Huinh, Simone 49
Hunnicutt, Arthur 77n, 126
Husky, Ferlin 182

"I Can't Give You Anything but Love" 18, 66
"I Fell in Love" 211–212
I Married a Communist 6
I Swing 48
"I Used to Be a Stripper Down on Main" **175**, 176
I Was a Communist for the FBI 6
"I'm Grateful" 211–212
"I'm Here to Stay" 180
In One Bed — and Out the Other 45
The Incredible Shrinking Man 31, 120
Inside the Mafia 156
Invasion of the Body Snatchers 6
Invasion USA 31

The Jack Benny Program 207
Jelke, Micky 18
Jergens, Diane 120, **121**, 122
Jet Pilot 15, 58, 110–112
Joe Smith, American 133
Johnny Olenn and His Group 128
Jones, Carolyn 18
Jones, T.C. 178
juvenile delinquency 7, 10, 25, 31, 92–93, 95, 119, 121, 123, 150, 162

Kadison, Ellis 189
Kallen, Kitty 86, 88–90
Kanin, Fay 115–116
Kanin, Michael 115–116
Kaper, Bronislau 111
Kellaway, Cecil 170
Kennett, George 169
Kent, Robert E. 156
Kerouac, Jack 142
King, James (Jaime) 199
King, Pee Wee 66n
King, Philip 46
Kinsey, Alfred 159n
Kinsey Report 159
Kissinger, Henry 46
Klushantsev, Pavel 191
Knight, Ted 172
Koch, Howard W. 27, 29, 47, 102, 105–107, 109–110, 128, 130
Krasna, Norman 58
Kubrick, Stanley 191

L.A. Law 205–206
Lahr, Bert 25, 89–90
Lamb, Gil 57
Landau, Richard H. 107, 110
Landon, Laurene 194

Lanning, Dennis 197
Lansing, Joi 182, 203
Lanza, Joe 105
Larry King Live 210
Las Vegas Hillbillys 42, 88, 181–183
The Late Show with Arsenio Hall 210
Laurie, Piper 9, 21–22, 65, 77n, 80–82, 209
Lawrence, Barbara 61
Lee, Bill 82n
Lee, Pinky 68
Leigh, Janet 15, 61, 111–112, 207
Leighton, Lee *see* Overholser, Wayne D.
Leinster, Murray 185
Lennon, John 39
Lewis, Jerry 5, 10, 179
Lewis, Jerry Lee 118, 123–124, 207
Liberace 57, 207
"A Lifetime of You" 211
"A Little Longer" 127
Livingston, Jay 88
Loeb, Bill 34, 39, 42
Loncar, Beba 180
Long, Richard 21, 64, 66, 207
Longstreet, Stephen 104
Loren, Sophia 8, 146, 212, 214
Love Is Better Than Ever 152
Lowe, Skip E. 52
Lubin, Arthur 77–78
Lubin, Joe 115
Lutz and Loeb 34
Lysistrata 85, 90
"Lysistrata" 88
Lytess, Natasha 15

Mamie (As in Mamie Van Doren) (CD) 211
Mancini, Henry 74
Mandel, Johnny 34
Mansfield, Jayne 3, 5, 7, 8, 9, 25, 27, 33, 35, 37, 38, 39, 42–43, 51, 176, 178, 182–183, 193–194, 208–209, 212–214
Margulies, William 109
marijuana 117–125, 133
"Marilyn" 51
Marsh, Tani 69
Marshall, Edison 72, 74
Marshall, George 85
Marshall, Herbert 163
Marshall, Peter 176n
Martel, Christiane 71
Martin, Tony 15, 61
Mason, Eric 172, **174**
Mason, Pamela 159
Maté, Rudolph 20, 67–68
Matheson, Richard 142
McClintock, Ross 46
McDonald, Marie 35, 176
McGlashan, Ian 43, 176, 178
McHugh, Jimmy 18, 20, 23–24, 66, 207

McQueen, Steve 39
Meadows, Jayne 162–163
"Meet Me Half Way, Baby" 138
Meltzer, Lewis 142
Mercer, Alan **17**, 52
Merlin, Jan vii, 9, 25, 92, 95
The Merv Griffin Show 210
Meyers, Lee 42–43, 192
Miller, Ann 15, 61
Miller, Frank 98n, 180
Miller, Glenn 23, 104
Miller, Mark 88n
Miller, Marvin 76n
Mills, Grace (Grayce) 95
Milner, Martin **54**, **166**, 170–171
Mister Ed 77
Mister Roberts 205, **206**
Mitchell, Gordon 193
Mitchell, John 46
Mitchum, Jim 142, 144
Mitchum, Robert 15, 58–59, 213
Moffitt, Peggy 152
Mohr, Gerald 137–139, 207
Monroe, Marilyn 1, 3, 5, **6**, 7, 9–10, 16, 20, 22, 24n, 25, 27, 34, 37, 43, 48, 54, 93, 95, 115, 130, 146, 165, 176, 194, 212, 214
The Monster from Earth's End 185
Montez, Maria 68–69
Moody, Phil 88, 176
Moore, Terry 48, 55
Morand, Don 37, 39
Morley, Jay A., Jr. 85, 98
Muhl, Ed 31
My Naughty Naughty Life! 48
My Wild Love Experiences 48

Nader, George 25, 80n, 82n, 88–90
Namath, Joe 42–43
The Navy vs. the Night Monsters 42, 183–188
Nelson, Lori 21, 27, **30**, **65**, 66, 77n, 102, 106
Nelson, Ricky 39n, 205, 207
Newman, Jack 16
Ney, Henry *see* Bogdanovich, Peter
Nicks, Dewey 199–200
Night Watch 210
The Nightcrawlers 185
Nixon, Richard 45–46, 133n
"Nobody But You" 211–213
Noonan, Tommy 9, 38, 43, 175–176, 178–179
Norrell, Norman 29
North, Jay 131, 133
North, Sheree 48, 176, 207
Nugent, Carol 156, **158**
Nye, Louis 165–166, 213

O'Brien, Margaret 152
O'Connor, Donald 77–78
Odell, Rosemary **70**, 72, 74
"Oobala Baby" 104, 106, 211–212

Index

The Oprah Winfrey Show 49, 210
Overholser, Wayne D. 98

Parr, Jack 57–58
Parsons, Louella 18–20, 24–25, 58, 207
Perkins, Millie 194
Perreau, Gigi 152, **154**
Perry, Roger 189
Pescow, Donna 196
Pevney, Joseph 71
Peyton Place 122
Photoplay 210
Pierce, Arthur 185
Pitts, Zasu 78
Plaatschaert, Alexander 35
Planet of Storms see *Planeta Bur*
Planeta Bur 191
Playboy 10, 16n, 38–39, 178
Playboy Mansion 48, 173
Playing the Field 48–49
Port Sinister 31
Presley, Elvis 7, 10, 29, 39, 47, 105–106, 207
Price, Vincent 59
The Prince and the Showgirl 34
Pritchard, Ted 47
The Private Lives of Adam and Eve 31, 167–171, 173
Promises! Promises! 35, 38, 176
prostitution 24, 122, 139, 155–156
Pull My Daisy 142
Pulp Fiction 5, 10, 126

"Queen of Pleasure" 211
Quinn, Freddy 39, 180–181

Rachmil, Milton 20
Rall, Tommy 88–89, 90
Randell, Ron 27, 107–108
rape 24n, 31, 88, 140, 142, 144, 156, 172
Rapp, Philip 81
Rathbone, Basil 182, 191
Ratliff, Dwayne 22
The Ray Anthony Show 27, 33, 207
"Razzle Dazzle" 25, 92
The Real McCoys 203, **204**
Reason, Rex see Roberts, Bart
Red Planet Mars 6
The Red Skelton Show 207
Rees, Virginia 66n
Reynolds, Burt 46
Reynolds, Debbie 9, 52n, 207
Rhodes, Robert J. 48
Richards, Grant 139
Richards, Jeff 126, *127*, 130
Richmond, Ted 20, 68n, 78
Rimmer, Robert H. 194
Rivers, Johnny 39
Rivkin, Allen 133
Roberts, Bart 72, 74
Robinson, Edward G. 18
"Rock Around the Clock" 7, 25, 93, 105n

Rockin' Boppin' Girls 213
Rodann, Ziva 31, 133, 162
"Rollin' Stone" 104, 211–213
Romen, Rachel 172
Rooney, Mickey 31, 77, **130**, 133, **169**, 171
Running Wild 7, **8**, 25, 55, 90–95, 105
Russell, Jane 15, 58–59, 207–208, 210, 212–213
Russell, John **103**, 106

"Salamander" 106, 211–212
Sawa, Devon 199
Saxon, John 25, 95, 207
Scandalous Follies 46
Schenck, Aubrey 47, 102
Schwartzman, Jason 199–200
Scott, Lee 81, 88
Screen Tests of the Stars 208
Sebring, Jay 39
The Second Greatest Sex 8, 25, 82–90, 95, 98, 176
See How They Run 46
"Separate the Men from the Boys" 212
Sex Kittens Go to College 31, **54**, 163–166, 169
"Sex Pots Go to College" 165
Shake, Rattle & Rock 139
"She'll Be Comin' Round the Mountain" 78
The Sheriff Was a Lady see *Freddy und das Lied der Prärie*
Sherrell, Pony 88, 176
Shulman, Irving 159
Silk Stockings 41
Simmons, Jean 48
Sin, Sin, Sin 31
Single Room Furnished 194
Skinner, Edna **86**, 88, 90
Slackers 10, 115, 197–201
Small, Edward 33
Smith, Joe 59, 61
Smith, John 20
Smith, Robert 133
Smith, Roger 205, **206**
"So What Else Is New" 211–212
Sobol, Louis 163
"Something to Dream About" 211–212
Southern, Lou **8**, 92
Spain, Fay 171
Sparks, Randy **161**, 162
Spelling, Aaron 18, 205
Spellman, Cardinal 149
Star in the Dust 8, 26, 29, 85, 95–100, 126
A Star Is Born 176n, 207
A Star Is Born World Premiere 207
"State of Turmoil" 47, 211
Steinberg, David H. 199
Sterling, Jan 120, **121**, 124
Stern, David 76
Stern, Tom 189

The Steve Allen Show 209
Storch, Arthur 41
Strain, Julie 199
Stump the Stars 209–210
Styne, Jule 25
Styne, Stanley 128, 138

Talbott, Gloria 152, **153**
Talent Scouts 209
Tamblyn, Russ 9, 93, 118, **119**, 120, 122–124, 195
Tarantino, Quentin 5, 126
Targets 191
Taylor, Elizabeth 22, 152, 207
Teacher's Pet 7, 29, **32**, 112–116, 208
That Girl from Boston 194
The Thing from Another World 184–185
Thomas, Derek see Bogdanovich, Peter
3 Nuts in Search of a Bolt 7, 38, **40**, 43, 48, 88, 174–179, 187
Thurman, Uma 5
The Tonight Show with Johnny Carson 38, 210
Top Banana 31, 165
Tormé, Mel 31, 133, **134**, 152, 155, 170
Touch of Evil 31, 119
Townsend, Leo 93
Travolta, John 5
Tryden, Doreen 82n
Tuttle, Lurene 106
Twain, Mark 169
Twitty, Conway **160**, 162, 165
Two and Two Make Sex 46
2001: A Space Odyssey 191
Two Tickets to Broadway 15, 59–61

Unseen Hollywood 207
Untamed Youth 7, 27, **28**, **30**, 49, 100–106, 107, 128, 211

Va-Va-Voom 212
Valentine's Day 203–204
Vampira 31, 133, 144, 165
Van Cleef, Lee 33, 138
Vanity Fair (magazine) 10, 52, 54
Vargas, Alberto 16
Vega$ 47, 205
The Vegas Connection 197
Vice Raid 33, 139, 155–157
Vietnam 43–45, 187
Von Sternberg, Josef 111–112
Voyage to the Planet of Prehistoric Women 43, 190–192
Voyage to the Prehistoric Planet 185n, 191

Wald, Jerry 58
Wayne, John 15, 111–112
Weld, Tuesday **164**, 165–166, 170, 207
Welles, Mel 121–123

Welles, Orson 31, 137n, 187n
West, Mae 13, 193n
"What Good Is a Woman Without a Man" 88
What's My Line? 209
Whoopee! 47
The Wild, Wild West see *Freddy und das Lied der Prärie*
Wildcat 35, 37, 89
Wilkinson, June vii, 172–173, 211–213
Will Success Spoil Rock Hunter? 25, 27, 46
Williams, Kenny 81
Williams, Tex 128
Wills, David 52, 54
Wilson, Earl 163
Winchell, Walter 137, 162–163
Windsor, Marie 27, 108
The Winning Way see *All American*
Women of the Prehistoric Planet 185
Wooley, Sheb 89
Wrightson, Earl 41
Written on the Wind 31
Wynn, Keenan 25, 95

Yankee Pasha 8, 22, 68, 69–74
Yates, Hal 57
"You Belong to Me" *19*, 67–68
Young, Gig 18
"Young Dudes" 211
You've Got to Be Smart 98, 188–190

Zadora, Pia 194
Zamparelli, Marc 58
Zugsmith, Albert 7, 26, 29, 31, 47, 98–99, 118–121, 124–125, ***130***, 133, 142, 144–145, 149–150, 152, 155, 159, 161–162, 165–166, 171